D1860375

UNEXPLORED BALUCHISTAN

UNEXPLORED BALUCHISTAN

A SURVEY, WITH OBSERVATIONS ASTRONOMICAL, GEOGRAPHICAL, BOTANICAL, ETC.

OF A ROUTE THROUGH

MEKRAN, BASHKURD, PERSIA, KURDISTAN, AND TURKEY

ERNEST AYSCOGHE FLOYER

GYAN

Published by

Gyan Publishing House
5, Ansari Road
Daryaganj, New Delhi-110002
Phone: 011-47034999, 9811692060
E-mail: books@gyanbooks.com

Distribution Network
gyanbooks.com
India, USA, Canada, UK, Australia, France

ISBN: 978-81-212-9116-3 (PB)
First Published, 1882

2nd Impression 2023

Printed at: Gyan Press, Delhi.

UNEXPLORED BALUCHISTAN
AUTHOR: ERNEST AYSCOGHE FLOYER

UNEXPLORED BALŪCHISTAN.

Woodburytype.

Yours truly
Ernest Ayscoghe Floyer

GRIFFITH & FARRAN, *London*, 1882.

UNEXPLORED BALŪCHISTAN.

A SURVEY, WITH OBSERVATIONS ASTRONOMICAL, GEOGRAPHICAL, BOTANICAL, ETC.,

OF A ROUTE THROUGH

MEKRAN, BASHKURD, PERSIA, KURDISTAN, AND TURKEY.

BY

ERNEST AYSCOGHE FLOYER,

F.R.G.S., F.L.S., ETC.

With Twelve Illustrations and a Map.

GRIFFITH & FARRAN,
WEST CORNER OF ST. PAUL'S CHURCHYARD, LONDON.
1882.

INTRODUCTION.

TO those who have studied the politics and geographical position of the countries between Persia and Northern India—countries, a knowledge of which is of the highest importance to Englishmen at the present day—the subject of "unexplored Balūchistan" can scarcely fail to be attractive. To others the very title may require explanation; for "Balūchistan," known or unknown, is not restricted within universally accepted limits. Roughly stated, we may describe it as the region situated between the longitudinal lines 57 and 67, bounded on the south by the sea, and on the north by a line sufficiently above latitude 28 to take in the Kuh-i-Basmān and Kuh-i-Nushādir. This delineation acccords with the Persian way of regarding the Shah's possessions east of Karmān and Bandar Abbas; and British India adopts the same general nomenclature for the Brahūi territory west of the Hāla Mountains. The point of junction—or line of demarcation—between Western or Persian, and Eastern or the Khan of Kalat's Balūchistan, is north at the Mashkid river, and south at the fishing village of Gwettār.

A glance at the most recent map of Persia will show how large a portion of territory comprised within the outlines here indicated needs specific definition, nor can the several blanks which have long characterized tracts such as Bāshakard, Rudbār, and Irafshān be disposed of by the term "desert" or "barren rock." So designated, or by the less definite if more significant word "unexplored," they cannot but be an eyesore to the geographer; while to the student of Oriental politics they convey the impression that if it be not culpable neglect, it must be questionable prudence, which keeps British India so ignorant of the *habitat* of her immediate neighbours and allies. More than forty years ago we styled our officers "Political Agents in Sind and Balūchistan"; and the former of these provinces has been actually in our own hands for little less than that period, while our relations with the latter have been continuous. It is, moreover, just twenty years since we established a line of telegraph for 400 miles along the Makrān coast, west of Karāchi; and this was prolonged some six years later to Cape Jask, with a submarine extension to the island of Henjām—a station overlapping the extreme limit of the Balūch country to the westward.

More recently still, the advance to Kwatta and war with Afghanistan, by strengthening the intimacy of our relations with the country divided between the Shah and the Khan, have afforded us new opportunities of examining its geographical features. But our troops have moved out of Kandahar as they may move out of Kwatta, and the blanks in the map of Balūchistan remain unfilled.

Some years ago, I ventured to make a suggestion with regard to the employés in the Government Indo-European Telegraph, of whom it could hardly be said, while exercising their professional duties at Fāo, Bushahr, Jask, Chahbār, Gwāda, and Pasni—telegraph stations on the coast extending from the mouth of the Shattu-l-Arab to Karāchi—that their lines were cast in pleasant places. It was to the effect that they should be encouraged and assisted in carrying out volunteer expeditions into the interior. Only capable and trustworthy men, it was understood, were contemplated for such occasions; and this not simply in the sense of scientific acquirement or fitness for geographical exploration, but men who would avoid wounding national susceptibilities and treading upon local prejudices, as carefully as they would observe the sun or the stars, register botanical specimens, or take account of fauna. My ideas were put into shape and submitted in an official letter; but the practical object aimed at was not favourably considered, and it was ruled unadvisable to give official encouragement to the movement of employés out of their respective spheres of work, even when a holiday had been earned or failing health demanded temporary change of scene.

Mr. Ernest Floyer was at this time one of the Government Indo-European Telegraph Staff in the Persian Gulf, and one of those whose tastes, attainments, and spirit of enterprise would have naturally singled him out as a competent explorer. Had my suggestion been acted on, and the presence of English telegraph clerks at points along the Perso-Balūch coast line, extending from the Shattu-l-Arab to Karāchi, been utilized under Government approval, I have no doubt that he would have been one of the first explorers selected; but he would then have had certain general instructions which haply he might rather have been without, or which he might have been tempted to consider more formal than serious. As it happened, Mr. Floyer moved away from his dreary residence at Jask into the interior, without any authority from his superiors, but at the same time under no veto to keep within the limits of a telegraph station: and he went unhampered by official directions. How he fulfilled his self-imposed mission, it is left to the reader to judge. It would be impertinent in this place to pass an opinion on the literary merits of his book—in fact, I have not had the leisure to read it with a critic's attention—but I have great pleasure in bearing testimony to its usefulness in giving life and reality to extensive tracts which, if little known, are full of interest, and should have an exceptional charm for Englishmen, owing to their proximity to British India. To myself, the unknown province of Bāshakard has always presented attraction. Twice I have crossed the Bampūr plains on its northern side: once I skirted it on the westward, passing up from Bandar Abbas to Sistān; and two journeys from Bampūr to seaports of Makrān have made me acquainted with the lands bordering upon its eastern frontier. Yet I have had neither time nor opportunity to do more than communicate with its chief by letter. It was reserved for Mr. Floyer to visit the capital of Saif Oollah. That fierce old Balūch was, at this period, in difficulties, and another functionary had been installed in his seat; but we are told some stories about him which illustrate his determined character.

Bāshakard, however, is not the only part of Western Balūchistan that has been visited by our enterprising traveller. He is to be found camping at places to east, west, and north of that Perso-Balūch province—always accompanied by one or two faithful natives, to whose adventures he pays as much regard as to his own, and whose individuality he brings out by frequent anecdote and example. Later on, he takes a more direct course to the west, enters Persia proper, and traverses the whole breadth of the Shah's kingdom, through

Karman, Yazd, and Ispahan to the Turkish frontier at Khanikin. Thence to Baghdad and Basra, there was little more land-travel to be accomplished, and from Basra to Marseille and London we need feel no surprise that the author has not attempted any narrative of his journey.

Mr. Floyer's removal from the inhospitable shores of the Persian Gulf to the direction of the Egyptian telegraph, and my own official residence in Cairo, have enabled us to renew the associations of bygone years. They explain, moreover, how I have been asked, and have consented, to write these few lines of preface to a book which might otherwise have been introduced under more brilliant auspices. It is not so easy to decline a spoken as a written request, although it be demonstrated that non-compliance is to the clear advantage of the applicant.

F. J. GOLDSMID.

CAIRO,

30th March, 1882.

CONTENTS.

CHAPTER I.

CHAPTER II.

CHAPTER III.

CHAPTER VII.

ON FOOT TO ANGUHRAN.

CHAPTER VIII.

CHAPTER IX.

WE ENTER PERSIAN TERRITORY.

CHAPTER X.

CHAPTER XI.

We cross the Mountains.

CHAPTER XII.

We reach Kirman.

CHAPTER XIII.

Life at Kirman.

CHAPTER XIV.

EN ROUTE FOR YEZD.

CHAPTER XV.

YEZD TO ISPAHAN.

CHAPTER XVI.

ISPAHAN.

CHAPTER XVII.

CHAPTER XVIII.

DOWLETABAD.

CHAPTER XIX.

KIRMANSHAHAN.

ILLUSTRATIONS.

ERRATA.

Page 332, top line, *for* tasbiah, *read* tasbíḥ.
Page 347, line 11—at Bairamabad—*read as footnote*,
"Balram, corruption of bárán, rain."

UNEXPLORED BALUCHISTAN.

CHAPTER I.

Illness.—Hiring camels.—On march.—Old Jellāl.—Jemohad and his family.—We reach Jagīn.—The river impassable.—Tājoo.—Balūch salutations.—The impassability of the river is exploded.—An anxious crossing.—Abdulla.—Male camels in the breeding season.—A day's ibex-shooting.—A night march.—Cross the Sadaich river.—We turn north.—Shūr hills.—*Chamærops Ritchiana.*—We change guides.—Men in buckram.—Camp in the Sārtāpi.

IN January 1876, having suffered severely during some years' hard service in the Persian Gulf, I was granted my long deferred privilege leave by Her Majesty's Government, and cast about for the best way of making the most of it.

I was at that time stationed at Jask, opposite Maskat, and I at first sought for some means of joining my friend the Political Agent there, but was compelled to abandon the idea, as the only bagla or native craft available had recently suffered shipwreck, and a steamer could not be expected in less than a fortnight.

The alternative then was a journey up country, and the Bashakard country seemed to promise best for such a trip as I proposed to make, but I was met at the outset by such fearful accounts of the ice and snow, that I soon saw it would be impossible to get natives to travel through a country which they described in terms which would have been exaggerated even for the arctic regions. There were, moreover, wars and rumours of wars, a full account of which I afterwards heard.

My native friends much pressed me to go to Mināb, urging that the road was good, much travelled, and everything was easy and straightforward. These considerations, however, naturally weighed with me in a direction quite contrary to that expected. I had long wanted to see what was on the other side of the range of mountains which runs down this Mekran coast on which I had spent so many years, and, excepting for my illness, this seemed as good an opportunity as I should ever have of crossing them.

In Sir Frederic Goldsmid's map Bint seemed a good place to make for, and it had advantages in that none of my people had ever been there, and I had just as much ground for dilating to my intended companions on sheltered valleys and sunny gardens as they had for warning me of the horrors of death from freezing. Bint was accordingly fixed upon as our first point, though I privately resolved that if I only partially regained my health, Bint should not be my limit.

Three days were consumed in ransacking the country for camels. The Balūchis are not an enterprising race, and, owing to the unknown nature of my destination, and the fear of cold, the seven camels I proposed to load were very difficult to get. It was now also the breeding season for camels, and all the full-grown males were more or less furious with must.

On the afternoon of the 7th of January seven camels

duly arrived, and I congratulated myself that only one seemed very furious. He was a big five year old male, continually roaring and blowing a large bladder out of his mouth; but, though he fully deserved the epithet of "Old Eblis" which he afterwards acquired, he was much more tractable than he looked.

Owing to my illness my baggage and establishment was much more cumbersome than would otherwise have been necessary, and included a hill tent, a bed, a chair, and a portable table. Salah, an Arabic mulla, accompanied me to investigate matters of religion and superstition; a wooden-headed Goanese was the cook, and a sturdy honest boy, called Ghulamshah, the table servant. Old Jellāl, a very Abu Zeid of Surooj* for shrewdness, carried my gun; while the five camel-men, who turned out jovial good-natured fellows, were under contract to pitch the tent and bring the wood and water. Toby also must not be forgotten, a good pious little dog with a black nose, who travelled on the cook's camel and at night took my bed under his especial protection.

After about three hours' wrangling about the loads, the men left for Bint, but as that evening was the feast of Kurbān I allowed them to make only six miles, stipulating that the following night they should get to Jagīn, about twenty-seven miles away.

I may just mention that the Balūchis here had barely sufficient knowledge of their religion to know that

---

* Stories of Abu Zeid of Surooj, the merry arch-rogue and swindler of Basreh, form many of the poems in the celebrated Arabic collection, "Makamat al Hariri," portions of which were translated by Preston, and published at the Cambridge University Press.

there was a feast, and all who could afford it put on a new shirt. But of the few we met next day on the march not one could tell me what feast it was, and all were glad to accept my suggestion that it was probably that of Kurbān.

As Salah and myself intended starting the next morning, I turned in early, after a melancholy attempt to do justice to the princely hospitality of the Jask Lancers, a cavalry corps who, armed with pig spears and mounted on donkeys, scoured the surrounding country for pariah dogs. A violent shower of rain fell during the night, just to warn us that we were not going to have fair weather always.

The morning was fine, and, mounting our camels, we plodded off to Jagīn across an uninteresting desert, the monotony of which was only broken three times by patches of date trees and wheat.

Our road for the first ninety miles lay along the sandy strip between the hills and the sea; for, though the villagers told us that a pass through the hills would be found nearer than this, I was anxious to meet a friend who was travelling up from Gwadur along the telegraph line.

Leaving Jask about 10 a.m., we, according to promise, made a short detour to pick up Jellāl. The old man's second wife had recently died, and Mīr Ali, his chief, had provided him with a temporary one until he should get a little money to buy one of his own kindred. The *locum tenens* was a young negress of violent temper, who had been probably too much for the Mīr's household. She had a rooted aversion to the old gentleman's four children, and, as we approached, we heard a hot dispute raging, the lady threatening that if he did not give her another two krans which she suspected him of having kept back she would starve his children.

A shout from us brought the old man out of his hut, driving his donkey before him with vehement blows and muttering curses on all women. His pet son—the one by his first wife—followed him crying and entreating him not to go, which wrung the old man's heart, and, added to his other family troubles, made him glad to get safe off.

Old Jellāl merits perhaps a somewhat detailed description. He was any age from forty-five to sixty, about five feet six inches in height, and of remarkably spare and wiry form. His legs and arms were thin, the same size all the way down, and covered with a coarse, crackly hide, which he greased whenever he could "do" the cook out of any ghee (clarified butter), or with the oil supposed to be devoted to my guns. His head was shaved and covered with a close-fitting skull-cap, rendered stiff in the orthodox manner by the grease of years. Huge, bristly, prominent eyebrows sheltered his deep sunken bloodshot grey eyes, with which a thin aquiline nose harmonized admirably. His short curly white beard was at present plastered up in what looked like a mass of black mud, and, as he trudged along before my camel, he detailed, in tones that would have drawn sympathy from a stone, how, owing to the domestic troubles before alluded to, he had been unable to get the henna for his beard until late last night, and consequently it could not yet be washed off. One likes to be tidy when going amongst strangers, and the idea of a Balūch (if old) is to dye his grey beard red and buy a new pow or "puggree." Jellāl was game to the backbone; endowed with extraordinary powers of endurance, he would trudge along at four miles an hour from morning till night, with his rounded back and legs as straight as if he had never realized the use of knee joints, or, I often thought, from mere economy of movement. He had been Mīr Ali's pet shikarri, but now his wind failed him for the hills and he stuck to plain game. At night he would—if he could get it—eat such a quantity of dates and swallow such bowls of māst, lach, dōgh, shilanch, cashk and the other forms of decomposed milk which are a Balūchi's staple food, that he would sometimes be unable to move for two hours. He was very loyal, and his work was very trustworthy; anything he tied on a camel never came undone, and if you had told him to call you at three in the morning he would always be up at half-past two with everything ready.

He could fast wonderfully, still his appetite was so insatiable that he never had any money. He was pleased to be the jest of the whole caravan, but with his querulous ever-wagging tongue he would, if he cared to, give such stinging repartees as would effectually turn the tables against his antagonist. His donkey was always a young one bought cheap in its infancy, and his solicitude for it was such that he rarely rode it, and would nearly double the day's march in his searches after tufts of the especial grasses his long experience had taught him were best for the "child," as he called it. He was well connected, but his appetite and want of grown-up sons had caused him to somewhat lose caste, for a Balūch of good family would die sooner than, even after a three days' fast, fail to share his food with any one present or show the least appearance of haste to eat. The poor fellows seem to regard their stomachs as the one thing of which they are ashamed, and for which they grudge expense.

Chatting with the old man, and pushing along as briskly as the wretched condition of the camels would allow of, we soon reached the Bahl, a small grassy hollow about six miles from Jask, and just then inhabited by the villagers whose head-quarters are Oushdāhn. Jemohad (generally pronounced Jemait), the head man, was another old friend and the shikarri of the Oushdāhn hills (each shikarri having a sort of hereditary right to the shooting of each hill), and he accompanied us some distance, recommending to our especial care his son Zangi, who was Old Eblis' attendant for the journey.

The Oushdāhn villagers have three camping places, which are about eight miles one from another, and in each they spend a portion of the year: Bahl, being a hollow, collects the rain, which produces a luxuriant crop of spring grass; when the flocks have eaten this it is time to go to Yekdār and look after Jemohad's "mach" or date grove there. The patches of wheat, too, previously sown there are now about eight inches high; and mat-huts, spinning-wheels, water-skins, and the favoured among the women are all loaded upon camels and donkeys, and off they go, followed by about a dozen large dogs, and perhaps half a dozen cows, and thirty or forty goats and sheep. Oushdāhn is next visited, after which they return to Bahl for the next spring.

Jemohad has four wives and five fine sons: Bangi,

Zangi, Jangoo, Dilwash and Shahi; all were shikarries, though Jangoo had married into a strange family and devoted all his energies to agriculture. The old man was never happy if he did not see them all pretty often; Dilwash—a corruption of Dil Kwash or "heart rejoicer"—had three days before returned from a journey to Chābar, and he was still in a clean shirt and the household generally in a state of fête.

From Bahl we took the sandy sea-shore and, passing Oushdāhn, again struck inland towards Shārināh, where we had tiffin under some pleasant shady date-trees.

I must not, however, forget to mention the solitary traveller we met. Mulla Saeed was formerly Abdul Nabi's head man, but after that chief's recent defeat by Mīr Yusuf in the struggle for the possession of Jask fort, he had taken service with Mīr Yusuf. Tall, lean, melancholy, very dark, with long straight hair, Mulla Saeed gives himself out to be an Affghān, but is generally believed to be a Hindoo. He was mounted on a fine camel, and his heavy English rifle was carried by a small slave boy who ran in front. He was a strange-looking fellow, and in the fluent Hindustani of his salutation to the feringhi one could not help noticing, in partial support of the Hindoo theory of his origin, the ultra-Balūchi accuracy of his pronunciation of the four-dotted R.

At Shārināh were a few huts, and the villagers came out to exchange notes. They all wore clean clothes in honour of the feast of Kurbān, the day on which the procession round the Kaaba at Mekka takes place. As I have explained, however, the mulla and myself were the only people who could say what the feast was.

Leaving Shārināh we pressed on to Yekdār, where

are more groves of date-trees. These groves being banked in and full of stagnant water, swarmed with venomous black mosquitoes, which infuriated both the camels and ourselves, and rendered driving along the narrow tops of the banks a rather exciting operation.

By the state of the date groves an idea may be formed of the antiquity of the owner's family. Here and at Shārināh the groves were almost all owned by Mīr Ali and his rival Abdul Nabi, and my men (who were all slaves or vassals of the former) were delighted to point out his tall full-grown trees and compare them with the parvenu's groves, which were all newly planted. The respective characters of these two chiefs—whose rivalry had for some time torn the country—were generally summed up as follows: Mīr Ali is the best man for the räiats, gives each slave a certain portion of his date-trees to reside amongst and look after, and allows him to marry and establish himself permanently. Mīr Ali, however, is old and behind the times. Abdul Nabi, who in his younger days, after his father's death at Mekka, was the other's *protégé*, made all his slaves soldiers, never let them remain long in one place, and constantly had them in attendance on his journeys intriguing for soldiers or other assistance.

About sunset we entered the belt of trees which fringe the banks of the Jagīn river, and found the camp just being pitched on the west bank.

We were not long in finding out that none of the men had ever pitched a tent before, and their good nature was far ahead of their energy in the matter. The first thing I distinguished in the darkness was three men at one peg, one holding it, a second tapping it with another peg (the mallet had been voted barbarously heavy), and the third sitting firmly by with the end of a rope in his hands. However, we soon got matters reorganized, young Zangi, a mere boy, showing himself especially anxious to deserve his father's recommendation; and after dinner we turned in to sleep to the sound of Old Eblis' hoarse roaring in the distance as he chased the other camels about; music varied by the hum of mosquitoes, and the plashing sound of frequent sand avalanches from the cliff into the river bed.

In the morning the jungle along the river bed swarmed with black and common partridges and grouse which had come from the plains to drink. Jellāl and myself sallied forth before the sun was up. The morning was lovely, and in about two hours we had made a mixed bag of a fox, jackal, wild cat, three black and a brace of common partridges. I should be ashamed to say how many shots I missed, but my nerves were utterly out of order, and the jungle was in places so thick that I could only hear the birds getting away. Jellāl caught two partridges with his hands, a performance much easier than it sounds, as these birds after two short flights will sit perfectly quiet in a thick bush, and if they can be seen may be pounced upon and secured in the hunter's puggree. The black partridges are even more difficult to flush than the brown ones, and completely exhausted the patience of Jellāl, who was only used to the latter sort. A new comer to the country, by the way, is always surprised to find these partridges at night roosting in the trees.

As the Jagīn river is a type of several which, coming down from the hills, cut a constantly changing route through the strip of sand down to the sea, a short description now may save time afterwards. The bed of the Jagīn is here half a mile wide, and composed of the richest silt, which, were the river dammed, would bear tremendous crops. The only advantage taken of it is the planting here and there of an inferior kind of cotton tree. At this time of year, also, the ground here is covered a foot deep with rich spring grasses, of which clover is the most common; there are, however, but few sheep to eat it, and the people ridicule the idea of mowing and stacking it as hay for the dry season.*

Returning to the tent we were met by the unwelcome information that the river was perfectly impassable, owing to an accumulation of very soft mud; the men added that they had been searching for a ford all the morning, but without success. This was a blow indeed. I immediately despatched Jellāl up river, and Tājoo, a camel-man, down river, and sat down to my breakfast with less appetite than ever.

Tājoo deserves a word of description, for he was my companion in a subsequent journey which took my Balūchis so far from home that their hearts failed them, and while they mutinied, he alone remained staunch. He was a broad good-humoured fellow, with colossal legs and a way of plodding along on them that seemed to defy fatigue. He paid great court to the cook, and became that worthy's very handy assistant, though he was, even for a Balūch,

* The inhabitants of Kishm Island, in the Persian Gulf, on the contrary, jealously preserve their grass and store it up in caves and storehouses for the hot season. A chance traveller through the island is not even allowed to turn his camel loose for five minutes' refreshment.

preternaturally dirty. The leather band round his head far from confined his long thick black tresses, which hung all over his face and shoulders. He owned three camels and shares in some others, and now accompanied us in charge of his pet Darchi, a light elegant female camel, hardly up to the weight of the tent walls, the cook and Toby, all of whom had fallen to his share. He had traded in donkeys to and from Oman, and was very proud of being able to converse with Salah in the latter's own language.

As the sun got high I was lying down on my bed, and listening lazily to the camel-men's conversation outside, when I head a strange voice, and lifting up the door, saw the men commencing the salutation with a tall Balūch armed to the teeth. Behind him stood his camel, held by a woolly-haired little slave carrying a long matchlock and a large Balūch banjo.

It was impossible to help laughing at the air of mournful resignation with which he kissed the hands of each of the camel-men, who in return gravely kissed his twice. Then commenced the salutation, which generally occupies four or five minutes, as it is impolite, or a mark of assumption of superior dignity, for one man to ask fewer questions about the health of another than the other does about his. This salutation is gone through by the commonest camel-man with any one he may meet in his own country, and I used to quite dread encountering any strangers on the march, owing to the delay caused, and the consequent disorganization of the line of march. Both men generally speak almost together after the first salaam or "peace" thus: "Are you 'fit'?" "Are you quite well?" "Is all well?" "Is your house (by which wives are understood) well?" During this they join hands, and each kisses the other's wrist three times; then "by the kindness of God all is well," etc., etc. Each then asks the other for news, both bashfully refuse to give any; they ask again, and each solemnly avers that the only thing of the least interest to him is the state of the other's health. One man meeting four men will sometimes go through all this with each one, but beyond that number the head of the larger party generally engages the one man in conversation, it being correct for a number to assume a superiority over one man.

After the conventional inquiry for news the visitor took his leave, and seeing that he appeared to be making straight for the river, I called to my men to ask him where he was going to ford it, and I could not help a feeling of surprise that it had not occurred to them to ask before; this was quickly followed by the thought that a personal investigation would give me a better idea of the real state of affairs than I could gain through the medium of my men, and putting on my hat, I went through the salutation with our new friend, and told him I would accompany him to the ford. We headed a procession and walked majestically towards the river, he being very careful never to get a step in advance, and to give me the precedence whenever the path was narrow. Our friend was a soldier passing from Abdul Nabi's camp to his head-quarters at Gabrig, and we afterwards heard that his business was connected with another attempt to retake Jask fort.

When we arrived at the water's edge the camel-men all assured him that the mud was too soft and the water too deep; but I can never forget the haughty air with which he turned round upon them and, grounding his gun, asked, "Who says there is mud? are not these my tracks of yesterday, when the water was much higher? No one would own himself responsible for the assertion, and, without more ado, he hoisted the little boy on to the camel and, taking off his clothes, walked through the river. The water in the channel was deep, and the ascent on the other side was steep, but the crossing was neither soft nor slippery.

Eventually tracing the statement as to the impracticability of the passage to one Dādoo, apparently the only inhabitant of the place, and a man who would have had perhaps no unconquerable aversion to selling us eggs, milk, and fowls for any length of time we might be induced to stay, I gave orders to load up and cross at once. After what had passed, it seemed only natural to find that the camels had been turned out to graze on the other side of the river. The sun had set before we had finished loading, but after two stampedes (caused by Toby leaping off his camel) we got under way. The worst came at the last in a sudden descent into about five feet of mud and water, and old Eblis, who followed close behind me with all the sugar, flour, and rice, very nearly swayed right over, being only saved by the prompt interposition of the camel-men's heads under the boxes.

It was a rather exciting half-hour standing on the shore watching the camels staggering through the cold, dark water. However, the food was safe, and each camel that scrambled dripping up the bank rendered our anxieties lighter.

We went just far enough from the bank to escape mosquitoes, and after successfully expostulating with Abdulla on the impropriety of pitching the tent so as to enclose three large milk bushes (a course which resulted in its being pitched in soft sand, and my narrowly escaping a horrible death through the fall of the tent-pole), we had dinner and turned in.

Abdulla was a good old fellow, but too feeble to do much good at tent-pitching. By virtue of his age, however, he had become head of the men, an arrangement which I refrained from disturbing until I could find a man more fit for the place, a time which never came. He was a regular magpie at chattering, and while the tent was being pitched, would keep up a constant stream of direction and applause. When all else failed him he would pick up a peg and expatiate on its beautiful shape: "Ah, this is a splendid peg, lovely peg this, got quite a point to it, hard as a nail," etc., etc.

The next morning was bitterly cold; we were up with the partridges, but the camel-men were difficult to stir; my own people had been provided with blankets, etc., but these men, though perfectly aware how cold the nights would be in the open air, had provided themselves with nothing more than their ordinary wide cotton petticoats, shirt, and sheet.

It appeared also that each camel's particular load had not yet been definitely settled, and we were not yet to get off without much wrangling, in which a small boy, Ismail, with a very shrill voice always took a prominent part. Three of the camels belonged to his elder brother Abdulla, and his invariable course was to plant himself opposite them and object shrilly to each separate article which any one proposed to put on their backs. Another source of delay was the "Pig," a camel who unless about twenty minutes were expended in tying him up so that he could not move a foot, invariably rose and shook his load off at least twice before it was securely tied on. I had unfortunately been unable to get a jemadar or foreman, and consequently had to do the driving myself; however, the loss was only felt for the first two or three marches, after which each man knew his camel's load, and understood that he had to do whatever stage I chose to make, even if he did not finish loading till noon.

This day's stage to the Gabrig river was twenty miles, and, after emerging from the fertile belt on the edge of the Jagīn, led over sandhills and salt plains covered with low bushes till we saw the date groves and trees of Gabrig in the distance. Salah and myself rode on ahead, the only excitement being passing two herds of camels, with whom my animal showed a disposition to engage in battle; but just after we entered the Gabrig belt of trees we fell into the very danger we had taken so much trouble to avoid, that of meeting mad male camels. While passing under a sandhill we heard a tremendous roaring, and in a minute three enormous camels charged madly down the slope in front of us. We retired precipitately, though we could not help admiring these huge animals and the rapidity with which they can move their apparently unwieldy legs; judging only from the sound of their feet when galloping no one could say that they were not horses, and pretty active horses too.

We passed here a rather good specimen of a Balūch

burying ground. On the top of some huge shingly mounds were fourteen or fifteen rectangular enclosures built of sun-dried bricks; the walls were about four feet high in the centre, but rose at each corner of the building to a high triangular peak. In these were the graves of the aristocracy, each grave being covered with white, crimson, or light green pebbles. Outside all over the surface were similar patches of coloured pebbles marking the graves of the poorer people. The walls of the enclosures are to a certain extent rendered ornamental by triangular recesses fitting one into another like an endless W, each triangle being filled up with lines of smaller W's. The only means of entrance was a hole through which a man might crawl on all fours.

Gabrig is so to speak the capital of Abdul Nabi, who owns the district enclosed on the east and west by the Jagīn and Sadaich rivers, and on the north and south by the hills and the sea.

Sport was reported to be very good in the hills behind Gabrig, so the next morning I sent for Rahi, a shikarri with whom I had had good sport on the Geigen hills, about seventy miles to the west, and, until his arrival, strolled about among the jungle on the river-side botanizing and shooting black partridges. At noon, however, Rahi had not arrived, so, as ibex shooting that day was out of the question, I strolled down to the village to arrange with him about to-morrow.

Rahi was a slave of Abdul Nabi, and lived in one of the six or seven mat huts which accommodated the latter's household and were placed near a cotton plantation apart from any other huts. I found him very ill, having had twelve days' fever and ague; however, we agreed that (being both ill) we would try a day in the hills, and make as easy work of it as we could.

It was eight miles from the camp to the Guarani hills, and the way was enlivened by meeting with a herd of about 700 female camels, into the midst of which my camel rushed me with the utmost violence. Our sport was much simplified by the presence in the low valleys of innumerable mosquitoes, owing to which the ibex were unable to feed there, and were to be found only on the tops of the hills. After about three hours we found a herd of nineteen, among whom three very fine white ones excited great hopes. Just at the end of the stalk, however, we came suddenly upon five other ibex, whom we had not previously seen; with two hasty shots I missed with the first barrel but killed with the second, the result being a young male with horns about six inches long. Rahi's triumph over Jellāl was great, for the latter, a consummate "*laudator temporis acti*," was down upon the new breed of shikarries, and had not failed to comment with considerable point on each false move the young man made in his pugging (*tracking*).

We got back to camp about sunset, or rather to the camping ground, for the camp had gone on to Sadaich, and its sole representative was Ghulamshah, in charge of a kettle, a bag of flour, and a tin of cocoa and milk. After some cocoa we discussed the respective advantages of going on to-night or waiting till to-morrow. There was a fine moon, and as the clouds in the north looked very threatening we decided on a move. Ghulamshah had a camel for himself and saddle-bags, Jellāl his donkey, and I my camel; and fording the river, which is about sixty yards wide, and rather muddy, we bade farewell to Rahi and trudged off over the sandhills. Camels always travel capitally by night, and ours, beyond an inclination to fight when brought together, went along well. The stage was twenty miles, and when about two-thirds through old Jellāl dismounted and turned in under a sandhill, promising to come on to camp early.

We arrived, as far as we could guess, at about 2 a.m., and found, as I had half anticipated, that everybody had gone to sleep and no tent was pitched. However, with the assistance of a tent-peg, it did not take long to rouse the men up, and, after I had pointed out that such a course would inevitably bring them to a bad end, we soon had some shelter. The wind was now blowing fresh, and the ground being mud and shingle did not give good hold to the pegs, but taking the precaution to be on the windward side of the pole I turned in.

It appeared to be in about half an hour that I was awakened by a great flapping, and rising found it about an hour before sunrise, and the windward corner peg was actually pulled up. I knocked it in and turned in again; but about nine o'clock I was again roused by a tremendous storm of wind and rain. The thunder roared just overhead, and the men soon rushed in with their bags, etc., and four were set to hold the pole, while two more hammered in desperation at the pegs; these were, however, far too short, and the men had to sit by the ropes till the squall blew over.

As soon as the weather cleared up, we took down the kanāts (*tent walls*) and spread them in the sun to dry, and I sent the men to cut four good stout posts which we carried with us, and which afterwards proved invaluable.

The Sadaich river, on the banks of which we were encamped, was now a roaring muddy torrent, and we could only congratulate ourselves that our night march had saved us from being shut up on the wrong side of the Gabrig, while our camp was at Sadaich. The day was spent in drying everything, and an unsuccessful search for a furious old wild boar, said to have taken up its residence close to our camp; while the servants enjoyed themselves immensely in bargaining for sheep, fowls, and ghee (*clarified butter*), with the result, after much animated discussion, of the purchase of one bottle of ghee, which I at once countermanded, as, though ghee is a necessary evil in the station, out in the jungle the sheep are very fat; they are moreover of the fat-tailed sort, and carry a large reservoir of fat in their tails.

Next morning was fine, and the river was (of course) pronounced impassable. However, the experience at Jagīn had decided me to take the matter entirely into my own hands; it was impossible not to see that otherwise we should be in a fair way to imitate the man who sat on the bank waiting till the river should run by. Sending men across with branches to mark the patches of quicksand, we got safely across, though at one time I almost feared I had been precipitate, for one camel got mired and fell. This was Tājoo's poor Darchi, but luckily her load was nothing perishable, being the cook and the kanāts, which were quickly removed, and the camel raised before she had sunk very deep.

Our stage this day to Sūrag was luckily a short one for five miles of the road were slippery mud. Salah and myself took a long detour to the south and found about 200 acres of wheat and cotton; the men ploughing, etc., were nearly all slaves.

Sūrag was the pleasantest place we had yet camped at, and I sat outside till late in the evening with a huge tree burning in front of me. We were, however, disappointed at seeing nothing of the friend we expected to meet, as one more stage east was all we could conveniently make before striking north.

Next evening found us at Kāshi, after sixteen very difficult miles over broken hills, without any definite road. At one time Salah and myself got into a *cul de sac* from which there seemed positively no exit, save by retracing our steps for upwards of a mile, a most unpleasant proceeding. Dismounting we prospected, and, discovering a dry watercourse which appeared to lead our way, we scrambled down into it, dragging the camels after us and fervently hoping that the baggage would have found some better route. Our difficulties ended here, for the nullah took us along for two or three miles, then into another nullah by which we got clear of the hills.

At Kāshi, also, there was no sign of our friend; so next morning, in a bitter cold wind, we loaded up and struck away north, ten degrees west, heading for the Karwan district.

The country here was composed of shingly banks and plains intersected by small sandy water-courses, whose course was marked by lines of long grass and low jungle. Wild thyme was abundant, and in places scented the whole air.

We had obtained a guide at Kāshi, an unfortunate old fellow with a remarkably fine head, beard, and Herculean shoulders, but one of whose legs was only half as long as the other. He had three donkeys which he rode by turns, was a chatty, good-natured fellow, but knew nothing of the route.

Crossing the small Kāshi river, at this time a chain of pools and mud, we skirted a large area of low salt mud-hills, covered with flakes of bright chrome sandstone. Leaving this on our left, we passed through four or five miles of shingly banks, and about noon arrived at Nowalag, some large salt mud-hills on the edge of a belt of trees in the district of Karwān.

I shall have so often to mention these salt mud-hills, that it will save trouble to give here a brief description of them, and refer to them in future under their native name of Shūr. They are high, sharp-edged ridges of a whitey-blue mud, and are fairly regular in shape, the section of the main ridge being an acute-angled isosceles triangle. From the main ridge spring numerous spurs or buttresses of the same construction as itself. The surface has generally a "noduly" appearance, and they are more or less intersected by veins of gypsum, varying from two to five or six inches in thickness; nothing ever grows on them, and they are found between and at the foot of the other hills, from the sides of which also patches of shūr mud constantly project; shūr means salt.

Old Jellāl added to his enormities in his companions' eyes by the unbounded and almost unfair demands he made on the hospitality of the inhabitants. Immediately on catching me up here, where I had halted for the baggage, he discovered some goat pugs, and was off on their track for a bowl of dōgh. On this occasion he repaid his host's hospitality by purchasing on my behalf a fine young lamb with four horns, a thing very common here.

Leaving Nowalag in a slightly north-westerly direction, we crossed the Karwān river four times, and arrived at the Jowdar* hills. The water here was fairly sweet, but the boulders were white with crusted salt. Winding amongst the Jowdar hills, we crossed and recrossed the river, the bed of which was now full of large clumps of fine pīsh, a plant or tree which in this country fills the place taken in England by the oak, ash, elm, bricks, slates, boots, matches, and a host of other materials.

The pīsh is *Chamærops Ritchiana*, a fan-palm, and grows in clumps in the beds of rivers running through salt ground. The root is a thick, black, fibrous trunk, which runs along the ground for about twelve or fifteen feet, throwing up at regular intervals branches which in favourable soil attain a height of nine feet. The fronds are sometimes four feet from the setting-on to the tip; but when so large they appear to lose much of their toughness, and those a foot or a foot and a half long are most esteemed. Like other fan-palms, it dies after flowering and bearing fruit once. It sends up from the centre a tall straight stem, from which at regular intervals numerous branches curve out in a horizontal direction, the whole having a pyramidal form.

The fruit is called Kunar or Kunal, and is eaten though not much esteemed; the young white heart

* Ju dar, a place with a rivulet in it.

of the tree is eaten like that of the date. Some trees produce a fluffy substance which, when soaked in a solution of trāt-wood and dried, furnishes admirable tinder; the leaves split into fingers and twisted together make tough ropes, the mats made of these leaves are particularly strong and lasting. In the hills, where the fan-palm is plentiful, houses are thatched with it, and rendered quite waterproof. It is carried from the hills to the plains on camels, a good camel being able to carry ten krans' worth (the value of a kran is one franc). The pīsh in the bed of the Karwān river resembled miniature date groves, and greatly increased the beauty of the river from the high banks.

The night was lovely, and we camped at Pūgūnzī, pūgūnz meaning the heart of the pīsh tree. Next morning Mihrāp, our guide, objected to the load on his camel; and luckily, as we were quarrelling, a man came up with a camel who was bound also for Bint, so we gave Mihrāp his *congé* and engaged Habībī, and, after a loading that lasted four hours and included seven pitched battles, we marched triumphantly up out of the bed of the Karwān, and after two hours over a high shingly plateau, we arrived at the foot of some perfectly barren hills; here three plain deer were disturbed just in the line of march, but, though I made a long detour, I could not get their wind.

After a mile along the base of these hills, we struck into them, and going slightly westerly, we entered the Tenk river. Tenk is the same word as Tang (*a pass*), and there are three rivers within twenty miles of each other all bearing this name. This Tenk had rocky sides and bottom, for we were now fairly in the hills, and there is but little level ground for about a hundred miles due north, when the level of the Lāshāri plains is reached.

We followed the course of the Tenk for about a mile, the bed being about four hundred yards wide, and the hills on either side from fifty to three hundred feet high. Here we met two men with camels loaded with pīsh. As I had not yet acquired sufficient influence with my men to prevent their exchanging salutations for a quarter of an hour with everybody they met, I was obliged to let them all sit down and converse, merely stipulating that one man should go on with the camels.

The news was that Mīr Hāji, Chief of Bint, had killed a brother of Hamam Shah, a great man of Sūrag, and that thirty men had just preceded us to take Mīr Hāji before Hussein Khan, of Kasser Kand, to get compensation. I pointed out the fact that the only pugs on the route were those of two camels and one donkey, and questioned the accuracy of the number given; but our informants immediately made it thirty-five, and it was apparent that before they reached their destination, Sadaich, a very considerable army would have gone up. The matter was a blood feud, the "*belli teterrima causa*" being a somewhat wealthy widow, whose frailty appeared to have been less carefully concealed than usual.

We were now aiming for the Sīhrān-i-Koh, or crimson mountain, a hill which in all lights was a soft rich crimson, and, leaving the Tenk, which was said to come to an end here, we branched off to the right, down the Sīhrāni nullah. Following this about a mile, we turned under the brow of Sīhrān, and, passing up a steep, narrow defile, we descended on the other side into the Gari river. Following this a short time, we crossed another steep defile into the Derāi nullah, and after another tough bit of climbing, entered the bed of the Sartāpi * river, and getting into some rather more open country, we camped about sunset.

---

* "Sart ap," corruption of "sard ab,"—cold water.

CHAPTER II.

Pitching camp.—The bivouac.—Ousted by the rain.—Balūchi powder.—Toby makes trouble.—" Inchruki dārū."—The Gidīch Valley.—*Nerium oleandrum*, the poison-bush.—Road-making in its infancy.—Gorgeous colouring of hills.—Irrigation in the Gari river.—Our reception at Bint.—Pitching camp under difficulties.—Bint, its products and inhabitants.—The literary and religious element.—Mīr Hāji.—The pipe of brotherhood.—Diplomacy in Balūchistan.—Disgust of Salah the orthodox at finding the *soi-disant* Sunnis to be Sūfis.

To those uninitiated into camel travelling, a sketch of an arrival at camp may be of interest. This evening, for instance, the sun had almost gone down upon us still on the march, for in this country places suitable for camping only occur about once in six or seven miles; we had thus very often the alternative of a very short stage or a very long one. Now our trusty guide Habībī received his wages per diem, and at the first halting-place after ten miles would swear solemnly that if we did not stop there we would not find another suitable place till midnight. In this the camel-men would clamorously back him up, quite indifferent to the fact that they could not possibly know anything about it. This, of course, after the first day, resulted in my taking the matter into my own hands, and refusing to stop anywhere till 4 p.m. There was a certain amount of responsibility in thus taking loaded and tired camels over an endless chaos of barren hills through dark evenings and in the face of the only man who knew the road, and I often laughed to myself at the meek manner in which the men submitted, when, had they but known it, they could so easily have compelled a halt; but we never came to serious harm, and indeed I never could have made the journey in the time allowed me had I not thus taken charge.

To-day, declining to stop under the Sīhrāni hill, and having also been much delayed by the quarrels over loading, we were later than usual; Salah and myself on ahead were thus glad to find a flat place for the tent in the Sartāpi river; that was the first thing which became apparent in the dim light, then water, then heaps of driftwood caught by the tamarisk trees in the now dry river bed. Our experienced eyes could not be deceived in deciding that the dark spots on the hill sides were lorti (*Tavernea Spartæa*); we dismounted and immediately found some trāt bushes (*salicornia*), the salt meat without which these camels cannot long retain their health and appetite.

Here was "lizzat," as the Balūchis expressed it. Salah set to work making tea, Ghulamshah hoppled * our two camels, took off their nose reins, and soon after we heard old Jellāl coming along in the distance abusing his donkey, the guide, the country, and many other things. How he brightened up when he saw our evident intention of camping.

"Ah, Sahib, capital place this, water, firewood, and fodder abundant;" and in two minutes he had tied his donkey to a bush, shaken out some of the grass with which it always arrived loaded, and, getting a handful

* Tied the two hind legs.

of dates from Salah, was off collecting driftwood. "Tent here, sahib, eh?" he would say as he arrived with a load. "Cook's camp here;" then he would go and badger Salah till the latter got the nargilla out of his saddle-bags, and gave him a handful of tobacco, for your Balūch is dying for a smoke when tired, and Jellāl was getting old.

Then we hear the merry voices of the camel-men, and old Eblis strides in with the cook's two heavy boxes, and announces his arrival by a thundering roar, showing that at all events he is not much fatigued.

"Al ham du lillah," is the cry, "marro shap bīta, manzila sangīn bīd" (*To-day it began to be night, and the stage was a heavy one*). "Where shall I put the cookhouse?" "Where the tent?" "Is there any fodder here?" "Trust the sahib for that;" and in six or seven minutes all the camels would be unloaded, hoppled and turned loose, and the men enjoying a feed of dates and a pull at Salah's nargilla, meanwhile discussing with Habībi the chances for and against the presence of the dreaded jūr or oleander.

Soon old Abdulla wonders, in a stage whisper, whether the sahib will have the tent pitched or not, and on receiving my answer "no," the men prepare for the night. Two take a long stick, and, slinging the three waterskins across it, go to the stream for water; two must go for firewood; Abdulla gets a firebrand from our fire and prepares a pot of rice; the cook quarrels with and bullies Jellāl, who takes it quietly enough from the man who controls his rations, and four more men make bags of their sheets and go off with short sickles to cut lorti. The night is heavenly, and I stroll about the camp and bully the cook at rather short intervals. By the time I have finished my dinner the men all come in and have their rice with—at this early stage of their journey—a little very putrid salt fish. (Their fish was sometimes so strong smelling that I had to make special arrangements for its separate transport.) I sit in my little arm-chair over a roaring fire. Ghulamshah makes the bed and covers all with a mackintosh, for the dew is very heavy. Then the men bring in their camels, remove the saddles, and come to Salah for pitch plaister for any fresh sores. The four grass-cutters announce gladly that they have seen no jūr, and Habībī, who has been busy with his own camel, assumes a "told you so" sort of manner.

The camels are all made to kneel with their heads to the fire, the lorti is apportioned out, and the feeding commences. It is a picturesque scene; the glare of the fire falls redly on the men's animated faces as they chaff one another and talk about camels and krans, the only subjects in which a Balūch is at home. Each man holds his camel's nose-string in one hand, and with the other makes up a handy wisp of lorti; then he draws the camel's nose down, thrusts one end of the wisp into its mouth, and pushes it in till the animal begins to chew. They afterwards consult with Habībī (in whom, since the triumph about the jūr, they have regained a temporary confidence), and, hearing it is safe to turn their camels loose, they do so. The transition is brief from a roaring fire with its animated surroundings to a few smouldering embers included by a ring of white-sheeted forms, some of whom snored fearfully.

The country immediately around us was low shūrs

of various colours from chocolate to dull yellow. In order to get away early we had not pitched the tent, and were lying in the bed of the river. It was awkward about 9 p.m., just as we were turning in, to find a steady shower of rain commencing. We lit fires in various places to show the way, and soon carried everything up the side of a hill near, and, wrapping myself in my mackintosh, I slept well. Scarcely any rain fell after all, so our change of camp was hardly needed but that rain might have fallen farther up the river and washed us out suddenly.

Next morning as we were having breakfast, while the men loaded the camels, a Balūch rode up, followed by his slave, also mounted; the former got off to pay his respects, but he had had all his front teeth knocked out, and his speech was difficult to understand. He was one of the parties interested in the before-mentioned blood feud, and was on his way to Bint, where we afterwards met him. His name was Kerimdad, and he had a great reputation for knowing all the routes through the hills. He asked, as usual, for powder, but used the word "marsala," and it was amusing to see the face of the cook, who overheard the request and fancied it an attack upon his treasured curry powder. Balūchi gunpowder is not good, and a careful analysis of its ingredients could not fail to surprise an English powder manufacturer. The best powder is made in Panchgūr, Mināb, and other small towns; that from Bandar Abbas is bad, being probably imported from Bombay. The Balūchis also make a sufficiently powerful sort in the jungle, using probably trāt-wood.

The next morning (which was January the 18th)

we followed the Sartāpi for half an hour between low shūrs, backed by hills averaging 800 feet, and then, ascending a steep defile, emerged on to a high, shingly plateau. Straight ahead was the Gou Koh, marked by Lieut. Stiffe in his latest chart as 6,400 feet high, and from which emanates the Gabrig (Gao rīg) river. To our right the almost parallel ranges of Ligandi and Sharīki abutted on to the path.

After about 2½ miles we rounded the N.W. end of Ligandi and saw the Band-i-Sharīki. These two very striking ranges are about 1,600 feet high, and impassable except in a few places even for a man on foot; they converge sharply towards the south-east, and a bitterly cold wind comes down the gorge. The Sharīki nullah, which divides the hills, contained a little brackish water; here we saw two flocks of sheep and goats feeding on the sand-hills, the vegetation of which consisted almost entirely of trāt.

About eight miles after Ligandi we passed between the end of the Sharīki range and a low hogbacked hill on the left; in the distance to the north were the blue tops of the Hashingān mountains; the end of Sharik was marked by a curious castellated hill, reminding one of a blanc mange shape. We had been ascending gradually while crossing this plateau, and as we entered the wide pass we obtained a more open view than we had enjoyed since entering the hills. Mountains all round as far as the eye could reach, of every colour from chocolate to sky blue.

Toby here was—unwittingly—the cause of a little excitement which may be worth mentioning. He generally rode with the cook, and was quite an adept at balancing himself on a swaying camel over rough ground; to-day, however, he had been allowed to run on his own little legs and "*hinc illæ lacrimæ.*" I was trudging along at the head of the caravan when word was passed up along the long line that Toby had frightened a man's camel and given the rider a severe fall. I was rather annoyed,—for of course it is unwise to travel with a pet dog even in such an unorthodox Muslim country as this,—but I had mounted Abdulla, who was rather knocked up, on my riding camel, and did not quite relish going half a mile back to investigate the matter.

Shortly afterwards I heard some angry conversation going on in the rear, and soon two very tall, white-bearded old Balūchis came riding up to me mounted on splendid camels; they both had enormous noses, such as are only seen on Balūchi faces. On learning from Zangi—who was close behind me heading the caravan with Old Eblis—that I was the "waja," one of them rode up to me, and, perhaps thinking from my insignificant appearance (for he had never seen a Feringi), that I might be bullied with impunity, he commenced a long and loud-voiced string of complaints. He related with much violent and offensive gesture how he and his holy friend,—both were Syeds (descendants of the prophet) he said,—were riding along, when an evil-minded and immoral dog or fox, as the case might be, belonging to me, had jumped at their camels and so frightened them that his friend had fallen to the ground; how he had drawn his sword and was on the point of cutting the dog into pieces, when the thought occurred to him that the dog was not his, and he had stayed his hand as became a holy man, and determined to refer the matter to me; "and now," he added, "what have you to say?" Loud speech of this kind must be met by louder speech in this country, and, under a certain amount of irritation at his language towards my doggie and myself, I proceeded to outtalk him. I commenced by telling him that I did not consider a person who could not ride a camel as either a man or a Balūch (a telling taunt where the men pride themselves so much on their camel-riding and their nationality). This beginning decided my men, who had hitherto been rather doubtful about taking my part against two Syeds, men not so common here as at Yazd and other places in Persia, and I saw that they were with me. I went on to inform him in my choicest Balūchi that my long experience of Balūchis had compelled me to come to the conclusion that, when young, they were not endowed with much sense, and when old they were, as a rule, absolute idiots. I finished by assuring him that, had he defiled my dog with his leaden sword, I would have beaten him black and blue, and by advising both him and his friend that next time they went on a journey they should get a couple of quiet donkeys to ride on.

The man was beaten on his own ground, and, in a whining tone, begged for a kaladar (*a rupee*) to buy some medicine; this being scornfully refused, he fell back upon the old cry "Inchruki dārū" (*a little powder*). Having my man now well in hand, I with great dignity ordered Ghulamshah to give him a little, at the same time instructing him in Hindustani to give him the whole flaskful. He expected a thimbleful, and it was grand to see his face, at first somewhat clouded at being referred to the servant, gradually smile, look cunning, and at last astonished, as the shiny black stream continued to run into the corner of his sheet until he had enough to last him about two years and to give him such a superiority over his fellows as he had never gained by his religion. We parted the best of friends, both Syeds imploring me to come and stay a day or two at their village.

After the Jamki (or *forked pass*) we commenced a slight descent; the ground was in many places white with salt, studded with luxuriant pīsh, and ornamented with vividly green agrich bushes. About 2½ miles from the Jamki (or *fork*) we suddenly broke upon the magnificent view of the noble Gidīch valley.

This valley was here quite straight for five or six miles, the bed was partly shingle and partly vertical, hard, blue clay strata. The valley from top to top was about a mile broad, the hills on each side sloping down to the edges of a broad belt of fine tamarisk and other trees, between which ran the smooth, dark blue river, at this time sixty yards broad with an average depth of two feet and a velocity here of about five miles an hour. Just to the right of our crossing place it rushes down a natural weir, caused by the projection of a stratum of the blue clay, which is almost of the consistency of rock. Altogether it would have been a charming camping place,—water, fodder and firewood were abundant, and the men did their best to make me stop there,—but it was only about two o'clock, and I knew from experience the value of the guide's assurances that we should find no other water till midnight. Habībī, as usual in such cases, refused point blank to proceed, stating violently that we were going to destruction; but as he followed when I led on, it was plain that mine was the right course.

After crossing the river, we turned to the east for about two miles through low shūrs, from the tops of some of which I noticed little streams of salt water trickling down. Then we went north over a fairly level extent of rocky plain, interspersed with shūrs full of six-inch thick veins of pure gypsum. In the blue distance far ahead was the lofty Band-i-Nīlag, the range through which the Fanōch pass leads, and probably a continuation of the Aphen-i-Band in Bashakard. We passed a nullah called Shīrīn Kandag, (*sweet defile*) unimportant looking here, but said to go to sea at Sūrag, and, leaving the Mīroi Koh on our left, passed on over another three miles of rough ground into the Hūrdin valley, which was white with salt, and where the pīsh flourished in wild luxuriance, the fronds being four feet long and the plants running seven feet high.

After some rough travelling and crossing many small black-watered, rusty-margined, slightly bitter creeks, we opened upon the Pāzgā valley just opposite a striking rock on the top of the opposite cliff, called Kŭnār Kanŭ. The Pāzgā here has a much wider bed than the Gidīch, but there is nothing grand about the view, owing to the hills on both sides being low and the river split into three channels, all hidden in dense kāsh* and kik grasses and gaz, jūr, and other bushes.

Here on the Pāzgā was the regular camping ground for all caravans passing between Bint and the sea-

---

[1] Kāsh, pampas grass.

board, and we found a caravan, which had arrived that day from Bint, carrying about ninety bags of dates, for sale at Sadaich and at whichsoever of the scattered mītags (or small settlements) on the way they might find purchasers. The men called upon us in the evening, and—as had done all the other people we had met since leaving Jask—commiserated me greatly on the wretched condition of my riding camel. This was a matter of indifference to me, as I had walked nearly the whole of each stage since entering the hills, and I never asked them if they had a better one which I could hire, for I felt sure they had.

Here also at Pāzgā is the jūr or gīsh tree, which is poison for camels. This beautiful bush (*oleander*) is fatal to all beasts except donkeys. Camels, goats and sheep will not, as a rule, eat it of their own accord, but a single leaf getting into the fodder cut for them would kill those who ate it. Some camels may be trusted to graze in the middle of it, while others eat any green shrub they see.

The morning of the 20th was gloomy, and Habībī said the river filled very rapidly, and that, if rain was falling up country, we should be unable to get out of the valley, which, soon after we left camp, narrowed to a width of about half a mile with broad low hills and shūrs on each side, thickly studded with gaz, pīsh and kāsh grass (*tamarisk*, *chamærops*, and *pampas*).

After about a mile and a half we struck the Kahir-gāzī; the strata were perpendicular and remarkably regular here, the bluish shūr mud being about six inches thick and the chocolate coloured sandstone about four inches.

Soon after we crossed into the Kalkīa district, and

following the small Kalkīa stream for about a mile, left it on the right bank.

The surface of these hills, which are composed of alternate strata of shūr mud and brown sandstone, is always covered with a thick layer of loose angular flakes of the sandstone ; the size of these flakes is proportionate to the thickness of the sandstone strata. This layer appears to be created by the rain washing away the shūr mud and leaving the sandstone ridges bare, which, from exposure to alternate heat and wet, crack off and fall all over the surface.

Here we came upon almost the first animal life we had met with since entering the hills. Flocks of rusty coloured birds were frequent ; they were the size of sparrows but of rather more elongated body, and their note exactly resembled the creaking of a loosely made rusty iron wire gate.

After two miles the sandstone strata were not alternated by strata of shūr. Ahead were two high hills to our right ; on our left were shūr with horizontal strata of gypsum for twelve feet from the surface, and above that was three feet of shingle and mud. After another mile and a quarter we re-entered the Pāzgā valley, the banks of which were regularly sloped, perpendicular strata of sandstone and shūr.

Here were two large rugged hills on our right and one on our left ; the former covered with huge boulders of a purple shiny stone. The view was magnificent, immense boulders of dark green, crimson, and purple, intersected by a network of wavy white veins. The hills were simply of every colour of the rainbow.

We crossed the Pāzgā river, which was here three times as large as at our camping place, then passed a shrine, called—like all the others on this route—Pīr Tarī, consisting simply of a heap of stones to which every passer-by contributed something. Men mounted on camels will throw their sticks on to it, and men on foot will pick up a stone and throw it on, and, should their suāss (*grass sandals*) be worn out, they will keep them till they come to a ziārat (*shrine*) and drop them there.

The origin of this puzzled me at first, but afterwards, while journeying along the pilgrims' road to Kerbela, I found ziārats exactly similar, and received, both from pilgrims and natives of the country, what I have no doubt to be the true explanation.

On the stony parts of the Kerbela road through Kurdistan these stone heaps are especially frequent, and immediately suggest the idea that they are crude attempts at road-clearing, and the natives all say that the mullas have given out that it behoves all true believers passing along the road, to cast at least one stone on each heap, to make the road easier to the holy pilgrims, thereby becoming part-sharers in the latter's sanctity. The custom has been introduced into Balūchistan, where it is certainly particularly wanted, while the reason for it is not realized by such splendid hill walkers as the Balūchis, who always aver that each heap marks the burial place of some saint. Often, when ahead of the caravan in Balūchistan, I have made a heap of stones by the side of the tract, and, when the men got near, have ostentatiously thrown a stone on to it, and my example was always unhesitatingly followed.

Rounding the foot of the right hand Kalkīa hill, we again crossed the Pāzgā, past two large snowy white boulders in mid-stream. The river here was twenty feet wide, with an average depth of one and a half feet; around us the hills were positively of every imaginable hue. Passing on up a very difficult defile, called the Rīdagon Darag, we entered a sea of hills of such rich and variegated tints as must really be seen to be believed.

After a mile and a half through this richly coloured sea of hills, we entered the small Hādar or Halirt river, on the banks of which are many small settlements. The strata here were perpendicular and wavy, as if the material had been moved when half consolidated. We passed between two of four conical hills called the Katal Janīn, a name which may or may not have an Arabic derivation.* One of these peaks was of a rich blood red. We were now heading for the Sigā Pūsht hill, which was about half a mile distant. All around were curiously shaped tall peaks, on which the chief shrubs were dihīr, agrich, and tūlări; the latter is, in Bạlūch phraseology, lorti's brother, and is another species of that much esteemed camel vetch, whose place it fills entirely in these latitudes.

At the foot of the Sigā Pūsht is another shrine, also called Pīr Tārī, and here abounded a sort of sweet potato, the leaves of which have no white lines and curl round over the ground like young snakes, instead

* Soon after leaving Marrick, the second stage on the Bahomadi route from Jask to Anguhran, the capital of Bashakard, is a pass called Katal Zan or Katal Janīn. I could get no explanation of the name further than that the camels, if not led, would sometimes break their loads against the sides of the pass. There is another place near Oushdāhndarrī, where the road leads up a narrow cleft in the rocks, which bears the same name.

of sticking up. Here also was much trāt jungle, and the road was crossed by another very faint track, along which came a solitary donkey, who stared at us in mute surprise.

In the hills we entered now the shūr strata are much thicker than the sandstone, which results in the flake covering being very thin and small.

Passing the Sigā Pūsht hill we entered a wide valley full of trees and shrubs. Here we re-entered the Pāzgā river into which the Sigā Pūsht stream runs; here was a fenced patch of wheat in the bed of the river, which was about a quarter of a mile wide and contained much tall kāsh growing to the height of thirteen feet.

We entered the Sigā Pūsht stream, the bed of which we followed about three-quarters of a mile, when we entered the Gari river again near the Gari Drāp (or Gari river hollow). The bed was white with salt, and here about four hundred yards wide. We passed a large settlement containing many extensive groves of tall date-trees, many fenced gardens of tobacco, beans, and spaces reserved for rice when the season should come in, about two months hence. The water appeared to stand here some time, judging by the presence of many water weeds, while the existence of siriks (or upper storied huts) on the tops of all the neighbouring hills betokened the presence of many consequent mosquitoes.

This was quite a delightful oasis in the sea of barren hills through which we had been travelling. Its irrigation was quite scientific, and there were many small well-built bridges. The walls of the gardens had the appearance of being built of English bricks, so regularly square were the flakes of sandstone of which they were composed. The strata of the hills here were alternately brown sandstone and good earth, not at all salt. To our left was a many-coloured mountain, which looked as if it had been struck by lightning, boulders the size of houses lying about it anyhow. One canal, which had been dug to bring the water direct from higher up the river, was upwards of a milc in length, and was crossed by two strong bridges of mud and stone.

Here we overtook a stout, good-humoured looking man, who was returning to his native place; he had very much the expression of a jovial English farmer, and hospitably offered us some of his travelling provisions of shilanch, a very hard and sour cheese. He said that Mīr Hāji's brother was the chief man at Gari Drāp, and that there were but three or four families of importance, the rest of the houses being occupied by servants and slaves.

We passed up the river bed, which was very broad and shingly, studded with bushes. Settlements are dotted all along this river; on our left was the village of Daskīr, and on our right Rah Gudār, while straight ahead was Tarampōg. The river here was very rapid, fifty feet broad with an average depth of one foot, and is said to originate from the Band-i-Nīlag and is with the Gidīch and the Pāzgā an almost perennial tributary of the Rapsh.*

Passing up the river bed we went between the villages of Tarampōg and Rendag. All around were

* I received many conflicting statements as to whether this river dried up in the hot weather, and think the truth to be that it would dry up in a very dry year, and continue running during the summer succeeding a moderate rainfall.

date and other trees, behind which were almost barren hills. About two miles after emerging from the river bed the road to the Fanōch pass branched off to our left past some date-trees, called Umkān. All the date-trees here were in a most slovenly condition, and Salah, who was used to the Basrah farming, animadverted on the owners in no measured terms, assuring me that if they were but properly looked after, the yield would be fully a quarter more than it is.

We were now heading for a large, conical hill called the Sī Pūrg, and one and a half miles after leaving the road to Fanōch, we crossed the small rocky-bedded stream Zangūtan, which here flows east, has but small volume with a deep bed, and a width of about three hundred yards. It is said to be a tributary of the Rapsh and perennial, but the latter is doubtful. We crossed the river by another Pīr Tārī, and camped about 4 p.m. under a hill, weather very gloomy and threatening.

I was convinced that Bint must be very close, but the guide, as usual, denied it, and his statement that no fodder could be got further on was accidentally corroborated by our seeing a string of donkeys carrying camel fodder towards Bint. We were content to camp, for, should it be at all a large place, involving a ceremonious arrival, we should perhaps be able to perform the operation better after a short stage than after a long one.

During the night it rained pretty steadily, and when the sun rose it was entirely obscured by an inky sky, from which a heavy, perpendicular rain poured down as if it never intended to stop. We had, in a measure, turned the tables on the camel-men, for had they taken our advice, they would now have been safely housed in Bint. They wore a mutinous aspect at first, but a little chaff at the badness of their nasīb (or *fortune*) put them into a good humour, and they loaded up in the pouring rain cheerily enough.

Bint proved to be about three miles away, and agreeably surprised us in being a much larger place than we expected. It consisted on first view of a high, steep hill crowned by a square mud fort surrounded by many other similar flat-topped buildings. On each side were a mile or two of date-trees, in front was a shingly plain sprinkled with grass, and on the right was the curious, conical hill Sī Pūrg. As we advanced through the rain we saw every flat roof covered with people, while numbers poured out from town towards us. We counted 140 before dismounting, and, in spite of the wet, they still poured out.

Kerimdād (the man who had overtaken us at Sartāpi) had warned the Mīr of our visit, and the latter had consequently deferred his journey to Geh, on the blood feud business before mentioned; and now, before the tent was fairly pitched, he sent word that he wished to come and see me.

The tent was pitched under great difficulties, owing to the crowd, the rain, and the elastic hardness of the ground, which sent the pegs flying into the air unless held down very firmly. The mallet, if once laid down, was not found under half an hour's search, for the ground being wet, it formed at once a convenient roosting place for at least five humped-up shivering natives, who completely concealed it from view.

Our ancient shikarri Jellāl had, it appeared, married the daughter of the Mīr's choush (or *head man*) and the two men immediately struck up a friendship, the choush (Keramshah) being very useful in expelling the crowd from the tent while the walls were being fastened up.

I was not clearly given to understand which was the Mīr in the procession which soon entered the tent, but naturally addressed myself to the fat, unhealthy man to whom the others gave precedence. He, however, spoke but little, and as his friends insisted on his sitting on my portable camp bed (an operation which, even after much practice, I dared not perform) he lost much dignity by finding himself suddenly sink to the ground and become overwhelmed under a mass of bedding.

I found conversation much more practicable with a spare energetic man who sat next to him, and who spoke good Persian, not using any ceremony but speaking directly to the point, and clearly. *This* was Mīr Hāji, the chief. He answered all my questions without hesitation, and freely asked me about anything he wanted to know. The fat man I found was Abd el Kādir, who was the elder brother, but took no part in the government, and rusticated at Gari Darāp.

Sheep at Bint are poor and dear, and both camel fodder and firewood are brought from a distance of four miles. The bringing in of firewood gives occupation to about thirty boys and donkeys, the latter of whom spend the middle of the day on the shingly plain, making a journey for wood morning and evening.

Most of the cloth worn is home made. The manufacturers sit in holes in their gardens before their rather clumsy treadle looms, and produce a coarse white cotton cloth, and coarse gauzy handkerchiefs, dyed red, green, and blue, and often embroidered with red and green silk, while the women make minutely embroidered skull caps.

Long cloths from Dizzak are much prized both here and elsewhere, the cotton of that district being described as of such long staple that a single seed fills the palm of one's hand. None of the productions could be of the least value out of the country, except, perhaps, the skull caps, of which our men carried away a good many considering their price was a dollar each.

Boots, belts, and leather pouches are cheap and fairly well made. Couzas (or *porous water bottles*) also are made from the blue clay of the Gidīch, a name said to be derived from the Gil clay, the "l" suffering a not uncommon change into "d."

Mīr Hāji readily gave me the definition of many names of places through which we had passed, but the untrained native mind has so much of the common sort of ingenuity, a little exercise of which gives so fatal a facility for discovering coincidences, that I only give them for what they are worth.

Bint, he said, was formerly the Arabic "beit," being applied when his great grandfather first built the fort. Sartāpi is possibly "Sard āb" (*cold water*), while Maskhūtān was given as the residence of that tribe ("Maskan," a residence, *Ar.*). This it undoubtedly is, but it appears rather a strain to drop the "n" of Maskan, which may be the first syllable.

After the Mīr's departure we received several of the pillars of the state, all of whom were immensely civil, and perpetually apologising for bothering us; and then, leaving the tent in charge of Jellāl and Toby

Salah and myself started for a stroll in the gardens. At this season of the year these were really delicious; they were well irrigated, and the borders of each water lead were a foot deep in luxurious spring verdure of more than a hundred different kinds. Mallow and clover were the most common, and a beautiful crimson iris, a dwarf purple one, and English celery were among the most noticeable.

As nearly as we could estimate, there were about one hundred acres of cereals, in the following order of their respective areas: English horsebeans, wheat, rice, barley, and a very small quantity of tobacco. Dates are abundant, but carelessly looked after. A man in the gardens pointed out nineteen distinct sorts, only one or two of which were recognisable in Arabic.

The ground destined for rice still contained last year's stalks.

The irrigation is carried on by a canal made by the father of Mīr Hāji, and the latter taxes all his subjects for the use of it. The arrangements for the distribution of the water are bad, some crops of beans drowning while others are withering. The stream is led into four fields, making a total of about six acres, daily, and the landholders (all great men) take their turns according to their rank, and not according to their acreage.

The ground is a stiff clay, more adapted for building forts than cultivation, and requires constant manuring. All the cotton is grown at Dasht, a word the meaning of which I could not definitely ascertain, whether it were a place, or generally the open country; it is, however, plentiful at Gari Darāp.

Returning to tiffin we found that Mīr Hāji had sent

us a sheep, a bag of about ninety pounds of dates, several māns of rice, shilanch (or *sour cheese*), and, on hearing that we wanted some mats for a cookhouse, sent bodily the entire dome roof of one of his circular cottages. After tiffin we received a deputation of the mullas of the town.

Religion is of great importance in the towns, but among the nomadic part of the population is entirely absent. The mullas of Bint represent themselves as Sunni of the sect of Abu Hanifah, while they are really unadulterated Sūfīs. None of the representatives of the literary talent at Bint were more than mere youths, and they appear to retain little of their religion after arriving at a marriageable age. They were a cadaverous, sickly-looking set, and constantly interrupted the conversation by ostentatiously remarking that they had forgotten to say their prayers.

The main subjects of conversation were, as usual, the tyranny of the Gajars (or Persians), and the Balūchis' intense desire that the English should take their country, an event they confidently expected to take place shortly. They asked eagerly for Hāfiz, but could not read the shikasta (*running hand*) of my MS. copy. They had better success with a Hereford Gūlistān, and much enjoyed droning over the stories at the end of Forbes' Persian Grammar. Two or three professed a knowledge of Arabic, but could not read a word in any Arabic book but the Kurān, their chanting of which was painful. We puzzled two of them very much with a very plainly written copy of some Turkish poems, and they failed to discover it was anything but Persian.

Here and at Bampūr were the only places at which

I was asked anything about my religion. One very vigorous old man, who had brought his son, and who prefaced all his remarks by poking me up violently with a thick staff, asked me to read him some Hāfiz, and, while I was singing one of the hackneyed old odes to an admiring crowd, he abruptly changed the topic to my religion, and called upon me triumphantly, as a sort of test, to read something from the Kurān. Believing at the time that the people were, as they gave themselves out to be, orthodox Sunni, I turned upon him with the greatest indignation, asking him fiercely how he dared to mention in the same breath, a volume of love song and the word of God. He left me at once, congratulating myself on the success of my rebuke, which the after discoveries of Salah led me to think was more due to the tone in which it was delivered than to the force of the argument it contained.

The evening sun was now striking on the wet walls of the tent, and rendering it very unpleasant; so, having got rid of my visitors with some difficulty, I strolled out through the gardens down to the broad river at their back. The gardens are about half a mile wide, and, towards the south, reach the edge of the river bed, which, however, is so broad and full of large loose shingle, that I did not get to the channel itself.

Returning to the tent, we made all safe for the night, Mīr Hāji having sent purposely to warn us of the thieving propensities of his subjects.

The barometer here gave approximately an elevation of 2,000 feet above the level of the sea, and the climate was nearly that of England, only that the sun at noon had more power than was agreeable.

I had, in the course of the day, mentioned to Jellāl my intention of making a rapid march to Bampūr; and he had been, unsuccessfully, canvassing for three good camels to carry him, myself, and two camel-men. The following day, however, we proposed to return Mīr Hāji's visit, when we would mention our difficulty.

Accordingly, the following morning we walked across the common, and, entering through a breach in a curious natural sandstone wall, climbed up some steep, narrow and filthy streets, whose uses for progression were subordinate to their value as manure beds. We had noticed every day donkeys passing into the town laden with Kik grass roots, and now found every nook and corner throughout the town spread deep with Kik grass and old rice straw.

The houses of Bint, Fanōch, Maskhūtān, and other Balūch towns, are simply built in what resembles an English crew-yard, or yard for wintering cattle in, and the smell at some seasons must be fearful. The quantity of rice straw lying about, the sparrows, and the substantial look of the well-thatched houses, give the place at the back the appearance of a very slovenly English homestead. The ascent to Mīr Hāji's house, which crowned the hill, was steep, winding, and, owing to the late rains, very slippery. There was no regular path, but the thick manure straw helped one's feet, and the various inequalities in the flat roofs gave one occasional hold for one's hands. Arrived at the summit, we entered a fair-sized rectangular room, along one side of which were, seated on their haunches, Abd el Kādir, Mīr Hāji, and various chief people of the land. A cradle, swung by goats'-hair ropes, ornamented with cowrie shells, occupied one end of the room, and contained the Mīr's fondly loved son and heir; while at the other end, opposite to the chiefs, was a large chahar pai, or fourfooted bedstead, on which I gravely seated myself. My men herded with the Mīr's men clustering round the door, joining in the conversation with perfect freedom and invariable respect. The mud-plastered walls were hung with many English glass bottles, wrapped in network of camel's hair, ornamented with cowries; and I noticed many curious brass rosewater vases, apparently of Russian manufacture. We had a brisk conversation about routes, trade, and education; the Russians, and the Affghāns, who have made themselves a terrible name here. I was often asked to predict how much longer the Shah would live. Then a very humble kaliān was produced, the bottom of which was an English cut glass decanter, which I smoked, without appearing to make a point of it, through the hollow of my hand, so as not to put the Mīr into a dilemma about using the mouthpiece after me. His men were evidently rather proud of his being able to sport a kaliān like a "civilized Persian." In my subsequent journeyings, I often heard it commented on that Mīr Hāji had smoked a kaliān with me, a fact here regarded in much the same light as Brigham Young's blessing a Gentile is among the Mormons.

Of course, during the interview, we did not mention our business. Of course the Mīr protested that his country, his house, camels, and men were all at my service; and of course I protested that the only thing that could bring balm unto my anxious mind was the assurance that he and his family were quite well, and that anything else was mere supererogation. After regaining my tent, I sent Salah with many civil speeches to the Mīr to get me three good camels that same night.

Now Salah had been rather proud of an opportunity for showing his superior intelligence and capacity for managing the barbarians, and went on his way revolving in his mind many elaborate diplomatic speeches, which should induce the Mīr to grant our request. Old Jellāl, however, accompanied him as interpreter, and completely put his nose out of joint; for, on arriving within earshot of the chief, he shouted out in his most peremptory tone: "The Sahib requires three camels immediately." Subsequent experience showed that the Jellāl style of negociation was the right one, involving as it did a kind of assumption of superiority on our part. It was, as a bit of brag, far more suited to the natives, who would have regarded civility as a sign of weakness.

The manners of Balūchis to their Mīrs are not unlike those of the Bedawin, who, when entering the presence of their chief, walk straight up to him, and brandishing their long stick, shout at him: "Salām Yā mahfūth" (*Peace, oh thou protected of God*).

This was nearly my last night in Bint, and I will here insert extracts from Salah's diary kept at Bint while I was at Bampūr:—

"The school was simply a side room branching out of the Masjid, which was about sixty feet square, well and neatly built of mud, and matted with pīsh matting. The Imam of the Masjid was likewise the schoolmaster. He knew a little Arabic, which he said he had acquired in Mekka. He knew also a little Persian, but the instruction is carried on in Balūchi. The average attendance is ten boys, some of whom read the Kurān, and some Hāfiz. One of the former, at my request, read the 17th chapter; he read it well, but, as usual in this country, with manifest total inappreciation of its meaning. The Imam said that when one of his pupils had finished the Kurān, he received from the boys' parents ten reals, and, during the date season, small presents of dates."

The next is translated *verbatim.*

"Then I entered the Masjid, and saw in the recesses in the walls fragments of leaves from the Kurān. I saw also a book wrapped in green cloth, embroidered with gold, and on my asking one of them 'What is that?' he replied, 'the book of Hāfiz, the Shirazi;' and when I begged to see it, he took it reverently in both hands and gave it unto me. And when I saw that it was really Hāfiz, I said unto him: 'Why do you put this book here, for verily it treats of wine, and love, and debauchery?' Then he denied this, saying vehemently, 'Speak not thus, for the book is clean and divested of all such matters. Where, then, should it be placed if not here?' And I answered unto him saying, 'This is a Masjid, the house of God, and there should be in it nothing but the word of God and the traditions of the prophets. This book is for the youthful and ignorant, nor is it in any way a religious work.' And he answered, saying, 'On the contrary; the author of this work was of the very root of religion itself; and as touching the matter you mention concerning wine and love, it is not at all as you imagine. "Wine" is the drinking in of the love of God; "Love" is a longing for God;' and he recounted unto me the meanings of various words even as they are given in the dictionary of the Sūfī sect. Now I was then silent, and verily, judging by appearances, it will not be long before the people shall have abandoned the Kurān, and set up Hāfiz in Muhammad's place."

I would have given much to have been present when the bigoted old Sunni Salah got nonplussed by the carnal views of his plausible friend.

The following again are extracts :—

"I asked him if, on the day of assembly for prayer, he used the whole 'Khutbah'; and on his answering 'no,' I inquired why, and he answered that there were here no well defined rules of religion, nor any known law against unbelief and wickedness, adding that in his views of religion the prayer of Juma should only be used in places where there were well defined laws and a just ruler.

"He also said that the people were of the sect of Abu Hanifah, their religion Islam; they are Sunnis, and abuse the Persians, whom they refer to as accursed Rafizis (deserters of their religion). There is no regular trade here; after a good year superfluous dates are sold to the Balūchis around, and sheep and ghee are sent to Maskat and Bandar Abbas, in exchange for cotton cloths and silk, the latter for purposes of embroidery. There is no coin in the country less than half a kran.

"Mīr Hāji pays annually to Mīr Hussain of Kasser Kand 2,500 tomāns."

In the afternoon the Mīr came to bid farewell, as he left for Geh on the following morning. He was accompanied by his favourite little son, whom my quinine had enabled to rise from his sick bed. He was about three feet high, but had read through the whole Kurān; a process here regarded in much the same light as vaccination in England, and supposed to shield the youth from all sorts of evil eye, etc. We gave him some skeins of raw silk, and to my intense joy, and Salah's despair, he begged for the latter's accordion. He left, and was soon mounted on his little gray horse, promising that the camels should arrive in about an hour.

CHAPTER III.

Start for Bampūr.—Our new companions.—Icy cold wind.—Camels dangerous at night.—Mountain scenery.—The Fanōch pass.—Fish and crabs.—Reception at Fanōch.—A Persian slave.—Jellāl as doctor.—The last of the donkeys.—The "Pai-i-duldul-i-Ali."—We emerge from the mountains and open on the desert.—Maskhūtān.—Quarrel about the cooking.—Our guide Kuli.—Marri, the valley of desolation.—A grotesque scene.—The Bampūr desert.—A gentleman on a cow.—Reception at Bampūr.—Politics at Bampūr.—I am an officer of artillery.—Messing with the Khan.—Barley water.—The position of Persian and Turkish soldiers compared.—A curious mill.—Awkward position on a cow.—Old Jellāl.—Leave Bampūr.—Jellāl's camel wants a breastband.—Small-pox.—A horrible banquet.—Frozen out.—A cold ride.—The Pai-i-duldul-i-Ali renovated.—"Home, sweet home."—Jooji and the fowls.

ALTHOUGH promised, the camels did not of course arrive that night, and the next morning there was a bitterly cold gale from the north. Contrary, however, to our expectations, about ten o'clock three magnificent camels turned up. Two huge ones were furious with must, roaring, foaming, and blowing bladders from their throats. The third, destined for Jellāl and the saddlebags, was a powerful three-year-old.

A short parley sufficed to engage them, though the men expressed great dread of the cold, and at the most would only promise that if possible they would do the journey to Bampūr and back in sixteen days. Now I had only ten days which I could possibly spare, and that would leave me only six days for the journey home from Bint to Jask, which I had determined to make by a new route. However, I trusted to getting up very early in the mornings and making friends with the two men whom the camel owner sent with me, and who could not be expected to be quite so sparing of the camels as the owner himself.

Some little description will perhaps be welcome of these our new companions on the road. First, as regards the hiring the camels. The spokesman in the transaction was named Shukari, pronounced here like the English word "sugary." He denied all interest in the camels, giving as his reason for appearing in the matter that his "waja" had ordered him to provide three first-rate camels; and that he had with difficulty procured three and consented to accompany them and their two owners to make a bargain with me, as the two men were too much afraid of the Feringi to be able to speak up to and make terms with him. He said that his honour was concerned in my getting through my intended journey safely; that the two men who would be with me were his "brothers," and he enlarged freely on the extreme cold we should experience, pronouncing the Persian word "sard" as "swart."

The two "musty" camels belonged to Abdulla, a short stout jovial little man, with a round nose, bright little black eyes, and an irresistibly comic vehement way of speaking. The three-year-old belonged to Barja, a tall powerful man with an extremely handsome, intelligent face, and a fine brown beard. Barja, in Persian, means handsome and fine-eyed, which our friend was to an unusual degree. Barja acted as Abdulla's elder brother, and it was amusing, when turning in for the night, to watch Abdulla wind himself up in his "pow," or headcloth, and lie down, and then call to Barja to come and tuck him up in his blanket, which office the latter would laughingly perform with all the tenderness of an English mother.

We started in silence against a bitter north wind, Abdulla and Barja first on the big camel, followed by myself and Jellāl with the saddlebags. My camel was very "musty," and I involuntarily "shikarred" three unfortunate individuals whom we met on the road, to their great terror. We cut off a large bend in the river, and then travelled up the bed, the sides of which were studded with gaz and other trees, under which were frequent heaps of dead bunches of leaves collected and laid by the natives to rot for manure. The wind was dead in our faces, and icy cold, accompanied by sleet and driving rain.

About 3 p.m. the men halted, and said it was impossible to go any farther, as, even were the weather good, the day was so far advanced that we should not be able to get through the pass before nightfall. Not very much unsatisfied with my first day's work, and feeling very unwell, I camped under the high cliff of a nullah which ran into the river, and the material of which was entirely mud and shingle.

Here was the first gaz roghān, or oil tamarisk, which we had hitherto met with, and we found afterwards that all the tamarisks in the Fanōch pass and those composing the Bampūr tree belt were of this sort. The fruit is collected and sold for one kran a mān (or *weight of* 6 *lbs.*), and the oil expressed from it for three krans per mān.

We had rather an exciting night, the account of

which, as it is a fair sample of the next nine nights, I extract *verbatim* from my note-book.

"8 p.m., turning in. Much trouble with big līro (*full-grown male camel*), whose true character is now coming out, notice his master's hand half bitten off. He won't eat, but rolls on the ground, crushing bushes.

"They will none of them eat, each handful of lorti being forced into their mouths, and so far down their throat that they must choke or chew. They chew reluctantly.

"10 p.m. New sensation, to turn in on the ground within six feet of three enormous līros, all frothing at the mouth with must. The two lesser ones have sided against the largest. Barja lies on one side of the fire with the reins of the two former round his wrist, and Abdulla lies on the other with the big one's rein round his. They have stampeded three times already, but none of us are as yet damaged. The big one is tied both hind and fore-legs, and has just invaded us on his knees and haunches, with the result of filling my bed with gravel.

"11.30 p.m. The big one has worked himself within a yard of my feet, and stretching his neck along the ground gone to sleep. I note with pain that he is within biting distance, and follow his example. Shortly afterwards awakened by our friend's arrival, backwards this time. After a fearful struggle with the two men he is extricated, one leg from the fire, the other from my pillow. I endeavour to conceal from myself the fact that I am directly in his route to the other two camels, whose destruction appears to be his object. The attempt is a failure, not to say a miserable one. Observing blood coming from the hole in his nose through which the rein-knot passes, the probability presents itself that said rein-knot will come out. A cord is passed up through his nose and tied through the hole, so that he cannot get away without carrying away three inches of his nose. His 'waja' then goes to sleep again, rein in hand.

"The men agree that they are not frightened for themselves, but fear for the smaller camels. Their reflections do not include me. Old Jellāl, to whom has been allotted the largest share of blankets, sticks himself under a tamarisk-tree and sleeps with great indifference. The struggles occasionally half wake him up, only to mutter a few curses at all camels and regrets for his chōk or child, by which he means his pet donkey, which he has entrusted to his relative Keramshah, whom he appears already to hate and distrust, feeling sure that he will starve the darling."

Early in the morning it was icy cold, cloudy, and there was a strong north-east wind. The men declared that it was impossible to proceed, but by distributing all my remaining rugs, and threatening to ride in my shirt-sleeves to disgrace them, I got them to start. After about five miles, sometimes paddling up the stream, sometimes along the banks of sand and shingle, we fairly entered the pass at Giri, a huge blood-red rock under which was a large pool, said to be very deep. There was a striking contrast between the deep rich colour of the rock and the pale sea-green of the pool.

About three miles farther on the scenery about the Kelāt-i-Zangi is wildly beautiful—a reckless jumble of hills and rocks of every imaginable shape, size, and colour. It is literally true that on this occasion, when everything was wet with rain, pure lamp-black was the only shade of colour not represented; and when I add that the main colours were bright red, soft crimson velvet, snowy white, purpled steel, and all shades of green from dark to emerald, I have said what I can to give a faint idea of the utterly grotesque magnificence of this extraordinary pass. Oxide of iron gives every tint of red, from the palest pink to rich crimson; lead gives every shade of yellow, copper gives green, and the untinged limestone snowy white.

Sitting now in a house where I know the temperature will soon rise to 110, it seems odd that I brought away no specimen, nor any sketch, and the reasons in my note-book do not seem half so conclusive as they did then. That my hands were numbed and could scarcely form a letter, and that my saddle would be soaked if I dismounted for five minutes, were not insuperable difficulties. The main one was, that I could not get any idea of the length or practicability of the remainder of the stage, so as to estimate how much time I could spare. The men could only say, "It's a long, long way," and they pressed eagerly on, muffled up to the eyes and silent.

They had never been through the pass in such weather, and feared lest at a place ahead there should be so much water that we should have to return all the way to our last night's camp to find a safe resting place. The river here filled its bed, on each side were steep rocks, so our progress was generally against a rushing stream about three feet deep; that is to say, between and over the huge boulders which filled it, and round which the eddies excavated disagreeably deep and sudden hollows.

From twelve to fifteen feet above the present water were the marks of high water, and the river foaming down with a depth and volume such as this indicates must be a sight inexpressibly grand.

The least degree of mossiness would render this pass impracticable, save in the dry weather, and the roaring of the water was such that my camel seemed at one time to lose its head altogether. By a vigorous effort he had scrambled up to the top of a smooth round white flint boulder, and after balancing for a few seconds, his next step should have been to drop his fore-legs over the opposite side into a raging miniature whirlpool four feet deep. Instead of this he turned round and round, roaring piteously, and from the excited shouts and gestures of the men there were evidently just grounds for apprehension that he might put one foot off the very confined standing place, and break his leg. As vigorous an application of the stick as my numbed condition would allow put him on the right course, and we struggled on for about four miles; when we opened on a straight piece of about a quarter of a mile long and piled up high on either side with huge smooth snow-white boulders. At the end, half-hidden in watery clouds, was a lofty hill of the Band-i-Nīlag range. This piece of the pass, though easy looking, was very difficult, necessitating that the two men riding double should dismount and go ahead, and find out a path.

Here we were near the end of the pass, and having heard that there was no firewood at Fanōch we halted to collect some of the dried uprooted gaz roghān bushes. Here we saw fish, about six inches long, and what surprised me more was a brown crab about an inch and a half in diameter. We found afterwards that the Bint people prided themselves very much on their fish, assuming for them a great superiority over sea-fish. They were long, narrow, and gracefully tapered, colourless underneath, and of a light ash colour on their backs.

We marched under a lofty perpendicular wall of purple rock, a section of the backbone of the Band-i-Nīlag; and emerging from the pass, and turning up the bank on our right, we entered the date-trees of Fanōch. A short mile to our right were the remains of a fort said to have been destroyed by the Affghāns. From the north, slightly on our left, comes a tributary to the Bint river of about one-fourth the latter's volume. Rounding a high dark purple bluff, on which was a small but very commandingly placed mud fortification, we ascended a steep hill covered with circular thatched huts looking like English wheat-stacks. Every foot of space between the houses was here laid deep in rice stalks, grass roots, etc., for manure. Chākar Khan was absent, and a slave of Mīr Hāji showed us into one of his master's houses which was empty, warm, and in the meaning of the word to which I had recently become accustomed, clean. Here, as soon as we were installed and my carpets spread, we received about a hundred of the aristocracy, and their manners, or absence of manners, were decidedly annoying.

Edwin Pierce, whose studies in the Balūch dialect have been as successful as laborious, used often to remark on the difficulty he found in persuading the natives that he understood and could speak their language. I had experienced this difficulty, but in the earlier parts of my journey candour had compelled me to attribute it to my imperfect knowledge of Balūchi. Now, however, the case was different, yet nothing that Jellāl could say would induce them to address a single word to me. They passed remarks freely about me, and when I showed any appreciation of them they nudged one another, saying wonderingly, "He understands." They would not believe that my clothes and big boots could have come from any place but Kirman, which place they spoke of much as English country-people speak of London.

We were much struck with one man who made himself very prominent. He was a huge, black-whiskered fellow, with enormous moustaches, a heavy swagger, and a deep hoarse voice. He wore Persian dress, had even thick worsted gloves, and knitted list stockings. His conversation was of horses, and I unhesitatingly put him down as an up-country Persian employed as a groom to Chākar Khan's two horses, but I was very much surprised to find he was a slave. My dress of a pea-jacket, white moleskins, and big boots took his fancy immensely, and I more than once heard him pointing out that "This was the style of the Shah," etc., adding: "Now you know the Shah is a wonderful king, any one oppressed or ill-used has only got to go to his house and say: 'Where's the king?' and the king immediately comes out and does him justice."

I could not believe that this man was a slave, but three people told me so, and as I had no opportunity of speaking to him privately and did not think my position justified open inquiries, I had to leave the matter unsettled. Murād Khan, Chākar's deputy, pressed me to take one of his horses, and get to Bampūr in two days, but I was not disposed to leave my small baggage behind, and only used his offer to point a violent harangue at my camel-men on their folly in persisting that the journey was a five days' business. As we got more fāmiliar, the people became very importunate for medicines for all sorts of diseases, chiefly for headaches of two years' (?) standing. I was soon tired of protesting that I had left all medicines at Bint; but Jellāl, without a hint, took up the rôle of doctor with a happy audacity only paralleled by Abū Zeid of Surooj. The grave way in which he would find out from a man where his pet shrine was and then tell him it was there, and recommend him to go and sacrifice a goat there, was not more amusing than their expressions of wonder at his apparent intimate knowledge of the locality. No twinkle in his rugged old eyelids ever betrayed the solemn and thoughtful manner in which he ordered powdered rice, solutions of gypsum, or pills of mud.

Chākar Khan's people sent us in a very good dinner, and I invited his eldest son to dine with me. He was a nice shy little boy, dressed in a goat's-hair frock-coat, deeply embroidered with red floss silk, the badge of "royalty," and wore scarlet silk trousers. I may claim the credit of having permanently settled his age; for, on my asking how old he was, his friends said they did not know, and referred to me. On my proposing, as a guess, "ten," they expressed great wonder, and considered my decision as an additional proof that Feringis know everything.

The houses here were some circular, and some oblong, the latter being adapted for a second storey. The walls were well and straightly built of hard blue clay. In the case of the oblong houses, trunks of date-trees were put across, covered first with mats, and then with clay. But the circular huts were the best, for the walls were twelve feet high, and the roof was a dome-shaped construction of date-sticks, covered with mats and thatched with pīsh leaves, the whole being kept in its place by a network of rope.

The muezzin here seemed a practical sort of man, for instead of inciting his parishioners to prayer in the orthodox but, to them, unintelligible Arabic, he paraded the streets crying, in Persian, " Biro namāz," (*go to prayer*). Murad Khan presented me with a capital brown cotton sheet from Dizzak (*small fortress*), after which for the fourth time we cleared the house, and making up the fire turned in.

Next morning was very cold, and in spite of strenuous exertions it was an hour after sunrise before we got fairly off, accompanied by about twenty men and boys mounted on donkeys, all provided with large mat bags for bringing in grass roots for manure and firewood. This was the last we saw of donkeys, which, being imported from Oman get dearer in proportion to their distance from the coast.

We passed the *Pai-i-duldul-i-Ali*, at this time a series of circles about a yard in diameter, rendered distinct by being bare of the shingle which here covered the flat plain we were traversing. These marks are said to be the footprints of Ali's mare, though doctors disagree on the question whether Duldul was a mare or a mule, and whether it belonged to Ali or Muhammad. We crossed one brackish nullah (or *water-course*) full of pizgh, a tall rush used for making soft mats, and passing over alternate stony plains and steepish stony hills, we entered a dry shingly water-course full of pīsh (or *dwarf palm*). Here was the last of the pīsh, and shortly afterwards the last of the hills. There was but one path, so I had been enabled to take the lead, and travelling fast, we made ten miles by about 10.30 a.m., and reached the boundary of the hills. Before us lay the desert, the mirage over which gave it exactly the appearance of a sea, while in the blue distance were the snow-covered Bāsmān and Tōrīk ranges. Our course had hitherto been north, but now we struck to the east. The country was sand mixed with red gravel, from the surface of which now and then a huge streaked red and white boulder protruded, and the whole was thinly studded with the golden tinted pīr, the vivid green agrich, trāt, and ishwarak—bushes for which the Latin equivalent will be found in the Botanical appendix. About 4 p.m. we crossed a dry nullah called Mūrgh, and an hour before sunset sighted Maskhūtān, situated among low hills, between which the barren sand changed to a light soil bearing thin grass and a few babul trees.

Here we overtook a small boy, panting under the weight of an ordinary donkey-load of firewood, a sight which rather aggravated old Jellāl, for instead of using his pet donkey for such labour at home he now found that he might have used some of the children of his second wife. Our Fanōch experience decided me to pass through the town and camp on the other side; so we held on our way, past date groves in which the water was standing a foot deep, past canals for irrigation, attended to by unwholesome looking people in Persian dress, and ascended the steep low hill on which the town was perched.

The Persian dress here was no proof of the Persian origin of the wearer. The Balūch of Mekran would scorn to wear any but a Balūch dress, and would particularly object to a Persian costume. Here, however, the Persian is more feared and the Balūch more ignorant, and they wear these dresses with a feeling modified but somewhat like that with which the African savage wears a red coat and no trousers.

The towns of Fanōch and Bint have been compared to English crew-yards but in Maskhūtān the manure had got ahead of the straw, and the town had every appearance of being built in a large pigstye. We passed through it, detailing Barja to purchase another water-skin for the desert journey; and crossing the broad river-bed, down which a shallow stream meandered, we camped at the foot of some low hills on the opposite side. We found a snug nook under some pīr bushes, and soon had the kettle boiling, when to our horror the entire population of Maskhūtān appeared, garments held aloft, wading across the river. I promptly seized my sketch-book, and nerved by despair scaled the nearest mountain. My sketch was barely finished when four perspiring men, dressed in their best clothes, toiled up over the ridge before me, and without a word of salutation of any kind sat down and began to criticise me. After about ten minutes they made up their minds, and coming up, the best dressed man asked me if I hadn't a rupee or an old shirt that I could give him.

Begging him to wait a minute I retreated to the camp, where I found Jellāl prescribing for about sixty diseased people. One woman who had been blind for twenty years, tasked the old man's ingenuity to its

DINNER IN THE BAMPUR DESERT.

The "Salt" question arises.

utmost, but he got rid of her at last with a small chip off my only cake of soap, which he recommended her to suck. An infallible specific could not have made her happier.

That night we had a grand quarrel over the cooking. Our meal was rice boiled, with some pieces of the legs of mutton which I had brought from Bint chopped up in it. This was generally prepared by Jellāl, and when I had eaten my fill the other three finished the pot. Some dates afterwards played the part of pudding. In such simple cooking there was only one point on which we could disagree, and we discovered it with perfectly human promptitude. There is no doubt that Jellāl did habitually put in too much salt. The salt was a hard blackish stony lump, and the old man's way of chipping off lumps with the handle of his knife was quite reckless. When pressed home upon the subject, he generally fell back upon the fact that our contract with the camel-men did not include feeding them, and would point out quite clearly that if they didn't like it they might leave it. This, however, did not conduce to such satisfactory relations as I was anxious to establish with the men, and I refused to hold his view of the matter.

After an animated argument we settled the difficulty by the apparently simple expedient of taking it in turns to cook, Abdulla officiating when it came to my turn, and it was amusing to hear each one chaff the other's cooking, and prophesy what luxury we should enjoy when it came to his turn.

The river here ran south, and the date groves, backed by low jagged hills, stretched some miles down the opposite or western shore. Just opposite us, the river bank was a steep cliff, which, being piled up with large white stones, made a pretty contrast with the rich green grass growing under the date-trees on the top of the bank. The water of the river was perfectly drinkable, but had evidently received contributions from some of the innumerable brackish springs which are found all over this part of the country.

There was a slight Persian element in Maskhūtān, and the inhabitants seemed capable of a rough division into three classes; viz., Persians, long-haired wild-looking Lāshāris, and wiry careworn Balūchis. The Persians have probably been introduced by Mīr Huti, who is in the Persian interest and communicates freely with Bampūr. The Balūchis here are of the Hūt tribe, and are vigorous men of great endurance. We engaged one old man for one rupee to take us to Bampūr in two days, and after one day's rest to bring us back in two more. Unlike any native we had hitherto met, our new comrade Kuli was immensely broad, short, and bandy-legged. His mouth was enormous, and his face a mass of carbuncles and wrinkles. He wore a skull-cap, a shirt and drawers, and an enormous kārch or reversible knife. This consisted of a strong blade 18 inches long, one half sharpened and the other jagged like a saw. The handle was a thick piece of wood like the handle of a razor, and the blade being fixed to it by a pivot in the middle, either end was available, according to whether it was purposed to cut grass or wood. These knives were common at Maskhūtān, and general north of it. The name is probably an abbreviation of kāh chīn, grass-cutter. Most of the others I saw were smaller than Kuli's.

Kuli proved a most disagreeable addition to our

mess. The other three men ate like gentlemen. There was no hurry, no tearing or gnawing; on the contrary, all was extreme politeness. Kuli, however, was a perfect ogre. I believe that he had never before seen food of any sort on three consecutive days, and I know he could never have tasted meat. Excepting the wool, horns and hoofs, he would eat ravenously any part of a sheep nearly raw, and he would gnaw and crack the bones with his teeth like a dog. After joining our party he had always in the breast of his shirt some old bone which he would draw out and suck at any leisure moment. We often met men with a craving for flesh and tobacco, but it was never carried to such an extreme or displayed so coarsely as in Kuli.

He was not to receive his rupee until we had returned to Maskhūtān within the stipulated time; so very early in the morning he arrived, wearing a good woollen blanket, and commenced a querulous tirade against the camel-men, which soon got us on march. As on leaving Fanōch we had been accompanied by a crowd of men going for grass-roots and firewood, on leaving Maskhūtān we had an escort of men on a similar errand, mounted upon cows, the stupidity and wilfulness of which animals gave us many a hearty laugh before we shook them off. At a subsequent period I had much experience in cow-riding, and of all animals in the world for stupidity, woodenness, pig-headedness, and obstinacy, commend me to a badly-fed cow. I am not at all sure that I exaggerate in saying that the fact of the people having to ride cows is partly responsible for a modification of the dialect, new and unique phrases being necessary to give adequate expression to their exasperated feelings. Before us was the desert, on our left the distant Bāsmān range, and on our right, at about three miles, the low ranges Baggink, Gasumāl, and Band-i-lāgi. At this period of our journey, Abdulla could answer no question except in rhyme and tune, and I will mention his answer to my question about the hills. I interrupted an apparently endless song about Feringi, about hunting, etc., with my question: "What are the names of those hills to our right?" Jogging along on his camel before me, he at once makes his answer fit into the tune he was singing:

> "Hama Koh, Hama Koh, Just a Kūni, Just a Kūni,
> ī Baggink wa Gasumali
> Gasumāl wa Band-i-lāgi."

After three miles, we crossed the stream Jeh, flowing eastward. Soon afterwards we overtook a caravan of donkeys, carrying tobacco from Mohterabad to Bampūr. They were a jovial party, and one youth, who was playing a flute, addressed me in Hindustani. He had been at Hyderabad, in Sinde, and in Karāchi; but when I asked what had been his occupation, he could only say "Karm wallah," or "labouring man." They all wore huge knitted list stockings, with a division for the toe-string of the suāss, or grass sandals. At eight miles we saw the pale blue Lāshāri range, two days' journey to south-east, and soon after passed a row of large, dry pits, dug to lead down to the water, the first set of Kahns we had yet seen. To our left were the date-trees of Dariabad, and after another two miles through scattered fir-trees we reached that complete picture of desolation, Marri.

Two hundred miserable date-trees in every stage

of withering decay and mutilation, leant this way and that, or rotted prostrate, over a dreary white salt tract, the glare of which was only relieved by brown rust and tricklings of black, poisonous-looking water. It made even the desert round it look comparatively hospitable.

Here we watered for the journey from a small hole scraped in the black gravel, a few yards away from a bitter stream. At this time of the year there would be water at Lūchān Chāh and at Geshkōk, but as our camel-men had never before travelled this route, Kuli and I had arranged a conspiracy to pass the first stage, Lūchān Chāh, and call the second one by its name. Here was a pīr, or holy spot, on which Kuli reverently deposited a handful of wretched dates. There was no mark of any sort to indicate the holy spot, nor could he give any account whatever of its antecedents. General Goldsmid, in his able account of Balūchistan, speaks of the number of "Shia" shrines in this Sunni country. With all deference for such an authority, I believe the facts to be as follows :—

Firstly, that throughout the country, from Geshkōk to the coast, nothing whatever is known of either the Shia or the Sunni religion, except the name and a few Arabic formulæ. Secondly, that not one Balūchi in five hundred will trouble himself to guess at the origin of any shrine. Thirdly, that, by the more sensible, these shrines are simply looked upon as charms at which the observance of fitting ceremonies is easy, may bring luck, and can do no harm; while the motive that leads others to add their stone, is just that which makes one sheep follow the one before him. As I have before mentioned, I have frequently commenced shrines, and seen them religiously added to by every member of the caravan, and I have also heard discussions as to whether a certain heap of stones was a shrine or not. I have elsewhere stated that the religion of the country is confined to eight or ten boys and youths in each town boasting a mulla; and the only fairly so-called Shia shrine I met with—the Pai-i-duldul-i-Ali—owes its permanence to its propinquity to Fanōch. In calling this a Shia shrine, it may be well to remember the difficulty as to the ownership of the Duldul.

To resume our story, however. The sand-grouse here were absurdly tame, and I learnt for the first time that Katangar and Chākūl, which I had hitherto considered synonymous, were two different species.

The white efflorescence which covered the ground was so active that an old grass sandal, which did not appear to have been there more than a week, was thickly encased in it. It was not salt, but had more the taste of stale soda-water, and was I think nitrate of soda.

We had much difficulty in persuading the camels to drink, and while the three men were making the usual uncouth noises of invitation, I collected some of the powder. When at a little distance, I turned round, and the aspect of our party struck me as irresistibly comic. Barja`is resplendent in my rowing "sweater," covered by a scarlet blanket, worn as a coat; while as a head-gear, he wears my huge London rowing-club muffler. Abdulla, a most excitable little man, is, as usual, having a fight with his enormous camel. He has a spare flannel shirt and another scarlet blanket, while his small black eyes twinkle out from under a huge dark plaid. His language to his camel is extraordinary, being a string of oaths, professions of belief in the unity of God, obscene curses, and scraps of the Fātihat, the opening Muslim prayer. He, of course, is quite ignorant of the Arabic, and the Divine formulas of Islam are merely fine hearty-sounding words to swear in.

Kuli is saying his prayers by the pīr (or *shrine*), and Jellāl sits tranquilly by munching dates, clothed in the remains of an old flannel shirt and an Inverness cape made of a third scarlet blanket. The natives' own clothes merely serve as waist-bands. I suppose a more extraordinary group of figures never passed through that desolate spot Marri. The men were everywhere very proud of the English clothing, and even at Bampūr, where I expected them to appear in their ordinary garb, they strutted about with the utmost complacency. Kuli soon hurried us on to the march, and as the rest of the stages were entirely over heavy sandhills, I shall simply give extracts from my note-book, joined together in readable form. Our chief anxiety was to espy camel fodder, for the camel-men had agreed to travel from sunrise to sunset, if I would stop for them to cut fodder whenever we passed a good quantity. My own private anxiety was to make the pace while we were travelling as good as possible.

"Course from Marri nearly east, at thirteen miles (from Maskhūtān) passed between low hills Dīrbūm three miles on the left, and Kahnōk three miles on the right; jungle, thinly scattered petto-bushes,* no other sort. At eighteen miles crossed the low Gangja

* "Petto," a spiny-leaved bush, undeterminable.

hills, the perpendicular brown sandstone strata of which were so regular as to give exactly the appearance of a well-ploughed rounded mound in England. Hills studded with small white prickly plant siggichk,* four-fifths of each little bush of which was dead, and quite white and stiff. At twenty miles, course N.E.; at twenty-one miles, view of open country, all sandhills. Crossed some large ones called the Allūd Rig. At twenty-seven, struck a dry nullah and followed it for a mile. Here to our right was Lūchān Chāh. The men had stopped behind to cut lorti (*Taverniera spartæa*) but I pressed on, hoping that they would not fall in with any wandering Lāshāris and get an inkling of our whereabouts. When they rejoined us Abdulla's jovial temper was gone; he had been bitten in the foot, and had had a bad fall from his camel, who never would let both men get up. At the thirty-eighth mile, on topping a very high sandhill, we saw Bampūr fort in the distance. Mutiny was gradually brewing, Jellāl, who was in the secret, pretending to join. We struggled through another two miles, and then, the men having four times dismounted and flatly refused to go any farther, we gave in, and camped at sunset. Then we had a grand quarrel, for the men knew enough of the distances to discern that we had arrived at Geshkōk, which was, in fact, about three sand-ridges ahead. It ended, however, in a hearty laugh, for they were good fellows, though terribly afraid of over-taxing their camels; and we congratulated ourselves on having brought plenty of camel-

* "Siggichk," a small leathery-leaved plant, undeterminable.

fodder, for there was nothing but petto here, and it was pitch dark soon after we arrived."

It was bitterly cold that night on the sand, and very early the next morning we were up and trudging over the high heavy sandhills. We soon arrived at Geshkōk, which, though marked as a town in Pottinger's map, exhibits no traces of anything of the sort. It is, as the name implies, simply a place in the sandhills where the rain-water stands for a long time, and whither consequently the wandering Lāshāris, the Bedawin of the country, occasionally resort, and pitch their goats'-hair tents. Four or five stunted pīr bushes offered very inferior camel-fodder; and though Kuli said that the pool would last three months more, I felt inclined to doubt it. Here we passed a camel-caravan, the members of which were still fast asleep, a fact significantly pointed out to me by my camel-men; and indeed, before our journey was over it was a standing joke against me that we always did pass caravans when they were asleep, and when, according to our camel-men, we should have been asleep likewise.

Two miles more travelling over deep sand; after Geshkōk we topped a high hill, and saw in the north-west a broad belt of trees in which the forts of Kasimabad and Bampūr were visible, the former bearing W. and the latter N. 70′ E. The roads here divided, and taking the path to Bampūr we entered a series of stony hills and shingly plains. At six miles from the corner the path between Kasimabad and Isfakā crossed ours. Here we met a donkey caravan carrying grain from Bampūr. They were accompanied by an elegantly attired Persian gentleman mounted on a benevolent-looking but obstinate cow, on which I found he proposed to ride to Isfakā. At six miles from the Isfakā crossing we entered the belt of trees, which were nearly all gaz roghān, and shamefully cut about by the natives for firewood. The belt was about two miles broad, and after crossing the broad shallow river which flows westward through the centre of it, we found ourselves in a network of well kept up canals for irrigation. The water was said to be led from here to Kasimabad, though I did not see why it should be, as that place was in the tree belt and appeared to be equally near the river.

Along the northern bank were many small huts built of rice-straw and looking very snug and clean. The trees near them were reduced to maimed stumps, and looked very melancholy. Still going north-east, we came to extensive arable ground, which two months hence would be sown with rice. Passing through this we approached the Bampūr fort, and after a steep descent into the courtyard, unloaded about noon under a magnificent kunār tree. The delight of hearing good Teherāni Persian, after so much of that slovenly Balūch dialect, was one I shall never forget.

The Khan was asleep when I arrived, but the *major domo* of the establishment led me into a large empty room which looked over a wide court surrounded by the officers' quarters, kitchen, granary, threshing room, etc. In the centre was a square raised mud platform, and near by, a tank from which kaliāns (the Persian water-pipes) were filled. One end of the room was soon carpeted, and I received some of the officers, who appeared agreeably surprised at my speaking Persian, and when, having lost my pipe, I called for a kaliān their delight knew no bounds. The soldiers were clean and well dressed, and were much puzzled to find out what could be the object of my visit.

Begging for privacy, I had a good cold douse, and donned my court suit, which consisted of a white coat and trousers, a clean shirt, a fez, and a loose pair of shoes; and the Khan waking soon after I was escorted into his presence by a considerable procession. There were three large walled gardens adjoining the fort, and passing through the first of these we received the salute of four sentries, who appeared from two guard tents, and walked up a gravel path to a very fine large tent, where we were received in a most cordial manner by the Khan. The tent was a very handsome one, and the walls were covered with various devices in green and red *appliqué* work. Across the centre of the tent, and occupying three-fifths of its area, was a raised oblong platform, half of which was carpeted, and used as a divan, while the other half was covered with a silk canopy, under which was a large bed and some cushions. Round the tent-pole was a trophy of guns, some really beautiful specimens of Persian workmanship being placed alongside of infamous "Brummagem" imposture. I was eagerly asked my opinion of the latter, and though I did not attempt to conceal that I thought them rubbish, I was glad to be able truthfully to dilate more upon the excellence of the Persian weapons than upon the inferiority of the others.

The Khan was an educated Persian gentleman, and was most hospitable, even to the extent of messing me at his own "table," a kindness I had hardly expected from him after seeing the length of his prayers. The month, however, of Moharram was approaching, and

I afterwards had occasion to observe that the Persians, as well as the Turks and Roman Catholics, fully appreciate the power of religion as a weapon for governing ignorant people. Throughout Irāk the tone of the Turkish press is this : "We are the elected of God, the Sultan is the commander of the faithful. We live in Islam bool, or the place of Islam (a corruption of Stambool). Be very careful how you do anything against men so highly favoured by God."

The Persians here had to speak to men more ignorant than the men of Irāk, and their cue was a rigorous performance of the outward observances of their religion, and great display on occasions of festival.

The preparations for the Moharram were extensive, and the Khan invited all the Balūchis to come and see the play, even men whom he had just threatened with a beating.

We sat talking till evening, our conversation including a great variety of subjects, and fresh visitors constantly arriving. The Khan inquired whether we had seen any symptoms of mines on our journey; and in a discussion of Mekran politics wished to give the impression that all the sheikhs of the country were under his control, an idea pretty nearly correct, with the exception of the coast tribes, which are under the Governor of Mināb. By a mere accident I considerably strengthened the suspicion that I was an artillery officer, a suspicion arising from the fact that I wore large metal buttons on my coat. I had come up the Fanōch pass with a constant attention to the possibility of getting my baggage through, and when asked by the commander of artillery whether cannon could come by this route, I unhesitatingly replied that small ones could. There could be no doubt after this that I was an officer, and I was not allowed to enter the fort or see the guns. I learnt, however, from an old braggart who headed the procession which escorted me from my quarters to the Khan's tent, quite as much as I should have done from a personal inspection.

I could not ascertain anything definite about Pottinger's assertion that the hill on which the fort was built was hollow; though there was every probability of extensive subterraneous excavations. One thing was apparent, that by no possible arrangement could the guns of the fort be brought to bear upon anything under one hundred yards from the foot of the hill.

The Khan messed well, and he invited four or five very good fellows to dinner, so we had a very pleasant evening. Just before dinner I got into a hopeless mystery through the Khan's trying to find out if I had not any beer or brandy with me. He finessed dreadfully for about a quarter of an hour, to my utter confusion, nor did I at once comprehend that āb-i-jō (*barley water*) meant beer. On my assuring him that when in a Muslim country I never used such things, he produced a mysterious bottle containing a decoction which he had himself made from dates, and kept by him in case of illness. This I declined politely.

At Fanōch I had been told much of the Bampūr military band, but here I heard nothing of it, nor of the bugle and drilling mentioned by General Goldsmid.

Bampūr is, for the country, a very large, well kept mud fort, crowning a high steep hill. It is about three miles north of the river, the interval being filled partly by trees and partly by arable ground. Along the banks of the river are about two hundred huts of rice straw, but the importance of the place lies entirely in the fort. To the south of this is the camp of the soldiers, who are accommodated partly in tents, partly in rice-straw huts. They work in the fields as day labourers, as, indeed, do most Persian soldiers, a fact which the commandant of some Turkish troops at a place where I was stationed used to mention with derision; while the truth was, that his men, to whom field labour was not allowed, got no pay, and were obliged to steal everything they wanted.

There are here two hundred artillerymen, nine cannon, from six to three pounders, with horses for three of them, and one hundred infantry. The arms were Enfield rifles, the English powder of which was greatly appreciated by our camel-men, whose former hatred of the Gajars was soon changed into a feeling of profound respect. The Khan's chief business seemed to be getting his tribute paid, pacifying the Balūchi blood feuds, and arranging the agriculture in the immediate vicinity of his fort. He gave seed to the small farmers, and, whatever the season, exacted a fixed, and not very small, rate of interest.

We witnessed many interviews in which the farmer protested that he had sown the seed but it had not come up, while the Khan stated clearly his opinion that the man had secreted the grain. In my own experience of agriculture in this country, I have always found that the men who hoe in the seed will, if not watched, bury large quantities in holes.

The artillerymen, too, frequently came and complained that they found it impossible to get fodder for their horses, and the Khan, to them, as to all others complaining of arrears of pay, read a letter from Mīr Huti, saying that the latter had collected about 700 tomāns* and would shortly bring it. I noticed that the kunār (Arabic "nabak") trees were the finest we had ever seen, and they must be very old.

A curious mill was at work in the square courtyard where my quarters were.† It consisted of a lever twelve feet long resting on a fulcrum placed three feet from one end. A man by standing on the short end raised the long end high in air. This was provided with a heavy iron pestle, and when the man jumped off it came down forcibly into a round mortar or hole in the ground. The wheat thus pounded was re-pounded and sifted by five Balūchi women, who sat and quarrelled shrilly in the court. We had been told that there were many camels here, but we saw none, nor could I find that any considerable number were away feeding in any distant pasture, as might have been the case.

Almost all loads were carried on cows, and the very smallest children seemed to be considered equal to the charge of one. We saw one poor child crying bitterly on the top of a mountain of grass piled on the back of a cow, who was grazing with perfect indifference, its master with the stick having left it for a time for some other work.

Old Jellāl had an interview with the Khan which will be told to generation after generation of his

---

* A tomān is worth about 8*s*. 4*d*.

† I have since seen a series of similar mills worked by steam at Damietta in Egypt.

family. I had mentioned his practice of medicine, and in the course of conversation had enlarged considerably on his wonderful shrewdness, and the Khan becoming interested sent for him. The old man arrived, smiling and blushing up to the roots of his hair at the honour; and thinking that the emergency required a special and new sort of salutation said, bowing: "Khush āmadīd Khan" (*you are very welcome*). The Khan, fairly taken aback at having the words taken out of his mouth, stammered and said: "And you also are very welcome." The servants served him with tea, brought him a kaliān, and humoured their master's caprice to the full, leaving the old man in such a state of bashful delight that he did not know what to do with himself.

This little civility to Jellāl was well conceived, and had the effect it was probably meant to produce, for the old fellow has never ceased talking of Bampūr and Mirza Hussain Khan, the number of whose horses I recently heard him giving at 9,000. In fact the number of conversations between "the Khan and me," and relations of what "I said to him" and "he said to me," that sprung from this interview could not have failed to gratify that nobleman's desire for popularity. The next evening was the 1st of Moharram, and I determined to leave in the afternoon, for I had no interest in seeing the religious ceremonies which take place during the first ten days of this month, and I could not but be much in the way.

The camel-men were delighted at the prospect of an early start, for they had come prepared to purchase carpets, shoes, sheets, shawls, and all sorts of articles of commerce, and had found shoes the only things

OUR STATION AT JASK.

procurable. We had agreed also to sacrifice a sheep on arrival; but the sheep here were bad and dear, so we decided to postpone our feast.

On the morning of the 28th I went some distance from the fort to sketch it, accompanied by the talkative old fellow I have mentioned before, who came to see I did nothing treasonable. On my return to bid adieu to the Khan he anxiously looked over my portfolio, and seemed relieved at finding no ground-plans, elevations, or other treason. After a cordial farewell we mounted and set off west through the tree belt for Kasimabad. The old *major-domo* refused bakshish point blank, while our talkative friend when offered a dollar said it was too little. Affecting great embarrassment I got him to give it me back, and rode off leaving him waiting for the five at which he valued his services. The Khan gave me a firman to all the skeikhs on our route to provide me with anything necessary, and old Jellāl began gloating over the way he intended to loot them with its help. But I pointed out to the men that having received voluntarily every possible kindness and hospitality from all Balūchis I had hitherto met, I could not think of accepting anything that might be given me under the compulsion of a Persian firman. Jellāl, however, was not to be done, and retained the paper. After crossing the river and recovering my pipe from a shrill young woman of the village who had found it, we halted for a few minutes that I might don my moleskins, which Jellāl had hitherto been carrying at arms' length. He had, according to orders, washed them directly on arrival at Bampūr; but, fearing they would be stolen, he had then in excess of caution hidden them away in a dark hole in the wall, and when I wanted to start they were soaking wet.

This gave rise to a rather amusing incident. I had been very angry. The manner in which I had thought it necessary to point out the old man's stupidity to him had reduced him to a state of terrified silence. We were crossing numerous canals, and I was riding ahead. Now some camels jump, and in doing so they will, unless they have a breastband, jerk the saddle back over their tails. This occurred to Jellāl, but he daren't say a word until, seeing that he must slide hopelessly over the camel's tail, I heard in a trembling voice, "Sahib! Sahib! th—this camel wants a breastband;" and, looking round, saw the old fellow lying along the camel's back, grasping the wool of its shoulders, with the middle of the saddle about over the animal's tail. The hearty laugh which none of us could resist, restored harmony amongst us completely.

A dull grey evening, with occasional moaning gusts of cold wind, closed over us as we passed through a quantity of withered silk-cotton-fibre trees (*calotropis*) and entered the half-ruinous mud enclosure dignified by the name of the Kalat-i-Kasimabad. I observed that although Persian was here rather more general than Balūchi, nobody attempted the proper Arabic pronunciation of Kalat, a fort.

The place looked wintry and desolate, and its few inhabitants melancholy and pinched with cold, as they huddled themselves up in handsome Rudbar "mashuks" or cloaks. The head man was a slave of the Bampūr Governor, and civilly enough showed me a respectable empty mat hut. Jellāl, however, had managed to secrete the firman, and while I was not looking produced it, and was already authoritatively demanding fowls, milk, eggs, etc., when I disgusted him by quietly taking the paper from the head man's hand before he had read a word, and putting it into my pocket.

The north wind blew violently direct from the snow-covered Basmān mountains, and in spite of a good fire and the unusual luxury of a hut, we hardly slept that night. We heard broken observations about smallpox, and our friends would not let us have any milk to drink; but the discovery that our comfortable house had just been emptied by that disease was reserved for the morning. When just about to start, I expressed to the head man a hope that I had not inconvenienced any one by occupying the hut. "Oh, no," he said, "they're all dead." "Ah!" I said; "smallpox?" "Yes," he answered; "God has sent it."

It was freezing hard that morning, and had we been in England there would have been no doubt that the white thick appearance to the north was snow. As it was, in spite of smallpox, I purchased a Rudbar cloak, and was afterwards very thankful I had done so. We struck away across the desert for Geshkōk, where the pool was covered with thin ice; nor did the weather become pleasant till two in the afternoon.

At 4 p.m., after a very fast ride, for camels go their best when furious with must as ours were, we arrived at Lūchān Chāh, merely a place in the desert with wells and a few stunted trees, and finding here some Lāshāris tending their camels, we thought it a good opportunity for our promised sheep. The Lāshāris made some difficulty at first, saying that we were at their huts, and the laws of hospitality demanded that they should kill for us. We however, agreed to accept from them a skin bag of "chāch" (a kind of sour milk), and bought from them a sheep for a dollar. The Lāshāris preferred to take away and eat with their families the stomach, etc., rather than just come and eat their fill with us. This arrangement having been completed, a blazing fire was lit, and there ensued a most horrible debauch.

The sheep was hastily slaughtered close to the camp fire, and without the customary invocation. The men commenced to skin it in the usual way, but their eagerness got the better of them, and reflecting that they could not prepare the skin and take it with them, they tore it off in patches. As soon as the flesh appeared, they pulled off pieces and thrust them into the fire to singe, and soon their teeth were engaged in singed and cindery morsels of the still warm body which their hands were skinning. Parts of the entrails were, as agreed upon, given to the Lāshāris, and the men huddled round the fire, each with his portion of the raw flesh on the sand before him, chewing and singeing, gnawing at the bones and tearing at the sinews with a feverish energy that was horrible.

It was no longer two men eating diffidently anything that might be left after I had finished. Here was a whole sheep which they had earned and determined to enjoy to the utmost. My humble portion of the liver fried in the fat of the tail was soon despatched; but a horrible fascination compelled me to sit watching the men till late at night. Jellāl's nearly toothless condition soon made him give up; but what I have before written concerning Kuli's performances conveys but a faint idea of the scene enacted by that ogre, Abdulla, and Barja. Abdulla had just had another bad fall from his camel, which objected to be re-saddled to go and fetch water from the wells about a mile away, and which, when his master was down, had bitten him severely. He was really frightened this time, and evidently determined to smother his feelings in a tremendous dinner.

The Lāshāris are fine wiry fellows, each wearing a "kārch" in one side of his waistband, and an apparatus for spinning wool in the other. When asked who was the Lāshāri chief, they replied that there were many chiefs, but the only one worthy of the name was Mīr Huti, of Pip, two days south-east. These men were Huts themselves, and said that in their wanderings they often reached Chābar on the coast. One of them sold me for six krans a coat which he had just completed. Its material resembled coarse strong woollen sacking, its shape that of a frock coat, double-breasted, with no buttons and the sleeves very clumsily set on. These men possess few camels, which must be able to eat all kinds of fodder, and they own many very small donkeys, goats, and sheep. They drive these with them wherever in the sandy waste they may find scanty dried grass, and carry the patches of woollen cloth, which, supported on small sticks, are regarded as tents, and which are in fact miniature copies of the Eeliaut tent. Next morning my upper covering was frozen as hard as a board, and the scanty spring plants which subsisted under the shelter of the now bare petto bushes were white with hoarfrost which did not thaw all day. When I awoke, Abdulla and Barja were still singeing, chewing, and gnawing, and appeared to have been at work pretty well all night, for there was only a head and a leg left of the sheep killed last night, and not even the offal had been thrown away. Just before leaving camp two large flocks of sheep and goats, in number about six hundred, were driven past us, causing us to wonder greatly where they could find sustenance. I may here mention that the natives when purchasing animals chiefly look to the vigour with which they feed. If the reader will watch a flock of sheep feeding in any place where the herbage is short and scanty, he will notice some bite off the short grass with a kind of nervous eagerness, and walk quickly over the patches intervening between the grassy spots. Others feed along leisurely, snuffing the bare patches to see if there is anything on them. A Balūch would have nothing to say to these last.

Soon we overtook a caravan of Lāshāris changing their residence. It consisted of ten minute donkeys and about as many men and women, but was spread over a line of at least five miles. The first whom we overtook were two women in men's tattered blue calico clothing, driving before them two donkeys laden with the goats'-hair tents of the family. The next member we met was a solitary donkey plodding along through the heavy sand, with, I suppose, an intuitive knowledge of the way. He was mounted by a jet black cock, who was evidently master of the situation, for he was sound asleep with his head under his wing. Then we overtook another donkey with the sticks of the tent and the family cooking pot, then some men, and so on till we had passed the whole caravan.

Wolves and obāras (*otis houbara*, a species of bustard) are very numerous here, and we saw no less than eight of the latter cowering down close by the track to avoid the keen wind. We passed Marri, where Kuli deposited some more dates, and getting off the sand on to firm ground, rode hard on to Maskhūtān. Here we left Kuli immensely happy with a whole dollar, instead of the stipulated rupee, for his five days' running and filling our masaks or water skins, passed on and camped about five miles on towards Fanōch.

The men were extremely indignant at the extra five miles, but it was evident we were going to have a snowstorm, and five miles extra before it burst on us might be of use to one tied to time as I was. Partly I suppose owing to their recent heavy meal, they did not recover their temper as soon as usual, and turned in vowing that I should not drive the camels on to Fanōch to-morrow. This, at the worst, could only have resulted in my having to walk the remaining three or four-and-twenty miles to Fanōch, where I could get fresh camels, and I was sure they dare not do otherwise than bring Jellāl and the saddle-bags safely in.

We awoke next morning covered in snow. We were lying against a thicket of pīr trees, and just as I put my head out a flock of little pīn kolaks * in them burst out into one of those warm gushing trills of soft melody compared with which, so long as it lasts, the songs of the nightingale and bulbul are but common chirping. My mind conjured up a picture of a

---

* One of the Timalinæ or Babbling Thrushes, probably *Heteromorpha unicolor.* No. 376, Jerdon's "Birds of India."

row of little soft brown birds nestling together on a frozen bough, and agreeing that it was so cold they wouldn't get up just yet. Their song is a long trill, beginning from a very high note and going down about an octave, dividing each note as nearly as I could guess into three. They only give it just when they wake, and its tone is indescribably melodious. After two long trills they disperse like magic, chirping and evidently setting to work hunting for some breakfast. Abdulla and Barja were still inanimate bundles, but near the fireplace was a second heap of smouldering ashes which I knew from experience contained the head of their sheep. The head, just as cut from the animal, is buried in the ashes of a fire, and the ashes again are buried deep in sand. The cooking lasts the whole night, and the result is delicious.

One call to old Jellāl was enough, and after a few very indecent observations on the filthiness of the country he had come to he soon had a blaze and roused up the camel-men. They consumed the sheep's head in silence, and, as I expected, declared it impossible to move till the snow stopped. After a violent harangue, in which my line was that this snowstorm would last three days—a statement I backed up by pretended reference to my prismatic compass, they appeared partially convinced, and though declaring that the camels would die, they reluctantly went to fetch them. I reduced my clothes to what was barely necessary, and made them put on the extra ones. We began the march about 9.30 a.m., the north wind sweeping the snow across our path and bedding us up pretty thick on our right sides. It froze hard, and my bare fingers were intolerably cold. Never while duck-shooting in the Lincolnshire marshes did I feel such a through and through shivering. I started Abdulla singing, but on trying to join in to keep the game going had to collapse with a melancholy quaver.

At about four miles we passed a caravan taking shelter under some pīsh, and my men immediately decided to stop. Jellāl and myself, however, pushed on, and finding themselves left behind, the camel-men followed. Again they stopped, and this time I said I would leave them and go on, and on their refusing to let me have a camel, started off walking. Again Abdulla came after me, and half laughing, half angry, said they would come on. My saddle this time was thick with snow, and I tore a long ridge of frozen snow from the inside of the breast flap of my pea-jacket.

Another three miles, and Barja, the large, the handsome, the shikarri, got down from behind Abdulla and scuttled away under a pīsh bush. He was a mass of blankets, but could not stand it. Abdulla made much of his own heroic conduct in abandoning his own brother and following me. It certainly was a very fierce snowstorm, and to give an idea of the cold I may mention that the skin of my right thigh, upon which the snow had accumulated and frozen, all peeled off in the next three days.

In another hour or so, to my joy, we turned to the south, and got along much better with the wind on our backs. About two miles from Fanōch it stopped, and the sun coming out we dismounted and made a fire. Barja rejoined us, and rallying him a little we singed some pieces of meat and had some dates. Remounting, we came upon the Pai-i-duldul-i-Ali again, and I was surprised to find the marks distinct, regular, and extending nearly a mile along the road, after which they turned into a ground plan of a house marked in white stones and evidently intended for a masjid. I carefully examined the spots, now about a yard in diameter, and fairly accurate circles. Where the snow had been blown away were, as I expected, marks of fingers. On my suggesting to the men that this was done by the priests on account of the Moharram, they laughed, saying it probably was so. They had not the least interest in the matter, and I have before mentioned that religion in this country is confined to the mullas and youths in the town.

We trotted on, and gained our old quarters at Fanōch. The men sat up late, telling yarns of the perils they had gone through, every sentence ending with "ispeet, ispeet, ispee-et cho shīra" (*white, white, whi-ite like milk*).

Chākar Khan was still absent at Geh, but his people sent us in a dinner very good in quality, but lamentably small in quantity. The thin, large wafers of ground rice were very dainty food. Our calculations for the journey had been pretty exact. My tea was out, three little Chākar Khans finished my sugar, and the eldest of them, on my giving him the empty cocoa-tin, asked whether it was made of silver.

Judging from the cold on the plains, I began to be afraid that I should have another difficulty to get the men through the pass, so next morning I rose about an hour before sunrise, and got Jellāl to make a fire. Outside was a cross-bar for suspending the water-skins of the various houses near, and every skin was as hard as a stone, with icicles two feet long hanging down from it.

The men, however, were now very obedient. Barja was ashamed, and I had told Abdulla he might keep the red blanket he wore as a testimonial.

The men were on the march by sunrise, I having gone on half an hour before them to take a sketch of the pass. I walked through the date groves, and was surprised to find those on the east side a perfect swamp from innumerable warm springs which trickled from the hills into the river. This, in the cold season, caused a constant steam to hang around the entrance of the pass. The first three or four miles were dark and cold, but the wind was moderate, and we got occasional glimpses of the sun as we zig-zagged through the hills.

The pass was about as full as it was when we passed it before; but it lost much of its wild beauty from the hills being dry. The same bright colours were there, but their velvety richness and deepness of tone were gone, and were now hard and matter of fact. We rode fast, and about four in the afternoon we sighted my tent; Toby sitting in front, Salah just going into it from the cook-house, and the Portuguese cook the centre of an admiring ring of natives, who were watching him trying to cook something.

The men were all delighted to see me. I was some four hours under the nine days in which I had undertaken to do the journey, and they were proud of my success. Poor old Abdulla, with the fever, roused up to kiss my hand. "Sharin atkagi, sharin atkagi," (*you have come along well*) was the cry, and even my two companions, who had declared it was a sixteen days' business, shared in the glory of the achievement. The time had gone heavy with them, nine days waiting; and everybody had told them that the sahib was mad to talk about doing it so quickly,—the camel-men wouldn't let him, etc., etc. It was a good hard ride such as Balūchis can appreciate, and, better than that, it was a promise kept, and kept under difficulties.

Everything in the camp was in perfect order, clean and swept; in fact, unchanged, but for one thing to be mentioned hereafter.

My first proceeding was to take off all my clothes and hand them over for inspection, together with those that the men had worn, and putting on others I then sallied forth to make the rounds of the establishment. The camels and men were all right with the exception of poor old Abdulla, who had fever, but whom two ten-grain doses of quinine fairly set on his legs. The other Abdulla and Barja took an affectionate leave of me, and I turned into bed, very well satisfied with my journey and its results so far, and, surrounded as I was by old friends, feeling very much as if I had got home at last.

Just as I was getting drowsy, however, an incident occurred worth recording. I have mentioned that I had with me a wooden-headed Portuguese cook—poor old José, or "Jooji" as the Balūchis averaged his name. He was a good cook, too stupid to make any exorbitant perquisites, and too proud to learn a word of Balūchi. He was a short little fellow with huge black beard and moustaches. He was fat and puffy, and his appearance as he came in on his camel after a long march was quite heartrending. He was immensely religious, and on his saints' days I used to hear him holding forth to the camel-men in Hindustani, and explaining that St. Francis was now walking about under the earth near where he was, and might, on the least provocation, be expected to turn up and want to know why he was not holding a service. And he would occasionally go to the length of explaining what excuses he would offer to his holiness; such excuses bearing mainly on the reprobate and barbarous condition of the people by whom he was surrounded. All this, being of course to them perfectly unintelligible, the men took with the utmost good humour. To-night, while waiting for sleep, I heard his voice outside addressing in choice Hindustani and with terms of most lavish endearment some person or other unknown, and imploring her to "come down and go home like a darling." "Ah! light of my life," he went on, "how can you behave thus cruelly? You know that this is a barbarous country and full of wild beasts, how can you remain there, keeping me up, when you know I want to go to bed!"

I gradually roused up on hearing this, and knowing that no one in the camp could possibly understand this Hindustani except myself, I had the curiosity to put my head out of the tent door to see what could be going on. José was shutting up the fowls of the establishment in a portable coop we carried. It was always rather a chase, and, as I have said, José was fat. He had, however, got them all in but the old cock, who, having eluded pursuit, had flown up to the top of the tent, and in that elevated position peacefully gone to sleep, regardless alike of the cook's blandishments and his ineffectual pokes with a too-short stick.

CHAPTER IV.

Mehdi, the gay deceiver.—Poor Ghulamshah.—My Prayer-book.—The Sadaich river.—Baggage goes astray.—Asking the way under difficulties.—We get clear of the hills.—River crossing in the Mekran.—A ducking.—A long night ride.—White men.

NEXT morning a more detailed inspection has to be gone through. All friendly as we are, "discipline must be maintained," as Mr. Bagnet says, and Ghulamshah and Jellāl are both on the charge sheet. Ghulamshah has been seized with a violent desire to trade, and has borrowed all the camel-men's money and purchased quantities of guns, swords, and shields. He is instructed that unless these things are disposed of before night he will be discharged. Old Jellāl, for once detected in using my name in an unauthorized manner, is reduced to the ranks, *i.e.*, to mess with the camel-men on dates and rice instead of with "Jooji," and get tea, sugar, and meat. The weather was cold, but not nearly so cold as at the top of the pass, and we settled to start for Jask on the following day. It was young Zangi's turn to go and fetch wood and water for the camp, and he was instructed to bring in all the camels. We heard much talk of a large caravan of Persian gipsies who had lately been expelled from Bint for stealing and had left for Jask. These caravans of Persian gipsies or beggars are rather common, and tales of their adroitness in cheating are rife in the land. They are often very wealthy, and not long ago the Commissioner of Sinde despatched from Karāchi some four hundred such vagrants, who arrived at Jask equally well provided with money and wits.

Mīr Hāji was still at Geh, but his wazir, Keramshah, had orders to supply all our wants. We demanded a guide for the Gabrig route to the sea and fifty māns of Bint rice. The Bint rice being only last year's crop had a strong wheat flavour, and was much nicer than the withered stuff some years old that is exported from India mixed with lime to keep off the weevils. The rice was ready and everything packed that night, but our guides were not forthcoming, though every assurance was given that they should be at the camp before sunrise next morning. We were, however, to leave one of our party behind. Poor Ghulamshah came to the tent in the evening and said in a faltering voice that he would please take his discharge, and sorry as I was I bade him farewell. The matter was this. While I had been away at Bampūr the camp had been rather dull; Salah's readings of Persian stories could not fail to pall, after a time, upon people with a very limited knowledge of the Persian language, as exhibited in the graceful anecdotes at the end of Forbes' Persian Grammar, and they were consequently very glad of the constant visits of one Mehdi. This Mehdi was a jovial young fellow, a capital singer, with an inexhaustible repertoire of Balūch ballads and a great talent for playing the flute. He had moreover a most winning, plausible tongue, and would have shone as, what is called in Bombay, a European loafer. Seeing Ghulamshah in a good service and drawing good pay, he laid himself out to captivate that guileless youth. He was an accomplished swindler, and not only borrowed Ghulamshah's clothes, but induced him to make the aforesaid purchases, on each of which he of course received a commission. When, however, the stern edict came out, which I have before mentioned, he was at first nonplussed, but, recovering, took Ghulamshah to his arms, swore he should marry his sister, and evolved the plan which will be developed shortly.

Next morning we were up early, but many delays arose. The loads had of course all to be readjusted, and the quarrelling lasted till ten o'clock.

Just before starting our guides turned up, and who should they be but Mehdi and Ghulamshah. Keramshah, the wazir, who was responsible, was of course not forthcoming. As far as their guidance went, these two knew no more about the proposed difficult route than I did: however, my men were good fellows and made no objection to taking my guidance. I had a good inkling of how matters stood, but said nothing, and gave the word to lead on. We were late at starting certainly, but I determined to make Pāzgā that evening; so giving my camel to Abdulla, who was still sick, I marched alongside the caravan with a long stick, and, as we were lightly loaded, kept the pace up to over three miles an hour.

We took, after crossing the Zangūtan, a more easterly road than before, and soon arrived at Gari Darāp. Here his perfidious "friend" left Ghulamshah to get some provisions for the journey from one of the huts. We never saw him again.

It was observed that he wore at the time a coat, shirt, and trousers, and carried a gun, shield, and sword belonging to his dupe. The latter, full of shame and mortification, walked bravely and stolidly on for two long stages,* refusing even the men's kindly offers of food, and too proud to go near " Jooji," his late comrade.

After the two days we had a general amnesty; both Jellāl and Ghulamshah were reinstated, the former literally crying over the back of my neck, and the latter kissing my hand with tears in his eyes and settling down to a much-needed hearty meal.

We followed our former route to Pāzgā, and, save noting that the rivers did not appear to have got any smaller, found ourselves travelling over fairly well remembered ground, in which nothing new could be found. We reached our old camping place about an hour before sunset, and had the tent pitched to punish the men for quarrelling over the loading.

Next day we got off about sunrise. Ramadhan, the one black sheep in our flock, tried to make some difficulty about travelling through unknown mountains without a guide, but from inquiries I had made, I felt sure I could find the Gabrig road, so I exhibited my prismatic compass and went ahead on foot to pioneer the route, accompanied by Jellāl and his darling donkey, whom he hourly commiserated in affectionate terms on the frightful treatment he felt sure it must have received at the hands of Keramshah during our absence at Bampūr.

After travelling about two miles among chaotic barren hills, we found three paths. Taking the one to the extreme right, we followed a creek bed two miles to the west, and then crossed the Gidīch, where

---

* A boy still in his teens.

we were assured of being on the right track·by finding the traces of a caravan which had spent the preceding night there. When I speak of roads, I must be understood to mean, not so much a path or track, but more an absence of obstacle, such as precipices, shūr banks too steep for a loaded camel to pass, cliffs, and huge boulders. Following the noble Gidīch river, we came to a settlement of two huts, and a flock of sheep and goats which had recently arrived from Sadaich. The inhabitants, when they had recovered from their surprise at finding a white man talking Balūchi, told us that we were on the right route, and that three miles on the path would divide, that on the left being the Sadaich route and that on the right leading to Gabrig.

The Balūch has no measure of distance. In a village two or three distances well known to all are used as standards of comparison. A new route will be described as farther than from Jask to Yekdār and not so far as from Geigen to Oushdāhn. If you ask a strange Balūch he will at first try you with his standards, and finding these convey no information, he proceeds as follows. He will turn round slowly, and face towards the direction; then, if it's very far, stand on tiptoe, or even get upon a sand-hillock, and stretching out his hand repeat in a high crooning voice "oo-oo-ooh," over there. From the height to which he raises his voice and his head you estimate the distance, but it is obvious that you must apply a correction, both for the "height of the observer," and the compass of his voice, and the method is not very satisfactory. A man from the huts kindly accompanied us up the right bank of the Gidīch by a path so very steep that I thought it best to wait and see the baggage up it. There was a better though slightly longer road to the north, but the baggage was close behind us and we resolved to risk it. They did struggle up, the men all collecting, and pushing behind each camel in its turn, and, on the descent, hanging on to their tails; but three camels shifted their loads, and caused half an hour's delay. We were now on a high shingly plain, and recognised in the distance the Band-i-Sharīki. At fifteen miles from starting we were about five miles to the west of the Jamki. Here a road crossed ours, evidently leading to Sartarpi, and now we overtook the caravan whose camping-place we had passed in the morning. There were seven magnificent līros, carrying, some ten, some twelve bags of dates each. Three or four donkeys accompanied them, some carrying two bags. The men were on foot, and the camels were spread over a good deal of ground, each feeding whenever he came to a lorti bush. The speculation was a joint concern, no one man owning more than four or five bags, and each owner being either present or represented by some relation. They were three days from Bint, making for Sadaich, but would sell a basket of dates wherever they found a hut, and would probably take back salt fish, ghee, and blue cloth. They were very courteous.

Leaving Sharīki to the left, and sighting our old friend the Sihran-i-Koh to the south-east, we marched another six miles over this level plain; at the twenty-first mile from starting descended by a steep path winding through shūrs into the bed of the Surini river, and after following its winding bed for two miles entered the Sadaich, of which it is a tributary. Here was such an admirable camping place that though we might have marched another hour we determined to camp. The sandy bed of the river was full of lorti that had apparently never been grazed upon, and was well-grown, plentiful and tender. A cliff seventy feet high to the north-west kept off the wind; almost every bush was piled up with drift-wood, and the water was abundant and delicious. The Balūchis, who are great connoisseurs of water, pronounced this the sweetest we had yet found. Here also were sweet potatoes and agghir, one of the three kinds of truffles with which Mekran abounds. Our friends of yesterday passed us soon after we had camped, and next morning, true to our custom, we repassed them fast asleep about a mile down river. By the way, it was at this camp we had a laugh at old Jellāl. I was then, as now, an extremely bad sleeper, and never allowed any one to sleep in, or even near, my tent. This night, however, was cold, and, as it was the night of the amnesty before mentioned, I relaxed the rule, and Jellāl turned in near the tent pole. But he had not been there half an hour before the most fearful snoring compelled me to hunt him out. He gathered up his bed and went away to where some men were still sitting round the camp fire. He evidently anticipated some chaff at his ill-success at getting a better sleeping-place than they had, and took up a plan of defence before they could speak by saying in an awestruck voice, "Verily, there is no God but one God! Do you know that you common people have no conception of the sanctity of our sahib?"

"What is it then?" they asked, startled out of their original intention.

"Verily," went on the old man, "I believe that if our sahib did but not keep a dog he would be perfectly invisible except to the angels, on account of his extreme holiness."

"Ah!" said a man, "and if he didn't eat pig" (this was Ramadhan).

"Eat pig!" said Jellāl, fiercely, "and who are you, to say the sahib eats pig? Do I not mess with Jooji? Do I not see everything he eats?"

Chorus of men: "No, no, he doesn't eat pig," and Ramadhan is sat upon.

I may observe that I did not eat pig, but the assertion to the contrary would not have met with such a prompt contradiction from Jellāl had not his position as one of "Jooji's" mess rendered it possible to argue that if I ate pig some of the pots in which his food was prepared must be unclean. "Now," proceeded Jellāl, when he had sufficiently prepared his audience, "Do you know why the sahib won't let any one sleep in his tent?"

Chorus: "Why is it?"

"Why," answered Jellāl, "so far from eating pig, (this was for Ramadhan) he spends the whole night in saying prayers, and, of course, he does not want to be interrupted."

He was implicitly believed, and I heard him a day or two afterwards clinching his argument by pointing out to some one that my huge Persian Dictionary was a Prayer-book.

But to resume. The Sadaich where we were now encamped was considerably larger than the same river when it debouches into the sea. Of the numerous streams in the hills but three or four get through the sand strip between the hills and the sea, and these very much reduced in volume; the rest are lost in the sand. This river Sadaich emanates from beyond the Band-i-Nīlag, through which it forms the Shimsan pass and gives a good road to the interior. With the exception of four or five ascents up the steep cliff on one side or the other, to avoid a larger bend than usual, our march hence led down the valley of this fine river. Sometimes a mile through tall rich spring vegetation (much *cardamine pratensis**), sometimes over rough large shingle thickly studded with feathery tamarisk, and sometimes down the broad shallow river itself. The bed, cut a hundred feet deep into the shingly plain, was about a mile and a half wide, and the present low water channel ran pretty regularly from side to side, leaving rounded corners called kuches (Persian, "kunj"). Each kuch had a name, but none of our men knew it, and each kuch throughout the march would have made a good camping-place for any one carrying his own food. With this preface I will extract direct from my note-book.

"*February 5th.*—One mile from camp, emerged from Sadaich valley up steep defile on right bank. Course west for two miles over shingly plain, leaving Sihran behind us; then down defile into valley, which from top of bank looked beautifully green and well wooded. Crossed to south bank, and followed this for about three miles; then up steep path over very high bank or cliff and crossed river twice in quick succession. Fourth crossing dangerous, unless made in right place.

---

* Cuckoo flower.

SADAICH RIVER.

Ledge of rock slopes up from east bank to middle of stream, and then ends abruptly in about seven feet of water. At fifth crossing river runs right across bed from cliff to cliff; high hills on both sides. After sixth crossing narrow pass. High shūrs on north and sandstone and shūrs on south.

"Between seventh and eighth crossings a kuch one and a half miles wide, very pretty, with much long grass and many trees; eighth crossing fronting a long, saw-backed hill apparently about six miles distant. After ninth crossing ascended steep defile on north bank. No vestige of a track seen yet since leaving camp, and we were very glad of the tracks of two camels which we found here.

"Shortly afterwards met a shikarri called Shamrād. His companion was on ahead with the two camels whose pugs we had seen, and which were loaded with pīsh for Sadaich. He himself was looking for gurand (*hill sheep*), which abound here.

"After two miles, turned south again, fronting the saw-backed hill of Sūrag. Crossed river again, and then turned four hundred yards *up* river on west bank. Receiving Shamrād's assurance that there was no road straight on, did not depute Jellāl to wait and warn baggage of our sudden turn. There *was* a road, or, at least, a possibility of going that way, and my negligence led baggage astray, for our pugs while crossing the river could not be seen on the rough shingle. Wound about through shūrs. General direction north-west, leaving Sūrag behind, and fronting for long Ilai range, west end of which is Gabrig and east end Sadaich. Saw three gurand close to road, which in the shūr clay became rather better defined, and

Shamrād left us in pursuit. Again entered Sadaich valley, and halted about an hour before sunset."

We were waiting for baggage to arrive, when a well-dressed man with a mounted slave and a spare camel passed us. They told us that soon after starting the next day the road would divide, and we must keep to the right for Gabrig. They were on their way to Bint, being servants of Mīr Hāji.

Night set in, and here we were, Salah and myself and our camels, and Jellāl and his donkey. We crouched over a fire, as the night wind soon got unpleasantly cool. We had given up our baggage for the night, and were regretting that we had nothing to eat, when, suddenly, we heard voices in the darkness. Jellāl rushed in the direction indicated, and shouted vigorously in reply; but the echoes in the hills all round confused us utterly, and it was impossible to say whence the voices came. At last, after much anxiety, the men arrived, both themselves and their animals, quite exhausted. They had missed our sudden turn, which cut across a bend of about six miles of the worst possible travelling, and followed the river till at last they saw our fire.

We had hit upon what had evidently been the camping ground of the Persians mentioned as having been driven from Bint, and were soon established in their quarters. We served out dates and rice, and soon cheered up all hands with the exception of Tajoo, whose beautiful riding camel, never meant for burdens, had been mired three times, and was quite "kein" or done up.

I should have much liked to give the camels and men a day's rest, but we were bound to go forward, and early on the 6th we loaded up, and crossed the river for the twelfth time, and made a south-west course for the south-east end of the Gurānī hills. After the thirteenth crossing we made a westerly course through much rich spring grass; and here we overtook Shamrād and the two camels carrying pīsh, and travelled in company for a time. Soon afterwards we ascended a steep defile up the right bank. From the top of this was a grand view of the broad, blue river, winding through a grassy, well-wooded bottom, hemmed in on both sides by fine hills. Passing an old burying ground, we parted from our friends, who took the Sadaich road to the left, and entering on a steep decline, soon arrived at a shingly tract covered with innumerable goat paths. Here were three huts; and we had been so much puzzled by the numerous goat-paths that immediately on seeing them the men rushed ahead to ask the way and have a smoke. But they found that the sole inhabitant was a toothless old woman, who, do what she would, could not utter a single intelligible word.

Our whole party followed up, and acting upon the usually-received theory that any one whom they could not understand must be deaf, commenced a vigorous yelling that would have been amusing had I not felt that time was precious. Old Jellāl, who had taken the lead, was the first to give in, and, wrought up to the highest pitch of exasperation, he recommended her, in a despairing yell, to go and get some one to bury her, and rushed off muttering and shaking his head. The old lady, who could produce no sort of noise but an eager gabble, on hearing this un-Muslim advice, retired into her hut. The direction in which she pointed was over an almost inaccessible hill, but taking a south-westerly course, we sighted a river which seemed to go our way.

Here we met a small boy who, however, was nearly as exasperating as the old woman had been, owing to a habit Balūchis have which had annoyed us throughout the journey, but I have not mentioned it hitherto, as I was under the impression that it was merely caused by my own presence. This was a habit of prefacing every remark or reply with a broad admiring grin, and "You are Balūchis, aren't you?" It was meant as a sort of compliment; and though I cannot think of any exact English equivalent, it meant pretty nearly, "You're sensible sort of fellows, ain't you?" The Lāshāris, when we first met them at Lūchān Chāh, had driven Abdulla to open reviling by their constant use of this expression in reply to a simple question about the road. It is one evidence of that strong feeling of nationality which is a prominent feature in the Balūch character.

By this youth's advice we forded the river, of which I have unaccountably omitted to note the name, but which I think must be the Haimanī, and after some delay, owing to two camels getting mired, Jellāl and myself led the way down its banks.

The place was overrun with goat-runs, and we with difficulty kept sight of the pugs of a camel which had preceded us. I may note here that the track of a camel going for a hundred yards in a straight line gives pretty sure indication of a road. With practice also it can be seen whether the camel is loaded or not.

After a quarter of a mile along the banks, we rounded a high bluff, and kept on a south-westerly course through some fairly open ground. In one of my detours in search of the road, I came across a beautiful little oasis in which were the remains of a very large date grove. The trees seemed all to have been dead for years, probably owing to a change of course in the river that previously watered them. There are in the Mekran many instances of whole tracts of trees being destroyed in this way; and though these are generally found where the river cuts its way through soft sand, and makes a new course yearly, still in the hills a landslip might easily produce this effect. Here the broad shingly bed of apparently the same river, Haimanī threw us off the trail; but two very high hills, one on either side, limited our choice of roads; and after passing through about four miles of high shūrs, we crossed a broad slope with a long, abrupt cliff on our right, and some high shūrs to the left. This rough slope, covered with loose stones and flakes of sandstone, severely tried the feet of men and camels, and we made our way without a vestige of path through shūrs for another three miles, and finding two good water-holes, stopped to refresh. Here were pugs of innumerable gurand and plain deer.

We now seemed to be getting near the limits of the hills, and marching over a flat salt plain down a nullah we came upon a little open place behind the Huni mountains. Here were huts, trees, and sheep, and after their long weary march over rugged pathless hills without a guide, my party evinced a strong desire to camp then and there. There was, however, still an hour to sunset, and ascending one more very steep defile we fairly emerged on to the open plain and camped under some bushes.

To-day's march had been from sunrise to sunset, and nearly all bad travelling for man and beast. The camels' feet were nearly all bleeding, and those of Jellāl, whose suāss (*grass sandals*) had given out, and his donkey, which was used to plains, were fearfully swollen. There was a small village near, and some of the inhabitants presented a type of feature different from any we had seen before. They were very clean cut, olive-brown in colour, and the eyes were very large and bright. The head man came and begged very hard and in a disgusting manner for a nargilla. When we killed a sheep, all the men importuned the cook for little bits of offal, which they singed and ate greedily. They wanted to purchase my mashuk, or Persian cloak—the "small-pox coat," and in fine I had to order them out of the camp. They had but just come to this place, having been formerly residents at Gabrig, but Abdul Nabi had extorted from them such taxes that they thought they should feel safer farther away.

We were now, so to speak, at home. Our course lay straight for the huge Markoh bluff due west. Instead of winding amongst pathless hills, our road lay spread before us over a soft sandy plain, for traversing which the camel's feet are well adapted. Only the two broad shallow rivers Gabrig and Jagīn lay between us and Jask, and next morning we loaded up very early in high spirits. Salah and I, on ahead, got first to the river, and, as might have been expected, came to grief in trying to rush the camels over a likely looking place without first sending a man over to sound the depth.

A river running across the sandstrip has a very

different appearance from the same stream while winding through the rocky hills. We exchange clear transparent water with firm shingly bottom for a broad rushing swirling sheet of muddy stuff through which you can see nothing, and the bottom of which is but one remove from a quicksand. The bed may be about three hundred yards broad, and, at this season, the channel of the Gabrig is about one hundred yards wide.

One bank, the one on which the everchanging stream impinges for the present, is a sand-cliff from two or three to even thirty feet high, and this cliff gives off every now and then an avalanche of sand which is whirled away as soon as it touches the water.

The other bank is a gentle sand-slope, and there are frequent sand islands, generally covered with a slippery slime very fatal for a camel, whose feet sometimes slip apart and split the wretched animal up.

The first operation on arriving on the banks of a river of this kind is to halt and send two men forward to walk across, and find out how the bottom is. They throw their clothes over their heads, and walk in with sticks, now and then staggering about and getting stuck in a softer place than usual. The rest of the men stand on the bank and chaff, while the sounders chaff back and yell "mīn! mīn!" or "quicksand." Sometimes they can go straight over, the mud and water averaging about up to their waist except in the deep channel under the sand-cliff, where it may take them up to their arm-pits.

Sometimes there is a bad place, the position of which is at once marked by a tamarisk stick. Sometimes it is all rather soft, and then the men all "betach," *i.e.*, march across and across, and tread down a path, thus reversing the order of things in Dr. Norton Shaw's "Traveller's Remembrancer," where it is said that a ford will sometimes be good enough for the first two or three to cross and impracticable for the remainder. Sometimes one camel is unloaded and led across and across. Again, if the camels are very heavily loaded, all hands turn to and cut armfuls of the never-failing tamarisk and lay it down across the river, treading it into the mud.

When the path is ready, the lightest loaded camel goes first with three or four men on each side supporting the load, and two behind with big sticks, to induce him, should he get mired, to use his utmost efforts at once before he sinks hopelessly deep.

One by one the camels are rushed across and driven up a small path dug out in the sand-cliff.

With a number of men the operation of crossing one of these rivers is simple enough, but it was a different matter for Salah and myself without any attendants.

However, we forced the camels down the slope, and chancing the quicksands, were soon staggering and slipping about in the swirling muddy flood. They got frightened, and waltzed round and round, trying to get back to the shore. We managed, however, to get them on to a small mud island in the middle of the stream. Then came the tug of war!

The next half was deep, and the only landing presented to us was a straight sand-cliff about three feet high. Beat as we might, and objurgate as we might, it seemed of no use. We were bound to go, however, as the shiny mud island we were dancing about on might at any moment lead to a fatal slip. At last, roaring with fear and utterly bewildered, they plunged in again; but finding himself unable to keep his legs together, down went my camel on his knees. Squelch went Ṣalah's just behind me. Water up to our thighs. By a vigorous application of a stout camel-stick I got mine up again, only to stagger forward two steps and down again. This time I had to get off as quick as lightning, for he threw himself viciously on one side, with the evident intention of putting me into the mud and rolling on me—this docile long-suffering ship of the desert!

We were hopelessly wet now, and Salah had to stand in the water holding the two nose-strings, while I went and cut a fresh stick, and he pulling in front and I battering them behind, we got them across.

We and our saddles (consisting of our bedding and blankets) were not in a nice condition to ride the remaining ten miles into camp, which we eventually fixed about half way between Gabrig and Jagīn.

At camp we had a thorough wash, a dinner, and half an hour's snooze; after which, tempted by the brilliant moon and our nearness to English friends, we remounted and set off for Jask.

We got, however, rather more of a journey than we expected, for very soon after starting the moon disappeared altogether behind clouds, and the difficulty and discomfort of a camel ride over extremely rough undulating sand-hills on a pitch dark night, requires to be experienced to be believed.

The circumstances under which I took my leave had rendered it impossible for me to be too particular about my choice of riding camels, and the motion of those on which Salah and I rode was, even on plain ground, and by daylight, when you could prepare for dropping suddenly over a bank or straddling over a nullah, as much like falling down stairs as it is pleasant to think of.

But to-night, strive as we would to pierce the gloom and make out something of the ground two paces ahead of us, we bumped, stumbled, and jolted in a most horribly spine-breaking, bone-dislocating manner. Suddenly, just in front of the camel, would loom up a huge sand-hill, and we would lean forward and grasp tight the front of the saddle, under the impression that the camel would have almost to stand on his hind-legs to climb up it, when, with a groan, down he would go into a nullah four feet deep, and the imagined mountain would prove to be perhaps a bush, but at all events anything but the *ascent* it was thought to be.

However, to turn back was as difficult as to travel forwards, so we pushed on, wishing earnestly for dawn, and consoling ourselves with the prospect of meeting with our friends at Jask.

Suddenly, before we expected it, we found ourselves among the trees which fringe the bank of the Jagīn river, and matters became critical, as this river has in places a forty feet cliff, and a camel's instinct cannot be trusted like that of a horse. Here we were compelled to halt for a time, but fortune was kind, and a glimmer of moon was vouchsafed to us, sufficient to show that we had halted exactly where a caravan had recently crossed; the tamarisk bushes all about having been entirely destroyed to form a path.

We expected much trouble with the camels, but the tamarisk road reassured them, and Salah, going first,

THE FORT AT JASK.

manœuvred his camel so skilfully as to prevent it from setting mine the bad example of lying down, and we struggled up the opposite bank just as grey dawn enabled us to see a dozen or so sleepy white herons standing in a shallow pool.

Jagīn was a favourite old head-quarters for shooting, and I had more than once pitched my tent on the very spot where we now halted. It has now probably been carried away piecemeal, for it was then perilously near the undermining river.

Remounting, we jogged along over a salt plain, past the Yekdār date groves, and over the sand-hills, until we sighted the Shārināh date groves, where we stopped about ten minutes to refresh on the unusually juicy Kŭnār berries (*Ziziphus lotus*). Taking then the track to the sea, we rounded the Oushdāhn headland ; at 3 p.m. we sighted Jask, and an hour and a half after that were shaking hands with white men, and being cordially congratulated on our safe return.

The men and camels dropped in during the next three or four days, and were sent off happy to their homes, with their waistbelts full of money.

CHAPTER V.

BY SEA AND LAND.

Preparations for a fresh journey.—Henjam Island.—Botanizing.—Ruined houses.—The Benoo Yass pearl-fishers.—Salt caves.—Curious well.—" Petrified date-trees."—Intense heat.—" Taking sights."—Transporting camels by water.—Kishm Island.—Sulky camel-men.—Lose my way.—Haji Ahmed's garden.—Old man and bull.—Breakfast.—A delicate question.—Kishm agriculture.—A thirsty walk.—A drink of water.—Sulky camel-men out-marched.—A barren fig-tree.—A late start and a long night-march.—Exciting moment.—Arrive at Kishm.—The wreckers.—Unfriendliness of the Sheikh.—Bearded in his majlis.—Difficulties of shipbuilders.—Start at last.—Among the breakers.—" There's many a slip."—*Terra firma* at last.—Bandar Abbas.—Mināb.—A Balūch army.—Left in the lurch.—Government donkeys.—A long march.—On board the steamer.—Curiosities of postal delivery.—Bahrein donkeys.—A race and a bathe.—Pearl-fishing.—Abou Shihr (Bushire).—Jask.

I REMAINED some time at Jask performing my official duties, digging tanks, planting trees and a date grove on the hitherto barren sandspit on which we lived; but soon commenced preparations for another and longer journey. The better to carry out these preparations, which included reading up botany, geology, entomology, observations astronomical, meteorological, etc., I obtained my transfer to Henjam, a small desert island in the Persian Gulf.

I must thank the officers of H.M.S. *Arab* for putting me in the way of learning to "take sights." They gave me the necessary books, I borrowed a sextant, improvised an artificial horizon by pouring quicksilver into the lid of a tin box, and made such progress that by the time my instruments came out from Europe I was quite handy in their use.

Salah, the Arabic mulla, accompanied us to keep the accounts of the establishment. Jellāl, the shikarri, came as caterer, for the island of Henjam is utterly barren, and we had to get what sheep, fowls, and ducks we could from the neighbouring island, Kishm. "Jooji," the Portuguese cook, came with much grumbling at going to a place where there was no ghee, while Ghulamshah also, and a couple of old women to grind corn, etc., completed the tale.

Henjam, to a person with nothing to do, is anything but a lively place. It is about five miles by three, and almost entirely composed of rugged hills, which look absolutely barren at first, but which to careful botanizing, in March and April yielded over a hundred specimens, the names of which, so far as they were determinable at Kew, will be found in an appendix to this book. One delicately pretty plant was a new species, and I was gratified to hear that it had been entered at Kew as "Reaumuria Floyeri."

This island must have had a curious history in the old piratical times. There are scattered all over it the ruins of thousands of stone huts, concerning the former inhabitants of which nothing definite is now known. Hundreds of huge tanks hewn out in the solid limestone, and plastered with an almost imperishable cement, are everywhere abundant. The patches in the hollows between the hills where a little soil has collected, have, in ancient times, all been jealously walled in. Rain was apparently much more abundant 300 or 400 years ago than it is now, and enabled people to add dates, beans, and goats' milk, to an otherwise never-changing diet of dried fish. At the north end of the island are the remains of an extensive town which boasted two masjids.

The destruction of this town comes within the range of tradition. The superior masonry shows it to have been a Persian colony, and the legend is very possibly correct which relates that it was destroyed by an Arab plundering expedition.

At the south end of the island is a small village of pearl-fishers, containing about 200 families of the Beni Yass from Debai, near Sharkah, as fine a tribe of men as one may wish to find.

We collected specimens of almost every insect in the island, to the number of 140;* my two native boys soon becoming expert enough both in collecting and preserving to save me much trouble. But the geology and mineralogy of Henjam are unique and interesting to the last degree.

The huge salt-caves are very wonderful. There is one especially fine near the centre of the island. Externally it is a tolerably lofty hill, of a rich deep crimson. But as you approach the eastern side you see it cut down the middle, and you face a straight wall of rock-salt, flecked out with boulders of crimson and yellow limestone.

As you climb up to the opening you scramble over masses of iron pyrites, specular iron ore, large bright green stones, yellow stones, and debris of all colours.

---

* This collection was entirely spoilt in transmission to England.

The blocks of specular iron ore are very heavy, and used by the pearl-divers as sinkers. Forcing a way down the narrow and tortuous cavern, which winds away under the hill, one cannot help feeling that this may have been one of the originals of the beautiful Arabian Nights caverns.

Iron pyrites, in the dull light of a lamp, looks very like gold, and the jet-like iron ore like splendid jewels.

At the end of 200 feet or so is a beautiful cave, where are not only huge stalactites of rock-salt, but all the roof and walls are covered with a beautiful salt efflorescence like the softest, purest snow.

Two officers of one of her Majesty's ships once accompanied me down to this grotto, and on their return spoke so highly of its beauties that two more men were fired with zeal, and went off with their lanterns to make the descent. They had, however, a mistaken idea of the grotto's size, and almost suffocated themselves in the attempt to let off a blue light in it.

Except at the pearl-fishing village, there are only three wells in the island, very deep, and rarely holding more than a bucketful of brackish water at a time. One on the south-west coast is rather a curiosity. Its water is strongly flavoured with bitumen, and its mouth extremely narrow, and yet, when your eyes become accustomed to the darkness, and you peer down the 120 feet to the bottom, you are astonished to find it full of pigeons. I only discovered this well just before leaving, or should have thoroughly explored it. It is probably connected with the cliff of the sea, about 200 yards hence, by a fissure, through which the pigeons find access.

It would not be right to leave Henjam without

mention of the curious phenomenon generally called "the petrified date-trees." In some banks of salt calcareous earth are a forest of curious natural pillars of very hard and heavy mud. It was long before I realized that they could not really be petrified trees. I quarried up one "tree," and sent it to the political agent of Maskat, but we remain in the dark to this day as to its origin.

The hot weather at Henjam is fearful. I had no less than five beds in different parts of the island, adapted for any winds should ever any arise. Perhaps the most used were one by the sea, and another on the edge of a cliff; but it was weary work trying to sleep with heavy warm dews, the air poisoned by the smell of seaweed rotting in the warm sluggish waves, and the wet-bulb thermometer rarely under 96° all night.

However, with the exception of one man who went out of his mind, we got safely through the year, and it was, I remember, in August, 1876, just after my new artificial horizon and two chronometer watches had arrived from England, that I received orders to move off to Bushire.

The few remaining sheep I had wandering about the island were soon sold, baggage made into camel-loads, and Jellāl despatched across to Kishm Island to get camels.

The Henjamis have a curious way of getting camels across the strait; they take two at once, and first compelling them to kneel down side by side, they tie every limb up as tightly as possible, then run a boat on shore in between them, and fastening them on outside the boat, they shove off and set sail. Camels will travel like this for hours, though constantly suffering almost total immersion from the waves.

The surface of Kishm Island consists principally of salt plains, intersected by low limestone ridges. It looks now just exactly as it must have done when it first emerged from the sea, and the traveller who crosses it in August without a tent, cannot but wonder for what high destiny it ever did emerge. At this time of the year, too, the inhabitants all go and live among the date groves at Mināb, on the main-land, and both camels and men are very difficult to obtain.

On the night of the 20th I was ferried across the straits, and after trudging three or four miles through complete darkness and over rugged trackless rocks, I stumbled upon my "camp" on a small mound near the village of Dīristān. We had a sulky lot of camel-men, and I could not even get a few camel-droppings to keep the fire up, so we were a prey to mosquitoes and jackals.

Next morning I sent the caravan off at 6 a.m., and started to walk; but almost immediately lost my way. However, after a great deal of hard walking I arrived at a fine date grove, the owner of which, Sheikh Haji Ahmed, made me very welcome, and gave me a mat under a shady kahūr tree, where I drowsed away the heat of the day. There was a well and small tank not twenty feet away, and as the stifling hot noontide came on, the birds and beasts all round got thirsty. It was curious to watch them. Each kind came, so to speak, at its appointed time. First ringdoves, then doves and blue pigeons together, then sparrows, then bulbuls, and last of all, crows. And it was most ridiculous to see how each kind bustled its predecessors away, with apparently the greatest indignation at their presumption. Soon it was the old men's turn, and tying their turbans round their waists, they one by one descended into the water in true biblical style.

The cows, it appears, were to follow the men in due course, and they could no more manage the matter without a squabble than their predecessors the birds.

One very old man remained after his companions, only his clean-shaven head above water, either lost in contemplation or perhaps half asleep.

An old bull who was leading the herd, came noiselessly along the soft dusty path, and put his nose down for a refreshing drink. But suddenly a round cocoa-nut-like appearance in the water caught his eye, and putting his nose down to within an inch of it, he gave a most stupendous sniff.

A yell escaped the old man as he bobbed under the water and presently re-appeared at the other end of the small tank, coughing, gurgling, and spitting, and abusing the bull in the most horrible language. "Oh, may a wolf tear you to pieces," "Oh, burnt up soul," "Oh, particularly illegitimate cow," etc., etc., and I roared with laughter.

The bull meekly, but with dignity, elevated its nose and chewed calmly till the excitement he had so unwittingly aroused was over.

Just now, however, a tall Persian in a clean shirt appeared, bringing in a large copper tray my breakfast. The usual two or three sorts of curries, a fowl cooked to perfection, buttermilk, curds, fresh dates, sugar, raisins, and pieces of thin wafer bread about two feet across, which serve as plates. All were soon despatched, the servant squatting politely a little out of sight that I might not be bashful. I had been wildly hungry, and I suppose my face must have expressed some remorse at the havoc I had made of the good Sheikh's viands, for the man took upon himself to gravely assure me that I had not eaten enough to support a little child.

Breakfast over, and still scorching noon. Nothing for it but "broadback exercise" under my tree, and there I lay, sometimes scrawling these notes on the roof of my pith hat, for I had forgotten my note-book, and sometimes lazily lighting a pipe and letting it go out after a couple of whiffs, watching the ants carrying off the datestones I had pitched about, and I believe not unfrequently asleep. I was agreeably aroused by a tremendous chattering and much not unmusical laughter, and turning over, found the tank and well surrounded by a bevy of damsels who were the ladies of my host's establishment, *and*—who evidently wanted to bathe!

As I became aware of their presence, they were holding an animated argument as to whether I could understand their speech or not, and it was settled that I looked fairly intelligent and would probably get some idea of their meaning if they spoke very loud. The difficulty was who would bell the cat.

I cut the matter short by assuring them that as soon as I could get on my coat I would seek another tree, and they thanked me, laughing merrily at the adventure.

I picked up my rifle and trudged off under the shady trees of the garden to where I found my host, also just roused up from his *siesta*, and we had a little conversation about the crops, taxes, etc. Wheat was little grown, as it generally came up smutty. Tobacco was rarely used, such as was, being imported. In the winter the gardens would all be deserted, and the people all go to the cities or stone-built villages. My host was very intelligent, and gave me much information.

At five we had dinner, and though the sun was still intensely hot, yet I had over twelve miles to go, so I trudged off with a man to put me on the right track for Suza.

Issuing from the garden on to the burning desert, was like going from a hot-house into a furnace, and Kishm in August is miserably barren. We recrossed the limestone ridge I had wrongly crossed in the morning by a curious semi-artificial cutting, and then had miles of breathless scrambling over scorching crags and plains a foot deep with fine salt-dust. Such a journey as we were now making would be impossible but for the existence at every two or three miles of a dome-roofed tank of rain-water.

The first of these godsends will never be forgotten. We had started too early in the afternoon, and in about an hour after dismissing my guide, all the blood in my body was boiling, and my brain seemed ready to burst my skull.

I was obliged to stop every hundred yards or so to avoid a sunstroke, which I knew from experience to be imminent.

At last a friendly dome-roof caught my eye, and I rushed up to a deep circular tank and seized with trembling hands the earthen pot used for drawing water.

Will it be believed, the rope was so old and rotten

that the mere jerk of letting the pot down broke half the strands through. How my hand shook as I gently drew it up again, with painful self-denial, only a third full. That drink seemed like pouring the water into a dry bag somewhere in my inside. The second drink was better, and after a third I positively sat down half crying with delight, and patched up the rope and boldly drew up a full pot. All this will never be forgotten. If I had fallen there, nothing but jackals and hyænas would have known anything about me for at least three days.

It was pitch dark and far into the night by the time I reached the fishing-village of Suza and found my camp. Ghulamshah had tea for me, but the camel-men had been obstreperous, and utterly refused to fetch wood or water. Prompt measures were necessary, so after questioning the men themselves, I discharged them all on the spot without a fraction of wages. They went off threatening all sorts of things; but the sequel proved that I was right. Their master had ordered them to come to Suza to take himself and family to his country quarters, and they had engaged to take me to Kishm, hoping to pick a quarrel at Suza, get paid up to date, discharged, and be at their master's disposal next morning.

All next day I sweltered under a barren fig-tree, the only shade I could get. The village was quite deserted, everybody having gone to the date harvest at Minab, and my men wandered vainly about inquiring for camels. Towards noon, hearing that there was a head man left in the village, I called upon him, and after some haggling he promised camels in three hours.

We waited patiently till 10 p.m., when I determined on a personal investigation. Lighting a couple of hurricane lamps I started with all my people, and after getting to two or three wrong houses in the dark night and narrowly escaping a fall into a limepit in a hasty jump out of the way of a horned snake which lay in our path, we got to the head man's house. He affected, and possibly felt, considerable indignation, but I had done with the *suaviter in modo* as regards this transaction, and by a little *fortiter in re* we soon found ourselves inside the courtyard. Here, behold, were our three promised camels! The old man only delayed to get increased hire for them. We rather got the better of him, however. He had a new kind of madman to deal with now, and I don't suppose camels were ever loaded quicker than these were. We were off at 10.45, and did not stop moving on till we unloaded at Kishm at half-past eight the next morning. And the old man, the sheikh, was still more disgusted, when, by the merest chance, just as we were leaving his stables, I observed his own pet riding donkey and promptly ordered it out too.

It was a frightful road, and pitch dark, but with one lamp in the van and another in the rear, and myself in the middle wielding a long stick, we were bound to march. The camel-men proposed to make two and even three stages to Kishm, but somehow they never managed to get halted. At about eighteen miles one was left crying in the track. Soon after, another lay down, declaring he was dying, and without even heart to reply to my jeering offers of a mount on the camels. These Kishm men walk no better than old women, and my Balūchis, who had been at a discount while inactive at Suza, and had had to submit to much chaff on their helpless and camelless condition, thoroughly enjoyed the turn of the tables. I had only one camel-man left at last, and him I had kept up by mounting him on the donkey, which I never rode myself. This march brought out the character of these people. One might travel a long while with Balūchis before seeing one leave behind a tired and crying comrade.

Just before dawn it was as dark as it is possible to imagine, and we had the most difficult piece yet to come. We had approached the sea, and were traversing a flat shore of slippery mud often fatal to camels and intersected by deep slimy creeks.

It was a weird and animated scene, and all petty annoyances were soon forgotten in the excitement. The flashing lights, the splashing water, the yells of the men, and their ruddy eager faces as they tore madly through the deep water from one camel to the other, beating this one, hauling at that, while the huge beasts staggered about roaring hoarsely and getting deeper and deeper every moment, and all around us spread the dark sullen water. We got so deep at one time that the horrible thought came into my head that in the struggles with the camels we had altered our course, and were heading out to sea. I strained my ears to hear from which side came the sound of waves, but they seemed to boom all round us. I was glad to see that the thought had not occurred to the men, and I had sufficient presence of mind to say nothing, thus preventing a panic that would probably have been fatal. Nothing could pierce the gloom that enveloped us, and the two hurricane lamps did more harm than good.

Though I racked my brains, I could find no clue as to the course we were going or the state of the tide. All I could think of was to put my two watches into my turban, fasten my rifle to the saddle, and keep on the alert for anything that might occur.

We were, however, too busy to feel the full weight of the suspense at the time, and after about ten minutes the water gradually shallowed and we reached sand again.

We had one more bit of bad road before us, which involved forcing the camels round a bluff against which the sea was surging with an apparently lazy but really irresistible force. The men's blood was up, however, from their late excitement, and they would have driven those camels through anything, especially as their owners, the Kishmis, were not present. The gray morning broke upon us plodding through a ruined village, and three miles afterwards we reached the sea, and passing under a high cliff to our right, two more miles landed us under a mimosa tree at Kishm.

Little or nothing need be said of the town of Kishm. The bazaars were poor but clean, and the one imposing building was the mansion of Sheikh Sagar, the Governor. The only fruit obtainable was a curious kind of almond called Gurumzangi, of which one ate the succulent outside skin and threw away the shell and kernel. The flesh was bright red, and the taste exactly that of a pear. Mangoes, melons, and barley are grown in the little oases which form the habitable portion of the island. Wheat, as I have said, almost invariably comes up smutty. Three kinds of truffles are common, and the leaves of a tree called Murt are powdered up and applied to the skin for prickly heat. As I could not obtain the unpowdered leaf I was unable to identify it.

I remained at Kishm for two days being unable to get a boat; for though the sea here was calm, there was said to be such a surf on the Bandar Abbas shore that landing was impossible. I usually spent my mornings in wandering about the bazaar and chatting with the captain of a 180-ton dhow which was hauled up on the sand for repairs.

This boat ran short of water on a voyage from Bombay to Bushire, and was coming into Henjam to beg, borrow, or steal some water from our tanks. By the merest carelessness she was stranded not a mile from her intended anchorage. The weather was calm, and some men from the island were employed to unload her on payment of a third of the cargo. Then Sheikh Abid from the pearl-fishing village on the south end arrived, and forbade the unloading until the captain should agree to pay half the cargo. And while matters were thus under discussion and the boat gradually breaking to pieces, up comes Sheikh Sagar and prohibits all unloading until he shall have received two-thirds. Now the boat was under British ownership, and the captain, a fine picturesque old Arab, with a white beard such as one reads of more often than one sees, telegraphed to the Political Resident at Bushire, whereupon promptly arrived H.M.S. *Arab*. Then we had a grand judicial investigation; I being as it were counsel for the captain (for the conduct of the sheikhs was a sheer piece of piracy), and translator between the captain and Sheikhs Sagar and Abid.

I had further to translate all the captain's "manifest" of cargo, which was written here, there and everywhere, on hundreds of dirty bits of paper. What a work it was! He had hundreds of logs of wood. Every one was of a different shape, size, quality, and species from every other one, nor would he let me off a single measurement. Then he had 680 baskets of tamarinds, pepper, ginger, cocoa-nuts, and each basket had a different consigner and consignee, and was of a different weight from any other basket. Then the sea was covered with his cocoa-nuts, and were these to be written down lost or saved. Altogether we had some hours of hard work.

As matters went very decidedly against Sagar, and I had to translate the captain's severe strictures on his conduct, it may be imagined that he did not care to show much hospitality on my arrival, and I remained under my tree all the while as I did not choose to accept the hospitality of any one of inferior rank. It was not, however, such a good berth as the barren fig-tree at Suza, for the shadow of the tree was so small that when I took my noonday *siesta* a man had to sit by me and poke me gently round as the sun descended. Sagar was "asleep" (that is, "not at home") when I called at his palace, which presents a curious appearance, owing to a bright green cast-iron staircase joining two portions of a ramshackle mud-built house. I bearded him, however, in the evening, by joining, in company with my friend the captain, the majlis or council, which sat every evening on a raised and carpeted square near the shore, where Sagar sat in state, and where I had enough to do to maintain conversations in three languages at once. The talk was mostly of pearl-fishing, taking salt to Maskat, bringing back silk headdresses, and the probable amount this or that man could pay for this or that monopoly.

A case of this latter was instructive. Four merchants had exhausted nearly all their funds in the construction of a bugla or dhow. Sagar sent orders that "the usual tax of 3,000 krans" (£125) must be paid before the thing could be allowed to start. After much deliberation, *i.e.*, haggling for a week and bribing people in the majlis to take their part, the merchants agreed to this sum. But their haggle had not been long enough, and they had failed somehow to impress Sagar sufficiently with the idea of their poverty, and he raised the amount to 4,000. And the matter progressed thus until, at the time I was there, the tax was 10,000. The bugla, not yet masted, was anchored off in charge of Sagar's men; and I met in the majlis two of the unfortunate merchants.

In the afternoon of the second day, through the kind offices of the old captain, I got a boat. But the artifices of Sheikh Sagar induced three of the men to desert at the last moment. The wind, however, was fair, and we were just strong enough to hoist the huge sail, so I decided on a start. I sent word to Sheikh Sagar that I was travelling on duty on behalf of the British Government, and that he should be held responsible for any mishap that befel me, and we got under weigh. We narrowly escaped running aground on the now deserted island of Hormuz, but with a fair wind we arrived towards evening off Bandar Abbas. The surf was running mountains high, and landing was impossible; but the steamer I wished to catch for Abou Shihr would arrive to-morrow, and with much difficulty, owing to our shorthandedness (all but myself and the crew were sick), we managed to get our unwieldy anchor overboard, and rode out the night near three cargo-boats which were also waiting for the steamer.

It was an eventful night. We dragged our anchor, and getting into the surf shipped sea after sea, wetting every morsel of food and rag of clothing we had. Suddenly, excited shouts came through the darkness, and the next minute we crashed into another boat. We cleared again, though I don't know how, and luck turned. Just as we had got our sail half hoisted, a strong puff came off the shore and carried us out to sea.

Our reduced crew of three behaved very well, and showed great activity and fearlessness. We got out again to near the three cargo-boats, and waited, wet and uncomfortable, for the steamer.

About ten she came in sight. The cargo-boats immediately weighed anchor and hoisted sail. We, alas! had received so much damage in the night that, try as we would, we could not hoist. We heard the hoarse rattle of the steamer's cable, and I thought I could even make out the white figure of the captain on the bridge, but we could not get on board.

The mail-officer passed us with the mails, and we all joined in a despairing hail without success. I should think his time was fully occupied with steering, and indeed it was surprising that he dared venture in that sea in such a cockleshell. On his return journey he came nearer than before, and we once more hailed with all our might, without success. I hoisted my pith hat (the only European article I had) into the rigging, but the steamer left us behind. At half-past twelve

(I knew that steamer's hours) those people sat down to a luxurious lunch, with clean table-cloth, glasses, plates. We were soppy and hungry, but we could not bridge over that three or four hundred yards.

We set to work to repair damages. Ghulamshah perked up a little, saying with a half-miserable smile, "This is the way we enjoy ourselves on pleasure-trips." Towards evening we set sail and ran down the coast to Suroo.

Here we grounded about three miles from the shore, and half-waded and half-swam the remainder of the distance through stuff it was impossible to call definitely either mud or water. The number of wading birds here was enormous, and indeed at first sight they seemed to be the only inhabitants of the country. It was a flat, low, sandy shore covered with salicornia. But there were date groves on ahead, and marching doggedly along, our clothes and boots saturated with perspiration, mud, and salt water, we soon found a hut, where an old man was busy separating a heap of freshly gathered dates into three qualities for the market.

It seems that we had landed three miles from Suroo, a small village where the wealthier merchants of Bandar Abbas have country houses, and about nine from the Bandar; so after a hearty meal off dates, and some delicious icy-cold well water, our host got us camels, and once more we were on march for Bandar Abbas, and about the middle of the night we were being royally entertained by Messrs. Gray, Paul and Co.'s representative at that port.

Bandar Abbas has been often described, and a short notice here will be ample. As must always be done with oriental towns, there should be taken for granted an amount of filth, decay, raggedness, and bad smells incredible by one who has not experienced it. The general aspect of the town is a long, irregular collection of oblong, flat-topped mud houses, of which every fourth one is in ruins.

The old Dutch factory, now the Governor's house, strikes the eye, and the town gains considerably by the six or seven tall wind towers which the wealthier men build. As one nears the town, the houses seem to acquire ears. These ears are large funnels or wind-catchers, without which no house would be bearable. The climate is hot and very unhealthy. Behind the town is a sandy desert, a salt-water river, and the huge Jebel Ginnoh.

But Bandar Abbas is, as its name expresses, only the port, and must not be separated from the perennial river, the picturesque scenery, and lovely shady gardens of Minab.

Minab signifies muddy water, but should convey no reproach to the river, for the gardens are due to the mud it has brought down. The place is about fifty-four miles over fiery desert from Bandar Abbas. It is the sylvan retreat of the merchants of the Bandar, and during the date harvest draws to itself all the able-bodied men of the country for a hundred miles round. Mirza Abdulla, the *locum tenens* of the Governor, was at Minab; and after being three days at Bandar, my host and I got camels at ten o'clock one night, and at seven next evening arrived among the date-trees, three or four miles below the fort. Here we turned in, and next morning sighted Mirza Abdulla's summer-house under a huge banian in a luxuriant garden of pomegranates, henna, vines, cotton, limes, oranges, and almonds. While breakfast was getting ready, a bathe in the river refreshed us immensely. Here we were at the foot of a range of low hills, and the river debouched from a rugged amphitheatre of rocks with a full, strong stream. Just opposite us, on the east bank, it had cut a bed two hundred feet deep through a deposit of mud and shingle.

Along the top of this hill were the lofty remains of what had been an enormous fortified camp, and here, in tolerably spacious bazaars, is held a grand fair every Thursday.

Having climbed up into one of the loftiest watch-towers of the fort, under guidance of a Balūch match-lockman posted there, we saw from the top the curious and almost unique sight of a Balūch army. Let me here premise that when I talk of Balūch I mean always Mekran Balūch, a race far different from and finer than the men of Eastern Balūchistan. At first they had been hidden in the river bed, and as they poured up over the bank they resembled nothing so much as a swarm of ants. Over two hundred tall lithe fellows were perched on the extreme ends of as many donkeys, their long, silver-mounted matchlocks nodding behind their backs, their silver-handled swords dangling from their left shoulders, and at least one pistol and a knife stuck in the waistcloth. Amongst these men were some fifty others mounted on camels. These are the intelligence branch, and they can ride, if necessary, ninety miles in a day. Here and there amongst this many-coloured cavalcade were nine or ten horses bearing the chiefs; and I was surprised to make out with the glasses the tall but bent form and huge white turban of that restless, hoary old intriguer, Abdul Nabi, of the Jask district, about a hundred and twenty miles down the coast.

I found afterwards that he had taken advantage of the fact that there was no definite governor of Bandar Abbas, to pretend to offer vassalage to the *locum tenens*, on the condition that the Jask territory which had so long been a bone of contention between Mīr Yusuf and himself should be ceded to him. He had of course brought every man he could raise to impress the Mirza with the importance of conciliating him.

From my elevated post I noticed that with considerable ingenuity water from the river had been led through a canal underneath the fort and irrigated other beautiful gardens behind it, and we spent the heat of the day in their shade sucking limes and oranges, and regretting that the pomegranates and the guavas were not yet fully ripe. There is, as nearly as I could gather from many careful estimates, an annual export of over 1,500 tons of dates, and at this season the mouth of the river is full of native craft.

The henna too is an important crop; a good deal goes to Bombay by sea, but more to Kirman and Yazd. Bandar Abbas is the port for Kirman and Yazd; at Isfahan the greater portion of the English goods come *viâ* Baghdad and Kirmanshahan. A loaded caravan will reach Yazd in twenty-seven days, and Kirman in twenty-four.

In the evening we went back and had a good dinner about 10 p.m. with the Mirza, small brass cups full of the white blossoms of the fragrant double jessamine being placed all round us.

ABDUL NABI.

On inquiring for our camels great search was made for our camel-man, but unsuccessfully. The Mirza was full of condolences, which were unusually hearty, considering that the old gentleman had himself annexed our beasts to make up a caravan of dates he was sending to Bandar Abbas.

We could not afford delay, however, and in about an hour some donkeys were produced which the Mirza assured me belonged to the Persian Government, adding that I should find relays along the road.

It was half-past eleven and pitch dark when we started, and after stumbling along for about six miles our donkey-men proposed to get fresh donkeys. I gave orders, however, that the present set should not be abandoned until their reliefs came, for to the best of my belief we were somewhere in the middle of a desert. We nearly came to blows over this, but eventually outbragged the opposition, and they went off in the darkness. I rather believe we all dozed off for about half an hour when I was awakened by voices. "I can't go." "You must." "My donkey's lame." "Government orders." "I've only one donkey, and three weeks now it's been carrying wheat, and it's only two years old; it's perfectly dead," etc., etc. It was not a cheering prospect, but I had promised to deliver up our donkeys on production of substitutes, and as I had not stipulated for good substitutes it had to be done. Our new four, which it was proposed, I found, should take us the remaining forty-eight miles of hopeless desert, were probably the most wretched donkeys in the world. On putting a leg over their backs they one after another sank down before they got even my moderate weight of eight stone on their backs. We accepted the situation, for we had to catch a steamer and could not wait. But another difficulty arose. The three "donkey-men" were one big boy and two little ones, all perfectly ignorant of the way. I managed to make it their interest to procure a guide by starting off straight into the darkness at random and driving the donkeys before me. I had not got far when I heard the eldest send for his father, who after much hard swearing saw that he must go and consented to start.

I need not detail the march. Any one can imagine a pitch dark walk over a hillocky tussocky plain of loose sand; it is enough to say that dawn found us wandering aimlessly about having taken a course at an angle of 45° with the one we should have made. However with light came a landmark, being the tops of a date-grove far away on the horizon, while before us as far as we could see stretched a dusty plain. At 5 p.m. we reached the date-trees of Kalangong, and all had a "square meal" of curry and rice and tea. I had found out on the way that the wretched donkey-men had the impression that all this journey was made for the Persian Government, and as they never dreamt that I should be so weak as to pay for what I could get done for nothing they were proportionately sulky.

Immediately on discovering this, I assured them that nobody had to work for Feringis without pay, and at once offered them double hire on the spot. This had a grand effect, and by six o'clock we were on the march again. But at 10 p.m. we had lost the way, or rather the direction, for there was no track, and had to lie down where we were. Next morning we were off by daybreak and got to Bandar Abbas by eleven, thus completing one of the longest marches on foot I had, up to that time, ever made; the distance being 51 miles as the crow flies. The smaller donkey-boy could not have been more than eleven, and yet by two in the afternoon that same day these fellows were well on their way back! Over and above their double wages I had given them a present especially for a good hearty meal, but they would not spend more than sufficient to buy a lump of dates each.

Next morning I was steaming up the gulf in a first-class English steamer. Lingah, the first halting place, is a long straggling line of houses and palm-trees fringing the shore for about two miles, and backed up by the enormous mountain Bostaneh, the top of which is now hidden in white fleecy clouds. It used to be under the rule of Sheikh Mathkūr, a fierce and truculent old man who was much feared. His son now reigns, and the Persian Governor of Bandar Abbas has recently been feeling his way to a more definite submission and more regular taxpaying in this part of the country. I believe no European traveller has ever traversed the country from Bushire to Lingah. The natives say it is very barren, without water, and overrun by a fierce tribe of robbers called Behlūs, who are of Arabic origin and who kill even darvishes. "Native information" has its value with those who doubtless know better than I, so I give it, though my own experience shows that it is very rarely trustworthy. But we shall have more on this subject hereafter.

Mulla Hussein, the steamer agent here, has rather an original turn of mind. He was induced to accept the postmastership some two years ago. His duties as agent made it necessary for him to come on board every steamer; so Her Majesty's mails, instead of being sent ashore by an English officer with a red ensign trailing over the stern of his boat, were delivered to the Mulla in the saloon.

Here all those who expected letters were in attendance. "It was their own look-out if they were not," our postmaster would say pointedly, and he would dive into the bag, fish up a letter, and cry out, "Here's a letter for Khajah Abdulla with eight annas to pay." If the eight annas were forthcoming the Khajah got his letter, but if he even ventured to suggest that the letter was fully stamped, or even to lessen the sum by haggling, it was promptly torn up, thrown aside, and another letter proceeded with. Such a system of postal delivery could not of course go on long, and he was soon suspended from office, though declaring naively that that was the best kind of post-office he could afford to keep on the paltry remuneration of fifty rupees a month.

Leaving Linjah we steamed away for Bahrein, the two seas, where the great nucleus of the pearl fishery is. There are but few large houses in Bahrein, one rather good one was formerly the residence of a British agent, but is now inhabited by a Parsee postmaster and steamer agent.

Towards evening we went to see this gentleman, and picking our way through two courtyards piled twenty feet high in pearl shells, we ascended to the rather lofty upper room. We found to our surprise that the roof was covered with Turkish soldiers straggling about in every possible attitude, and most of them snoring to such an extent as to suggest sawing wood. They were the escort of the taxes just forwarded by the Governor of Katīf and to be taken to Bussorah by our steamer. We hired some of the enormous Bahrein donkeys—many of which, though I have never measured them, I should say were at least fourteen hands—and trotted off to one of several lovely fresh-water basins for a bathe. We were a jovial cavalcade scampering along that night in the cool air and under a brilliant moon.

Who that has gone from the glaring scorching sunlight to the cool pure moonlight can help wishing that the moon system of illumination was more generally in use? I know I thought so, but soon dismissing the notion as unscientific I rode on with the rest.

We had gone on in a very decent way hitherto, but mischief was brewing. P—— was our gay first officer and rode like a sailor, and could not regard an expedition of this sort as complete without a race. Now the jovial but botuliform Ff——, though anxious to gratify everybody, did not see his way to this. He was not used to donkey riding, his stirrups were only about six inches long, and he had every reason to believe that his girths were merely adapted from some portion of his attendant's garments. The matter, however, was not quite under his own control, for the mixture of iron chains and bandages which represented the bridle generally came out of his steed's mouth when he pulled it. An accidental discovery by J—— settled the matter. His attendant had constantly walked along by the side of his donkey, with his hand on the animal's back, and J—— soon noticed that this operation materially improved his speed. So at last he suddenly seized the hand and behold it was grasping a sharp peg! This was fastened by a short string to the saddle, in which was a socket for the peg when not in use.

This was enough for P——, whose speed had only been restrained hitherto by his ignorance of arguments adapted to his steed's comprehension, and in a minute we were all flying over the plain only to bring up at the tank. A strong spring gushed out at one end of a large basin hewn out of the limestone rock and made a perfect bathing place.

When we arrived, it was full of men, women, and children, who sometimes spend the whole of these lovely nights in the water like so many hippopotami. They did not seem inclined to move at first; but as one white form after another bounded into the air and disappeared headlong into the water, they fled precipitately, one aged damsel being frightened out of her wits by P——'s coming up from his dive just behind her.

It was a delightful bathe, and a jolly ride home; and next morning we were steaming away for Bushire.

Our course led us through a fleet of about three hundred boats engaged in pearl-fishing. Each boat had anchored, and the ten or twelve oars were placed half on each side projecting over the edge of the boat in a horizontal position. Each oar had a rope dangling from the end, and to these ropes the divers clung. As we passed through them we saw sometimes the whole ten black shaven heads bobbing about at the end of the rope. Then first one would disappear, then another. Soon they began to reappear, hand up their bags, and prepare for another dive. I have examined and timed many divers, and cannot but think Mr. H. Emmanuel's statement as to the length of time these men can remain under water much exaggerated. I never yet met one who could remain longer than one minute, and forty-five seconds is a good dive. They are a hard-worked and badly paid class.

Bushire, or Abou Shihr, the father of cities, is by far the largest town in the Gulf, and I should think contains more filth and strong smells in proportion to its size than any other town, the ordinary use of streets being quite secondary to their use as sewers. The town is of tolerably modern foundation, placed on a peninsula which is said to be gradually rising from the sea. The Armenians, of whom there is a strong colony, and the wealthier merchants, have all country houses and gardens at from three to six miles from the town, and during the famine two or three tolerable roads were made for about this distance, enabling them to drive in to business. Bushire is the port for the Shiraz and Ispahan districts, and much opium is sent to China, and sugar imported from Batavia, called by the natives Patoua.

Here I received from England the completion of my equipment of instruments, and with these, and a load of enormously thick felt coats and blankets, I left Bushire for Jask, my old station in the Mekran.

All the way down I was either taking sights or working them out, and soon got pretty handy with my sextant. After a prosperous run, I arrived at Jask and renewed acquaintance with many old friends.

CHAPTER VI.

WESTERN BALUCHISTAN.

Geigen.—The caravan.—Jellāl stays behind.—"Marro assuchi."—Buying camels.—Honesty of the people.—"Great expectations."—The Tang-i-Duhl.—A crisis.—Alishah.—Rain again.—An elderly man.—A' bad day's sport.—A swarm of locusts.—Rumours of disaffection.—Difficulty in keeping dead reckoning.—Pitch plaister.—Dazaka.

IN a short time my equipment was ready, and on the 29th October, 1876, I left Jask for Geigen with ten hired camels under an engagement to go as far as Anguhran, the capital of Bashakard. At first we camped near Geigen village, a picturesque place, situated amongst fine mimosa trees at the foot of the huge sandstone Geigen bluff, and we remained here two days. Here we witnessed a curious Balūch ceremony of sacrificing a sheep at the commencement of the sowing season to propitiate the "nadr lillah," a corruption of some Arabic phrase, of which no Balūch could tell me the origin. Then we marched round the bluff, and camped under the shade of some trees, in a valley near the Geigen river-bed. Here we spent four more busy days, making triangulations, taking sights, experimenting on different ways of carrying the big chronometer, doctoring the natives, and, last but not least, buying camels. After much consultation and questioning, I had decided that I could do better with six picked camels of my own than ten hired ones, and I accordingly, with much haggling, possessed myself of six beautiful "līros," as the full-grown camels are called. All had splendid reputations for having done marvellous journeys with unheard-of loads, and I had a personal knowledge of the powers of two of them. Before we finished our journey I was very fond of my camels. They were splendid specimens of their breed, and there are more numerous and more widely different breeds of camels than of horses. No one could help admiring their massive shoulders, colossal forelegs, and smooth shining brown coats.

First came the leader of the caravan, the Jamaiti līro, an old camel, but one of proved strength and endurance, and my readers may possibly recollect him as "Old Eblis."

Then the beautiful mahri, or riding camel (mahr, a rein), a powerful three-and-a-half-year-old, and the youngest of the troop. He was almost intelligent, and used regularly to invade my tent in the evening and nose out the date-bag.

The big Jaski came next, who carried the cook's heavy boxes; and it was grand to see him swing away with them with a stride nearly a foot longer than the others. His only fault was that he was "nesh," *i.e.*, he had cut his canine teeth, after which a camel's strength and endurance no longer increase, though they do not yet begin to diminish. There were no special points about the other three. They all did their work admirably, though some perished in the attempt.

The men of our small party merit a slight description. First Brahim Mahomed, a line-guard in the

Government telegraphs, was granted leave of absence by the authorities to accompany me as my head man. He was a tall handsome fellow, of good position and a thorough gentleman. Excepting that he was hardly severe enough with the men, he served me well; alas! only too well, for the poor fellow never returned to his beloved country, and his bones lie buried in a strange land. He was a good comrade, and I should like to have seen him before he died, and know that he did not remember any severities I may have used towards him when exasperated by delays, disobediences, sicknesses and other incidents of travel. But as a brighter picture let me draw Tājoo—Tājoo the broad-shouldered, the colossal-legged, Tājoo the preternaturally dirty and the naturally goodnatured; whose ready chaff and hearty laugh never failed, however bad our destiny—Tājoo who, however fierce might be my humour against the men, would always come and coax for a bit of meat, a little curry stuff, or some little luxury; who was staunch in mutiny, and in his broken Arabic, of which he was so proud, more than once warned me of an intended desertion, for Tājoo had travelled with us before and knew our conditions, which the other men had yet to learn.

Next on the muster roll come Brahim Khamīs and Dād Arrahīm, whom I bracket together. They were two high-spirited young fellows of good property, and of the same high family as the Jemadar Brahim. In fact, the latter had persuaded them to come more as companions to himself, than as actively useful to the caravan. They were wild flighty youngsters, and gave a good deal of trouble before they fairly settled down to the collar. Poor Dād Arrahīm died also, and was buried not far from Brahim Mahomed. Abdulla Daduk, the next man, was a curious little fellow with a hooked nose, small twinkling black eyes, and a curly black beard. He did his work steadily, but had a sharp tongue, and had more share in spreading discontent than I was at the time aware of.

Hassan was a tall powerful old man, of low family and unrefined manners. He was a good camel-man and understood firing, but his chief peculiarities were, a voice of extraordinary power, and a persistency in using it that beggars description. He still retains the name I hastened to give him, of Hassan Kharāwāzi, or Hassan of the donkey's bray.

Kāsim was a little wizened old man, who might have been cut out of a piece of wood, for his arms and legs were all the same size throughout their length. He was an extraordinary pedestrian, and is said, I believe truly, to have done two hundred and fifty-four miles in five days.

Alishah was a curiosity indeed, a little short, fat, round young fellow, without an atom of dignity or solidity of character of any sort. He was very clever, had been a line-guard, but a more utterly careless, good-for-nothing ne'er-do-weel never existed. His tongue was never still, and he would talk, laugh, sing, lie, brag, tell anecdotes, and chaff from morning to night. He would admit ignorance on no single subject, and, though despised for his barefaced lies, he was a valuable addition to the party owing to his splendid accomplishments as a mimic and a minstrel.

Ghulamshah, whose honest brown face grins at me now as I write this, is a strong-headed, careful-handed boy of from fourteen to sixteen. He is a Balūch of good family, and spent all his childhood wandering over the country about Rudbar and Bampūr.

Some idea of his value may be gained from the following summary of his performances. He accompanied me during a journey of seven months, and crossed the lofty snow-clad mountains of Kurdistan in the depth of winter. During this time he cooked all my meals for me, packed and unpacked all my instruments every day, and took charge of and wound the chronometer when I had to leave camp. He never broke anything, and never but once left anything behind. He was trusty in mutinies, never tired, and never frightened.

Such was the permanent staff of our expedition. I had some years' experience in the country to guide my choice, and had I to repeat the journey I would not alter a man. My old Bampūr friend, Jellāl, at the last moment elected not to come. The conflict between his allegiance to me and desire to share in such an adventurous journey on the one hand, and his growing old age, his new wife and pet son on the other, fairly convulsed the old man's mind; and when the die was cast and we actually started without him, he rushed about like a madman, beating those who had advised him to stay, and abusing even his own pet son.

On the fourth of November I weeded my stores, and sent back two camel-loads. I then had a farewell review of all my patients, to one of whom I had the satisfaction of completely restoring her eyesight. It was a young girl, daughter of one of my old shikarries, and her eyes were so bad that though the solution of nitrate of silver was four times the usual strength it did not produce the least effect at first. I told her that when it began to burn her it would be a sign that she was getting well. On the fourth day I noticed a decided improvement, and immediately I dropped the solution into her eye she screamed, "Marro asuchi! Marro asuchi!" * and putting her arms round my neck sank almost fainting on the ground. Both she and her mother were so profusely grateful afterwards, that, fearing scandalous tongues, I handed her over to my medical assistant, Ghulam-shah, who completed the cure. To-day also I bought my last camel from Brahim's uncle. The following is the recognised form of dialogue for concluding a purchase :—

Seller: "Now have you taken this līro for thirty-five kursh (£8)."

Buyer: "I have taken it."

Seller: "You have taken it, and if it be blind, lame, diseased and useless you have bought it for thirty-five kursh."

Buyer: "I have."

Seller: "And I take God's oath, that as far as I know, this līro is perfectly free from any blemish, that it is a good strong beast, and that I have not concealed anything from you."

Chorus of bystanders: "It's not lame, it's not blind," etc., etc. "You may put seventy māns on its back," etc. And we shake hands solemnly.

I had here an instance of the scrupulous honour amongst Balūchis. I wanted to send a large sum of money back to Jask, and as I was on the point of

---

* Balūchi for "Imrōz mīsūzad" (*It burns to-day*).

sending off Brahim with it, he happened to look out of the tent. "There's a man," he said, "just going; he'll take it," and he ran out and called to a man just disappearing among the bushes. This was a perfect stranger to all of us, but he duly delivered the money; and when in secret I hinted to Brahim doubts about its safety, the tone of his reply, "He's a Balūch," made me feel quite ashamed. One tribe of Balūchis will "chapao," or plunder, another tribe directly they get a chance, but petty theft is unknown among them.

We had not much difficulty in getting a guide, as Hammal provided one of his henchmen, Gazo by name, a good-natured whimsical fellow with a great turn for taking things coolly, and making quaint remarks when in any difficult circumstances. Everything was in perfect order by the evening, and I turned in to bed with my mind full of pleasurable expectations.

Next morning, the never-to-be-forgotten fifth, I was up betimes, and simply putting on my huge hat prowled out with my gun and butterfly net. It may be that I have not experienced many pleasurable sensations, but I certainly know of none to compare with mine on this morning. The cool air, the tamarisk trees covered with dew, and the gossamer webs more brilliant than strung pearls; from every bush the cheery ringing note of the partridges; the complete feeling of solitude and self-dependence, the proud feeling of proprietorship as I see the white top of my tent, and watch my string of camels being led down to drink; the exulting thought that for months I should be passing through new and strange countries seeing much that no white man had ever seen before;—I cannot describe the happiness of that morning. It is a feeling reserved for explorers only, I think, and more than balances the losses, delays, illness and troubles, which specially befall them.

At noon on the fifth, Brahim returned from Jask, whither he had been sent for the mails, bringing some English letters, and a mackintosh from my friend P——. His arrival was the signal for loading up, and in half an hour the tent was struck, and we were heading straight at the impracticable-looking wall of mountains. A river-bed, however, is a guarantee for a passage of some sort, though of course it sometimes presents obstacles by jumping over precipices. In our march of to-day we were warned of an extraordinary funnel-shaped pass, which in rainy seasons rendered the road impracticable for about a week. I thought, however, but lightly of the warning, for as yet there were no signs of rain, besides which we had received so many warnings that they ceased to have effect. All the Mekran streams are highways, in fact the only means of communication between the interior and the coast. We wound about up this most tortuous road, walled in on either side by lofty overhanging crags of every weird fantastic shape, and evening waned and found us still struggling along and beginning to wish for some chance of pitching camp. Presently huge dark clouds begin to mass themselves overhead, and an enormous roar echoes throughout the cliffs.

"Hakal kun, hakal kun" (*drive along*). "Oh, my brothers," shouts Gazo, far away in advance, "hakal kun, for if we don't get through the Tang-i-Duhl first——." The alternative was too awful for him, but the nervous energy in his voice was convincing.

As the sky darkened over us a few big drops splashed sullenly into the water at our feet, for the torrent bed had narrowed considerably, and contained a foot or so of water with awkwardly deep holes at frequent intervals. Darkness came over us so fast that by half-past five we had but the gleaming strip of water to guide us. At times the thunder roared sullenly, and twice the lightning showed in intense relief the lofty crags that hemmed us in on both sides and the small insignificant handful of men and camels wet and struggling along at the base like ants.

But there was some courage in our little handful, as we were soon to prove, or but little would ever have been heard of the expedition.

Suddenly from the front came back the shout of "mīn, mīn" (*quicksand*). In a minute I was on the spot, and found my riding camel plunging hopelessly about in a deep pool with a bottom of soft adhesive clay. Gazo was "mīned" too. We had to be quick; the men all left their camels, and with a long pull and a strong pull the "mahri" was literally dragged across the bad place to firm standing ground. "Quick, my children," shouted Brahim; "Betach! Betach!" (*tread it down*) and the men began trampling backwards and forwards, treading a path for the camels. One by one, all the men helping, these were rushed across, while with the busy excitement we almost forgot the ever-increasing storm and the dreaded Tang-i-Duhl still unattained.

And now, before we recognised it, we were at the entrance. It was not fifteen feet wide, and the walls of smooth sandstone would have defied a cat. Our impatience became a fever, and with remorseless blows the camels were urged along.

According to Gazo's earnest assurance, at any moment we might meet a blinding roaring torrent of water which would sweep men and camels down the gorge, like chips in a mill race. At last we came to the Duhl itself. The danger of being caught in the pass was evident, and I did not know at the time how short the really dangerous part of it was. The bed of the stream here had at first been a mere fissure, the surface rock hard, but that underneath soft. Consequently the water had hollowed out a tunnel about fifteen feet broad (the word "duhl" means pot, or cylinder). Just above this on the left the stream was augmented by a cascade which was silent when we passed, but in about fifteen minutes afterwards was pouring down tons of water.

The bed of the stream in the "Tang," and for some hundred yards below, was quite smooth and free from boulders, showing the force of the water. We plunged into the Duhl, and after a few anxious minutes the hitherto almost breathless caravan was shouting, talking, and laughing as if it were a relief merely to hear their own voices. We were out of danger now, for the torrent bed immediately opened out, and there were at the sides numerous "kuches," or flat ledges, above high water mark on which we could take refuge. Most of us were too thankful for our escape to care much about reaching any particular "kuch," and loud were the remonstrances at the imperturbable Gazo as he stolidly struggled and scrambled up the gorge, though the lightning, which was now almost incessant, revealed to us place after place suitable for camping.

Gazo, however, had in his eye a certain corner which yielded firewood and camel-fodder, for he was determined that his first day as guide should be a success. But the rain was upon us. Above the thunder roar came another sound, hoarser, persistent, and steadily increasing. "Howr an! Howr an!" (*It is the rain*),* cried the men, whose experienced ear told them more than mine told me, and we tore on for the next kuch, and at ten minutes past seven, for I had time to look at my watch, we were perched on a high corner of rock overlooking the ravine, down which already began to rush a swirling angry stream, a foretaste of what was now imminent. For a while we all stood stationary on our rocky refuge. The thunder and lightning were incessant. The wind blew a tornado, now from this side, now from that, and this mysterious rushing roaring sound, which I had never heard before, got louder every moment. The noise approached, and in less than four minutes our road was a maddened torrent ever increasing in depth and speed.

While we were yet looking at it, down came the rain; and it rained torrents.

The men, at first dismayed, now knew the worst. They were quickly stripped to the skin, and with many a jovial jest and laugh were setting up the tent. In half an hour the rain stopped, we had a fire, and in spite of some little anxiety about the still rising torrent around us we slept the sleep of the righteous, only being awakened once by the stranding on our rock of a good sized tree.

---

* The same word is used by these people for the rushing torrent and the rain that produces it, showing how closely the two things are associated.

On the sixth we did not strike camp till afternoon, as I wanted to sketch the "Tang," and also to get a meridian altitude, for it may be imagined that I did not make a very good dead reckoning of the course from the last camp. I was amused at Alishah this morning. He had appointed himself table servant, but on coming in to lay the table he found it covered with sectional papers, compasses, etc., to avoid disturbing which he carefully arranged everything on a sack on the wet muddy ground. He could never restrain his fun, and would sometimes stop at the tent door with a basin of soup he was bringing to me, and finish at his leisure a furious chaff with the camel-men.

While at breakfast a caravan of three Bashakardis came by with ten active little donkeys. They eagerly asked how we had spent the previous night, and I accompanied them back as far as the Duhl. The gorge was still impracticable for camels, but the active little donkeys clambered round pools through which camels would be compelled to plunge. On the way we found a solitary duck, which one of the party shot with a bullet from his matchlock, and which was afterwards identified by Professor Newton as the common shoveller.

In explanation of the extraordinary suddenness with which the streams become full, it may be remembered that the hills are all perfectly barren rock, and the water runs off them as off a slated roof. Then the Geigen near its mouth, where we were, receives nearly all the water from an area of hills about forty miles broad and seventy long.

In the afternoon we marched to Marrick, for which place we had been making when overtaken by the rain, and here again we endured a most tremendous storm. In spite of our being well out of the bed, we had to dig a bank round the tent, and in a short twenty-three minutes the cooking-place, where a comfortable dinner had been simmering, was a muddy stream, the creek half full, and every two or three minutes a bore coming down made it three feet wider. Hailstones rattled about us an inch long, which had all a small black nucleus, so I collected a few for the purpose of scientific investigation. These having melted, Alishah drank, afterwards industriously polishing up the tumbler on a corner of one of my blankets.

At 5 p.m. the sun was shining brightly again, and I enjoyed a delicious evening sitting out by a big log fire, with the pleasant thought that camel-fodder was good and plentiful, and the dreaded "jūr" or oleander entirely absent. Camels are the legs of an expedition like ours, and always demand first attention.

As long as the soft warm climate lasted, I always used to have my dinner by a fire close to the camel-men's fire, and enjoy their jokes, chaff, and absurd stories. Balūchis are the best fellow-travellers in the world. In times of difficulty they get excited, shout, and work like demons. In camp they were always merry, and their conversation cleaner than any similar set of men I ever heard. They have a strong appreciation of the ridiculous, and inexhaustible good nature.

Next morning (7th), it was all six men could do to hoist the tent, heavy with wet, on the camel's back, and almost immediately after starting we came to a difficulty. A waterfall from the rocks above had scooped out a large basin in the solid rock; and this was not only full, but its sides were coated with slime.

We had to cut down tamarisk bushes and tread them in as a path for the camels.

About 11 a.m. we emerged from the hills, and felt as if we had at last got inside the country. Before us stretched a salt mud-plain, so cut up by deep water-courses, as to force us to take a most roundabout road. There were many short ranges and clumps of barren red hills in front, and we aimed for a bluff of the Sihr Koh or Crimson Hill. As I was on ahead of the caravan I suddenly came upon two men with camel-loads of pīsh.

Now I happened to be just then in, to a Balūchi's way of thinking, a most undignified condition. Ghulamshah with the "mahri" was behind with the caravan, which, by the winding nature of the road, was hidden from view.

Here was an extraordinary apparition in preposterous and unsanctified clothing, and with a thing on his head two feet in diameter. Imagine the astonishment of these tall sinewy fellows with their aquiline noses and curly black beards. They had never seen, and possibly never heard of a Feringi, but to them I was evidently first a human being, and secondly totally unarmed. They, of course, were armed to the teeth; in fact, the sword, shield, gun, knife, bullet-pouch, etc., formed the major part of their dress, which was merely supplemented by a scanty cloth round the waist, grass sandals, and a skull-cap. I verily believe that had they "spied" me before I saw them they would have stalked and shot me, not from any malice, but just to see what I was. I had, however, a note-book and prismatic compass, of which last I had previously experienced the effect; and as they came near I took a round of bearings, and ended by fixing the leading man and ostentatiously making a note of him.

Though the men were not superstitious, the steady gaze through an unknown instrument as usual rather disconcerted them, and they made a slight *detour* and would have passed on their way. This, however, I did not wish, for I was eager to ask questions about the road, camping-places, etc., before us; and assuming great authority I called them up.

At being spoken to in Balūchi they got a fresh access of confidence, and, muttering to one another, grounded their guns close in front of me, and commenced a torrent of questions: "Who are you?" "What are you?" "Where do you come from?" "Why do you speak Balūchi?" "We are Balūchis." "Where's your camel?" "Where are you going to?" etc., etc.

I waited quietly until there was a pause, and then said in a slow and dignified manner, "Salaam aleikum."

It took at once. Their self-respect and politeness were both touched. Their intense curiosity had led them into a serious breach of good manners, for even the commonest Balūchis will exchange salutations in a most punctilious manner. The one false step was irretrievable, and with the loftiest politeness I could assume, I pursued my advantage and went through the entire salutation.

"Peace be with you."

"And on you be peace."

"You are welcome."

"May you be in safety."

"Are you well?"

"Is all your house well?"

"By God's kindness all is well."

"Give news."

"I have none; and am interested only in your good health."

We were just beginning all over again, for it is impolite to be the first to stop, when the caravan hove in sight. As camel after camel came round the corner, each led by one of our jaunty devil-may-care fellows fully armed, the faces of my two heroes went through a series of dissolving views, and I heard one say to the other in a resigned and awe-struck tone, "Well, I've lived nearly 3000 years, and I've travelled over the whole of Balūchistan, but I never saw a man with so much property as that in all my life!"

His intellect had to receive another jolt, however, for I took out my note-book and wrote a note to a friend at Jask announcing the success of my expedition so far. He had never seen a book, paper, or writing. As he fingered the leaves his surprise was very quaint. "Oh, what thin, thin, thin!" and "how white, white, white; white as milk, Wallah!" "And he just rubs it a little with that stick, and it makes black foot-marks. This is indeed a wonderful thing!" Then on examing the pencil he detected the lead, and with glee showed it to his friend, saying, "There you see, that's how it marks, its heart is black."

As the caravan had now got some way ahead, I handed my friends over to Brahim for a cross-examination, and mounting the mahri which Ghulamshah had made to kneel close by, I rode on to the front.

I have not, I believe, explained that the mahri had a double saddle. In the front seat rode Ghulamshah with the big aneroid, telescope, thermometer, binoculars, pocket sextant, and my dinner or lunch. I invariably walked, for the convenience of taking bearings, botanizing, etc., and Ghulamṣhah kept close by me; and if my investigations delayed me till I fell far behind, I could jump into the hinder seat and in a few minutes regain my lost ground.

We swung past the caravan at about six miles an hour, and reaching a sort of cave where there was a shade, proceeded to lunch. The inevitable rain, however, overtook us, and at 3 p.m. we camped on the banks of the swollen Sharīfi Khowr as shivering and well-soaked a band as it is easy to imagine. The Sharīfi here flowed through a broad well-treed valley, and the camels had a good feed off Kahur (a species of acacia) which they had not seen since leaving Geigen.

It was disappointing on boiling the thermometer that evening to find that after all our struggles through the rocks and hills we had only made 600 feet of ascent. We had seen so many ibex, hill sheep, and other animals worthy of hunting that I was easily persuaded by Gazo to halt for a day's sport. We could dry the tent too, and as the camels had a long journey before them, they would be all the better for the rest.

Next day we awoke to a lovely morning. I was quickly dressed, and soon hauled my little arm-chair out of the damp tent and sat over the fire impatiently watching preparations for breakfast. It was one of those mornings worth years of one's life. Every sense was full of the most intense enjoyment. The contrast of the smell of burning wood with the clear cool air; the incessant scream of an old woodpecker from an

CAMP AT SURAG.

adjacent tree, apparently the only bird in the country; —every little detail impressed itself deeply upon my memory. It was a picturesque camp, there on the banks of the brawling muddy Sharīfi which was to guide us for the next two marches. The tent was pitched on a patch of green spring grass, and at our back was the purple and red range of hills called Oushdāhndarrī.

A few feet off, round the remains of their fire, lay the men, still wrapped in their huge felt coats, which they called "Bālbālaks," or "hairy-hairies." They refused to acknowledge the Persian name, saying, "No, no; we're Balūchis, and we call them Bālbālaks."

Ghulamshah soon had some eggs and tea ready, and Gazo was set to work on dates and bread. I took for myself the old double Westley-Richards that Brahim carried on the march, and gave Gazo, as my second gun, another double Egg, which it was Dād Arrahīm's privilege to carry. We started just as the sun rose over the hill and flooded everything in its warm grateful light. Striking up a steep ravine into the Oushdāhndarrī hills, we soon found traces of game plentiful. But I also soon found that my friend was but a poor shikarri. He was dreadfully clumsy with his feet, and made as much noise as two ordinary men. Added to this he was afflicted with a violent cold in the head, and at a critical moment, when everything depended upon absolute quiet, he would be convulsed with paroxysms of coughing. He appeared to cough with every part of his body at once, and produced noises that a hippopotamus would despair of emulating. When I add that he had a slight cataract and was partly blind, it will be clear that he was not likely to be a very valuable assistant. It was impossible to be angry with the old fellow; and though we frightened away two herds of hill sheep by the noise we made, I enjoyed an exhilarating scramble, added considerably to my botanical collection, and obtained some valuable bearings for to-morrow's route. This district is perfectly uninhabited; we had only met five men on our route from the coast, and for two days afterwards we saw none.

The morning after our unsuccessful hunt we started up the Sharīfi river, a tributary to the Jagīn. The bed was just here much confined, and full of huge boulders, so we were glad to climb up the steep clift and cross a flat shingly plain, which cut off a considerable bend.

Here we encountered one of those extraordinary migrations of locusts which have so often been described in the East. These insects were so thick as to produce a shade over the earth like that of a thin cloud. They were all of the red edible kind, and as fat as possible. The living in our camp was so good that the men disdained to eat them, though I saw Abdulla squeeze out the yellow fat of one or two and eat it with great relish. All the men seemed to regard them more as luxuries for the table than as destructive to the vegetation. They however rapidly devoured the spring grass that covered the low-lying patches, and the leaves of the shrubs fringing the watercourses that here and there intersected the plain. These locusts, by constant travelling, can at this season keep themselves supplied with food; but as the hot weather comes on, and every green thing is burnt to a cinder,

I think they are probably all starved to death. I remember something of the kind happening in Henjam. Some sustained themselves by eating camel droppings, and many more by eating the dead bodies of their neighbours, but by June there was not a locust to be seen.

There were numerous charz (*obara*), flocks of sand grouse, and sussi, the yellow-legged partridge, and I wasted a good deal of time stalking some of the first.

At 2.35 p.m. we again struck the Sharīfi. It had here cut itself a bed three-quarters of a mile wide, and the perpendicular banks of mud and shingle were sixty feet high, the stratification being much contorted. The bed was full of zahren karrag (*calotropis gigantæa*), and the beautiful but cordially detested jūr (*nerium oleander*). It may be worth mentioning that coast camels are peculiarly apt to eat this poisonous shrub, as they are frequently fed on timmr (mangrove bushes), and cannot tell the difference. Karsh (pampas grass) flourished luxuriously, and the pīsh (*chamærops Ritchiana*) though small was of good tough quality. Succulent lorti (*Taverniera Spartæa*), that prince of camel fodder, was abundant, though trāt (*caroxylon fœtidum*) was absent. Trāt is the camel's Worcester sauce, and without it, or some similar bitter shrub, no Mekrani camel can keep his full health; but we were destined to see no more trāt.

At about three miles from where we had entered the river we came upon a small patch of date palms, near which was a solitary hut, and here we pitched our camp. The owner of the grove was busy lighting clumps of karsh, that the smoke might keep the locusts away from a small plot of wheat he had farther up. He was much terrified at our cavalcade, but eventually condescended to sell us some curds and eggs at an exorbitant price. Here also we killed the last of the three sheep we had brought with us from Geigen. This sheep had in point of fact to be killed to save his life. As long as he had company he would walk along with the caravan; but when his two brethren disappeared he wandered so much from the track and so obstinately refused to be led, that he was tied on a camel, and a rope pressing on his gullet he was discovered *in extremis* and his throat promptly cut.

During the march I had noticed much earnest conversation between Brahim and the two young fellows, and here the first signs of faintheartedness appeared. This was owing to the beautiful and copious rains that had fallen. These two men, being of good position, could command a great deal of labour. The rain this year had been more abundant than for many years previously. Now, in Mekran the amount of wheat that can be sown is regulated by these two things, the amount of labour procurable and the amount of rain. The position therefore was this: These men had started on a long and arduous journey into unknown and hostile countries, and just as they left, and while yet close at home, came the opportunity of living in affluence at home without going any dangerous journey at all.

All these things were duly reported by Brahim, who added that should these two go back the whole caravan would be broken up.

I revolved matters carefully in my mind for some time before coming to a decision. One thing, here hard measures were out of the question. A single rough speech would have been ample justification in everybody's eyes for their going off home in a huff, and we were still uncomfortably near home.

Again, to yield to the hints thrown out by Brahim of promises of extra pay was equally out of the question, as lowering to my dignity, and by creating a precedent indirectly compromising the success of the whole expedition. No, I would refuse to believe it; and calling up Brahim I told him vehemently (for it was necessary to impose upon him, too, to a certain extent) that I could never believe it; that I had known Balūchis for years, and as for their ever doing such an unmanly* thing as giving their words* to accompany a man and then running away at the beginning, it was impossible. If, now, it had been Alishah (object of their special contempt), or any of the common herd, why they perhaps might do such things, etc., etc.

It had the desired effect, at all events for a time, and every stage farther from home made my position safer.

Next day we had before us what at this early period of the journey we considered a stiff march, for we were nine hours *en route*, and for the last two and a half were picking our way up and down tortuous rocky watercourses in utter darkness, in great uncertainty about the right direction, and anxiety about the poor camels' feet.

However, we must not anticipate the somewhat eventful journey which actually landed us within the boundaries of that wonderful country, Bashakard.

---

* Both literal Balūch idioms, "Nā-mardī" (*unmanliness*); "Lafz deaga" (*to give one's word*); also, "Wati lafz awart" (*he eats his words*).

We were, "according to native information," to find many astounding things here. Much of the country was impassable, being entirely in possession of huge hairy demons called "Hirsh," in form like men, but endowed with stupendous strength, enabling them to tear up trees and use them as clubs. Then, again, there were forts of massive structure, built actually by Rustam himself in the olden time. We were to see many other objects of interest, and such things as we did see are faithfully described in the following pages. It was at least a virgin country which, though it has been marked on the map since the days of Pottinger, had never yet been entered by white man. Even Major St. John's map, which I found published when I came home, places the capital, Anguhran, at forty miles from its true position.

On the morning of the 9th we were delayed some time by the camels. They had been hoppled behind and before, for fear they should get access to the oleander, and in their struggles they had pulled out of their noses the wooden knob to which the rein is fastened. This, though generally tolerably easy of remedy, was with my huge beasts fully half an hour's work. They were in pain about the nose, especially the big Jaski, who flung his powerful neck about, and made such savage bites that it was all five men could do to hold him.

These matters having been arranged, we started up the river-bed, passing a small patch of young wheat which my men recognised as "Sunaiti," a kind only suited for the hill country.

Our route was pretty enough, through groves of the feathery tamarisk and flanked by most picturesque rock scenery. We missed in the mornings the cheery note of the "Kofinjah" partridges; the sussi, or yellow-legged bird, has no note; and we had not yet arrived at the country of the kabg, or red-legged, with their steady going, low toned kuk kuk kúk, kuk kuk kúk. I noticed to-day the curious fact that camels perspire only at the back of the head—that is, male camels do; females are said not to perspire anywhere, but as mine were all males I could not verify the assertion.

Dead reckoning when travelling in this hilly country is excessively troublesome, owing to the impossibility of getting any good distant landmark. To-day from 10.15 a.m. to 5.30 p.m. I find noted forty-four accurate bearings with a prismatic compass,* and on comparison with other days I find this hardly as much as the average; there are also seven altitudes of hills, each with a paced base of from half a mile to a mile.

At 2 p.m., on arriving at a spot where the Sharīfi received three large tributaries, we left the main bed to follow the easternmost channel. Here, on rejoining the caravan after a round of bearings, I found a general halt, and the men all consulting over one camel.

As I got near there was a general shout, "Hi, waja! Hi! come along quick in the name of God. The medicine's broken, and it's burning the camel and all to pieces."

This was of course absurd, but I could not for the life of me guess what could be the matter, and rode

* On plotting out, only three of these were found to be unnecessary.

up full speed to where the men were standing. Two sticks of pitch plaister in the saddle-bags had been melted by the noonday sun, and were dripping down over everything and giving forth a tolerably powerful aroma which had alarmed the men. They were always in a great fright about my medicines, for Hasan had to carry in his hand a leather bag containing strong nitric, sulphuric, and muriatic acids for testing minerals. Though these were carefully packed, the bag slowly charred away day by day, and the men saw this and expected all the other medicines to burn things too.

Beyond finding all my spare socks hopelessly gummed together, there was no damage done, and we resumed march. There was a curious shrub here, called by the natives pūn, and probably allied to the Vincetoxicum. Hundreds of straight, fleshy green branches grew up from a common centre. They had no leaves, and exuded an acrid white milk. When the shrub died, these all broke off from the root, and, radiating from the centre, resembled an inverted tassel.

Evening found us still winding up the torrent bed, and soon the walls converged together and we were threading our way at the bottom of a deep chasm. The walls were about 300 feet high, of laminated blue clay with occasional lamina of quartz. The strata were vertical, and the edges being towards us presented the appearance of having been streaked with a fine tooth comb. The water was strong with iron, and either that or some other ingredient turned the clay in the bed into a hard blue stone.

Soon Gazo began to hunt for a ravine leading out of this chasm, and up which he said lay our route. We found two or three, and at last halted, lit the

THE DAZAKA PASS.— NIGHT COMING ON.

hurricane lamps, and set out to explore one which Gazo, very much like an old setter, would not leave, though he could give no reasons for preferring it. It turned out satisfactory, and with a tremendous struggle we got the camels up a steep ascent. On reaching the top we had an equally rapid descent, and after crossing a small stream it was decided that we had arrived at Dāzakā and we camped. We had made some ascent to-day, and the barometer marked 27·265, being about 3,540 feet. We were obliged to take Gazo's word that there was no "jūr" round about, and the camels were let loose to browse on the few kahur trees which we ascertained to be there.

CHAPTER VII.

ON FOOT TO ANGUHRAN.

An embassy.—A durbar.—An Arab in difficulties.—Guides and the route.—A horrible murder.—Bashakard politics.—Negotiations. —*En route* for Anguhran.—The Rais Ali's mountain stronghold. —Bashakard scenery.—A horned snake.—A night in a Bashakardi hut.—Demons at last.

NEXT morning I was up very early, anxious to see what my new domain was like. There were traces of the hand of man in the shape of an old wall which had probably at one time enclosed a patch of wheat. Close by, too, was a huge old male date tree, sole survivor of all the female trees which had at one time filled the plot of ground over which he now stood sentry.

While enjoying a breakfast of cold leg of mutton, pickles and cocoa, for hitherto we had retained all the luxuries of civilization, Alishah announced the arrival of an embassy from Rais Ali, the ruler of Bashakard, whose establishment I learnt was at the foot of the lofty Aphen-i Band, near which we were encamped. Anxious to produce a good impression, I had a scarlet cloth thrown over my arm-chair, ordered coffee and kaliāns or water pipes, and then summoned my visitor. There entered with a somewhat proud salaam a tall Balūch, who, to judge from the quality of his arms, and especially the quantity of silver plating over the barrel of his long gun and the handle of his sword, was a person of some consequence.

Though careful not to show it, he evidently felt considerable astonishment at my well pitched tent, comfortable carpet, and, more than all, the ring of double barrels round the tent pole.

My men had ranged themselves on my right hand and on my left, and affecting not to understand the language, I set Brahim to converse with him.

He was evidently duly impressed with our greatness, for he was content simply to answer questions; and when he did pluck up spirit to ask whence we came, Brahim was too well trained to answer.

The coffee was not much appreciated, as coffee though highly esteemed as a mark of politeness, is not much liked from its bitterness. Nor was the kaliān, which was prepared with good Shiraz tobacco, much liked, as it was too mild for the Balūch taste. Like Arabs, Balūchis smoke extremely acrid pungent stuff, and cannot appreciate a delicate flavour.

His mission was a pressing invitation from Rais Ali, whose encampment was only a mile off, and thither he had come to guide me. Having ascertained this, I, rather to his surprise, took up the ball, and told him that I had some business with the sun about noon, after which, should things be favourable, I might think of his proposal; I hinted also that as I had not had the honour of seeing the Rais himself, it might be advisable for me to pay my first visit by deputy, and with that Brahim took him off to talk over the real business of the meeting. My observations for a meridian altitude excited great interest, and I had often afterwards occasion to notice the difference between the effect on these ignorant but fearless-minded Balūchis, and that on the more civilized but more superstitious Persians.

Brahim then came with his report, which was favourable to our immediate departure. Mīr Yusuf (of Jask) was at Rais Ali's, as also Mīr Shahdad, a brother of the first-named, and with both of these chiefs Brahim was "dastgrift," that is, each had sworn an oath to protect the other.

As far as danger to be apprehended from Bashakardis, Brahim repeated what he had said all along, that one Mekran Balūch (or Balūch *par excellence*, as he is rightly considered) was worth six men of Bashakard, and that the men would only look to me for protection in the unknown regions beyond.

At half-past twelve we loaded up and scrambled over the rocks for about a mile and a half due west. On the way my attention was drawn to Tajoo, who was walking alongside my camel behind the caravan, and indulging in the most extraordinary and uncouth gesticulations, from which I gathered that he had some communication to make to me. Seeing that I apprehended his object, he commenced to dig up word by word, from the depths of an extremely chaotic memory, a sentence of Arabic, in which language he had acquired fragments of some fifteen or sixteen words. Had I not had at Henjam an opportunity of studying the Batinah dialect with some *quondam* pirates from that coast, who were windbound for nearly a fortnight, all my Arabic studies of four years would have availed me nothing; and as it was, a conversation such as that upon which we now entered had in it many of the features of a game of "Buz." With some patience, however, I melted down his communication to "Gy yesīrūn, al ithnain, yabghūn fulūs" (*They are going, those two, and want their pay here*).

This, however, did not disturb me much. We were going to be three or four days in camp, during which all men would draw full pay. My two friends would of course stay for this. Probably they would never have the pluck to tell me they were going and then go. They would wait until the very moment of starting, when it would not be worth my while to take any steps of retaliation. Thirdly, though they had presented three extremely plausible reasons for wanting an advance of pay, I had, without arousing their suspicion by a refusal, always been unable to attend to them just at that moment.

Soon we rose to the top of a high "Bir," or smooth laminated blue clay mound, and slipping and sliding down the opposite side, found ourselves in a deep gorge, which we followed right up to the very foot of the Aphen-i-Band, towering 3,000 feet above us, and here our guide showed us almost the only flat place where it was possible to pitch a tent. Until the tent should be pitched, my carpet was spread on the ground, and my arm-chair placed at one end, and thus we awaited the Rais and his friends.

First came Shahdad and Yusuf, Mekrani chiefs from the coast; and some of my men, who stood in one or other of the various degrees of vassalage to them, hastened to acknowledge it by kissing hands.

These two tall powerful-looking young chiefs were very much esteemed for their liberality and manliness, and the greetings between them and the men, though tempered on the one side by graciousness and on the other by cordial respect, were more like those of old friends than of lord and vassal. There is something in the wild hand-to-mouth life these fellows lead, which inevitably brings the real man into his right place, and refers the imitation man to his.

Our swarthy friends were soon seated on my left hand. We had met before on the coast, but years ago, and it was not until Brahim had explained that it was "Falower" (the Baluchi for Floyer), that we became really friendly. We talked of old ibex hunts in Geigen and Parkoh hills, and I ascertained that the chiefs were here to negotiate an alliance with the Rais, the main point of which was that the latter should lend them some men to assist against the perfidious Abdul Nabi, whom the reader may remember at Mināb.

Presently our ambassador of the morning, Durrgosh, or the "Pearly-eared One," arrived, and said that the Rais would be here immediately, and in fact at that moment a body of men were seen scrambling up the precipitous path, and after some hand-kissing the great man was seated at my side. But he was a very singular kind of great man, and Brahim's stories of the pusillanimity of Bashakardis were in a fair way to be realized.

On my left the black-bearded, bushy-eyebrowed Mekrani Mīrs, with huge turbans, handsome scarlet cloaks with silver fastenings, and waist-belts positively stuck full of pistols and knives, to say nothing of the sturdy henchman waiting on each with his lord's sword and shield.

But on my right what a contrast. A gross fat man of sallow yellowish complexion, without beard, moustache, or any other manly attribute, a very Emperor

Claudius, wearing just a cloth round his waist, and a long, not over-clean white shirt, without even a particle of scarlet silk embroidery, the badge of royalty, down the front. His manner was boisterous cordiality and cringing self-abasement. The kaliān, when offered to him, was refused. "No, no, he was a plain old man, and didn't understand such fine things." A plate of barley sugar is handed round. With ostentatious humility he begs that he may take two pieces for his little son, and when presented with a bottleful is uproariously grateful. Abdulla comes up and says that the ground is so rocky that the tent-pegs won't enter it. He is off! "I'll knock the Sahib's tent-pegs in," and in a minute he is squatting on the ground with a tent-peg between his legs, hammering away with a very moderate-sized stone, amid the laughter and gentle deprecation of my men.

In the middle of the tent-peg dilemma, up swaggers Brahim Khamīs with a bundle of camel-reins in his hand. He has been letting the camels loose to graze. On hearing the difficulty, his scorn is too great for utterance. It actually swells him out. Brahim the Jemadar takes him by the arm, and picking up a peg, quietly places it in the right position: "Strike, my child." The "child" stalks up to the massive mallet and picks it up, his legs perfectly rigid with indignation. Carefully measuring his distance, he whings the heavy mallet back over his head at arms' length, and whack, whack, until at the eighth stroke the peg head is fairly buried. Still scornful he goes the round, and drives every peg in exactly the same way, and then with lofty indifference stands by and lets the common herd tie the ropes.

It was always a treat to see this sturdy young fellow drive a tent-peg, a thing by no means so easy as it looks. Brahim Jemadar was good, but was so tall that, unless with a specially long-handled mallet, he had to stoop at each blow. To look at the little Brahim you would think that he was simply swinging the mallet round his head. It never seemed to stop. As soon as it had done its work with a thundering crash on the peg, it was dexterously twisted off, and before you realized it, was again on the upward swing. More than once, in elastic shingly ground, I have seen large three-foot tent-pegs fly from fifteen to eighteen feet in the air under the doughty strokes of this young hero.

As we laughingly resumed our seats after this incident, there arrived at our Durbar a man whom to my astonishment I recognised as a Persian. When I heard him welcomed as the Muhassil, or tax-gatherer, I began to see more how matters stood. Here, no doubt, was the key to the Rais' extraordinary behaviour, his aping of poverty and humility, intended of course to impress the Muhassil with the idea that he had beggared himself to supply the amount of taxes required.

Mahomed Beg was as evil-looking, foxy-faced a man as I ever saw; but I had hardly time to greet him, when down came a torrent of rain and hail, and we hurried into the tent *en masse*, as fast as we could.

The tent, however, was not as comfortable as it might have been, for the wind blew down the gorge with such violence, that while the storm lasted four or five men had to sit outside and hold the tent-ropes.

When the storm cleared off, my visitors took their departure, the Rais providing for all our wants in the way of dates, flour, etc., and saying that he would come and see me again shortly. The rest of the afternoon was spent in receiving visitors of inferior rank, and doctoring patients, chiefly ophthalmic.

I must not, however, forget a visit from an unfortunate Arab, rather a singular person to meet in these mountain fastnesses. He was a horse dealer, from Maskat, and what extraordinary chain of circumstances had brought him here, where there were only two roads practicable for horses, I could never find out. His servant was ill with fever, and he himself had had toothache for three weeks. Just as he was showing me his mouth, which was terribly swollen, we heard outside the rink-a-tink of the iron pestle and mortar in which Ghulamshah was pounding coffee. His whole bearing changed at the old home sound, now so trebly dear to him from long absence.

"Sidi," he said, nearly biting my finger off. "Sidi, hadtha kahwa?" *(Is that coffee?)*

We rejoiced his heart, by giving him as much as he could drink, and by sending after him a small bagful.

Towards evening the Rais was ushered into my tent, with a certain degree of secrecy, and accompanied only by the faithful "Pearly-eared One," who, I found, had married his sister.

This looked like business, and after tea and kaliāns (my tea and kaliāns were, by the way, the only things of the kind in the country), I duly propounded my necessities,—guides to Anguhran, and should the road prove impracticable for camels, as I had heard it was, donkeys, for which I would pay well.

The Rais was no longer the buffoon of the afternoon, but a shrewd practical man, and laying his hand on my arm, and speaking in a rapid impressive manner, he answered thus:

"Waja," he said, "I don't know who you are, or where you come from. You may be as you say, a Feringi, merely going on a visit to the Governor of Kirman; or you may be an agent of the Feringi Government, of which I have heard, and come for some purpose, I know not what; or you may be a messenger from Maskat, for you are said to be an Arab. I do not know what you are, but you shall have my safe conduct as far as Anguhran."

This was good so far, and I professed my gratitude, and Brahim incidentally placed a tin of gunpowder in the "Pearly-eared One's" hand. I then asked about the roads, and his answer was equally decided, and, though I didn't think so at the time, equally sincere.

He said: "It is perfectly impossible for you with your 'dashti' (*plain*) camels, to go by the Anguhran route. It is true that the Muhassil is going that way, but his case is very different. He rides a trained and practised horse, and he has only six donkeys, the whole of which do not carry as much as half the burden of one of your camels. The only path possible for you is by Telling, and I will give you a guide for that route, and you shall go by no other. And if you insist upon going to Anguhran, I will give you a guide thither, but you must go no farther, for beyond that are a bad people with whom I am at war, and with whom my safe conduct would be your death warrant, even were it not enough that you have come from my country; for seeing that I have not plundered you, they would know you for my friend."

We then chatted on other subjects, and soon afterwards he took his leave, begging that in the morning he might bring a friend, who was suffering from ophthalmia.

I will here give a slight *résumé* of the political events in Bashakard during the last two years.

The six provinces of Bashakard were under six governors, who, until the end of 1874, paid allegiance to a clever and fierce old man called Seif Allah Khan, who had, about twenty-five years ago, consolidated his position by building a huge fortress at Anguhran in the centre province Daroser. Early in life, in one of his innumerable fights, he had incurred a blood feud with the tribe of Ghulam Abbas, ruler of Daroser. This, however, had been expiated by many deaths on both sides, and all seemed tranquil. Seif Allah Khan's power, won by the sword, now seemed firmly established, peace reigned for some years, and many date groves were planted. The subordinate provincial governors were in a state of unwonted unison, and an unfortunate tax-gatherer, ill-advisedly despatched from Kirman, was murdered off-hand.

But the proud intolerant mind of Seif Allah Khan still rankled under the loss of a near relative, who had fallen in the blood feud with Ghulam Abbas. The sore was kept open by the father of the dead man, by whom he was constantly urged to wield the great power which he had acquired. Yielding at last, Seif Allah Khan resolved upon a foul and horrible deed, a crime which has no parallel in the annals of Mekran or Western Balūchistan.

He had been on a journey, and on his return, Ghulam Abbas, with all the leading men, came to visit him. In the great gateway they were received with a volley which stretched, it is said, seven of them lifeless on the floor.

I was told that Seif Allah Khan alleged as a reason for this diabolical act, that Ghulam Abbas had been intriguing with the Persians. However that may be, the whole country was raised upon him, and the Kirman Government, who always keep a watchful eye for cases of dissension among the chiefs of Bashakard, professed great indignation at the murder, and sent down thirty horsemen. In a country where none but chiefs ride horses, this of course was regarded as an almost invincible army. These horsemen, though a month before they dared not have put a foot in the country, were enabled, now that the master hand was gone, to penetrate to Anguhran. Seif Allah Khan, however, had shut himself up in his fortress, and they could do nothing. Rais Ali, governor of Pizgh, where we now were, was chosen from the other governors as being of the Ghulam Abbas family, and he was promised the governorship if he could deliver up Seif Allah Khan. This last he of course would not do, as one Balūch would never deliver up another to the hated Persians.

Making a feint of acceptance, he gathered men, and in a half-hearted way besieged the fortress for nearly a year. At the end of this time, the water in the wells became undrinkable, and terms were made. It was then found that there were only two or three of the besieged left, the rest having one by one escaped. Those remaining were allowed to go unscathed, Seif

Allah Khan fled in safety to Marz, the province of which he had once been governor, and Rais Ali returned to Pizgh. So far, so good: Rais Ali was successful, and governor of Bashakard. But the position had its penalties. Soon came the Persian tax-gatherer, saying, "Now you are governor of Bashakard, where are the taxes?"

Early next morning, while I was still brushing my hair, an operation which always excited unqualified astonishment, the Rais and his son were announced. The latter picked up a copy of Hāfiz which was lying about, and began to read with great glee, while his proud father almost burst with self-gratulation. The latter had come, he said, to take leave of me for to-day, he was going to see the tax-gatherer off. His little son, however, an exact reproduction of his father, was deputed to supply all my wants. He repeated all he had said yesterday about the roads, and took his leave, saying that Mahomed Beg was going to call on me, and that that gentleman wanted something to make him drunk. Mahomed shortly after came in, and in a circuitous manner asked for spirits. I had not a drop of anything of the kind, and said as much, but in an indirect way, and followed it up by questions as to the real state of the direct route to Kirman, thus giving him to understand that he might get what he wanted if I got what I wanted, namely, the truth as to the road's practicability for camels. He answered that if I was really an Englishman, and going to see the Governor of Kirman, it would be his pleasure to assist me in every way; but he added, with what he meant for a crafty smile, he had seen me reading Persian books, and if I were a naib, or perhaps a sultan, we should be brothers. He would get my camels through for me somehow, and we should go along together.

I replied coldly that the Governor of Kirman would be able to judge as to whether I had been misled or not as to the nature of the direct road, and begged him to confine himself to a simple statement on that head, could my camels travel it or not?

He was here supplied with a glass of liquor ammoniæ and water flavoured with essence of peppermint, which fearful mixture he appeared to relish vastly. He then began a rambling speech, saying that I could not expect to travel anywhere in this country with "dashti" camels, that my men were on the point of leaving me, that my baggage was enormously cumbrous, etc., and ended by advising me to sell the camels and hire donkeys and accompany him. On the whole, his main idea seemed to be that I should accompany him, doubtless with visions of prospective brandy. He was bowed out, and, I heard afterwards, made Brahim a small present to see if any spirits were to be had.

My next visitor, in the middle of breakfast, was an unfortunate old chief, Mahomed Mīr Ḳhānjān, governor of the province of Marz, and almost blind from ophthalmia. This was the man of whom the Rais had spoken, and I very quickly determined how to steer with him. My answers were rather curt at first, and I went on eating eggs as if unaware of his presence. But the poor old fellow would stand a good deal from one who might restore to him his eyesight, and at last he implored me to do something for his eyes. To this I replied, somewhat bitterly, that it seemed as if the Balūchis of this country were not Balūchis at all, that it was all beg, beg, beg, and that when I just asked for a small thing, such as guides for the Anguhran route to Kirman, I was met by what was worse than a flat refusal, namely, equivocation; and with that I called for more of the flat unleavened cakes which were our bread.

The old man was thoroughly roused. Seizing the arm of the faithful fellow who guided his steps, he said angrily, "This my own servant shall guide you to Anguhran, or anywhere you will. You shall pay him nothing, but you shall give him a paper to me whenever you discharge him, saying whether he has served you well or not. Only," he added, "if your dashti camels cannot go through, and if you are obliged to abandon all your baggage, it is not his fault. You say you can get them through, and you may try; all I can say is, that no camels, even hill camels, have ever yet done the journey."

This was enough for me. I rose and took the old man's hand: "My father," I said, "we two are trustworthy; I will not take your servant, nor will I take the Anguhran route." After some more conversation I examined his eyes, and made him a solution of nitrate of silver, and told him its use, and, putting my hand on his shoulder and looking full into his almost sightless face, added, "As you have spoken truly to me, so may my medicine cure your eyes." Just then a tall active young fellow named Pīrū looked in at the tent door, and announced that the Rais had sent him to guide me to Anguhran.

This was rather sharper work than I expected, but I soon decided to start, as on my return I could easily re-open the question of routes, and should have much additional experience to guide me. Brahim was duly instructed in the careful winding of the chronometer, and also told to make all inquiries about the country he could think of. Ghulamshah packed up a couple of mackintoshes, a small portable kettle and saucepan, tea, flour, and dates, Australian beef, tobacco, aneroid, max. and min. thermometer, prismatic compass, sketch-book, notebook, and a dry pair of socks. Gazo took a spare pair of sandals, and in spite of all delays, by 10.30 that forenoon we were fairly on the way to unravel the hitherto unfathomed mystery as to the existence, position, size, etc., of Anguhran.

We had a stiffish climb before us, and as we loaded the donkey with our baggage, I heard the old Rais, who appeared to be always going but never gone, come up to Pīrū and warn him solemnly not to deviate from the track he had told him to go, for we were certain to be robbed, and he had a great dread of being called over the coals by the Feringi Government, of the powers of which he had a very exaggerated conception. For the first half-hour we were climbing up and down steep rounded mounds of brittle laminated blue clay, which ran from three hundred to five hundred feet high, and which sustained no vegetable life whatever.

Turning round towards the huge Durini hill,* under which we had been encamped, Pīrū pointed out, almost at its summit, two or three little green thickets nestling in its cavernous irregularities. Here was the Rais' eyrie, and hither in the frequent times of disturbance he collected the flocks and inhabitants of all his

---

* Local name for the end of the Aphen-i-Band or range.

little outlying villages. Pīrū waxed quite enthusiastic in describing his lord's lofty castle. Here was a perennial spring of the sweetest water, the source in fact of the stream in whose bed lay our camp; here were green kŭnār bushes for the young goats, and patches of wheat. Here the Rais had planted pomegranates, and there were three orange trees, and in fact it was quite a little paradise.

"Ah," I answered, "please God, when I return from Anguhran, I will go up there and see this lovely place."

"Yes," he replied, "but you might wander about many months without finding the road; and, indeed, should you not kill yourself by falling down, the watchers would not know you, and would throw rocks down upon you. But if the Muhassil has gone, and you are very active, like an ibex, perhaps the Rais will let me show you the place. And there you will, if there are no clouds, be able to see the sea."

This last was probably true, for about twelve miles to the east there was, in this same range, a peculiar notch which was visible from Jask, and of which before starting I had taken bearings, and by latitude observations we were only sixty miles distant from the coast as the crow flies.

Soon we got again amongst the old sandstone rocks, and into a broad and deep dry water-course, where we found a small village of three or four families and as many mat huts, all the property of the Rais. Here Pīrū tried to hire another donkey, and I at first agreed to wait. But as he commenced the negotiation by sitting down to smoke some of the tobacco I had given him, I carried him off without waiting for the end of it, and we trudged along up the river-bed. This was, where possible, dammed up by solid stone dams sixteen feet high, and the oblong patch of rich soil thus produced planted with numerous date-trees, the fruit of which is said to excel all other dates. I believe, too, that it is not usual for date-trees to grow at such an elevation as they do in Bashakard, where they are found 2,770 feet above the level of the sea.

These patches of soil were covered with long grass, which presented a most curious appearance, being almost buried in masses of hailstones. Each hailstone retained its individual shape and size, something that of a sparrow's egg, and the whole resembled masses of frog spawn. After crossing more shūrs, and still keeping a general course of N. 20° E., at 1.47 p.m. we topped a high cliff and found ourselves overlooking the most magnificent view that even this picturesque country had yet shown us.

Far below at our feet sparkled a brook of crystal clearness, rippling and splashing along over a bed of jet black stone relieved by a network of white quartz veins. The brook was fringed on either side by a narrow belt of tall graceful date-palms towering from out of the rich green setting of a thicket of bistil * bushes. At the back rose sheer 600 feet a frowning black cliff, on the edge of which was balanced an enormous block of pink stone, and all around were rugged hills of all colours. I have been found fault with in England for not sufficiently admiring the beauties of nature, and I had been brought to think that I was incapable of thoroughly appreciating fine scenery.

---

* A kind of pepper.

The grand sight before us, however, drew admiration from all. "This," said Pīrū, exultingly, "is Shahr Baghi.* Have you any such place as this in your country?"

I sent the men down to the foot of the cliff to make tea and get our noon meal ready, and sat myself down on a flat rock to meditate upon the extraordinary country I had entered upon. Behind me, as far as the eye could reach, lay what might be called a purgatory of chaotic scorched-up rocky crags, range after range of which we had laboriously toiled across. Before me ran a stream of clear rippling water fringed by green trees and long grass, making a little garden of paradise. As slowly and meditatively I filled a well-earned pipe, a slight snort attracted my attention; and looking round, I became aware of a flock of fourteen beautiful mountain sheep, regarding me some with indifference and some with curiosity. They passed slowly on within sixty yards of me, one grand old fellow who had been leader remaining to continue his scrutiny until far behind the rest. As he trotted off with a couple of complacent little snorts, I could not help thinking of the old Bashakardi, mentioned in my sixth chapter, who had lived 3,000 years but never seen such an astonishing thing as my caravan, and I wondered whether the old ram would go off to his family with a similar observation. While thus musing, a small avalanche of rocks was displaced to my left, and there appeared the good-natured face of Ghulamshah announcing that tea was ready, so I slid and scrambled

---

* Shahr Baghi (*the garden city*), a name common in many corrupt forms, as, Shahr Bawegh, Shahr Babeg, etc.

down to where an armful of branches had been placed as my seat on the brink of the rushing stream.

Tea and dates were soon despatched in a bower of fine alder trees forty feet high, and on a carpet of a diminutive wild peppermint, and in twenty minutes we were again on the march after registering the barometer at 26·6 (3,246 feet). Here, where except in the torrent beds there is no soil, the stratification of the rocks is everywhere exposed to view, and in some cases most curious. The Rastu mountain, which we were now to cross, resembled nothing so much as an enormous tortoise, while across the torrent bed just ahead of us ran a succession of natural terraces of which the natives had availed themselves for date groves.

From the top of Rastu we had a very extensive view. Across the northern horizon in the farthest distance ran the lofty Marz range, which, with the plains on its northern side, forms the province of Marz. To the east, as far as the eye could reach, ran range after range of low hills. These were the Gavr and Parment provinces, the least hilly of the whole country and producing good camels. Around us were three or four tall rugged peaks rearing their heads about 1,000 feet above our present level, where the barometer indicated 26 (3,858 feet). As we pressed on, another herd of twelve mountain sheep wandered carelessly by. They looked very beautiful with their ruddy fawn-coloured hair, and I own this time the sporting instinct was very strong. But business had to be attended to, and I had no gun.

At 4 p.m. we were picking our way up a narrow chasm, the sides of which were beautiful blue and purple marble veined with white. Soon afterwards, we crossed a small valley in which were the remains of thirty or forty date-stick huts, and this, Pīrū informed us, had been the camp of Rais' army when on the war trail to capture Anguhran. Then we struggled up a huge Bīr, as I shall in future call the mounds of laminated clay which I have before described. This was Bīr Jamal, a name undeniably Arabic, though Pīrū indignantly denied it, and at its summit the barometer marked 25·82 (4,071 feet). It began to get rapidly dark, and Pīrū, who with characteristic quickness had soon discovered Gazo's easy-going nature and given him the donkey to drive, began to call back to him to hurry on. Poor old Gazo struggled on bravely though he was pretty tired, and he had at times to almost carry the donkey round corners and hang all his weight on its tail going down steep places. He would only soliloquise in his whimsical way, "Ah, if only Tajoo and Alishah were here just to see a little of this kind of luxury, I should be quite happy." Tajoo and Alishah had made him their especial butt always in camp, and he would dearly have enjoyed seeing them in the same predicament as himself, with a tired donkey, a dark night, and a road full of precipices. And if they had been there he would have laughed at them and done all their work. The donkey, like all these Bashakard donkeys, was preternaturally active over the hills, and seemed to have equal parts of monkey and ibex in its composition, but it was getting tired and hungry.

Just as the darkness closed in, we were rather startled by an incident which might have had serious results. I was picking my way down a chasm close behind Pīrū, when suddenly with a loud yell he flew into the air. I then became aware of a loud hissing somewhere close in front of me, but I couldn't for the life of me make out where. "Snake!" yelled Pīrū, and *I* flew into the air,—backwards,—knocked down Gazo, and we both slid, rolled, and scrambled down over the exact spot whence the hissing appeared to come. Pīrū came to the rescue, and before we could struggle to our feet he was dangling triumphantly the bruised and mangled body of a hideous horned snake.

At 6 p.m. a light was seen below us, then the barking of dogs was heard, and we were led by Pīrū to the hut of one Jaafir, one of the Rais' head men and now in charge of this village.

After a free fight with a quantity of savage dogs, we effected an entrance. Where walls and doors are all made of ragged matting, it is difficult in darkness to ascertain which is which, and we made considerable havoc on a wrong side before a gruff roaring voice from inside explained our mistake. When we arrived, the mother of the family was just preparing supper of thick slabs of unleavened bread baking on a broad, thin flake of sandstone. Three pretty little girls and two thin-armed but vigorous-looking little boys watched the operation with considerable interest, while the burly old paterfamilias, a very gorilla of a man with a broad good-natured face, was blackening his eyelids with antimony and in a general way dressing for dinner.

The father and two sons wore simple homespun kilts, while each had a sort of coarse cotton plaid which he bestowed about him with much natural grace. It would appear that the plaid pattern is the easiest to weave, for it has been the first effort of the Highlanders both of Balūchistan and Scotland. We received a hearty welcome when Pīrū had explained who we were.

The old mother squeezed out of the skin a profuse allowance of ghee in our honour, and a little boy was set to work with a stick to dig out more dates from the mass in the basket. Presently old Jaafir said to Pīrū: "The waja knows of course that he is very welcome to share our meal, but he knows it is very coarse food; and if he have with him any of his own food, let him cook it, I shall not be ashamed."

It was a delicate piece of politeness on the old fellow's part, and had I been unwell I might have been glad of it. As it was, however, the only thing I begged permission to add was a bowl of tea sufficient for all parties. This, when diluted with hot water to the condition of *eau sucré*, was much appreciated. Then came a great luxury, in the shape of a handful of a small dried fish called Metoot, which the old man with conscious pride instructed his wife to produce. It was curious to see the politeness even over this rarely attainable delicacy. The guests positively refused to touch another fish when they were half finished, and the host had to distribute the remainder in small bunches all round.

During the evening the married daughter came in to see the stranger, and we had one or two other visitors, all announced by a furious onslaught by the dogs. The biggest of these was a very fine shaggy animal answering to the name of "Chambur," derived, according to his owner, from cham or cheshm burīdan, "the cutter-out of eyes."

At about 9 p.m. we all turned in where we were, and then our difficulties began. The hut was only fifteen feet long, eight feet wide, and in the centre seven feet high. All round the wall were stuck little young branches of kŭnār bushes, and tethered opposite these were over thirty little baby goats, who were practising eating on the young leaves. Then there were four old mother goats, who bleated, snorted, and were otherwise troublesome all night.

One end of the hut was of course occupied by the host and his wife, with their children and the miscellaneous assortment of spinning wheels, old saddles, and cradles which form the furniture of a Balūch hut. The other side of the fireplace, that is, the other end of the hut, was devoted to Pīrū, Gazo, Ghulamshah, myself, the goats, and a stack of firewood. In accents of the most venomous sarcasm, I said to Pīrū, "Don't you think that poor donkey had better have been brought inside too?" "No," said Pīrū reflectively, "I think he'll do where he is." I have often found my sarcasms fall flat, but never so fearfully flat as this, and I felt very abject. We got through the night somehow, though I had to get up once and tie Gazo's legs up to the wall. He was so fearfully reckless with them, that had this ingenious idea not occurred to me we should have got up in the morning and found "we were all dead men," or something of the kind. The goats, too, "sucked all the goodness" out of the lappet of my mackintosh collar.

When I awoke, the old mother was already cooking more slabs of bread. The keen misty morning air came pouring in at the open door, where peered in at least twenty hairy noses belonging to as many old goats just released from their stable, and come to look after their young ones. Of these, however, some were still too young to go, and it was amusing to watch the selection. The smallest girl planted herself gravely in the doorway. She was a plump little thing, not three feet high, and very active with her hands, hardly missing a kid that her brother inside shouted to her to stop. The fondness of the two boys, too, for the quaint little goats was very interesting, and often before letting them go they would take them up in their arms and give them a hearty kiss on their snub noses. There was an air of hearty good nature all round, which made the recollection of this camp very pleasant in our minds.

At 7 a.m. I strolled on ahead of the others, enjoying the still morning air and wonderful rock scenery.

The camp of last night was a small village of six mat huts, placed as usual in the bed of a water-course. They and their inhabitants all belonged to the Rais, and they appeared contented and simple people.

Our road to-day was down a torrent bed instead of up it, and after a brisk walk, at 9 a.m., from the top of a small Bīr (bar. 26·3, 3,552 feet), we sighted in the distance the imposing fort of Anguhran.

I own to a feeling of satisfaction at actually seeing this place. We had not had a long or arduous journey to it; still, in a perfectly wild and unexplored country, many accidents may happen to prevent one's reaching any one particular spot.

We pressed on in high spirits, and were trudging along a wet stream bed, when I suddenly noticed some to me quite new footprints. "Ah! ha!" said Pīrū and Gazo in a breath, "perhaps you'll believe us now, those are the pugs of a female hirsh and its baby. There, don't you see? it's been walking on its hands and feet, and (pointing a little farther on) there it wanted to look about, and stood up straight." Here was a wonderful discovery! There was something in these demons then, after all, and I eagerly asked questions about them. Had Pīrū and Gazo ever seen them? How tall were they? etc., etc., for the idea seized upon my mind that it was a kind of ape, and to find apes here would indeed be a discovery. The gist of my friends' information was this: They were originally descended from a cross between the donkey and the human race. They were extremely fierce, and much more cunning than men. They opened the caves in which the grain was stored, however cleverly they were hidden. They climbed up the date-trees and picked the dates. When seen by man, they stood up erect and did not run away. They would tear up a tree as a weapon. Finally they were the size of a well-grown man; they were covered with long black glossy hair, and had no tails.

I took a careful sketch of the footmarks, and that was all I could do at present.

As we marched on, more pugs were seen, and then more, until at last there must have been twenty hirshes passing along this path. At half-past nine we arrived at Shahr Pahtik, a place where the torrent bed widened, and where, a quantity of silt having been deposited, cultivation was carried on. Here in this little green oasis grew figs, limes, mangoes, maize, alder, willow, and Koh-i-Sang, a handsome tree I have been unable to identify. Following up the torrent bed, which widened rapidly into a broad valley, at 10.30 we arrived amongst the numerous date-trees of Anguhran, and camped beneath the hill on which the fort was placed.

CHAPTER VIII.

Seif Allah Khan's fortress.—The river system.—Balūch marriage difficulties.—Nightmare hyænas.—The Kagar Koh and ancient fort.—Leave Rais Ali's.—Watched off the premises.—Fowls and eggs.—Geological researches unappreciated.—Partridge shooting extraordinary.—More murder.—Stealing the guns of the watch.—The demons are bears.—Camels in trouble with bears and snakes.—Start for the spring of oil.—The Khan lectures on botany.

I HAVE forgotten to mention that about an hour after leaving Rais Ali's, a man had come running after us with a letter, which he gave to Pīrū; and now while the kettle was boiling for tea, Pīrū left us to deliver this missive. While I was shaking the dust and shingle out of my shoes, I observed that first one, then two, and gradually several, armed men began to appear among the date-trees, and, after inspecting us, to quietly disappear again.

However, I did not at present see my way to taking any notice of them with effect, so we peacefully continued our meal, Gazo supplying a luscious addition by climbing up the tree under which we sat, and cutting a solitary branch of dates which were still hanging.

Presently loud and angry voices came along the path. "I won't go; he has escaped. He left last night. Where shall I find him now?" etc., and soon

Pīrū appeared accompanied by two strangers, who saluted shortly and continued their argument.

It seemed that the letter Pīrū had brought was to the head man, warning him to be careful of my safety, and instructing him to pay the Muhassil some money when he should arrive. The two men were the Muhassil's servants, who were protesting that they had not been instructed to detain the head man, who had left, and that now it was too late to pursue him. Pīrū explained that the armed men were merely watchers looking out for Seif Allah Khan, should he endeavour to return.

The massive but now partly ruined fort of Anguhran, which would hold two hundred men easily, and four hundred in time of war, is perched on the very apex of a narrow tongue of land or cliff formed by the convergence of two broad and deep torrent beds.

These two rivers come from S.S.W. and N.N.W., and after confluence go off to join the river Jagīn with a S.E. course. It is a coincidence that on the prismatic compass the bearings are 135°, 235°, and 335°.

The hill on which the fort stands is about 360 feet high, and, being formed of a conglomerate of clay and shingle, is not quite perpendicular, though only accessible on the S.W. side, in which, near the apex, is the only entrance and the only well. The ordinary path up is narrow, tortuous, and very steep, and would be rendered very difficult by the destruction of some artificial steps which now make it practicable.

The walls are lofty and very massive. From the base about seven feet upward they are built of large boulders of rounded stones, and above that of a tenacious clay.

The citadel and chief quarters run across the fort rather nearer the apex than the centre, and are still in fair repair.

Behind this is the main court, to which no one was allowed access but the soldiers. The walls are pierced for matchlock men, and a platform for them to stand upon is contrived in the way usual in this country, by a kind of thick inner wall about eight feet lower than the main wall. Outside the northern wall is a dry fosse, about twenty-five feet deep and twenty broad, cut straight across the peninsula, leaving only a narrow passage between each end of the fosse and the cliff. In both courts, which are overlooked by the chief's quarters, are the remains of neat rows of mat huts in which the soldiery lived.

The food of the fort lies all around in immense date plantations which fill the valley, in elevated spots in which are also grown wheat, maize, pomegranates, etc.

The well, which is near the entrance, formerly reached to the bed of the river. It was choked up by the besiegers on the capture of the fort, and is about the only effective piece of destruction they perpetrated, as they could do little harm to the strong walls.

The fort is of roughly triangular shape, about a hundred and eighty yards long by sixty broad across the centre. At the foot of the S.W. face are two buildings which formerly served as masjids, or mosques, and which would afford good cover for a small attacking party.

Such was the almost impregnable stronghold of the fierce old Seif Allah Khan, which only yielded after a year's besetment, and it is now so little damaged that should his family and adherents wait patiently and accumulate wealth by their flocks and agriculture, he will reign again, and from the centre keep the whole country in strict order.

There is but a very small channel of water in the torrent beds which here meet, and the contrast between the bed and the stream is throughout this country very marked.

In some cases the stream has evidently followed natural valleys, while in others a now small brook has equally evidently forced a road a quarter of a mile wide through solid rock, while in the case of the Sharifi river, up which we marched, it had cut for itself through amalgamated mud and shingle a bed sometimes a mile wide and from sixty to a hundred feet deep.

It might be said that the rivers did their work in the rainy season when flooded, and the Tang-i-Fanōch, described in a former chapter, as also the Geigen river, which had shown us the road from the coast across the mountain belt, may be instanced as cases of this. In the former, high-water mark may be seen fifteen feet above the summer level, and in the Geigen river we ourselves saw the floods. But in many other cases, such as the Sharifi, the Gaz Shirai (sweet tamarisk), and the two other streams which join at Anguhran, cultivation is carried on in the river-beds down to the very verge of the channel. It would seem that either at some previous time there has been enormous rainfall, or that the present outlets to the sea have not always been open. The theory that the water which originally cut out, *e.g.*, the huge bed of the Sharifi river, has since been diverted to another channel, will not hold good; for the whole out-turn of water from this country, from the Rapsh, in longitude 59° 25′ E., to the Mināb river, in longitude 57° 5′ E., even when multiplied by ten to compensate for the enormous loss while crossing the sand strip from the mountain belt to the sea, would hardly fill the Sharifi bed.

But it is time to get on the march again, for the sun is over the meridian, and I have determined to return to Pizgh by a new route called the Sardasht route. There seem to be difficulties in the way, for I know nothing of the route but its name. Pīrū protests vehemently that there is no such road; that any deviation from the road by which we arrived will lead us into a waterless country inhabited only by "demons;" and that should we escape these creatures, the best fate that awaits us is to fall into the clutches of Alaroussan Khan, who will rob me and kill him (Pīrū) offhand.

It came out by degrees, and with much cross-questioning, that Pīrū had married a daughter of that family, and that afterwards he had either been unable or unwilling to make up her price, so her parents had indignantly reclaimed her and commenced a hunt after Pīrū.

This would be the commencement of a blood feud: for should they succeed in killing Pīrū, Pīrū's relations would commence a hunt after his murderer; and so it would go on until the matter would become so serious that overtures would be made about paying the extra amount. This kind of marriage is not uncommon. Ghulamshah's brother had to be left behind in Jask, as he could not enter Bashakard. He had married a woman of Pizgh, and paid for her completely, but when he went down to the coast she refused to follow him so far from her friends. He demanded repayment. and her friends demanded that he should come and live in Pizgh. Ghulamshah himself, who was recognised as belonging to Ghulam Hussein (the brother), would have got into trouble on the matter had I not been very peremptory about it. Most Bashakardis go about with their lives in their hands on account of matters of this kind, and an instance will occur in the sequel.

However, I had during this discussion definitely ascertained that there *was* a Sardasht route, and when I assured Pīrū that no one would dare to touch any one under my protection, he reluctantly consented, and by 2 p.m. we were fairly on the march up the Pahtik river-bed. There is nothing like persistence in these matters, even when there are hardly any grounds for it, as in the present case.

At the commencement I had only an indistinct remembrance that some months before, while prosecuting inquiries about Bashakard, the Sardasht route to Anguhrán had been mentioned, but had I not been firm, I should have had to go over the same ground twice, which is always an unpleasant thing.

Presently we came to an encampment of three huts, and were in the process of hiring a donkey for Ghulamshah, who was footsore, when who should appear but the Muhassil with fifteen or sixteen men, among whom was my blind friend Mīr Mahomed Khanjan of Marz.

They had come by the Sardasht route, and seemed very much surprised at my having come by any other.

They were in ecstasies at the performance of the rough, wiry pony on which the Muhassil was mounted, and said I should now see for myself how far the road was practicable for my camels.

The Muhassil promised to announce my arrival to the Governor of Kirman, and we trudged on our way. Soon we turned out of the river and entered upon a long valley of salt clay, which was a great relief to our feet after the incessant climbing over rocks.

Little need be said of our walk henceforth. We turned aside once to inspect a warm and intensely bitter spring, a sample of the water of which I much regretted being unable to bring away.

At 4.25 p.m. we crossed another neck of the Bīr Buland, where the barometer marked 28 (1,820 feet), and at 4.55 we reached the bottom and prepared for camp. Night closed in rapidly, and we got into a snug little dell and set fire to three or four tall karsh bushes (*gynareum argenteum*). By the lurid blaze of these grand torches, we cut grass for the two donkeys, collected firewood, and finally had a hearty meal of tea, bread, and dates, and then turned in one on each side of the fire under a beautiful starlit sky.

I remember even now the quiet beauty of that night, for I was sleepless, and two or three times I replenished the old familiar "G.B.D." All was not, however, as peaceful as it seemed, and as the fire waned, the donkeys, tethered near, began to be uneasy, and snort distrustfully.

Fatigue, however, gradually overcame me, and I slept the sleep of the weary.

Soon it seemed that out of the burnt and blackened karsh bushes there peered the grinning mouth and powerful fangs of an old hyæna. I shouted to drive him away, but his shoulders and body gradually emerged, and he came straight towards me with the horrid open-mouthed teeth-showing snarl habitual to these brutes. Indignantly I seized a half-burnt log from the fire and hurled it at him; but it seemed to vanish as it left my hand, and the brute still stealthily approached. As I looked in astonishment and almost anger, behold another close behind him, and another. There is a rustling in the reeds, and the whole karsh thicket seems alive with them. Suddenly behind me rises slowly and gradually, more and more distinctly, a low, thundering sound, and then,—can that be the ring of iron ramrods?—with an almost superhuman effort I rise to my feet, seize a half-burnt log from the smouldering fire, brandish it round my head, and—awake!

It is a dream; dates and half-baked bread for supper will have their way. The ringing of steel ramrods, however, still continued in the thicket to my left. A thought flashed upon me,—my saddle, that was my pillow, is gone.

I plunged in the direction of the sound with a shout. Three or four dark forms slunk away growling from my saddle. The steel stirrups ringing on the rocks as it was dragged away made one part of my dream, but the rest, I fear, was wholly attributable to my hearty supper.

Gazo and Pīrū lazily looked up, asked, "what's the matter," and decided to have a pipe, and in ten minutes more all was peace again, and thus we remained till morning.

Nov. 13th, 6.40 a.m. Again on march, after noting the minim. thermometer at 55. The "demons" had prowled about us in considerable numbers during the night, and I reflected a good deal on the extreme shortness of their toes, which did not correspond with my theory that they were apes.

About 9 a.m., after good honest walking over hills and plains, we sighted a most remarkable hill. This, Pīrū informed us, was the Kagar Koh, and on it are the remains of a massive fort, built in the ancient bygone times by Rustam and the Pehlevis. It is totally unlike all other hills near it, most of which are stratified and have a definite dip and strike.

This has the appearance of a huge white pillar, 1,000 feet in diameter, projecting up from the crater of a volcano. On the top are seen old walls and three trees.

I at once determined to ascend this at all hazards. There was, of course, the usual opposition from Pīrū, who at first said the ascent was impossible; then that on the top was a very sacred shrine, and that if any one heard that he had taken me there, they would kill him; and many other good and solid reasons, until I got angry, and told him roundly to keep his lies to himself, and to do what he was told.

Those who have never lived among an extremely ignorant people with no written language, can form no idea of the difficulty of obtaining correct information from a wild Balūch, even when he has the will and the knowledge.

Take an ordinary guide who has travelled the route for to-morrow perhaps a hundred times, and who is extremely anxious to oblige you. You might be tempted to sing out to him, "Oh, Hussein, how is the road to-day?" "Oh, the road's all right, Waja." "Is it a long stage or a short one?" That is too intricate for him, and he says, "Eh?" "Is it a long stage?" "No, it's not a very long one." "Is it a short stage?" "No, it's not a very short one, but we shall get there this evening all right, I know the way."

Now travel through whatever kind of country you might,—and there is a considerable variety in Bashakard,—you would get the same answers to these questions. Should the road lead over a sandy plain, or through broken hills and down rocky water-courses, you would get but one answer to your questions.

The man would willingly describe the road if he could; but he cannot project his mind far enough ahead of the real present. Put him on his memory, aud you will have more success. "How long ago was it that he travelled this road?" "Who was with him?" "What load had he?" etc., and such like questions as may stir up a sluggish memory.

But the only way to get useful information about the road, is to sit with the men while they talk and chat about the next day's stage.

I believe no primitive uncultivated mind is to be trusted in the least on any abstract subject. It would be difficult to find a parallel for this mixture of totally unroused reasoning powers and high moral character.

This is a long digression, and it must be remembered that I had just silenced Pīrū's scruples about ascending the Kagar Koh, and that now, after a severe scramble, we have reached, as it were, the neck or rim, where the perpendicular part rises from the cone.

It seemed a tremendous height now we were close under it, and some ravens, jackdaws, and hawks, the only birds we had yet seen, looked like swallows as they soared out from the cliff above.

But an insuperable objection to our getting higher soon became apparent. It was the only one which Pīrū, experienced in my manner of treating objections, had omitted to mention—it was impossible. The next twenty feet or so were perfectly impracticable; and an avalanche of huge water-worn boulders was all that remained of a stone staircase which had formerly given access to this wonderful natural fortress. We were now about 500 feet above the ground, and the summit could not have been less than 500 more from where we stood.

Away nearly east, and some fifteen miles distant, was a similar hill, which Pīrū said also contained remains of fortifications; but I could nowhere hear the vestige of a tradition about their builders. They were attributed to the ancient times, "the age of Rustam and the Pehlevi."

Due south, a thin, spiral column of smoke rises from the chaos of ridges and peaks stretched out below us, and we gird up our loins and start for where Gazo and Ghulamshah are making tea.

Henceforth it was merely a matter of hard walking and taking bearings, both of which are sufficiently explained on the map. Suffice it to say, that at 4.30 p.m. we were receiving a most hearty and cordial welcome from the men, and all the kettles in the camp were boiling in preparation for a tremendous wash.

The chronometer was all right—that was the first thing; but the thought of it had so preyed upon Brahim's mind, that he declared he had been unable to sleep, for fear something should happen to it.

My two young malcontents were very sick indeed, unable to work or do anything but lie wrapped up in their "hairy-hairies" and moan. After a careful examination of their tongues and pulses, I assured them of my intense sympathy for their sufferings, and gave them each a rousing dose of Warburg's fever drops, which is, I suppose, without exception, the nastiest stuff in the whole world.

Next morning we bade farewell to the Rais, obtained from him two guides, and after getting a meridian altitude at noon, we left by a desperately hilly road for the province of Jangdā. Soon after starting, our good-natured, much-enduring guide Gazo left us. He had fulfilled his task of guiding us to Anguhran, and was all anxiety to return to his recently married wife at Geigen. He took a handsome bakshish in addition to his pay, and a letter to a friend at Jask who had kindly undertaken to act as my agent. This contained instructions to pay none of my two sick friends' allotments to their families until further news; also, should they arrive without proper certificates of discharge, to seize them "and cruelly entreat them."

Having thus loaded my gun, I was careful not to weaken myself by firing it off prematurely, and contented myself by darkly hinting that I had written letters to Jask.

Meanwhile my two sick friends were mounted on camels, and I spoke of them always in low tones, as of men who would probably be afflicted with a grave illness on account of their conduct in promising to accompany a sahib on a journey and then wanting to return halfway.

At 2 p.m. the disadvantage of having two guides became very apparent; my guide having taken one path, and the one with the luggage having taken another, and we were compelled to get upon the tops of hills and hoot.

They had got on ahead when I was taking bearings, and we followed along a very picturesque valley. During the struggle between Rais Ali and Seif Allah Khan, the hills to our right and left had been lined with little walled places for sharp-shooters, and these were still numerous, and in good order; and at one time, happening to turn and look behind, I saw no less than three black heads bob down.

The "Pearly-eared One" was walking and talking with me at the time, so I had nothing to grumble at, but it did seem at one time as if there might be something in the Rais' instructions to follow only one particular road.

At 3.10 we clambered out of this water-course, and after two or three terrific hills, scrambled down into the broad well-wooded valley of the Sharifi river. Here was a beautiful valley, and it contained such abundance of camel-fodder, that I determined to halt for a day.

This evening I put four inches square of cantharides blister on the back of the necks of my two patients, and next morning both were up and bustling about, leading their camels to water. Thus this affair was settled for the present, and harmony was restored.

On the 16th we marched along, up rocky water-courses, winding amongst endless barren hills, and camped near the Barahing hill. It was very absurd to hear the Balūchis boasting how terribly the Bashakardis were afraid of them. On the road to-day we had met a man who stuttered dreadfully in his speech. This complaint is unknown on the coast, and was at once ascribed to intense fear.

The "Pearly-eared One" was a great delight to us. He was gradually proving to be the prince of guides, and by far the most intelligent man in the country. On leaving one camp, he would point out the bearing of the next, and this, as checked by a back-bearing from the second camp, so accurately as never to be 5° wrong. The value of such a man was of course inestimable to a traveller lost, as it were, in a maze of high hills. He was a great scholar too, and carried with him a large and well-thumbed Persian manuscript, from which in the evenings he would chant in a high droning voice for hours, a most odd medley of the religious, superstitious, and meretricious. This was at times inconvenient, as he considered himself personally responsible for my safety, and invariably slept across the door of my tent, and before going to sleep he would always refresh himself by first singing, and then translating to the admiring Balūchis, a few gems from his repertoire.

On the 17th we moved on to Bun Keram, the stony road telling frightfully on my poor camels, four of whom were lame, two badly. To-day we turned out of the Telling route, and went in a more northerly direction, for I began to be much exercised about a mysterious fountain of grease said to exist in the hills, and to be used for lamps as well as to be a specific for the mange in camels. After much discussion, I persuaded Durgosh to diverge from his intended route, though he declared that we were all risking our lives, as the place was inhabited by men of the Seif Allah Khan faction.

Our camp to-night was in the broad and fertile valley of the Gaz Shirai or sweet tamarisk river, which reaches the sea at Sirik. The jungle was very dense in some parts, and was delightful after the barren hills. There was, too, a small village near, and as I stood on the small smooth spot which I had chosen for camp, and watched our camels gradually filing up the ascent and kneeling round me to be eased of their loads, I was electrified by hearing first one, and then three or four distinct clucks. Not a doubt about it, it was a hen, and Brahim was immediately despatched to secure her, and as many eggs as possible. It is a curious thing that Balūchis look upon the idea of eating an egg with the greatest disgust, regarding it in the light of a fœtus or embryo. With me, however, the case was different, and very often my stomach totally refused all food but milk and eggs. For some days now, mutton and dates and bread had been my fare, and though that sounds luxurious enough, still, when one is unable to eat any of the three, one yearns for other things.

There were here many acres of fertile alluvial soil, and I noticed that it was so light, that the bullocks required no goad while ploughing.

The encampment here belonged to Rais Ali, but the men were very uncivil, and refused to sell anything. They were, however, sorry for their refusal when they learnt that I was a doctor, and I eventually got from two ophthalmic gentlemen, two fowls and eleven eggs (all there were) for two small quantities of solution of nitrate of silver.

I met here with the first cases seen in the country of consumption and tapeworm. Nor must I omit to mention that here we found the first vestiges of fossil remains in Bashakard, namely, the cast of a scallop shell (? *Terebratula sufflata*) and a lump of dark purple stone, which close examination proved to be a kind of coral.

I find here noted in my note-book some rather unkind reflections on the total want of appreciation in the Balūch mind for geological researches.

This evening, on arriving at camp, I had as usual my pockets full of specimens, and as ill luck would have it, before I could disembarrass myself of them, Durgosh came up and asked for the matches. To my dismay, they are under the specimens, and I slowly begin to turn them out. He looks rather surprised at the first, more so at the second, examines carefully the third and fourth; at the fifth he sits down opposite me, as if prepared for any number more; but at the seventh he bursts into an uncontrollable roar of laughter, in which he is joined by all the camel-men, who, attracted by the extraordinary spectacle, were standing breathless round me.

My pocketful of rocks was altogether too much for them; and weeks afterwards one of them would recall the circumstance to his friend's memory, and they would all go into fits of laughter.

Next day, the 18th, I had to wait for a meridian, and we did not get off till 1.15 p.m., and even then we had not a very bright look-out. I had four camels out of six badly lame; before us lay a fourteen mile stage over rough angular boulders; and, as we were to-night to arrive at the stronghold of our warlike friend, the relative of Seif Allah Khan, to-night was, according to the "Pearly-eared One," our last night of life. Dar Pahan or "the open country," did not belie its name, and as we travelled on, the hills gradually got lower and the valleys wider.

Durgosh to-day distinguished himself in a remarkable manner as a sportsman. He began with a "kabg," or red-legged partridge, which he killed "fatally ded" at twenty yards, with an A A A wire cartridge; shot another at sixty-four yards, with an old brown Bess (three or four of which I had purchased at three shillings each) which was loaded with a miscellaneous assortment of shot of all sizes, gravel and other things; he got a third with a gun which I assured him was not loaded; and towards evening, when it was too dark to see, he banged the head clean off a "sussi," or rock-partridge, with a 12-bore bullet from my old Westley Richards. He always presented arms at the first cluck, and with gun at shoulder, finger on trigger, and body bent double, would tear recklessly over hills and rocks, until he fairly ran the wretched bird to earth.

As the darkness closed in upon us, and the rocks and hills began to assume the weird fantastic shapes always produced here by night-fall, this man called me a little way off the track to show me a little nook in the rocks where, but a short fortnight ago, he and his brother had perpetrated a most bloody murder.

It was of course in pursuance of one of these dreadful blood feuds. The murdered man had been travelling alone from Jangdā, and his two assassins had followed him carefully for five days. Very early on the morning of the sixth day, they came upon him still asleep, and carefully withdrawing, Durgosh's brother loaded his gun with twelve bullets, all the two men could muster between them. Then with the utmost precaution they crept back over the rocks, and drawing their swords in readiness, the brothers fired. The wretched man was almost rolled round by the shock, rose, staggered a few paces, and fell and was immediately hacked to pieces.

All this my companion not only related to me with much gusto, but actually acted for me—creeping over the rocks, stealthily pointing his gun,—then, reversing his position, he lay on the ground, started at the imagined shock, rose, staggered forward, and fell with a groan. This relation, with the wild scene, the solitude, and the eager lifelike way in which the acting was performed, made a powerful impression upon me, and I could only wonder at the perfect indifference to death these fellows displayed. Soon we were disturbed by distant shouts from the men crying for the guide; and indeed well they might, for such a trackless chaos of hills could hardly be found in any other country than this, and we hurried on to put the caravan in the right way.

It was not till 6.15 p.m. that Durgosh decided that we had arrived at the village of Hussein Khan, and though we could see nothing of the village, we camped. At the sounding stroke of the mallet wielded by little Brahim, and the flashing of my two hurricane lanterns, which were invaluable on such occasions as these, the inhabitants were aroused. There seemed to be a considerable number of the men; nor was their appearance over friendly as they came and looked suspiciously at us, speaking amongst themselves in undertones.

We were evidently in the land of thieves, and here

any one moving about at night was sharply questioned. The men all turned in under arms, with their guns under them, and I hoped fervently that they might shoot neither themselves nor the camels. I was busy with the stars till late, when Durgosh came in reporting that the chief recognised me as an old friend and was coming to visit me to-morrow with a large present.

Just as I was going to bed, in came Tajoo nearly bursting with suppressed laughter. He had stolen from under the men every single gun in the camp, and now deposited them by my side in a bundle.

I hesitated at first whether to wake Brahim and make him set a watch, but he was very unwell and the men were so tired that we might have set as many watches as we liked but could not have kept them awake, so I decided to trust to Durgosh and keep the guns in the tent for fear some outsider should imitate Tajoo's feat.

When daylight came, we found as usual that we were in a broad river bed or valley much of which was under cultivation, and close by us ran the river, while at a little distance were about thirty mat huts.

While at breakfast, Brahim came in with a dreadful report of the camels. The four that had been lame were lamer than ever. "Seif kuta" was the expression, meaning that the horny sole of their feet was worn through, and in truth they left bloody marks wherever they put their feet. Nor was this all. The big handsome Jaski līro had one leg swollen the size of an elephant's, and the Jamaiti līro had got into trouble with some wild beast during the night and had received a fearful clawing in the neck.

This last was unanimously put down as the work of a "hirsh," and there gradually dawned upon my mind a suspicion as to what this mysterious animal was. Had he a tail? Yes, a very short one, but hardly visible owing to the length of his hair. My hope for ape discovery was a mistake. It was a bear.

It was odd that the Persian word "khirs," a bear, had never occurred to me, but I was led astray by the great insistence on his walking upright and his wrongly imputed absence of tail. The Jaski līrọ's swollen leg, however, was a most serious matter. I had not the faintest idea what was the matter, but to exhibit my ignorance would have been fatal; so I did what I could to promote discussion, and then authoritatively decided the majority to be in the right.

With much solemnity we administered two table-spoonfuls of strong liquor ammonia, and whether it was snake bite or not, the camel was able to march next day, and the case was added by my men to my list of marvellous cures.

Soon a body of men approached, amongst whom, Brahim whispered, was Hussein Khan; but which he was I was at a loss to make out, for all were in exactly the same dress. However, I put myself at the head of the procession and led the way to the tent. Here it soon became apparent that the leader was even worse dressed than the men, and indeed his men murmured a good deal to mine afterwards that their chief had not even a turban to put on when he went to see a stranger. And yet this man was wealthy, had many men and plough oxen, and was nearly related to the late ruling family. But this is the way here; when a family meet with reverses, they live quietly, and by agriculture and a little trade they gradually accumulate the sinews of war, and when prepared, strike another blow for supremacy.

Our short interview was mainly about the ancient forts and this fountain of oil of which I had heard. He mentioned one fort, at the base of which was an inscription, but it was merely "Turn to the right," in modern Persian, and hardly seemed of much interest. He spoke also of having heard of another, which gave a list of prices of dates, ghee, and other things; but he seemed vague as to where it was, and refused point blank to entertain the idea of taking me there, nor could any offer induce him to alter his mind.

It seems probable that the country about 58·30 E. long. and 27 N. lat. is inhabited by a Persianized race in a much higher state of civilization than the men of Bashakard, who make carpets, but not having the dyes, are confined to black, white, and brown, the natural colours of the wool. There are three villages of the name of Seit, all more or less known by repute to Balūchis, and all of which are said to produce these carpets, suggesting the idea that the word "Seit" has some meaning bearing on the subject.

Hussein Khan, however, readily promised to show me the oil fountain, and at 9.35 a.m. he, I, and Durgosh with his donkey, started across the river in a northerly direction.

The river was full of small fish of two kinds, and a small crab of a dull greenish brown above and a dirty white below.

Three or four hundred yards of very large shingle thickly studded with tamarisk brought us to the steep bank. Kabg, sussi, common partridge, Goa sand-pipers, and blue pigeons abounded, and we left the enthusiastic Durgosh behind engrossed in the sport. He missed something, however, for we crossed soon afterwards about twelve acres of marshy meadow land and flushed seven ducks. One of these was afterwards bagged, and was identified by Professor Newton as the common teal.

The rest of the way was hard scrambling, and it came on to rain like a waterspout. I had a spare mackintosh, and with some difficulty managed to get Durgosh manœuvred into one, but much as he admired its wet-resisting qualities, the confinement of the garment was quite too much for him, and in less than ten minutes he struggled out of it with a sigh of intense relief.

Wet always adds much to rock scenery by deepening and softening the colours, and I was admiring the desolate grandeur of the scene, when, as we topped a hill, we came upon life in its most picturesque and harmonious aspect. A tall powerfully built old shepherd with a handsome white beard was leaning in a very fine position upon a long and gnarled staff. Round him crowded innumerable sheep and goats, the glossy black hair of the latter contrasting well with the snowy wool of the former.

Much as we admired the contrast between the white-bearded old shepherd with his homely flock and his rugged wild surroundings, the importance of getting fresh meat for the camp was obvious, and we made a descent upon the old man. He was, however, exorbitant in his price, and I was obliged to acquiesce in my companion's decision not to purchase.

I was often obliged thus to go without meat when I would have been glad to have given double the price asked, for my reckless display of money would have roused endless suspicion and trouble.

At last we struggled up a steep torrent bed full of pampas grass, and the increasing size of the boulders showed us that we were getting near the fountain head. The regularity with which the stones gradually decrease in size from the head to the embouchure of these streams is very remarkable, the smallest pebbles being of course carried farthest down by the water. A curious instance of this on a gigantic scale will be described further on.

Soon the gorge narrowed, and the pools of water were covered with a sort of iridescent scum. The rocks at the bottom were coated with a black deposit, and now and then ornamented with white feathery fungus, such as is seen in coal-pits. I could not preserve specimens of the fungus, for when picked it collapsed in much the same way as a sea anemone when taken out of water. My guides, on seeing the quantity of water in the torrent bed, began to exclaim that we should see no grease; and they explained that the grease fountain being just in the stream course, the least rain washed away all the accumulated pool of grease. We gradually became aware of a very old and powerful smell of rotten cabbages, which affected the natives' noses horribly.

At last we came to the "fountain," which would be better described as a source. A huge boulder of hard sandstone, the size of a railway carriage, jutted out of the side of the hill into the water-course. One end of this was quite black and greasy, and from no one particular place, but as it were from every pore, there oozed a kind of oil the colour of sherry.

But little oozed out in the cold weather, and what there was was carried away by each freshet. But in a dry summer, as far as I could gather from various native accounts, as many as eighteen gallons are collected and carried away to Mināb to be burnt in lamps.

The ground underneath the stone was black and saturated with the oil; and pieces of earth, when once lit, burnt freely, but with much smoke and a strong bituminous smell.

Very little research satisfied my friends, who soon adjourned to a neighbouring rock and there sat, a most ludicrous spectacle, with their eyes blinking, their noses grasped convulsively, and barking out, when the coughing would let them, "Ai kih būăsh ziādi girān!" (*Oh, but its smell is most fearfully heavy!*)

I bottled off a pyretic saline bottle full of specimen stone, and we took our way homeward, receiving, as we climbed along the rocky path, a lecture on botany from Hussein Khan, who had something to say about every plant and shrub we passed. I unfortunately lost the specimens of the only plant of much value, which was one, the root of which was used as soap, and which, without any preparation whatever, possessed the most wonderful bleaching properties. It was a little round, flattened bush with pinnatifid leaves, having a white silky gloss upon them. The root was like that of a carrot, but fibrous.

As we neared our camp, we passed through the Khan's extensive date groves, where were also many very large pomegranate bushes, which the Khan said, with some pride, had been brought from Bam by one of his ancestors.

When we got home, we found the camels so much better that, to-morrow's stage being a short one, we resolved to start.

CHAPTER IX.

WE ENTER PERSIAN TERRITORY.

A ruined village.—Welcomed as traders in fish.—Bivouac stories.—Ancient burying-ground.—Telling.—Another postal curiosity.—More doctoring.—Mutiny again.—Successful tactics.—Our new guide Hussein.—We try to become Persians.—The "wide wide world."—Difficult passes. — Manujan. — Quack doctoring.—Bustards.—Bargah.—Red-legged partridges.—Kahnu.

NEXT morning we followed the Dar Pahan river, and camped on a small, well-treed plain called Zamin Mulla. There were only two things worthy of note on the road, one of which was the remains of a very large village which had possessed several water-wheels for grinding corn, and other signs of wealth.

The river that had supported this village had, it appeared, during a heavier flood than usual, broken through some obstacle that had previously kept it up, and now left the village three miles to the south. The other was an extremely steep and sharp-pointed cone of shūr clay running up more than 600 feet high, and exceedingly regular in shape. This was called the Safit Gunj, and was a most remarkable landmark.

Zamin Mulla is the most westerly village but one in Bashakard. We were now on the caravan route between Mināb and Bashakard, and the people at a small village here took us for traders, and rushed up making most importunate inquiries for dried fish. The men entered into the joke at once, and made the poor people's mouths water by eloquent descriptions of the beautifully salted fish that my boxes contained.

There was a capital minstrel at Zamin Mulla, and we sat up very late singing, playing, and telling stories. Our new musician played a fiddle of peculiar

BALŪCH MINSTRELS.

make, and both his choice of music and his execution were so excellent, that I offered him a large sum to accompany the expedition. Two of his tunes in particular ran in my head for days afterwards, and will be found with one of Alishah's melodies in the appendix. There is about them to my mind such a jovial rhythm, that they were doubly delightful after the weird, mournful flute to which we had so long been accustomed.

It was to-night, too, I remember, that one of my anecdotes over the camp fire fairly brought down the house. Many extraordinary instances had been related of the climbing powers of the Bashakardi donkeys; and at last I was appealed to as to whether the donkeys in my country could climb as well as those of this. I was obliged to say loftily that in my country we didn't ride donkeys, but that an acquaintance of mine had once turned his horse out to graze, and had found him in the morning, after a very long search, quietly sitting up in a date-tree eating the dates. *

The men quite caught this as a satire upon the incredible yarns of the Bashakardis, and went into fits of laughter. The great Hussein of the donkey's bray was occasionally permitted a solo, which was the only painful part of the concert. He had a wonderful power of sustaining a note for a long time, and the men would sometimes sit perfectly breathless with anxiety to see whether he would think of a fresh note before his breath was exhausted over the last one.

I often thought it was rather like a lot of children watching a humming-top just "dying." They know it must break down soon, but ever as they put out their hands to pick it up, it gives another lurch and spins away again. A Balūch song is more a series of vocal gymnastics than anything else; and yet I have sat and listened to some of them for hours. Hussein, however, was a bad specimen of a soloist.

---

* It would never do to admit in such company that our country was not a mass of date-trees.

Another amusement is a relation, half recitation and half anecdote. Some story, generally of a journey or a shooting expedition, is told with great rapidity and vivacity of manner, and every other sentence is made to finish with some kind of refrain or chorus, "Man goftum ting," "Lā māhū kathálik," or "La hani dilum hā abu," * that has no meaning as bearing on the story, but sounds ridiculous from being brought in in such incongruous and unexpected positions. Next morning we were all very ill. I felt quite knocked up myself, and Brahim could hardly move. On consideration we unanimously decided that the sheep Hussein Khan had given us was bad.

We were evidently leaving the hills fast, and I had a quarrel with Durgosh for bringing me back to the coast. It appeared, however, to be true that this was the only practicable path. Meanwhile he assured me that we had only one more westerly stage to make when we should start north. It was evident from the features of the villagers, from the vegetation, and the birds, that we were close to the sea coast.

Next morning we made a rapid march over smooth plain to Telling, a large and flourishing village, under the governorship of the Pearly-eared One's father. On the route we passed through much fine and diversified scenery, sometimes in a well-treed plain, sometimes winding amongst hills of grotesque shape and most brilliant colours. At 1.10 p.m. we crossed the Sindrik stream, which gives name to a very large

---

* Persian: "And I said ting."
Arabic: "No, not like that."
Balūchi: "Oh la! and now my heart is happy."

village on its banks higher up, and which joins the Dar Pahan stream a few miles south. At 1.35 p.m. we reached the boundary of the Gurrū district, the westernmost limit of Bashakard. Here was a remarkable collection of ancient tombs, extending over more than four acres of ground. The tombs were oblong, square, or circular enclosures, formed by strong walls about six feet high, the only entrances being very small doorways from two to three feet high.

Scattered among these were many other graves, ornamented in the Balūchi fashion with red, white, and green pebbles, and about the centre of the whole were the remains of two well-built plastered houses which may have been masjids (or mosques). This graveyard was generally attributed to the "Gours," which in the Balūch mind means foreigners of any kind. As far as I could judge, it was the burial place of a former race of Balūchis who had employed Persian masons to build the masjids. The graves seemed to be of two distinct periods, those of the second having been put there owing to those of the first having invested the place with a certain amount of sanctity.

But I was at a loss to discover any traces of a town or village such as might have produced this burial-ground, for neither Persians nor Balūchis carry their dead far from their houses except under special circumstances. It happened, however, that the strange regularity of what appeared to be the strata on the neighbouring hills struck my eye, and going to the spot I found distinct traces of very old but very extensive fortifications. In another hour we were riding through the fertile fields of Telling, where indigo and castor oil seemed to thrive wonderfully, and at 3.15 were encamped in what might almost be called a park. It was a beautiful place in the midst of fine tamarisk, kŭnār and kahur trees, and though the tallest was not forty feet high, still it was years since I had seen any taller, and everything goes by comparison.

Soon we had a visit from Durgosh's father. There was much to tell on both sides, for during the son's absence in Bashakard there had been wars and rumours of wars. The Persian Governor of Mināb had sent thirty horsemen and carried off one Abbas, the chief of a neighbouring village; and Durgosh's father, ever ready for an encounter with the hated "Gajars," had collected his men and gone after them. Shots had been exchanged, but the rescue party had been obliged to return empty-handed; and fearing retaliation in the shape of a night attack, they had driven off their flocks and herds to a neighbouring mountain, whence they had but just returned.

I had a busy evening's work in altering the packing of various boxes as experience had shown me would render the contents more readily available for use.

The camel-men had some grand games at wrestling, etc., and for once in the journey there ensued a quarrel. They were living too well, eating meat every day, and I stopped the supply of that article, though not altogether unaware that a storm was brewing.

I was much amused by a villager coming in to show me a letter he had got, and of which he was immensely proud. It had been entrusted to him, he said, months ago, for conveyance to Kariūn, and when I naturally asked why he had not delivered it, he said, "Oh, he had not had occasion to go that way yet!" It was too absurd. Letters travel about this country for months, exciting a sort of reverential awe in the minds of those permitted to see them, and a pride in the bearers. As to who they are for, and what are the contents, no one ever seems to dream of forming a conjecture.

We had a laugh, too, over the *Illustrated London News*, which Durgosh was never tired of poring over with Ghulamshah as showman. They came to the picture of the Prince of Wales' diminutive pony, which Ghulamshah correctly enough explained. "No, no," said the men who were looking over Durgosh's shoulder; "that's a wolf." "But it's a pony," expostulated Ghulamshah, indignantly; "go and ask the waja if it isn't." "Not a bit," they replied; "that's all very well for you. We're Balūchis, and we call that a wolf." That was enough for them; it might be whatever it liked, but they had settled it was a wolf, and it was a wolf.

Next morning we were busy with astronomical observations, after which came innumerable applicants for medicine. Spleen, a withering of the limbs, and ophthalmia, were the commonest complaints among the men, whilst among the women I had patients suffering from various ailments.

Owing to Durgosh's representations that I never gave medicine for nothing, all came provided with a fowl, and it was the funniest sight to see before the tent door a sort of avenue of old men, each squatting down and holding an old hen by the legs. Then the women's great aim was to have a private interview, and many were the stratagems to get me away quietly behind the tent, or into a thicket, where they could explain their special ailments. There were many pretty girls, always accompanied by an aged grandmother or aunt, between whom and themselves there seemed to be a good deal of sympathy and affection.

The main difficulty we experienced was to provide some receptacle for the solutions of nitrate of silver, for all my spare bottles were gone long ago. They brought gourds, cocoa-nut shells, and all sorts of things, and I had to put a great many doses into small sections of reed in which the joint formed the bottom.

One poor old fellow was a sight to touch any one's heart. He was quite blind, and had no one to take care of him, but, guided by the voices and helped by a long stick, he was slowly making his way towards the tent. As he approached he stumbled, and in the effort to recover himself, the fowl which he had hitherto been grasping escaped. There was a slight laugh at his expense, as he made an awkward snatch in the direction he conceived it to have gone. He stood for a moment with a hopeless expression on his blank face, and then said with a sigh, "Well, now I may go home again." Meanwhile I had asked his name from Durgosh, who was standing by me, and just as he turned round I called him by it. "Come," I said, "my father; by the decree of God your fowl has run away, but He is merciful, and your medicine shall not be wanting." Then two of my men brought him up to me. His gratitude was very fervent, and I remembered it for a long time.

But there was a storm brewing in the camp, and from what I could hear it was open mutiny, the only difficulty being who should bell the cat. Durgosh, who was quite *au fait* with matters, and whose friendship was most sincere and valuable, came and talked the matter over with me.

The upshot of it all was this. I had been very harsh with the men for any trifling derelictions of duty, and at the present the remembrance of this obtained the ascendency over that of many little kindnesses received. They were going to a country of ice and snow, to which Balūchis had never before been, and where it was impossible for them to live. It was known that the people there were hostile, that there was no camel fodder and no dates. Finally, that on setting out I had promised them warm clothes, and as yet they had received none, and they had decided to demand money, and send two or three of their number to Mināb to purchase clothes. Such was Durgosh's view of the case; but he had no advice to give, and in fact paid me the compliment of thinking that I could manage best myself.

I determined to bring matters to a head at once, for I was very angry, and calling Brahim in, I proceeded to give him instructions for to-morrow's march.

Brahim was an excellent fellow, but he had not sufficient firmness or independence of mind to elect definitely to serve either me or his comrades, or, as they ought to have been, his subordinates. He should have known that in the position I had made for him he could have led them with a thread had he but been resolute, and that if, when the first man broached the subject of desertion, he had treated it properly, it would never have been discussed again. As I expected, he was taken aback when he heard my intention to march to-morrow, and with many excuses stammered forth much of what I had previously heard from Durgosh.

I took his statements one by one. As for my harshness, I said that the men had yet to learn what discipline was; at the same time, it was not for me to call to mind many kindnesses done to them. As for the cold in the country we were going to, it was more cold than it was possible for them to conceive, that they were mere children, and could know nothing about it, nor was there any one here who could tell them except myself. As for my promise of giving them warm clothes, that had been fulfilled by my giving them the felt coats and carpets; and in this matter I asked, "Was it true that the men wished him to tell me that if I did not give them warm clothes they would return and leave me?"

He reluctantly admitted that this was, in point of fact, what they did say.

"Very well," I said, getting warm, "then I'm to be servant and do what they tell me, and if I don't they'll punish me; that's how it is to be, isn't it? and perhaps I'd better load the camels too! Whose woollen coat is Brahim Khamīs wearing? Is it mine or his? Whose cloak is Dād Arrahīm wearing? and to whom do the things that Hasan and Kasim are wearing belong? Do you think for an instant that I will negotiate on such a footing as this? Send all the men here at once. Do you think that I don't know how cold it will be,—that I don't know that those felt coats don't give any warmth,* not any more than

* These felt coats are very stiff when new, but after having been worn fit themselves to the body and give great warmth. Our Balūchis had hitherto only slept on them, and not worn them.

boards? What sort of a master am I that you should have found this out and not I?" and I again told him to send the men here.

The men, however, had all gone to fetch the camels in, and Brahim began to reason the matter, which, as he commenced by putting himself entirely in my hands, it was only politic to let him do.

"But," he commenced, "you did promise the men warm things, and I never thought you referred to the felts; and I have always told the men that you would give them all sorts of clothes; and what are the poor fellows to do with their thin cotton shirts and drawers?"

I replied, but in a milder and more placable tone, that so long as the men threatened to abandon me and break their promise, it did not matter what promises I had made, for I would be bound by none of them.

"But," he urged, "you did say once or twice that they should none of them ever be cold. If they promise to go with you, will you give them clothes?"

But I refused to make any promises whatever. "The men," I said, "shall come with me unconditionally. What I have promised shall be performed so long as what they promised shall have been carried out."

"But," he repeated, "you did promise that they should never feel the cold, didn't you?"

"Yes," I answered; "and you should know whether I generally do more or less than I promise. The men shall behave to me like men and like Balūchis. They shall trust me fully and unconditionally, and if they can't do that they may go"——I am afraid I said, "to the d——l."

With that he went off, leaving me outwardly calm and master of the situation, but inwardly fuming with rage and uncertainty. I had but one card left, which was to hold out the terrors that awaited them at Jask, should they return without a written permit from me.

I might, after all, have to come down from the high horse on which I had mounted, and use measures of conciliation. That would indeed have been a bitter pill. But I knew the men I had to deal with thoroughly, and my instinct did not fail me. That evening I ordered Brahim to kill a sheep and invite to the banquet all who were coming with me, while he was to warn solemnly all those that were not coming that they had better not be found about the camp next day.

What Brahim did say I do not know; but the tent was never struck nor the camels loaded up with more cheerfulness, alacrity, and thorough good humour than it was the next morning. The fellows had made up their minds to trust me, and there were no half measures about it.

The result was the more gratifying in that the place was so situated that desertion would have been quite simple and easy had they decided upon that course. Never was I so rejoiced in my life; but my only confidant was Ghulamshah, for had I exhibited my delight it would have betrayed that I had been anxious about the matter.

Durgosh accompanied us a good way on our road, and afterwards entrusted us to the care of a guide called Hussein, of whom more anon. He gave me the marvellous donkey on which he had ridden, and I gave him a good old Colt's revolver which he much coveted. Our course was nearly east, and at 3.45 p.m. our new guide brought us to a halt, saying that we should not be able to reach Sarnay that night. It looked a bad beginning for our guide, for the day was yet young to camp, and I noted the time till sunset carefully, with a view of comparing it with the time we should take in reaching the proper camping place the next day.

Hussein was a middle-aged man, about thirty-five, with handsome features and a black beard. He was the most singularly stupid man I ever had to do with. Had he been made of wood, he could not have shown more complete indifference to everything around him. To questions about the road he had but one answer, which was that it was all right, and that he would bring us to a good camping place, where water, fodder, and firewood should be abundant. He speedily became the butt of the whole camp, and his simplest action would bring down storms of chaff. Did he even go to cut firewood, a shout from Tajoo or some other wag would announce his return: "Ah, poor dear Hussein, poor creature! look at his firewood. Green! green as an onion!" The chief labour of the camp was speedily put on his shoulders. Did the wood run short, Hussein had to rouse out and get more; was water wanted, or did one of the camels stray, it was all the same, until I often felt inclined to interfere on behalf of the unfortunate stupid.

On leaving Telling we had received instructions to say that we were of such and such a tribe and family, and already the men began to make the most ridiculous attempts in jest to behave like Persians.

I hear Brahim call out in Balūchi, "Oh, Hussein, go and fetch the donkey!" *

Chorus of men, "No, no; you musn't speak like that. We're in the country of Rūm now. You must say, 'Bring the quadruped!'" †

"No, no," sings out Tajoo; "animal—animal—that's what we must call it." ‡

Here is a difficulty at once, and they consult on this crisis. Then Alishah, as spokesman, calls out in a firm voice, as of one delivering an ultimatum, "Oh, Hussein, sit down the donkey!" §

And the wretched Hussein, who was a genuine coast Balūch, was henceforth assaulted in every conceivable kind of mangled language.

Our next day's march was a most interesting one to Jagīn, a village with a fort belonging to Chiragh Khan, a gentleman whom we shall meet further on.

Soon after leaving camp we passed through a narrow defile, on either side of which were remains of considerable fortifications. We were informed that here, about ten years ago, there had been a grand battle. A large band of Bampūri Balūchis and Persian soldiers, accompanied by what Carlyle would have called a Tolpatchery of Lasharis, under Mīr Ahmedi, had got thus far on their way to plunder Mināb. Here they were met and signally defeated by the Mินābis, assisted by levies from the ships in the Mināb creek. It was a curious natural pass, the bed of the stream being from one hundred to one

---

* Balūchi: "Karra biār."

† Persian: "Charwar biar."

‡ Arabic: "Haiwan."

§ Mixture of Hindustani and Persian: "Charwar bito."

hundred and fifty yards wide, and just here cutting through a perpendicular wall of rock a hundred yards thick and about thirty yards high. We were surprised to find here a cormorant and two specimens of a snipe.

The valley which we were ascending gradually opened out, and instead of scrambling over rocky ground covered with shingle, we were trudging over a fertile alluvium, and constantly meeting with proofs of man's presence. Now it was a herd of cows cropping the sweet grass along the stream edge; and once we passed a party of men beating out the seeds of indigo plants.

At 11.22 a stream called the Seruken joined ours from the east, making at the junction a large triangular area of the richest land. Soon we reached the date plantations of Sarnay, and crossed a valley of fertile grass of the kind called "kik," or, in some parts, "female pampas." This is only fit for cows to eat, and just here the few inhabitants are large cow-owners. There are here some fine, tall spreading trees, called by the natives "jam" trees, which, I regret exceedingly, I was unable to identify, and which I never saw again. They are the finest trees in the country, and in the distance resemble ash-trees. The fruit is described as black, edible, but full of stones. We met one camp "flitting." There were six men, four women, and over a hundred cows, while the mat huts and other property were bound upon two or three steady old bulls. They stared immensely at our caravan, which, though small, presented an imposing sight. Every man was armed to the teeth (except myself), and each walked at the head, and held the rein of, his own particular camel. Abdulla led the van with the big Jaski, and each camel followed in his proper turn. No straggling was allowed; and the man whose load required adjustment on the march, involving a quarter of an hour's stoppage, generally heard of it afterwards.

These and many other little details of march the men had now learnt, though not without difficulty; for they were a wild set, and had never obeyed any one before.

There was now, too, a general good feeling throughout the camp, far better than had been before the decisive affair at Telling. The men were pleased with themselves for having chosen the right course; the road seemed so much easier, and the country so fertile, that they had ceased to dread the journey, and began more and more to rejoice in the prospect of visiting Kirman. So there was a general nose-in-the-air, defiant kind of aspect as they swaggered along, and a tendency to depreciate the new country we had entered upon, and to ridicule everything it contained. On this head they got delightfully snubbed in camp to-night. They had from the outset identified the wretched Hussein with the country through which he was guiding them, and always held him responsible for everything wrong. To-night the water was not to their taste, and they immediately attacked Hussein.

"Ah," he said, coolly; "you must put up with it to-day. Further on it's all right; nothing but melted snow."

There was a general groan and collapse, and it was some time before they attacked him again. Stupid as the old fellow was, he now and then decidedly turned the tables on my impetuous youngsters, and the mention of snow generally sobered them down.

To resume our march, however: at 1.45 the valley opened to about twelve miles in width, mostly studded thickly with kahur trees. We rode through over two hundred acres of newly ploughed land, which was so good as to yield fair crops every alternate year, though most corn-land in this country is only sown once in three years. Further on we passed a drove of over two hundred donkeys, who seemed to thrive very well indeed on the rather dry grass. We passed also to-day the first of very many flocks of snow-white sheep and goats. There were about three thousand, all covered with the same thick glossy hair, the goats only being distinguishable from the sheep by the different shape of their horns. They all produced the soft, long down called kurk, which is exported in small quantities from Bandar Abbas for the purpose of mixing with the wool of which Kashmir shawls are made. Even at Bandar Abbas it realizes from two shillings to half a crown per seven pounds. This fine silky down grows out amongst the wool, and can be combed off with the fingers.

The men in charge of these sheep were the first Iliauts we had yet met, and pointed out as their home a little green clump of date palms, just visible, nestling at the foot of the mountain range that fringed the western edge of the plain upon which they pastured their flocks.

At 2.50 p.m. we reached a large rain-pool, and finding fodder for the camels plentiful, we camped. I shot here starlings identical with the English species, as verified by Professor Newton, and larks which appeared to be the same as the English skylark. The fort of Jagīn was on the skirts of the hills, and out of the line of march.

Next morning, loading up at 7.50 a.m., we passed through the Jagīn village of about forty houses, of the same shape as thatched cottages in England, and saw nearly a hundred men engaged in reaping about thirty acres of millet.

From where we were now, the plain, down the middle of which we were travelling, seemed to be oval-shaped, and our course to point to the thin end of it. We were hemmed in on the right by the lofty hills of Bashakard, and on the left by a similar wall of hills, which had no definite name. I was amused at the reply of one of the shepherds, of whom I had asked, "What is there behind that range?" "Oh," he answered, "there's another country"; then, evidently expecting that I was under the impression that the range was the edge of the world, he added: "The world is very broad here."

We were off by 8 a.m. on the 26th, and *en route* for Manujan, of which place Hussein had long been singing the praises. As yesterday we had commenced the march over fine earth and ended on coarse sand, so now we began on coarse sand, gradually increasing to fine shingle, and then large shingle.

At 1.28 p.m. we entered the thin end of the oval I have before mentioned. The pass was about two miles wide and very hot, while the shingle, which would seem to have all come from these rocks here, became absolute boulders, very trying to the camels' feet. The pass gradually narrowed, and at last we had to climb through a narrow cleft in a wall of rock.

As we emerged we saw a most lovely view. We were on a sort of island of bare massive purple rock. Before us lay, as it were, an oval lake of rough boulders, quite flat, and unrelieved by tree or shrub. But to the right was a broad green line of feathery tamarisk, fringing and hanging over a beautiful dark blue river. The blue sparkling water, and the soft green of the trees, formed such a contrast to the rocky plain, and was so refreshing that I sat till my caravan was far ahead; not exactly staring at it, but feeling a sort of enjoyment at the knowledge that it was there.

We crossed this lake of boulders, having some bother with a huge dry water-course, fifteen feet deep, and with very steep sides; and by another cleft in a second natural rock barrier, we got into another but smaller boulder lake, about half a mile in diameter.

Out of this we struggled through a path which without blasting materials would fairly stop any artillery unless carried on camel back, and which, though widening a little at about four feet from the ground, proved a severe trial to my boxes. It was a narrow winding fissure in the rock, with lofty jagged sides, and about half a mile long. The donkey came off worst, for the fissure was hardly a foot wide at the bottom, and the camels' height raised them well up into the broader part. The tent stuck fast for a long time, but we eventually got through on to a valley covered with kŭnār trees and passing round to the south of a small volcanic-looking mountain we camped upon the lovely plain of Manujan. Behind was a date grove and a handsome little wood of kahur, while in the stream in front of the tent I found the English potamogeton, which I had not seen since I had left Lincolnshire. I received visits from the head men of the huge ruined fort, and after they had got over their astonishment I found them civil and intelligent.

There are three roads hence to Marz, and thence they join and make one to Anguhran; probably the one by which the Muhassil had travelled.

After the interview I got one of the men to come with me up to the top of the rock and name for me the various mountains.

It was a grand view. The plain, here green with waving grass, here brown with ploughed land, and there yellow with the stubble of last year's crop, stretched away to the east for twenty miles. Beyond that ran the Ginou mountains, looking at this distance like a continuous range, though in reality this is a long and more or less fertile valley reaching to Bampūr. With the sweetwater Manujan stream running across it, besides the Halīr and others, it was a noble patrimony, and it all belonged to that clever drunken scoundrel Chiragh Khan. I thought that with a couple of thousand a year this would be a charming place. I would purchase sixty or seventy miles of this valley, repair the old fort, keep a small army, preserve the neighbouring mountains for the shooting, and with a cargo of books now and then from Mināb one could begin to enjoy oneself. The wheat here is a good sample, the wool is unsurpassed, and the already fine quality of the dates might be much improved with a little attention. The only difficulty would be to arrange matters with the present possessor.

Next morning, the 27th of November, we wound past the fort, and across much cultivated ground and immense thickets of stunted kahūr which here grew like oak scrub, and after a short march we camped literally in a twenty acre "plough-field," studded like a park with magnificent kahūr trees, the branches of which swarmed with wood-pigeons.

The few people were a fat Persian-looking race, who could do nothing but grumble at the heavy taxes and beg for medicine.

I was very busy mapping and writing that afternoon; so I put a guard at the tent door, with instructions to make every one wait till evening. When the appointed time came, Ghulamshah brought out my armchair and medicine chest, and I proceeded to examine my patients. As usual, they were nearly all perfectly well and hearty, and had only come for medicine from a sort of feeling that it was a good thing to have and that it was gratuitous. One man indeed did tell me that he had "a boil upon his soul," and two others were ophthalmic; but after that, the remainder, to the number of fourteen, were in such case as I myself could only envy hopelessly. So we made the fourteen squat in a row, and I made them a little speech. I began by pointing out that they all appeared to be suffering from the same disease, and all from the same cause. They had all evidently overworked themselves, they had too much taxes to pay, and they did not get enough to eat. To this they all assented eagerly, murmuring among themselves, "He is a doctor without doubt." I then went on to say that this sort of thing was unknown in my country, and we had consequently no medicine for it (how the faces fell!); but that during my last visit to Mekka, the holy and sainted man Syed Abdulla, of whom they had doubtless heard (they would not own that they had not), had given me a small bottle of an elixir which he assured me was made with the water of Zemzem, and was infallible in such cases as theirs. I explained that this was too holy a thing to be sold, and that I should give it them free as I had received it, only I begged that they would not pollute it by touching it with their hands, but would simply open their mouths. There was some discussion at this, and I nearly spoilt the whole by laughing outright as I caught sight of Brahim peeping from behind the tent in a state of perfect coma from astonishment. Ghulamshah had a sore tongue for two days afterwards from trying to keep from laughing; but at last the consultation came to an end, and our patients had decided to accept the holy remedy.

They were got into a row with their mouths open, and Ghulamshah went gravely round with a bottle of croton oil and a match. Dipping the match into the bottle, he dropped a drop upon each man's tongue.

I never saw such a variety of expressions in my life. There was the man whose turn came next, with his mouth wider open than ever, and snorting with anxiety. The man who had just had it, squeezing his lips together swallowing it down, and looking round at all the other faces to see what they thought of it; and there was one lanky goat-bearded old man who came up just as it was beginning, and who consequently did not understand the operation, and who would peer into the bottle each time, and then peer into the man's mouth as he received it, and then plant himself opposite him and watch him curiously, as if he expected him to burst or come out all over spots.

I believe we all enjoyed this each in his own peculiar way, and always afterwards the mere mention of Ab-i-

Zemzem (*water of Zemzem*) sent the men into a broad smile.

I have forgotten to mention that I had brought from Jagīn a poor unfortunate young fellow the whole of whose right arm was one running sore. He could not sleep for the burning pain, and his stomach revolted against even the best food that could be procured for him. His mother described, with tears in her eyes, how but a year ago he was the most active man in the whole camp; and now, for no fault, there he was rotting away before her eyes. On examining the sore I found nothing that looked very fatal, and thought that could the blood but be brought right it would heal. On looking at his tongue, however, I was horrified to find his whole throat eaten away, and began to fear I had done wrong in touching him. But it was no good abandoning the case now; so I took off a lot of foul old bandages of lime and ghee, washed him carefully, and bound him up with lint and abundance of zinc ointment. He was much exhausted by the pain of the operation, but by the aid of an opiate I gave him he had a good night's rest, and appeared so much stronger in the morning that I was encouraged to allow his request to accompany me; and after a tolerably hearty meal on four eggs, "rumbled," he mounted an old black donkey which had had one ear cut off for trespassing on corn-fields, and accompanied our caravan. The man was so little trouble and so very grateful, and began to heal so well, that when two more men proposed to accompany me from Sar Kahur I willingly agreed, and I afterwards had reason to know that I had been more indebted to my cripple troop for confidence, civility, and even forbearance from attack, than to all our guns and shields put together.

On the 28th we were on march by 8.12 a.m., and striking nearly east across the head of the plain in order to get round a spur of the range to the west. The plain seemed to be alive with charz or bustard, and I mounted the mahri and made a *detour* to get a shot; but they all cowered at my approach, and I could neither see nor flush a single one. I got a handsome old fox though, who was probably sneaking about on the same errand as myself.

At noon we entered a small range of high shingly mounds which ran across the north end of the plain, and at 1.40 p.m. camped amongst some very extensive date-trees, just in time to get observations for longitude before the sun got behind clouds for the rest of the day.

There were no people or huts at Bargah, the owners of the date groves having probably, now that the date harvest was over, gone to plough up their wheat land.

There is a picturesque rapid stream running through the place, and the number of kabg (*partridges*) was something astounding. They were kuk-kukking away, just fifty yards from the tent, like so many young guinea fowl.

Presently, in peeped the good-natured, black-bearded face of Tajoo, who looked significantly at me, and showed a gun in each hand.

I was obliged to turn out, and found about thirty fine males in an open space, strutting round, bowing, and behaving generally like the pinnated grouse do in a "scratching place" in America: I do not know whether this has been observed in any of the "perdrix" tribe before. The kabg is identical with *perdrix rufus.*

After shooting a brace as they ran before me like barn-door fowls (nothing on earth will flush them towards evening), I left him to provide supper and returned to camp.

Next morning when we started, the thermometer standing at 47° warned us that we were getting into colder regions. Soon after leaving, we crossed a curious low ridge called the Ab washur, or turning of waters, and hence it is credibly asserted that water flows south to Mināb and north to Kahnu.

At 10 a.m. we passed the Garaki hills, of whose inhabitants we had been constantly warned to be on our guard. They are professional robbers, and work with impunity, being of the same family as Nur-eddīn Khan, governor of Kahnu.

The Garaki hills are an imposing mass of rock about six hundred feet high, about two miles long, of a rusty iron colour. The strike is north and south, and dip east about sixty degrees. There was one solitary tree visible near its summit; but otherwise it looked utterly desolate and inaccessible to man.

After a steady easy march with occasional showers, at 1 p.m. we struck a low-lying shingly plain covered with petto bushes, which we had not seen since leaving the coast, and at 3 p.m. we passed some curious green marble tombstones, of which more hereafter, and finally pitched our tent a little below the large village of Kahnu.

CHAPTER X.

Kahnu.—"Your is have some spirits."—A poor slave.—Irrigation.—Difficulties as a doctor.—The Haliri river.—Butter unexpectedly.—Washing clothes.—Dosari.—Camp in a graveyard.—Nasir Khan.—His brutish secretary.—Persian tax-collectors.—An indigenous pointer dog.—Our new guide.—The "exalted places" are unable to make good their position.—Thoughts of home.—Dasht-i-Kuch.—Persian carpets.

KAHNU is a place of considerable importance, being, as the governor expressed it, "on the road to everywhere." It lies at the confluence of three broad shallow valleys from the north, south, and west.

If the reader will imagine himself in the middle of the junction of the valleys, and will face due east, he will see dotted thickly over the face of the slope before him some four hundred good-sized oblong yellow reed huts, in the centre of which near the top he will observe a large space enclosed by a mud-wall, and containing the three or four somewhat bigger huts of the chief himself. Quite at the summit of the slope, and in a most imposing position, stand the ruins of a considerable fort.

The whole valley is, as is natural with such an admirable drainage, very fertile indeed, and produces besides wheat, mulberries, and dates, the valued red dye Runask. The houses are large and strongly built, the frame-work being of fasces of strong cane-like reeds, and the whole covered with pīsh matting.

It is a somewhat busy place, supporting three traders, who, however, generally come here from Kirman on their way to the coast for further stores, and the goods they sell here are mostly such as will not go down anywhere else. The result is that young fellows go about in a perfect burlesque of the ordinary Persian dress. I saw one who had dressed himself up to visit me, a description of whose costume will suffice. He had the ordinary white calico trowsers, but his coat was of bright pink broadcloth, embroidered with black imitation lace, and he had managed to make the full skirts stick out almost horizontally all round him, presenting much the appearance of an overgrown little girl of forty years ago, with a new dress on. The men here wear the same sort of two-thirds Persian dress that seems universal throughout the whole of this long valley, running between the high table-land of Persia and the mountain range along the coast.

Supplies were difficult to obtain at Kahnu, and I find in my note-book an indignant remark, "Pay a halfpenny for an egg, and if you want it under a month old you must take reserved hens."

Very late in the evening, when busy working out dead reckoning, Chiragh Khan was introduced. He had a fine, intelligent face, and was very tall and well-made. He was accompanied by a tribe of servants, and one man, a kind of secretary, was a pink and pimply creature in complete Teheran costume. The Khan spoke Balūchi very well, and entered into conversation with Brahim, in which he showed such intimate familiarity with all and each of the extremely intricate degrees and kinds of feudal clanship or kinship, that I at once decided that he must have been a Balūch.

While this was going on, what was my astonishment to hear from the pimply man in broken Hindustani, "Sahib, have you got any spirits?" * I chaffed him a little by pretending not to know what he meant; when suddenly his master said in an aside, "Pour out," and he quickly drew from his pocket a large quart bottle of brandy, and a brass saucer, in which he poured out for his chief a liberal peg.

When the Khan had drunk this, he received a large piece of gauze as a handkerchief, and then a sweet-meat. The secretary then proceeded to help himself, and *then* it was offered to me.

This was too much. Not content with boring me by calling in the middle of the night, they must come with a bottle of brandy in their pockets, and give unmistakable signs of intending to finish it in my tent. I got up, and I said they might go. And when they rose to go, I told them what I thought of them.†

I am afraid the Kahnuites must have thought me a very violent-tempered creature, for next morning I had a blow-up with the old man Nur-eddīn Khan himself. I found out afterwards that it was fever that had made me so irritable, though of course at the time itself I thought that I was calm and even-tempered.

But Nur-eddīn Khan had arranged for me to visit him at 9 a.m. And I was anxious to be as punctual as possible, so as to get some observations of the sun

---

* Verbatim: "Tumhare daru pas hai." (*Your is have some spirits.*)

† "Nur-u-Din's brother, Chiragh Khan, is an open and unmistakable drunkard."—*Extract from a paper read before the Royal Geographical Society, by Sir Frederic Goldsmid, Jan.* 27, 1873.

before starting. After 9 a.m. the sun rapidly got so high as to be of little use. Of course, however, as the hour approached, the mihmandar (*guest-receiver*), who was to be introducer, began to make excuses, "The Khan was asleep," etc., etc. "You had better go and rout the son of a burnt father out," I said; "for if I'm not in the majlis by 9 a.m., I shan't be there at all," and I sent him off to the Khan.

The desired effect was produced. In less than five minutes, down came another mihmandar, much more respectably dressed, and evidently of much higher authority, who said that the first man was a fool, and was now being beaten for his impertinence (a lie), and begged me to come to the majlis at once.

It was but a short interview, for I was ill-tempered, and snubbed the Khan in every way, and moreover, I was anxious to get back to the sun.

With reference to last night's affair with his brother, he made a kind of semi-apology, saying that he thought the Feringis drank spirits. I replied curtly that the lower classes and the women did. He mentioned the visit five years ago of Ma-jor Gen-eral Goulmit, a name he had evidently taken much trouble to learn, for he pronounced each syllable as a separate word. I acknowledged Sir Frederic, but affected to disbelieve the visit.* After a little more of such conversation, a fat, jovial merchant, who sat on the Khan's left hand, and who was anxious to obtain from me a bottle of eye-wash without payment, whispered,

* I had now struck, and for four or five days I followed the route taken by the Mission of 1872, under Major-General Sir Frederic Goldsmid.

"His heart is black, they used him very badly last night."

I had made my point, which was to show my displeasure at my treatment last night, and became more amiable, gave a sketch of the Russian and Turkish nations (between whom war was at this time impending), and before the Khan had time to recover himself, bade him farewell, put myself at the head of my procession, and marched off to my camp. Orders were given to load up smartly, while I took the sun and received four or five of the leading men of the place.

I cannot omit to mention one poor fellow, a slave of almost pure African blood. He was so fearfully emaciated that he could hardly stand; yet he had no appearance of disease. He said he was dying of starvation, and I really believe he was. His story was that he had belonged to Ahmed Khan, a relation to Chiragh Khan. Ahmed Khan had come to Kahnu to hunt with Chiragh Khan, bringing this boy as his groom. The boy fell ill, and failing in some feat of activity which seriously affected Ahmed Khan's chance in the hunt, he had been beaten so much that he could not stand. When he could walk again, he found Ahmed Khan gone. He was perfectly destitute. No one would employ him, for he was still Ahmed Khan's slave, and no one would give him food without work.

I referred to my friendly merchant who was standing by, and was still friendly, his bottle of eye-wash being as yet in my pocket. Save that he did not know what fault the boy had committed, he substantially corroborated the story.

And I said, "Do you mean to say that this boy is dying quietly before every one, and not one will give him a piece of bread? Verily and by God, you are Muslims every one of you, and if you don't get to heaven and enjoy its fullest delights, then there is neither faith in God nor His prophet." I shouted to my men, who by this time had loaded the camels and stood around, each one at his camel's head waiting for the route. "Oh Balūchis," I said, "now we have indeed left behind us our own country, and entered that of the noble and powerful Gajars. Last night you saw the chief of this country as drunk as a female pig, and now you see a son of man starving in the midst of strong fat men because he is too ill to work."

"Ah, miskīn bīchāra (*Ah, poor helpless creature*), I've got some bread," said two or three immediately, producing their food for the route. But the poor fellow couldn't eat bread, so Ghulamshah fed him with alternate sips of tea from my road bottle and bites of a hardboiled egg. In five minutes Brahim was holding him on in front of him on his camel, and we marched out of Kahnu.

We passed down the valley through numerous plantations of date-trees with extensive and good irrigation.

I got into conversation with a rough old labouring man whom I found regulating the water supply, by damming up this rivulet and cutting open that with a long-handled spade. He lived in a hut near which we afterwards camped. He had never been into the town, as he called Kahnu, and looked upon its inhabitants as altogether a superior race, amongst whom he would be quite out of place. He and his two sons were responsible for all the water leads of two or three miles of date-trees, not having only to keep them in order, but to lay out and plan the whole system of irrigation. It is curious what a low place agriculture, or any employment requiring unskilled manual labour, holds in this country.

At 3 p.m. we came to a plain covered with the most luscious trāt (*caroxylon fœtidum*), which was such a find for the camels that we halted at once and camped on the spot that they might get a good stomach full.

Here the agriculturist brought me his daughter. She appeared to have a kind of *phlegmasia dolens*, and both her legs were swollen and as hard as wood, while a pain in her chest was such that she could never sleep. I could do nothing with her but give her an opiate to get her one night's rest. The poor parents were profuse in their gratitude, and left praying that I might eventually arrive at the unspeakable bliss of being buried at Karbala.

I must here explain in self-defence, that over and over again I had to give medicine, and even receive payment for it, in cases where it was perfectly useless. It was impossible to persuade people that I did not know what was the matter with them, or that I had no medicine which would do them any good. It was in vain that I would point out as forcibly as possible, thus :—

" You admit that you have been suffering from this disease for twenty years, and yet you come to me and expect me to cure it in one minute. The God that has afflicted you with this disease, has not given to me the power to take it away by merely looking at you or touching you."

It was impossible to make them believe a word of this or anything like it, and they would go on praying and beseeching for "just one little drop of medicine," "only just give one look at him or touch him," in a way that made one miserable.

Then they would go away and bring perhaps a bowl of sour milk, very probably all the food the family had for the day; and if I persisted in my inability, they would say sorrowfully, "What can we poor things do? we can bring nothing else." The only reason to which they could ascribe my refusal was that I wanted a higher price.

I found at last the only way, in cases beyond my reach, was to say that I feared I could do no good, but they should have the best medicine I had, and we would remember that God was merciful.

The man with the rotten arm, who had come from Jagīn, was now fairly convalescent, and with many expressions of gratitude he started back home. He took a note to the doctor of the telegraph staff at Jask, explaining the treatment that had been pursued, and two others to friends in England. Either his gratitude failed him, or he had a relapse and could not undertake the Jask journey, but the letters never arrived, and are I suppose to this day wandering about Balūchistan, the wonder of all beholders.

Next morning we were *en route* by 7.30 a.m., and at 1 p.m. crossed the famous Halīri river. It was now a rapid rushing stream thirty yards wide, with an average depth of 4½ feet. It was a beautiful river, fringed on either side by dense thickets of tamarisk, willow, pampas grass, and reeds; while the scene was enlivened by numbers of magpies, cormorants, and tall stately herons, while innumerable black partridges filled the bushes.

Where this fine stream goes to, as also where the Bampūr river goes, has still to be determined. It only remains for some one to travel direct through the Rudbar country, say from Kahnu to Bampūr, with a slight detour south, to disclose this mystery. Meanwhile I may be allowed the theory that they unite and reach the coast by what is there called the Sadaich river, which I know for certain originates north of the mountains through which it comes by the Shimsāni pass. The extent of the sandy desert about latitude 27° and longitude 59° has, I feel sure, been very much exaggerated, it being generally described as spreading over much country which I have reason to believe is very fertile. Two such streams of sweet water as the Halīr and the Bampūr could not be lost in the sand so near together without producing an immense area of fertile swampy country. One of my people spent the whole of his childhood in wandering about the Rudbar country, and remembers well both the rivers far beyond the present limits of European exploration.

I would not wish to quote his reminiscences as an authority in matters requiring scientific accuracy, but had these two streams both sunk underground in or near the same place, the result must have been a swamp, fertile ground, or anything but a desert. His notion agrees with mine (though perfectly independently formed), that they find their way to the sea either by the Gabrig or the Sadaich.

To-day was a long march, as we had started at 7.30 a.m., and it was not till 5 p.m. that we camped by the side of an underground stream, under a huge kŭnār tree.

Here we discovered that a skin of fresh milk which we had purchased at Kahnu, had, from the jolting motion of the camel, turned to butter. By adding a little warm water to the contents, and giving it a vigorous shaking, we not only obtained about a pound and a half of beautiful butter, but more than a gallon of delicious buttermilk.

It is curious that while the only luxury a Balūch has is milk, he should never use it in any of the three forms of it which we do. Fresh milk, cream, or fresh butter, a Balūch will never touch, except, perhaps, he might use the latter to grease that pride of his heart, his hair. Fresh milk he instantly "búnds," or turns into a sour jelly. He does this either by putting into it some sour milk from a former brew, or by the juice of various herbs which he knows by experience. Milk thus prepared is call "māst." It only becomes properly sour on the second day, when with a little salt and pepper it is the most nourishing food that can be desired. We used, each and all of us, to eat immense quantities when we got a chance.

Now in the present case we had fresh milk and bunded it ourselves; but, having to travel in the middle of the operation, the milk was no sooner bunded than it got churned too. This was the first time we had got beyond the māst stage. The māst was always too tempting, and was immediately devoured. However, in this case, we churned it.

Now, we ate the butter, but a Balūch would boil it down to roghān (better known by the Hindustani name "ghee"), keep it in a leather skin, and squeeze a little into his dough when making bread, or into anything else he may be cooking. Roghān is the grand luxury of Balūch life, and of any country where hot suns and dry winds have to be encountered. To welcome a friend, a man opens the string of his grease skin. It is the first thing that goes empty in hard times, and the first thing he gets filled when fortune begins to shine again. To be without it, is dry bread and water. To have it, is bread and butter, buttered toast, tea with cream in it, etc.

But from the butter manufacture is left the butter-milk, called "dōgh." This is boiled, and the remainder is "luch"; this is pressed and dried, and becomes "shilanch," or in Persian, "kashk," a hard white biscuit of very sour cheese. This is powdered, and, boiled with savoury herbs, is very palatable.

These are the main divisions of Balūch dairy farming, but there are many other stages, each called by some local name, and the pride of some special camp, just as in England each dairy wife has her own peculiar way of arriving at universal results.

We are, however, still camped under a spreading ziziphus, near a stream or line of water-holes, which divides the districts of Kahnu and Dosāri.

This evening, Brahim Muhammad set the example of washing his clothes in the stream, and the rest, fearing unfavourable comparison, were compelled to do the same. A Balūch of the highest family will wash his own clothes, but it is the manner that makes the difference. With him, there is no squatting down on haunches in an undignified position, and rubbing awkwardly with both hands. No. His garments are four in number: strong cotton drawers, fitting close from below the knee, and neatly embroidered in red by his eldest wife; over these, a long cotton shirt, also embroidered at the neck, breast and cuffs; a large turban and a thick cotton plaid complete his equipment, while for the march he puts on gun, sword, shield, pistol and sandals. In his saddle-bags are a duplicate of each garment, but unfortunately it is so long since we have camped near a suitable stream that all want washing.

The mode of proceeding is this: each chooses to himself a pool, always near enough to his comrades for friendly conversation and banter, and tying his turban round his waist, he puts his clothes over his arm, and descends into the water. Standing erect, he takes the extreme end of some garment in his hand, and swinging it over his head brings it down flop, with all his force on the water. A party of these fellows make a noise like a general engagement. When sufficiently clean, they squeeze the garment tolerably dry, and at once put it on. And even further north in the cold weather, they took a pride in keeping up this custom; and sometimes afterwards, with the thermometer at 45°, I have found them going about with simply their wet cotton garments on.

Here was plenty of ardūr, and had we but known it, this was the last really good feed my camels were destined to have. While passing through a small thicket of kahur, we suddenly came upon a small herd of most magnificent looking camels. Their huge bodies and short colossal legs, and more than all, their tremendous shaggy coats of tawny wool, took us all aback with astonishment. To our unaccustomed eyes they were perfect polar giants, and I looked askance at my tall lanky smooth-coated wiry-haired animals, and wondered how they would stand the tremendous cold we expected. I lagged behind, and got into conversation with the herdsman. These monsters were mere youngsters, not yet put to burden! They were from Kirman, and whole troops more were shortly expected. It was the custom for all up country camels to spend the three or four spring months in the plain of Jiruft, eating the succulent ardūr.

"Would my camels eat dough?" he asked, "they would have to be fed upon dough as soon as I crossed the mountains."

I questioned him closely.

"Was there no place where any sūrag, mihishk, or other salt grass grew?"

"No," he said, it was all "dirmonah," (a wretched little strong scented plant which nothing but donkeys will touch). I might find some "puzhelle" (a caroxylon?); but in that country the seasons were different, and everything died in winter.

The man's conversation was not cheering, and I gave him a kran and rode on.

Next day we were at Dosāri by 2 p.m., a very Persian-looking village, one house boasting a "bādgīr" like a church tower. A bādgīr is for the most part a plain square mud tower, but the topmost twelve feet require more description. All four sides are open, so as to allow of the freest access to wind from any quarter. Thin mudplastered walls are built across diagonally from corner to corner, and the wind, thus confined in a V, goes of necessity down into the room below. This is the most expensive kind of wind tower. Others are made in the form of a hood, or the orifice of a snail-shell, with the open end facing whence the prevailing summer wind comes.

We camped near the graveyard, under some broad-spreading kŭnār trees, and close by some gardens and thickets of calotropis. The tombstones were of the same stone as we had seen at Kahnu. Each was a coffin-shaped monolith of a pellucid seagreen stone laid horizontally over the grave and covered with inscriptions mostly of an orthodox Shia nature.

I noticed that when two stones were wanted to form a fireplace, a villager unhesitatingly brought two fragments of tombstones, and I thought to myself, what a fuss there would have been if *I* had sent for two tombstones for such a purpose.

The green marble was quarried in the hills, and exported to Kahnu. Dosāri is a small village of huts and date-trees, scattered in a long line along the foot of the huge snow-clad Jamal Bariz range. The governor, Mīr Nāsir, lives in a burnt brick enclosure with the bādgīrs before mentioned. I had purposely camped some little distance from him; but he soon found me out, and sent me a quantity of roghān, two sheep, and some flour. I sent him a pound of my best "Bygnauth mixture," and a five-pound packet of coffee, here considered a great delicacy. My men made very merry over camping in a graveyard.

"Well," said Brahim Muhammad, "I always knew we should have to sleep in a graveyard some day."

"Oh," cried Alishah, "but this is a perfect enjoyment; we can get buried without being dead!"

"Ah," said Tajoo, "you remember, when you used to say you would die of the cold, the sahib used always to answer, 'Oh, there are plenty of burying grounds.' Now, you know, this is really extremely convenient, and you'd better not lose such an opportunity."

Three or four very amiable men from Kirman, now

visitors to Mīr Nāsir, came and called upon me in the afternoon. They were very polite, and exhibited none of the staring astonishment I had met with at Kahnu, and asked no impertinent questions.

I was busy all that evening doctoring, and was much troubled by an Iliaut family, who were encamped outside the village, in black goats'-hair tents. The father and mother brought me the daughter, a fine, handsome girl of about sixteen, with rosy cheeks, and altogether looking the picture of health. It was, according to the father, a case of the inevitable "bād grifta ast." All natives have their peculiar way of expressing a sickness. Even in England, the Lincolnshire "He's nobbut badly," expresses much more than is seen at first glance.

Among Balūchis, anything the matter with the legs or arms is expressed, "My foot is dry," "My bone is dry." If altogether out of sorts, he will say, "My heart is dry," "My heart and body are dry;" but if his stomach is out of order, he has "bād gipta" (*taken wind*), an expression which is invariably used as an all-sufficient and complete statement of the case: and I used to be utterly exasperated when, in reply to all my queries of "Where does it hurt?" "What's the matter?" etc., I could get only a complacent, "Oh, bād gipta." The expression may have arisen from the great prevalence of indigestion and flatulency induced by the coarse food.

However, in the case of the damsel in question, I gradually localised the disease to her right arm. This I examined carefully, but could find nothing wrong with it, and indeed could only wish I could show such a good arm myself. Appetite was good; but I could not get rid of the old couple. After endless perseverance, I got them to show me some small, roughly circular patches where the skin had simply undergone depigmentation, and which, though of no importance (and even common in Balūchistan), were a bar to her being sought in marriage. How these people expected me to find out these spots from their telling me first that she had "bād gipt," and then that she had a bad arm, I cannot say, but they did expect it.

Next morning the Khan came to call upon me on rather a screw of a horse, but with its mane and tail knotted in the most accurate manner. He was immensely polite, said but little, and said he was very deaf, a statement which might or might not have been true. A young fellow with a handsome open face and brown curling moustache accompanied him, and did most of the talking. This was a lieutenant who had brought a message from the Wakil-al-Mulk at Kirman, whither he shortly intended to return. He readily gave me much information about the road, but said I should take weeks to get my poor camels there. There was, moreover, no fodder after Dasht-i-Kuch, and unless my camels could eat chopped straw they would starve. He himself was travelling with one servant, and both were well mounted on strong horses.

The matter of no fodder was rather awkward, as every one agreed that the only camels that ever came across the mountains came and went empty merely for a run "at grass," and that these camels were all trained to subsist on balls of dough, which none of my camels would touch.

The conduct of my men here was gratifying. They heard that all camels required warm clothing for the mountain journey, and as they were led to water I saw each man had strapped his "bālbālak," or hairy-hairy, on the back of his camel, thus voluntarily depriving themselves of one of their two felt coverings just when they began to want them. It was partly from pride roused by the idea that their cherished Balūchi līros could not go where other camels did; but I was grateful to them, and shook old Brahim warmly by the hand. They began already to feel something like a countryman in London, and while being extra truculent and scornful in their bearing towards the Persians, were more than ever willing and devoted to their "waja," myself.

We had a short audience with the Khan, and saw something of "splendour and barbaric gold." The walls of the room we waited in were covered with the most beautifully executed mouldings in the finest plaster of Paris. But here and there in niches a small bent piece of copper had been stuck full of stinking castor oil; these lamps making above them a huge black smear, and below them a sort of permanent dribble of oil.

The cook came in to make the tea, and *did* make it with great swagger. He had begged, borrowed, or stolen a new green coat for the occasion, but he had not taken off his old shirt, the filthy state of which language is feeble to describe. Some of the servants going about the yard were in absolute rags.

We had to wait some time, and were much bored by the governor's secretary, who came and sat with us, evidently with the idea of getting some information about us. He was the last man I should have chosen as a confidant, being an uncouth brute who spoke always in a kind of yell. He set upon me first with a brutish impudence; but after listening in silent scorn to a string of questions, such as "Where do you come from?" "How much money have you?" "Are those your camels?" etc., I turned from him and addressed the assembly. "And where," I asked, "did you discover this kind of beast, with a voice like an ass and a smell like a camel?" That choked him off for a time, but soon he was asking Brahim how much pay I gave him. Brahim was very modest on such subjects, and readily confused; so I had to snub him again, saying that, judging from the appearance of the present company, Brahim was much better off than any of them.

Soon the Khan came in fresh from the bath, paring his nails and bowing in every direction. He sat at a large open bay window looking over the courtyard, an arrangement which enabled him to receive private communications from one side without the people on the other hearing. He seemed immensely busy, opening note after note, and either writing answers himself or dictating them to the braying secretary. The notes were all simply accounts of taxes paid in or not paid in, and generally ran as follows:—After compliments, "Mahomed Taki has paid in nine tomāns more, and promises three tomāns more when his brother comes back from Kirman." "Ah," says the Khan to his secretary, "Mahomed Taki—thirty-seven tomāns, isn't it? Tell him the Diwan requires the money immediately. (To the assembly) What am I to do? The Government insists on my paying twice as much as I can, and these men must pay up."

By attending to the conversation, I find that my

friend the lieutenant is the third messenger sent from Kirman to get the annual tribute from him. The first two have failed, and he fails also. The wily old Khan with his deaf ear for ever puts them off. But he is playing a deep and dangerous game. He has got a year's taxes secreted somewhere, and declares he hasn't a penny. But he has a wise man to deal with in the Wakil-al-Mulk, and must play his cards carefully and well. If he can get away with this money, he will be able by its power as a bribe to obtain another and a far richer governorship, perhaps from the Wakil-al-Mulk himself, who will accept the inevitable and wait till his turn comes. Mīr Nāsir knows his own game, but plays with his life in his hands. The Wakil-al-Mulk will get the hidden money *as a bribe*, and the very success of the stratagem will prove its author's fitness for a higher post. But should he fail, let him look to himself.

This is an ordinary every-day occurrence, and, in fact, fairly well represents the process by which the taxes are levied. A Persian will suffer anything sooner than pay money. There is a feeling of shame connected with it, a feeling of being outwitted. It is quite a taunt to tell a Persian he has paid money away, and he never boasts of how much money he has spent on anything. "Base is the slave that pays," would be rendered in Persia, "Fool is the slave who pays."

And if it is difficult for the accomplished petty governor to get the money out of the more ignorant agriculturists who live under his thumb, how much more difficult is it for the governor of a province to get his money out of his subordinates who live a hundred miles away, and who are as skilled as he is in lying and all arts of intrigue.

I shall show in a future chapter how the system affects the agriculturist himself.

There were six or seven well-to-do looking farmers sitting round the majlis, and the lieutenant, though maintaining the utmost courtesy towards the Khan, now and then held whispered conversations with one or other of them. These farmers, with whom the petty governor communicates direct, lend seed and bullocks for ploughing, and in general lead all the operations. They have a blunt clumsiness of manner, much like some of their representatives in England.

I was much surprised to see lying in the yard what was to all appearance a genuine English liver and white pointer. On inquiry I found that he was indigenous to the country, of a distinct breed called "tolah,"* and used for the same purposes as an English pointer. He was a handsome dog, but looked as if he would train soft.

Guides were promised to Kirman, and returning to camp we prepared for march. Poor old Hussein, the much-bullied and long-suffering, was sent back with his waistband full of krans, and a letter to Durgosh, giving him a good character, which he showed great disposition to tie round his arm as a "tawiz," or charm.

Our new guide did not turn up, so we started without him over a sandy plain covered with trāt, petto, and kahur, and with an occasional patch of wheat

* "Tolah," corruption of "tora," a jackal, which animal in Balūchistan is called "tolag."

and barley. At three our guide joined us, breathless with running, and driving before him three or four donkeys.

He was such a specimen as is rarely seen out of Persia. Apparently about seventeen years old, he was nearly six feet high, immensely broad, with huge fleshy limbs, and a round pink and white face, as of a somewhat dishonest cherub. This fellow in England would have been a lout, but here not a bit; he had a fine free movement, and though regarded by the men as an overgrown infant, he did our trifling six hours' walking a day with the greatest ease. We were now marching up a sort of arm of the plain, about forty miles broad, and heading for a spot north-west, were we could commence to climb the huge wall of the Jamal Bariz hills.

During the march, we crossed two or three foot-paths, betokening an amount of inhabitants which we were quite unaccustomed to. But indeed this whole fertile plain of Jiruft is inhabited at, from a rough estimate, the rate of about a village of 200 people to every ten miles square.

At 3.50 p.m. our cherub called a halt in a thicket of kahur trees, by the side of a clear artificial rivulet of sweet water. It was rather a short march, and a little bird whispered that our friend had business of his own at a village near, and I called him up and warned him of the consequences which would ensue on his trying to deceive us. His speech was absurdly flowery. I was never less than a "majesty of exalted place," and even the men were all "exalted places," a thing they chuckled grimly over. When, however, they tried to assume this lofty position with regard to him, in such matters as fetching wood and water for the camp, our clever friend left them very far to leeward. They always chose their times badly, just when he was on the point of saying his prayers.

The men were thoughtful to-night. The sandy plain, the thickets of tamarisk and kahur, swarming with partridges and francolins—all made it seem like home. It was Bahomadi;—it was Jagīn;—it was Sūrag; and each man called to mind some particular part of his own dear sandy desert, and imagined himself to be camping there.

To my mind, there is nothing more cheery than the ringing note of the kofinjah (*partridge*), and nothing more homely than the regwar (*francolin*), and I could easily believe I was back again at old Jagīn, camped in the thickets on the river banks, with M——y the other side of the camp-fire, and a day's fun in prospect for to-morrow. Without these two birds, camp-life in Balūchistan certainly would lose some of its charms. In the breeding season they both cry all day, but at other times only mornings and evenings, the kofinjah getting up first, and the aristocratic regwars following about 8 a.m.

Next morning we were away at eight, making very good going over the plain. At 10.30 a.m. we passed a village called Tihūn, where I saw some fine cows, which reminded me strongly of the breed called Bahrein cows, in the Persian Gulf.

It may have been a coincidence only, but our cherub, without my mentioning my idea, gave a long and circumstantial account of these people, stating them to be Arabs from Bahrein.

The word Arab is of course often used in the sense

"wanderers," but the presence of the cows was curious. Here also I noticed several handsome nearly white hawks, of which I could not procure a specimen.

Due west, apparently about forty miles, were the Isfanaka hills, whence the river Halīri is said to rise, It joins the river Shur below the village Surjaz, the Shur being the water outlet of the mountains to W.N.W. of us.

At 12.40 we camped at Dasht-i-Kuch,* a small arm of the plain running into the hills.

Here we found many men who remembered Sir Frederic Goldsmid's mission, and spoke in very kindly manner of the "old but active man who understood the language."

Here they brought many carpets made on the Jiruft plain, but the patterns were all the simple zigzag, the easiest to weave, and the colours were not brilliant. The dyes are brought from Kirman, and we were sorry to find that the cheap non-lasting English dyes, which will sooner or later ruin the Persian

* Since my return I have seen this place mentioned by Sir F. Goldsmid as Dasht-i-Kusht. This, probably more correctly "Dasht-i-Khushk," would mean "the dry plain." With all deference to so eminent an authority, I will retain my own version of the name. It is as I heard it, and its meaning, "plain of the corner," or "corner plain," is more in accordance with its position. Dasht-i-Kuch is in a corner, but is by no means a particularly dry place. While on the subject, I may mention that we differ on the name of the next camp. My guide called it "Sagdir," a word meaning "blackberry," and the name seemed perfectly satisfactory, for here, as nowhere else, the blackberry was twining over every rock, and was, in fact, almost the only shrub in the place. Sir Frederic has "Sakhtdar," meaning "a difficult country." But in an interview he preferred my version of the name.

carpet trade, were here well known. The only points by which the Persian carpets could hope to maintain a place in the English markets, are the intricacy and peculiarity of pattern, and the brilliancy and lasting quality of the dyes which by slow and tedious processes they extract from the Runask and the Zarili. The provincial governors are introducing English and French patterns, and cheap English dyes are so common that, go where you will now to buy carpets, the red colour at least must be carefully tested.

Our friends here prognosticated the worst results from our attempt to cross the mountains in this weather and with such transport; but indeed we were so used to this, that we should have been uneasy had they failed to do so.

What was more to the point, they told us of three or four kahur trees in amongst the hills, and the men were despatched to cut what would give the camels two days' feed.

CHAPTER XI.

WE CROSS THE MOUNTAINS.

The climb commenced.—Sagdir.—An inhabitant.—Mountain scenery by starlight.—The Ushteroon Gudar.—The Bag-i-asp-i-Ismail Khan.—We see our way out of the mountains.—The cherub exhausted.—The Mahri's misadventure.—Flat ground again.—Antiquarian discovery.—Our first caravanserai.—The camels too tall for once.—Snugly ensconced.—Poor Ghulamshah duped once more.—A mill.—The cherub gives trouble.—Puzzling the Persian.—The young lieutenant.—No camel-fodder.—Ridiculously large radishes.—"Lā, hani dilam *hā* abu."—Hospitable reception at Raiūn.—An amusing incident.—The camels break down.—Poison.—A weary delay.—Raiūn.—Kirman illuminated in honour of the Shah having purchased Baghdad.—Persian steel-workers.—Glass-blower.—Remove to the old fort.—*En route* again.—The end of the cherub.

NEXT morning, it was December 5th, we were away on the road by 6.40 a.m., winding along the foot of the hills with a gradual ascent. Soon we travelled along the northern bank of a tributary of the Shur river, which in spite of its name was sweet enough, and, judging from the flocks of large white, and black and white herons, contained numerous fish.

At 8.17 the Surjaz village bore 210, distant 10 miles, and after a laborious two hours' crossing the talus of a huge hill we turned up and the steep ascent began. The road was a shingly stony water-course, flanked on either side by grand cliffs and masses of rock, sparsely covered with shrubs.

Here I had reason to be grateful to Dr. Shaw's "What to observe;" for, acting on his precept, I carefully observed the vegetation on this side of the range, though I never thought of finding such marked and characteristic difference between this side and the other as I did.

One of the shrubs looked exactly like majgūk (capital camel fodder), but it was as bitter as a bitter almond, and useless to us. At 12.27 we reached the first summit, 5,770 feet. Across a shallow valley, and at 1 p.m. reached second summit (bar. 24·45), 5,523 feet. Halt to breathe camels, who snort, rumble, and groan in most heartrending manner. There is a huge mountain just on our right, about 1,500 feet higher than we are, covered with snow. Across another valley, and at 2 p.m. the third summit (bar. 24·5), 5,469 feet. Then we crossed a sheltered valley swarming with droves of kabg (*partridges*). I contented myself, however, with shooting three, being anxious to pay every attention to the road. At 2.30 we forded a rapid rushing, bounding torrent, which, in the reckless way it dashed itself about, seemed to harmonize well with the wild desolate grandeur of the scene around. I got wet through in trying to jump this, for I had stayed behind and was on foot, and I was not sorry when half an hour afterwards our cherub called a camp at Sagdir. A misty rain or rainy mist made everything dim and wet, and our position on the very brink of a chasm forty feet deep was not without its difficulties. Two ibex reluctantly vacated the spot as we arrived, flying like shadowy spirits at a bullet from my Westley Richards. This was the usual place for halting, and two deep but low caves close by had often been used as sleeping places. My men, however, scorned the idea of making jackals of themselves, and slept in the open. There was no fodder, the only tree being an occasional "Ban" (much like *pyrus terminalis*) and the shrubs being blackberries and the omnipresent "badam."

To our surprise, we found little patches of soil cleared of rocks and sown with wheat. The people, it appeared, lived in the plain during the winter, and camped here among these grand hills in the summer. One would think that the very fact of spending half one's life in such scenery and air as this would tend to ennoble the men both physically and mentally; but a specimen who arrived clad in a mass of woollen rags, and who whiningly expostulated with us for letting my donkey crop the young wheat, was not by any means a startling exhibition of physique or intellect.

We had slaughtered a sheep, and as this patch of wheat was the only piece of ground where it was possible to pitch a tent, we compounded with him by giving him a lump of meat for the hire of it. He was much pleased, and left for Maskun, where he said lived the Katkhuda.

The weather cleared up towards evening, and we had a glorious night. I turned out of the tent about nine to look at the thermometers, and saw a scene I shall never forget. Above us, the deep blue sky and clear shining stars; all around, huge black mountains without sign of life, and only awful in their desolate blackness and shadowy immensity. What a contrast to the little nest of warm-hearted, eager-tempered life at my feet. There, in every conceivable attitude, lay my companions; while on the other side of the now smouldering fires knelt the six sturdy camels who had carried our burdens so gallantly, and who were now peacefully "romasting," as the natives call chewing the cud, of their somewhat scanty feed of kahur. I came out with the common practical idea of simply reading the thermometers and making up my mind whether to take a "polaris" or not, but I clean forgot both, and went and turned into bed as happy as possible without doing either.

That night the min. thermometer registered 36°, and the camels, in spite of their felt coats, were shivering with cold.

We were on march by 8 a.m., and at 8.35 reached the summit of the Ushteroon Gudar, or the Camel's Pass, called, I imagine, on the *lucus a non lucendo* principle, for it is fearfully steep for camels. Here the barometer showed 6,780 feet. At 9.30 we passed a sort of oasis in the endless miles of rock in the shape of the Bag-i-asp-i-Ismail * Khan. It is a large grassy mound, and it is related that when Ismail Khan, father of the present governor of Kirman, levelled and widened this road across the mountains, he personally encamped there for many days. As for the road, it is impossible to conjecture what kind of animals travelled it before Ismail Khan's engineers took it in hand. Here the barometer showed 7,250 feet, and away to the west stretched an endless sea of mountains, range after range gradually softening away into distance.

We resisted the cherub's longing to camp at Maskun, but I called a halt just before noon, and in spite of the

---

* "Bag" is Baluchi for a "herd" of camels, etc., but I never heard the word in Persia.

clouds managed to get a very fair meridian observation for latitude, and an hour and a half afterwards one for longitude. Between the two I took a gun and strolled off after some kabg. These exasperating birds, however, would not rise, and ran up all the steepest hills they could find, kuk-kukking away in the oak scrub (as if delighting in my fatigue), and quite using up my patience. I was amply rewarded however, on reaching one hill-top, by finding the whole of that arm of the Jiruft plain up which we had marched from Dosāri spread out before me, and I got some capital cross-bearings of hills which I was fortunately able to identify from outline sketches made when I first saw them.

Higher and higher we went, the barometer at 2 p.m. showing 8,070 feet; at half-past, 9,250 feet; and at three, 9,260 feet; while wet and dry bulbs were 46°, 51°, and a strong cold wind set in from the south-west.

At half-past three we reached our highest point, 9,310 feet, and at last saw our way before us. The road ran north down a short steep descent, and lost itself in the thick oak scrub. Then far below us it re-appeared a dim line leading away across a broad desert plain running east and west, behind which rose a faint purple range called the Darzin hills.

About thirty-five miles to the west, half hidden in the clouds, ran a long dark-blue ridge of mountain. This is the Sardū route from the low-lying Jiruft plain to the high plateau. It joins our route at Raiūn, but owing to its immense altitude above the sea is only practicable in summer, when it is generally preferred as being cooler, more direct, and having two or three caravanserais.

Behind, softened by the mist, lay the ranges we had

just crossed, a sea of hills, here slightly clothed with oak scrub, and spotted now and then by a tall dark cypress tree.

I was on foot, far in advance of my caravan, and sat down to sketch the fine prospect. Presently up came our cherub—but what a cherub! pale, hollow-eyed, languid and breathless, he flung himself down on the ground, and called God to witness that I was killing him.

"But, cherub," I said, half-amused and half-indignant; "you the big, the strong, thus exhausted by a little hill like this?"

"Ah," he said, "but the illustrious majesty doesn't know that this is the second day I have fasted, and that neither water, tobacco, nor bread have gone into my mouth since Dasht-i-Kuch."

I gave him a good "talking to," about the absurdity of keeping fasts on a journey, quoted for him the verse of the Kurān by which fasts are not compulsory on sick people, travellers, etc., and while thus engaged the men's voices were heard and Tajoo appeared leading my riding camel.

We halted here to cut firewood, for the cherub said we should find none at the next two camps, after which Tajoo and I marched on ahead.

It was very steep, and I soon left Tajoo behind. Presently I heard the camel roaring tremendously, and immediately afterwards, to my intense surprise, Tajoo shouting with laughter.

I hurried back, wondering what could possibly have happened, and struggling up the hill I found Tajoo almost speechless with laughter, sitting on a rock with the camel's rein in his hand, while there was the camel prone on his nose, roaring piteously, the saddle on his neck, and all my dinner, instrument cases, tea bottle, etc., which had been slung on the pommel, hanging in graceful festoons on either side of his head.

"Well," said Tajoo, when he recovered his speech, "this is the most extraordinary illegitimate hill *I* ever saw."

This is the part of the pass that gets blocked up by snow, which it is easy to imagine gets drifted into the ravine representing the road, and renders it impassable.

At half-past four we finally "landed" on flat ground again, at a small grassy corner of the plain, which was, of course, fertile just in the immediate neighbourhood of the mountain. I was casting about for a suitable place for the tent, when my eye caught a mound that was evidently artificial. Here was a chance! Was I about to discover the remains of an ancient temple? I rode up—evident remains of domes buried in a large tumulus of clayey mud. I turned a corner. Here was a brick wall and an arched doorway. With considerable misgivings I got off, lit a match, and descended into this dark and subterranean abode, and this was our first introduction to a caravanserai. Here, in this howling wilderness of rocky mountain and barren plain, was a dry water- and wind-tight building, about thirty yards square, capable of holding men, camels, baggage and everything. True, it was almost underground, had neither chimneys, windows, nor doors, and smelt considerably of the stable; but it was all the warmer, and we were uncommonly grateful.

The Balūchis were in ecstasies. "This, then, is a

beautiful country! Wherever we go they make big houses ready for us. Well, the tent's done for now; this is better than a tent, isn't it, waja?" Ghulam-shah produced a candle, and we went in and made a more detailed inspection. Two broad main passages crossed in the centre, while each corner was a little private room, stable, or pigstye, as the taste of the observer might lead him to consider.

A plan of operations was soon arranged. A fire in the centre, the camels in one arm, I in a second, and the men in a third; the fourth was the passage to the doorway.

A difficulty, however, arose at the outset. The camels, even unloaded and with their packsaddles off, were just about six inches too tall to enter the doorway. The stupid creatures would not stoop or abate one inch of their now unnecessary height.

We made them kneel, and tried to get them to shuffle along on their knees, a thing they can do very well if they please, but they would rise suddenly and bruise their humps against the roof, and I could not at all afford to have my camels with sore backs.

We got out pick and shovel, and started digging away the floor of the passage, but the terrific smell of the manure of ages warned us to leave that alone if we ourselves wished to be able to sleep inside, and we were in the absurd predicament of a man arriving at his house on a cold wintry evening and then being too big to get in.

It was the aged Kasim who got us out of our difficulty. He had been tired out on arrival, and had been sitting down by the baggage rubbing his poor old stiff legs. The old man's age and sagacity had soon procured for him this exemption from camp work, and directly he saw the difficulty he was as usual up to the mark. He replaced the packsaddle on the mahri, the smallest camel, made it kneel down as far inside the doorway as he could get it; then, with a battery of blows from behind, the unfortunate animal rose, knocked a brick or two out, and struggled in. The rest followed without difficulty, their humps being protected by their saddles, and we were all snugly ensconced in our dwelling.

It was the first time that many of them had had an opportunity of examining a house, and their remarks, as they examined the vaulted brick roof and peered into the little corner rooms, were very amusing.

It was unanimously decided to be a "mazani sowab," * and equivalent to at least ten pilgrimages to Mekka for the man who built it. At this point, however, their enjoyment was considerably damped by Ghulamshah recollecting an occasion when, at a place north-east of Bampūr, the roof of a caravanserai fell in during the night and severely injured his parents and their cattle.

We soon began to find serious inconvenience from the smoke, but at last, tracing its peculiar pungency to some sticks of cypress we had brought, we rejected them, and afterwards managed better. The camels had only half an appetite for their kahur, and would evidently be in a bad way should we not find fodder or some change of diet on the morrow.

About the middle of the night I was awakened

---

* "Mazani sowab" (or "thowab"), a great act to be rewarded in heaven hereafter.

by strange voices in the place. But whoever it was, was holding an amicable and even affectionate conversation with Ghulamshah, so I turned over and slept again.

In the morning, we found a stout old Persian had arrived in the night, and was now saddling up his four or five mules to cross the mountains. In voice and feature he was exactly like Ghulamshah's father, and that ingenuous youth, having in the course of conversation found out that his visitor's name was Ghulam Reza (the name of his father), had made him some tea, and opened his heart to him completely.

When we were starting, about an hour afterwards, behold! Ghulamshah's pagri (*turban*) was nowhere to be found; and what a chaff there was when the theft was clearly traced to Ghulam Reza. "Wash gap bita," "To manni pit ī," * etc. And the unfortunate young fellow, whose goodness of heart and unwillingness to suspect people was constantly bringing him into trouble, was thoroughly roasted. It was also remarked as ominous that we were robbed the first day we got into Persia. The thermometers were 47° and 43°, and it hailed violently as we left camp and proceeded north down a mountain stream.

After about an hour and a half, during which Tajoo and myself "potted" over a dozen kabg and sand-grouse (*Pter. arenar.*), we came, to our great joy, upon some tamarisk bushes. These, though not of much use to the camels, would at all events change the taste, and enable them afterwards to finish their kahur. So we stopped, and while the men cut young branches I

* "It was a sweet and beautiful conversation." "You are my father."

took sights both for latitude and longitude. Then we wound our way down the stream, which grew wider every minute, and made a pleasant shrubby path amongst small sandstone hills.

At noon we passed a little stone hut containing a mill and miller. The mill was of most ingenious and unique construction, and the same kind as we afterwards found in Kurdistan. The water was taken from about a quarter-mile up stream, in a small canal, and thus the necessary fall was obtained. The cherub here began to give trouble. After his two days' religious fast he had set to work and actually eaten everything he had been able to lay hands upon, and drank quarts of cold water. The result was he was quite unable to keep up, and we, who were utterly ignorant of even the name of our next camp or the direction in which it lay, were frequently brought up and delayed until he pleased to come up and do what he was engaged for. As long as we were travelling over dry ground we could get on by keeping the same general direction, but down in a tortuous river-bed even that became impossible. At half-past two we debouched into the plain and followed its general direction north-west. We did not fairly go out into the plain, but kept so near the hills on our left as to be constantly going up and down hill crossing the huge talus. To our right stretched the smoothest, barrenest valley I have ever seen, simply a sea of sand, the opposite coast of which was formed by the Darzin mountains, behind which we were told was another sand ocean formerly inhabited by bands of plundering Balūchis, who alone knew the secret of the few and hidden wells.

I overheard Brahim ironically thanking God that we had at last arrived at the land of rose bowers and nightingales. At 4.15 we camped on the rocky, barren ground, the town of Bam being just visible nearly due east.

The caravanserai and two or three mud huts, comprising the village of Sarvistan, were visible when we camped, but a few heads of puzhelle (a salt grass) induced us to halt, considering that a bird in the hand is worth two in the bush. Little stinking bushes of dirmonah (*wormwood*) about a foot high grew between every rock and stone, and with puzhelle formed the entire flora of this part of the "rose garden."

Next morning was very cold. The men were striking the tent and loading up while I was sitting over a fire a little distance off drinking my tea. Suddenly, to our surprise three Persians bandaged rather than clothed up to the eyes, and mounted on mules, came trotting and jingling up. The leader, seeing our camp, found an opportunity for smoking a kaliān, which he carried ready with him; and riding up to the first man he saw (by chance Tajoo), called out to him in a bullying authoritative manner to bring him a light, and quite unnecessarily swearing at him to make haste. Tajoo had never been spoken to in that tone before, and seemed to feel only contempt for the man who could use it. He looked him quietly up and down, and then turned round to us with his most whimsical face and said, "Now this, indeed, is an excellent Persian man. If they're all like this, we shall have some extraordinary enjoyment." *

* "Īn diggar zabri Ajjam mardi an, agar drustan cho abi mȧ bāz lizzat agindoṅ."

The man did not of course understand a word, but just then caught sight of Brahim, who looked very imposing in a big ulster. "Come here," he cried; "are you the owner of this caravan? Come and give me a light."

"You had better go and make your salaams to the waja, first," said Brahim, and I then called the man up. He was a genuine Persian, and in a moment changed from bullying those he considered his inferiors to servility to one who might perhaps be his superior.*

He was, he said, going to Dosāri to get the tribute from Mīr Nāṣir. "Ah," I said, "and these are the bags to carry it in, I suppose. It's something like getting blood out of a stone, I should think, for the miserable creature doesn't look as if he had ever seen a thousand tomāns in his lifetime. However, you'd better make haste, for you're about the tenth man we have seen going to get the tribute from Mīr Nāsir."

He was rather disgusted, but did not quite understand my off-hand mention of such a sum as one thousand tomāns. Brahim offered him the wished-for light, and I heard him say, sneeringly, "I suppose the sahib has enormous quantities of money: all these boxes are full of it, eh?"

"No," said Brahim gravely, "these are all full of sand, which the sahib has brought as a present for the Governor of Kirman, whose country hasn't got any."

The three men jangled off, not quite knowing what to make of our incomprehensible caravan, and we finished our loading and got on march.

---

* I was dressed for riding this morning, and probably owed this estimate to my enormous riding boots. They were often valuable in this manner.

At about 10 a.m. we marched into Sablistan, a small village of thick walled, square mud huts, with very small doors and no windows, arguing great cold. There are two or three mills here driven by water, the millers of which charge five per cent., *i.e.* grind twenty māns and take one. Another feature of the village is "pies," of cut straw, which is preserved in winter just as wurzel is in England. Soon after arrival, my friend the curly-whiskered lieutenant arrived on a powerful white horse, shortly followed by two or three lightly loaded mules.

He came to visit me, and chatted unreservedly over his tea. Mīr Nāsir of Dosāri, and Nur-eddīn Khan of Kahnu, were, he said, utterly faithless people and no power on earth could get the tribute out of them. This was the fourth fruitless journey he had himself made, and he was now going back to fetch the general and some troops.

He said that Chiragh Khan was governor of Bashakard, and was amused when I told him that the Bashakardis knew nothing about it.

Imam Ali Khan, he said, was the man who had subjugated the Balūchis; first taking Bam, then Nurmanshir, and going thence to Charbar. He died about seven years ago. The young lieutenant spoke almost enthusiastically on his military qualities, and afterwards, at Kirman, I was surprised to find that there was a good deal of truth in what he told me.

To-day was the third day since the camels had had a "square meal," and we were beginning to get anxious about them. They would not touch dough lumps, or barley in any form, and we did not know what to give them. Once more, however, our good fortune did not desert us. A large troop of camels from Kirman passed on their way to eat the spring grasses on the Jiruft plain. One of the men told us that under the hills about three miles away we should find trāt and ardūr, so three of the men went off with the camels, and our minds felt easier.

But they got but a very miserable feed, for everything was dead and withered. The climate on this side of the mountains is like that of England, and everything withers in the winter; while just across them, on the southern side, the winter is the sign for rain, and for everything to become green.

In the evening I heard a great chaff and laughing, and presently Brahim brought me in what he called a specimen of the radishes of this country. The men were always eagerly on the look-out for anything new, but, far from admiring or wondering at it, they would uproariously chaff its owner. In the present case they had been having great fun with a native about the ridiculous size of his radishes. They went to great trouble, and in the most absurd broken Persian, and with shouts of laughter, they told him that it was quite preposterous for him to grow such radishes, that if he wanted to see proper radishes he must come to their country, and much more to the same effect. Now the things in question were turnips. There never was such a confusion. The men had not seen turnips before, nor could they learn the name, and the native did not know what "Gurgu" (the Balūchi for *radish*) was, nor did he know the misconception they were under, and he fairly gave it up and bolted amidst yells of laughter. I afterwards bought, a quantity of turnips at the rate of 77 lbs. for 10*d*., and for 5*d.* I got thirty-four eggs. The camels ate the turnips freely, but it was a mistake to give them, and nearly all were sick afterwards.

Next day, December 9th, we had an uninteresting march up the barren plain which has already been described.

We were surprised at seeing very good and well-baked tiles laid along the road for walling in the Kahns; they were short sections of a cylinder, about two feet in diameter and six inches deep.

The cherub was very ill to-day, and I had again to put him on my riding camel, and at one we camped in the bed of the Tahrut river. The place was picturesque enough in amongst the trees, but it was bitterly cold, and the poor camels ate but sparingly of the tamarisk.

Next morning we were away at eight. All the still water was frozen, and in order to regain the road we had to cross the five or six little streams which composed the river. It seemed hard on the men to commence a thirty mile march by getting their boots and stockings * wet through, and the small donkey Durgosh had given me was told off to bring them over by twos. Only Brahim Khamīs despised this method of crossing, and driving his camel into the first stream made a bound to get on to its back behind the load. Unfortunately he missed, and after a hard struggle fell flat on his back in the icy cold water.

But was he abashed? Not a bit. As he picked

* It was very absurd to see these fellows swaggering about in Bushire shoes and home knit stockings. To the last also they never realized the importance of putting on the stocking first and the shoe afterwards.

himself up, the moment he got his breath, he was out with the old quotation, "Oh la! my brothers, *ain't* I happy now!" *

It was a long dreary march that day, and it did not improve matters that the plain sloped upward towards evening, and we saw our destination hours before we reached it.

Towards evening I was delighted to come upon some patches of salt grass. The men were overjoyed, and congratulated themselves that now their camels would have a fair chance, and cut large quantities.

It was nearly five o'clock and quite dark when our caravan slowly wended its way amongst a quantity of mud-brick houses. The inhabitants were all safely shut up from the cold, and after a few fruitless efforts to find a caravanserai, I was compelled to call a halt, and commence a determined attack on about the only house which seemed at all inhabited.

Soon a stout old gentleman came bustling out, and with many expressions of delight at finding a sahib, he found a place for the men and camels among the ruins of a house.

After seeing men and camels safe for the night, I followed old Kabala Hassan to his own house, and was soon comfortably installed in a small mud-walled room without window, but comfortably lighted by a blazing wood fire.

Our host was a jovial, ruddy-faced fellow, the devoted and willing slave to three strapping buxom

---

* An old story he often told over the camp fire, where a man gets into all sorts of ridiculous and unpleasant positions, but always brings out that observation "*Lā*, hani dilam *hā* abu!" (*Oh la! and now my heart is happy!*)

wives, and four jolly, rosy cheeked little boys, the image of himself.

We had many callers, in spite of the lateness of the hour, and all were very polite and decorous.

One Muhammad Reza, who had married a daughter of Kabala Hassan, and lived next door, did with many cautious questions produce a bottle of wine, very much the best wine I ever tasted in Persia, and like hock; we made some kebabs on a ramrod, had a kaliān, and turned in.

The houses of Raiūn are divided by a court, the rooms facing south being for winter use. I was in the now empty summer rooms, and next to me was a room used as stable or lumber room, and in this it appeared some of my men proposed to sleep.

Now, Hassan, in a very characteristic manner, had gone to bed first, and just as I was dropping off to sleep I heard a whispering and scuffling outside his door.

The doors of the rooms here had intricate wooden locks, far beyond the ingenuity of a Balūch, who never gets farther than tying his door (should he have one) with a piece of goat's-hair string. Kabala Hassan had locked Hassan's door upon him, thinking no one else was coming. Here then were these shivering men, dying to go to sleep, not only unable to get in, but baffled by some mysterious and unseen contrivance, and mortally afraid of making a noise and waking me.

Hassan was at length awakened and made aware of the state of affairs, but he soon found that he couldn't open the door any more than they could. His despair was most ludicrous, but so were the remarks of the men outside. "Oh you poor Hassan!" "Oh you're quite dead now!" "After all this long journey, and then you make a grave in a Persian house!" "Oh now you are quite sealed up!"

Old Hassan stumbled about inside, making various ineffectual scratchings at different parts of the wall (I believe he never found the door); but at last it seemed to occur to him that if any one had an interest in persevering until the door was opened, it was his friends outside, and to their intense amusement and aggravation he abandoned the pursuit, and was soon snoring as loud as ever.

At this point I got up, and had a try at the door, but being unsuccessful we started to shout for Kabala Hassan. This deceitful old gentleman we found had been listening the whole time, and gloating over the success of his lock.

Next morning I was up early and picking my way down the frosty lane to where my camels were. Alas for our marching to-day! the Jamaiti līro, and my poor mahri were too evidently ill. The drooping head and dull eye showed only too clearly that the journey had been too much for them, and I knew by hard experience in former days that a camel that once gets ill, or is a little over fatigued, seldom or never recovers.

And my head camel-man and right-hand man, Brahim, where was he? Ill too, worse luck; and to my rapid questions as to what I had better give them he could only answer languidly, "the sahib knows best." But the grave aristocratic Dād Arrahīm, and the fierce, rebellious little Brahim Khamīs came to the fore. How they buried all old scores and differences when I appeared to be in a difficulty, the reader will readily gather if I have been at all successful in sketching these men's character.

We had a consultation, and agreed that, judging from the state of the bowels, the camels had been poisoned.

Yesterday, while on the march, they had cut a quantity of salt grass exactly like trāt, and this they had fed to the camels. Only these two had eaten it. They were favourites with their attendants, and had often been given bread and other unusual things, and so had learnt to waive their own instinct, and eat whatever their master gave them.

But a close examination of the grass by daylight proved that it was anything but trāt, and Kabala Hassan and Muhammad Reza, who came up presently, assured us that odalik (undetermined), was fatal to all animals, should they eat it before drinking of the water of the country where it was found.

The long and short of the matter was, we were here ten weary days, literally sitting and watching the bowels of these camels. And then there was no fodder in the place, and Brahim got very ill, and Kasim, poor old man, game as he was, began to fail.

I will not inflict upon the reader a continuous diary of our prolonged residence at Raiūn, but merely give a brief account of the place, and beg the reader to bear in mind that we were rather anxious-hearted all our stay.

Raiūn is a large well-built thriving village, not crowded together, but each house standing on, roughly, a quarter of an acre of well kept, fertile garden, surrounded by high mud walls; and in summer, when all the vines, poplars, figs, walnuts, etc., are green, it must be a delightful place.

There is a small but busy working bazaar, shaded

during summer by two huge plane trees. The streets of the town are cleaner than usual, from the fact that numerous rivulets, constructed for irrigating the gardens, run rapidly down them.

The village is on a slope, so that these rivulets, which are on the surface, about the middle of the village, are, at the upper end, sixteen feet under ground, and only accessible by kahns.

The arrangement of the gardens is generally the same. A row of tall, slender poplar trees, a tree considered next to the cypress in point of beauty, runs round the garden, inside the mud wall. Between these a few willow bushes, and, if the man be rich, an occasional rose. The garden itself is, at this season, full of lucerne only, grown in oblong beds. This is at frequent intervals cut down to about an inch from the ground, but the roots soon send forth a new crop.

Grapes are said to be excellent; Kabala Hassan declared, however, that the jackals devoured great numbers, saying that when the grapes were unripe the jackals howled all night, but that when they were ripe they "gobbled" in silence.

The women are fine strapping creatures, and it is curious to observe that, though wearing the white Persian dress in the streets, they wear in the house the multiplicity of short petticoats and exhibit the handsome bare legs of the Kurdī women, whom they closely resemble both in face and stature and their charming freedom of manner.

It is a very contented little community: they make their own felts, glass bottles, wine and soap and knives. The governor is a Shahzada as usual, and invited me to dine with him; but as the messenger naïvely observed that all the party would get drunk as quick as they could, I did not care to risk the effects of "bad-masti." I went, however, one evening to have a game at chess (in which I was beaten hollow), and was amused at the systematic way in which the doors were shut and his excellency proceeded to acquire an appetite for dinner by various glasses of wine and imported brandy.

The Persians drink always before eating, and I observed that he never called for a glass, but made a motion with his hand, which was sufficient for the single servant who attended.

There were great rumours that Turkey was at war with Russia and getting beaten, and a courier arrived on the 12th announcing that the Shah had purchased Baghdad, and that the town of Kirman had been illuminated in honour of the glorious acquisition of the Persians' most revered shrine.*

The Shahzada's son was a fine young fellow, very fond of hawking, and I was glad to be able to completely cure the damaged wing of one of his finest hawks, for which he was very grateful.

The Shahzada is only a "warming-pan" for a young scion of the hereditary governing race, Kasim Khan, who was just of age and about to take up the reins of government.

I was credibly assured that as many as 18,000 lbs. of opium were produced here yearly.

I think that should Persia ever increase its wealth to any considerable amount it will be through its opium.

---

* I learned at Kirman afterwards that the illuminations had been in honour of the governor's birthday.

The cultivation commenced at Yezd, which place, though known to European fame chiefly by its silk, owes now most of its wealth to this plant. Professional cultivators were imported to Isfahan, where the area growing opium increases yearly; and Kirmanshahan, which a few years ago knew it not, has many promising plantations. However, Persia and its prospects do not belong to a book professedly about wilder and pleasanter countries.

Here we found some remnants of the ancient Persian art of working steel. I had ordered some knives, which when brought proved quite useless from the softness of the iron. Whereupon I fell to taunting the man, until his wrath arose, and he went away saying that that very night he would bring me a knife which should cut my Balūch axe-head, of which I had been boasting, into two pieces. And he did bring me such a knife, which I have now, and the axe-head is cut and gashed all over by exhibitions of its quality to friends.

It is an odd coincidence that I am just reminded of this knife as I sit in my tent at Mazar in the Syrian desert (where we are emulating the Israelites) and through the tent door I see Ghulamshah split a sheep's head down the middle with it preparatory to "sousing" that luxury.

We paid a visit to the glass blower, a perfectly new experience to all my men, but it was odd how they immediately seized the ludicrous aspect of the operation. Brahim Khamīs went into screams of laughter at the bursting cheeks and distorted expression of the glass blower, and at night afterwards used to "bring down the house" by mimicking the operation.

What makes Raiūn more cheerful than usual is the absence of ruined buildings, which so invariably form the major part of a Persian town. The reason is, that up to the last thirty years the people all lived in an enormous fort, the remains of which, in a fair state of preservation, still crown the top of the hill. The fort contained 3,000 families, and the houses of the governor and the great men were very large and neatly plastered. The woodwork, however, has now been removed, and the roofs in most cases have fallen in.

On the sixth day the two sick camels were a little better. A stiff "rīk," or diaphoretic, composed of a whole sheep boiled to rags and poured down their throats, had at last cleared their stomachs, but the poor things were a piteous sight, quite blind and hardly able to stand.

We would have given anything now for just a little lorti, a handful of trāt, or any other of the sweet shrubs of their own country with which to tempt their appetites, but in this inhospitable land even the little scraps of ardūr were all withered up by the cold. However, there were some little patches in shady places in the fort; so, as soon as the camels could stagger along, I removed there and took possession of the very extensive range of stables.

Here we remained four more days, taking sights and meteorological observations, and wandering about the old fort, and never failing to bring back an armful of the greenest and most succulent ardūr we could find.

At last the mahri's constitution pulled him through, and he looked fit enough to start if not loaded. The

Jamaiti līro, however, was old, and could not improve. Their blindness we had cured. I had treated the mahri with a very strong solution of nitrate of silver, while Kasim had cured the other by the native remedy, which is remarkably quick and efficient for this kind of blindness, which is called "spool," and consists of a thick white film over the eye. We burnt some shells (some precious fossils I had collected) and ground the unslaked lime to powder. A quantity of this was put into a tube (a reed) and blown suddenly into the eye. The lime combining with the moisture burns the film away, but before it can have time to burn further and injure the eye, the eye waters so much from the pain that it washes the lime out.

The Jamaiti līro would not die, and I could not make up my mind to desert him. I felt a kind of sympathy for my Balūchis when they indignantly refused an offer from the business-like Muhammad Reza of thirty krans for his hide.

In my dilemma, old Kasim and Hassan of the donkey's voice came to my rescue. Give them, said they, a sufficient store of firewood, rice, flour, and a cooking pot, and they would remain till the party returned. I gratefully accepted, and our spirits rose a hundred degrees at once, at the thoughts of once more getting on the march.

We left with them the tent also, as we were now in the land of caravanserais, and would no longer require it. Our guide the cherub, whom we had not seen since arrival at Raiūn, was not to the fore. He lay dying, we were told, the result of his imbecility in fasting during a hard day's march, and then gorging quarts of water, raw turnips, dates, and any stuff he could lay hands upon. These *soi-disant* Muslimeen of Persia have no business to fast on the day's march, and the Kurān is sufficiently explicit on the subject, if they would only take the trouble to read it, instead of so much Hāfiz, Sheikh Saadi, and other obscene authors. Seeing that, after having been paid to guide us, he had invariably been at the rear of the caravan, I sternly refused all appeal for bakshish, even to defray his funeral expenses.

CHAPTER XII.

WE REACH KIRMAN.

A troop of Persian officers.—Ragged rascals.—Hanaka.—The first ice we saw.—Mahun.—The menagerie.—An obstinate cow.—Al hamdu lillah.—Kirman at last.

ON the 14th December we struck camp, and wended our way down the hill, from the foot of which, looking back, we got a striking view of Raiūn village, crowned by the imposing old fort.

We crossed a valley containing the stubble of several acres of wheat, and a host of recollections of "the marsh," and Lincolnshire generally, were aroused by a snipe getting away from a small unfrozen rivulet with a genuine "scaape" that made my heart thump. Then a steep and rugged ascent followed, and about half-past two an incident occurred which opened my eyes to the necessity for further adaptation to the customs of the new land we had now entered.

I was trudging along on foot, anathematising an icy wind which blew straight in our faces, and having been poking about, trying to grub up what was to me a new plant, I had fallen far behind the caravan and was left alone with Tajoo. Just after we passed a small barn-like stone building, which we had been told we should see, and which was a caravanserai without water, there broke upon our astonished gaze a large cavalcade of Persian soldiers, mostly officers and their servants, splendidly dressed and capitally mounted. Directly on spying us, the leader—who turned out to be a "Bimbashi," and as the word implies, nominally in command of a nominal thousand men,—sent a young officer to demand my presence. Now directly the cavalcade appeared, I had suddenly become conscious that neither Tajoo's nor my own personal appearance was very imposing. It was some years since I had been within a thousand miles of an European tailor's shop;—again, I had been travelling for months in the wildest countries, and had distributed my wardrobe amongst some fifteen or sixteen men. I was painfully aware of a large reddish leather seat to a very old pair of Bedford cords, which years of jungle washing had made about seven inches shorter than usual.

These everlasting cords are still a joy to Ghulam-shah; and I am sometimes tempted to instruct some of our Bedawin to lie in ambush and strip him.

Please pardon this digression, but a detailed description of our appearance would be too harrowing to Mr. H. Nicoll if to no one else, and I prefer to gently suggest it in this manner. Any way, we were sufficiently conscious of our shortcomings to make us all the more anxious to stand on our dignity, and to the naib's civil request, that I would "come and see the Bimbashi," I replied with much pointedness of expression, that if the Bimbashi wanted to see me he might come here. The matter, however, was pleasantly settled, by the arrival of my curly-whiskered friend on his white horse, who rode up, and by his extreme kindness of manner, and insisting on my riding on his horse, that I might appear in a fitting manner, entirely changed my mind.

The Bimbashi was a gentleman and very civil. His curiosity was much aroused by my caravan, which of course he had passed. He easily believed that I was the owner of it, but as for my travelling through these deserts for my own pleasure, my using camels instead of mules and horses, and my bringing those fierce ignorant Balūchis with me instead of intelligent Persian servants, these were things that he could not understand. He however was civil, but his youngsters annoyed me very much. It seems the expedition had been sent from Kirman, to rout out our old friend Nur-eddīn Khan at Kahnu, and thinking they might entrap Tajoo into an admission, two of them swore he was well known as one of Nur-eddīn's men. Others swore that they had known me last year in Kirman, that I was a Russian, and used to ride a black horse. I promptly lost what little temper I had; told the Bimbashi that his youths couldn't lie worth sixpence, and they had better go back to their old disgraceful trade, and I shook hands cordially with the man on the white horse, and strode off over the plain.

I have often laughed over the matter since; it seemed so natural to go and have a quarrel with a well-dressed man, because we were ragged.

It was nearly dark before the handsome new brick-built caravanserai of Hanaka appeared before us, beautifully situated among high snow-covered mountains. These caravanserais are the one institution of which Persia can fairly boast. I have not yet visited any land where, even on little frequented roads, you find at intervals of twenty miles warm stabling for any number up to 1000 mules, and clean water-tight little rooms for their owners.

The cold weather was intense. The thermometer marked 21° in the morning, and Brahim, disgusted at the complaints of one or two of the men, gave them every rag he had and slept in a thin cotton shirt sooner than the Balūch reputation for hardihood should suffer at their hands. The fact may stand by itself without embellishment.

Next morning was fine and sunny. The merciless north wind gave us a respite, and we started cheerily enough, though the thermometer stood at 32° and the barometer showed 9,330 feet above the sea.

The way was down a little mountain stream. This was the first ice the men had seen, and the fun and chaff over first walking on the water put every one into a good humour. It was amusing to watch the different characters of the men as they attempted this new risk; not that they feared the getting wet, but all Easterns have an intense horror of being done or looking foolish, and the man who fell in would never have heard the last of his ambitious attempt to walk upon water. To see the stately grave Dād Arrahīm balancing himself in ungraceful attitudes, and pawing away at the ice with one foot and with the other on the bank, was enough to send us all into fits of laughter.

It was an opportunity to correct a bad impression which had arisen about a perhaps too frequent reference to burying grounds. Our cherub, though in his own country and over a route he had often traversed, had once or twice declared that he was dying. I had replied that he was at liberty to die when he liked, but that he had better wait till we came to a burying ground. This, partly from the men being down-hearted at the time, and partly from their not understanding Persian, was regarded as anything but a joke, but even almost as a prophecy. So I seized the opportunity when their spirits were high, and catching little Abdulla Daduk behind I shouted to him, "Hurry up! hurry up! Hussein (the cherub) says we're all going to die of the cold, so we must get along to a burying ground." There was a hearty laugh at Hussein, and a little ridicule was successfully thrown over an idea which might have brought trouble, but which was thereby completely extinguished. "Wallah," I used to think to myself sometimes, "Heilat i beni adam bisīar and" (*The wiles of mankind are very great*). This, a quotation from old Jemait the shikarri, belongs to a story which often made the men laugh, especially when told in his well-known drawling bass voice. Once, while shooting in the mountains, I heard from behind a hill most direful howls and screams. Thinking that a wolf or leopard had seized a child, I rushed to the spot. To my surprise I found a little shepherd girl peacefully driving her flock before her. As I looked, she gave another scream, and I turned to Jemait for an explanation. "Ah!" said the old man with an air of paternal wisdom, "don't you see what she's doing that for? The goats think she's a wolf, and hurry on to get out of her way." "Ah!" after a thoughtful pause, "the deceit of the sons of man is very profound!" * The road was through barren hills

* The Syrian Bedawin use the same trick.

and a barren plain, but at 2 p.m. we sighted a large village, and at once distinguished the green glazed dome and lofty, slender minarets of the great mosque of Mahun. This is, I believe, one of the finest buildings in Persia. As long as you see it from a distance, you cannot but admire it as a single idea simply but grandly carried out, but when you approach nearer, the amount of elaboration, often in glaring bad taste, destroys your first impression entirely.

There is a capital caravanserai here, and I encamped there at first, but an old gentleman soon came and insisted on my going to the Wakil-al-Mulk's rest-house, so after seeing the men all comfortable (we had to buy firewood here instead of cutting it as usual), I went next door and was inducted into a most charming house. The great room was lofty, well plastered, and carpeted with the beautiful felts that this country produces. The large window looked over a long garden railed in from the road, and down the centre ran briskly a babbling shallow brook. Here at last was a rose garden, and although I could not help a feeling of effeminacy at sitting on carpets and living in a clean house, I managed to bear up, ordered a dinner to match, and bullied Ghulamshah till it was ready.

Meanwhile, however, a strolling menagerie arrived, consisting of a newly caught and very savage lion, and, without exception, the most hideous monkey I ever saw. The lion, a magnificent tawny beast, was held by eight men with ropes all pulling in different directions. The men crowded round from the caravanserai, and were hugely delighted at the two animals, both new to them. The monkey, however, "fetched" them most. The lion was evidently regarded as an assumption of superiority over their country by the Persians, for there are now no lions in Balūchistan. But the monkey took them by storm altogether. "Wy, wy, wy, wy, there is no God but one God. This is wonderful, this is powerful; it is the son of a man completely, verily; this is very much too heavy" (unbearably wonderful). But the scene changed like magic when Ghulamshah arrived with three fowls. The lion got their wind, and in a flash from a majestic tawny statue he was a raging fury. The men, however, stuck to him bravely, all except one at his neck, who paled and wavered at the furious roars and bounds made apparently directly at him. But the master of the menagerie, whose nice attention to dress, suave manner, and Teherani hat had led me to misjudge him, stepped forward quickly and took the rope from him, saying calmly, "never mind, never mind," and the animal was pacified.

Next morning a short twenty miles over a flat, sandy country brought us in sight of Kirman. But on the way an incident occurred that showed the extraordinary obstinacy of cows. I saw a man ploughing in the light sandy soil with a pair of oxen in pretty fair condition. As I passed, one of the cows fell down as if exhausted. After wearing himself out by beating it with all his might for nearly five minutes, the man commenced a series of the most revolting cruelties. It makes me angry even now to think of them, but I will just mention that one of the least barbarous was forcing his iron-pointed goad with all his force into its nostril and wriggling it about there. Still the cow lay as if dead. I was alone and on foot, so I scrambled over the heavy sand, hastening to interfere. But to my surprise, as I approached, the cow jumped up and set to work pulling hard. It was a perfectly healthy vigorous young creature, and for a mere caprice endured most barbarous ill-usage sooner than work. I talked to the man about the matter, and he said it was one of the best cows he had, but took fits of sulkiness which required the methods he had adopted. My cow riding in the Bampūr country had given me an insight into a cow's capacity for obstinacy, but I never saw anything like what this cow endured, and I am quite sure that though a mule's obstinacy has become proverbial, a cow's far exceeds it. In Balūchistan we sometimes burn a camel's head with a hot iron and make him eat a white cock, but this is when the camel is not obstinate, but completely exhausted, and life and death depend upon getting him up on his legs again.

Mahun is a pleasant little village with a rapid stream down its main street, bordered by trees and festooned with yards of green and scarlet calico fresh from the dyer's hands (the chief industry here seems to be dyeing). It is to Kirman somewhat as Brighton to London, or Poonah to Bombay, and the road was thronged. Towards evening we wound our way for about three miles through the ruins of old Kirman, guarded by the remains of a huge rambling fort perched on the ridge of hills to the east, and sighted the fair smooth battlemented mud-wall of new Kirman. At 5 p.m. on an icy cold evening, on December 21st, we filed slowly through the huge gate. When inside, I turned round to the men with a fervent "al hamdu lillah," which was chorussed by all of them with a will. We were at first confounded by the streets and houses, and we knew not where to stay the night. But I had heard much of the generosity and nobleness of the Wakil-al-Mulk, and, having hired a guide, insisted on being taken straight to his palace. We prowled along through endless streets and narrow bazaars, whose lights frightened our camels out of their wits, and at last were told to stop in a huge "maidan," or walled enclosure for exercising the troops. I refused, however, to stop anywhere, and swaggered and bullied the unhappy guide until he offered to take me to the sentinels at the gate of the palace. He remained behind quaking. I walked up to the sentinels, said I was an English traveller, and had come to stay with the Wakil-al-Mulk. They were rather staggered, but said they would send for the Nazir, or chief of the household. I, however, refused to wait, and accompanied the soldier into a large oblong garden surrounded by quarters. Here we seemed likely to come to a stop again, but luckily a man came by, a servant of His Highness' doctor, a man who had been nine years in Paris. In effect he came and examined me, reported to His Highness that I was without doubt an English gentleman, and I was welcomed with the utmost cordiality. My poor camels were unloaded and stabled by the Shuturdar (the Wakil has many hundreds of camels). The Wakil sent me a gracious message, saying how gratified he was that I had thrown myself so trustfully upon his hospitality. We had dinner, and turned in to sleep before a blazing oak fire, having completed the first stage of what proved to be a most eventful journey.

CHAPTER XIII.

LIFE AT KIRMAN.

A Persian palace.—Interview with the Wakil-al-Mulk.—His knowledge of English.—Alleged discovery of coal.—I nearly put my foot in it.—Comfortably installed.—Persian carpets.—Daily routine in Kirman.—The Commander-in-chief of the forces.—The box sextant.—Topics of conversation with the Khan.—Irrigation and windmills.—The Bazaars.—The Mint.—Kashmir shawl manufactory.—The College.—The Dungeon.—A prisoner released.—The Hindu colony.—Our mess.—The Khan's treasurer comes over.—Parting with my Balūchis.—Take leave of the Khan.

NEXT morning we received visits from numerous officers of the household, and were enabled to take a survey of our position. The palace was like most Persian palaces, an oblong enclosure about two hundred yards long by fifty yards wide. At either end are the royal quarters, the one suite being used in summer and the other in winter. Down either side of the oblong are the quarters of the principal officers, each having from two to four smallish rooms; and the space in the centre was occupied by a few untidy shrubs and trees now languishing with the cold. This oblong was the nucleus of the court, there being all round ranges of stabling for camels, barracks, prisons, guest-houses, baths, harems, and new gardens in course of being laid out.

However, this is enough of bare description for the present. We were soon summoned for an interview with the Wakil-al-Mulk, whose curiosity had been excited to the highest pitch concerning the unknown European who had forced his way into the palace at night, accompanied by a horde of savage-looking Balūchis, who came from places the very names of which had never been heard,* and riding on camels hairless and shaped like greyhounds. I was ushered into a long room handsomely carpeted and curtained, the produce of native industry, and leaving my slippers among a number of others at a sign from my introducer, I pushed up the curtain that served as a door and walked into the reception room.

The Khan had evidently meant to make an impression. He had got on four thick coats of handsome broadcloth, and over all a coat of the beautiful tawny fur the Persian nobles import from Russia, and which, lined with expensive Kashmir shawls, makes a coat fit for a king. He had also seated himself on a tall chair, minutely inlaid with pieces of different coloured wood, and I often smiled afterwards, when we became more sociable and all sat together on the floor, at the amount of ceremony thought necessary to overawe poor me.

The commander-in-chief of the forces and other pillars of the State were sitting on either side of the room. The Khan motioned me to a smaller chair on his left hand, and we went through a round of bows with the utmost politeness. A few questions and answers served to assure him that I was what I represented myself to be—merely an English traveller.

* These fellows never said they came from Mekran, but each gave the name of his own village, and with considerable pride. I suppose none of them had ever heard the word "Balūchistan."

He spoke highly of Major-General Sir Frederic Goldsmid and Major St. John; and as I had had the honour of serving under the first-mentioned officer, I found at once an excellent introduction and guarantee of respectability. The Khan knows four words of English, or, as he counts them, two. They are, "Major-General Goldsmid" and "parliament." It was really amusing to hear him pronounce the first. He paused before commencing it, halted on the second syllable for breath, then dashed off the rest without a trip. As for "parliament," he would never let me refer to "Mashwarat Khana"* without interpolating with a grave complacency that nearly upset my gravity, "Ah, parliament." He asked much of the countries I had come through, and was, like all Persians, anxious to know if I had found any mines. I explained that I had seen indications of mines in several places, but thought that they could never be worked owing to difficulty of transport and absence of fuel. He eagerly interrupted me, "We have found the stone of coal." He said that specimens had been sent to Teheran, and offered to send horsemen with me to investigate the place where it was found; but I never succeeded in getting there. While talking about his conquests among the Balūchis in the south, I nearly "put my foot in it." I was relating a thing that occurred some years ago: the Telegraph staff at Gwadur had been so reduced by incessant fever that out of eleven Europeans hardly one could rise from his bed. Tents were promptly sent up by Government, and we established a camp in a comparatively healthy, elevated spot.

* "Council house."

The appearance of so much canvas, coupled with the knowledge that a similar camp had been erected at Jask, gave an impression that the English were going to occupy the country; and, to snuff out promptly any such presumption on our part, the Balūchis commenced to build a fort in a retired place called Ras Tīz, where there were plenty of convenient stones. I related this story as funnily as I could. The Khan said: "Yes, *I* ordered that fort." "And *I* built it," said a member of the circle.

The Khan gave me a detached house in a garden, with ample accommodation for myself and my men; he also attached to me two servants, and a man to precede me when I walked in the streets. I then made my adieus full of gratitude, while he professed to be much charmed with my conversation; in fact, he either sent for me for an hour's chat every morning, or strolled round to my house with his handsomely attired suite to watch me taking observations of the sun.

I was charmed to be installed in a house of my own, for constantly being exposed to irruptions from strangers at all hours, day or night, was tiresome; and I opened my boxes, took out all my instruments, books, writing materials, sketch maps, etc., set up my little table, and furnished the room most comfortably. While thus engaged, twelve servants arrived, and each placed in the large reception room a huge tray of fruits, sweetmeats, pistachio nuts, etc., made a solemn salaam and exit. We had a roaring oak-wood fire, and a capital breakfast was served from the Khan's own table, his cook taking the opportunity to bring it himself to inspect me. The carpet of this room was curious and characteristic of modern taste in Persia. It was a large and valuable one, the pile was of the richest, and the colours and arrangement of the border were beautiful; but the centrepiece was an ugly representation of an English coach and four.

The Nawab came soon after, *i.e.*, the doctor whom I have mentioned as having been nine years in Paris. He had most polished manners, was always handsomely dressed, scrupulously and daintily clean, and as jovial a boon companion as I have met. He introduced to me all the callers, and they were numerous; but I shall only mention the most interesting. The Nazir, or chief of the household, came to see that my firewood supply was ample (and not wasteful either I found), and I could not have been treated with more royal generosity. If in after-pages I have to write unkind things about the Persians, the Wakil-al-Mulk must always be held a golden exception.

Our stay in Kirman was most pleasant, though the daily routine varied little. In the morning, early, a stroll through the somewhat dreary snow-covered high mud-walled gardens. Then observations and a visit to the Khan, breakfast, callers, and a stroll in the bazaars, finishing off with a tremendous wine party, often prolonged into the small hours. The doctor, who, I believe, will not mind my saying that he had but little medical knowledge, devoted his energies to the manufacture of wine, in which he excelled all the inhabitants of Kirman; and it is said that odd bottles of the choicest brands found their way into very good society.

Of our callers, the most amusing was the commander-in-chief, who had received instructions from the Wakil to learn from me the art of using the box sextant. He was a short bull-necked fellow, in a handsome fur coat, rather blind, and with a whimsical expression of face, and a way of prefacing every observation by "F'arz bukunam" (*And I beg to represent that*). A pocket sextant requires practice to hold properly, and more still to see through,—and the commander was short-sighted, and his fingers were all thumbs. He persevered gallantly, for the Khan made daily inquiries, and I believe was only playing a joke on him all the while, but he never attained much result. Despairing of making him understand the theory of measuring heights, I translated him a simple table of multiplicators for each angle with a base of 100; he could sometimes work out this on paper, but when it came to the practical observing, he was always at fault. We used to give an hour a day to it, and practise on a tall poplar in the garden. I think nothing in the way of scientific instruction could be funnier than this. After going over our previous day's work on paper, we would adjourn to the garden. The old commander would then laboriously measure 100 feet with my measuring tape from the base of the poplar tree, pettishly cursing the snow and mud, and being scrupulous to a quarter of an inch. He would then take up a position irrespective of the end of his base line, and try to see the tree through the sextant. The contortions he went through in endeavouring to effect this were ridiculous enough, but he would sometimes actually stalk the tree, sextant painfully grasped in both hands, with much the action of a "chasseur" going to shoot a wagtail. On one occasion I inconsiderately laughed out loud, and he detected me. The next day he brought to his lesson a French logarithm book. This he could not read, but it was evidently meant to check undue levity on my part, and inspire proper respect for his scientific attainments. I am to this day unable to tell the reader the height of that poplar tree.

On an inspection of my aneroid barometer he achieved to his own satisfaction a great triumph over me. After turning it over and over several times close to his nose, he held it out just in front of him, and looking me full in the face with his head a little on one side, said, "Now, if I might make an observation, where does the high in place wind up this barrowmeeter?"

The high in place loq.: "But I never do wind it up."

Comm.-in-chief loq. (cunningly): "Do you *never* wind it up?"

The H. I. P. loq.: "Never."

Comm.-in-chief loq. (pointing to keyhole at back used for regulating it, and looking round triumphantly for applause): "But, if I might make the observation, what then is this for?"

The daily talk with the Khan was always looked forward to with pleasure. He threw off all reserve, would invite men skilled in various crafts to meet me, and excite free discussion on all subjects. Taking the chief topics according to their importance, the irrigation system comes first.

Roughly to describe this, the reader should imagine a round basin with a smooth sediment of earth in the bottom. The sides of the basin represent the hills, and the earth the detritus of the hills washed down by the rain of ages which forms the soil of Kirman. If the rocky bed under Kirman were as uniform as the basin, the rain from the hills would slide equally down to the bottom as it were of the basin; and it is to find out the irregularities that taxes the ingenuity of the kahn diggers, who are a craft to themselves. The deepest kahns at Kirman are about eighteen feet, and the tools used in their construction are, a short-handled broad-bladed hoe; a very rude windlass for pulling up the mud, which is not even worked by a handle, but by pulling round the circumference by hand; and a water level called a "shuturgulu," of which no one would show me a specimen. The kahn diggers guard the secrets of their craft carefully, and that is I think all their craft consists of.

I proposed pumps, and laboriously described the Lincolnshire windmill pump; and seeing my listeners interested, constructed a working model, using the brass case of a broken thermometer as cylinder. They recognised the model, and I was rather mortified when after all my trouble they quietly said, "Oh yes, we got one of those from Bombay." I found on inquiry that they had actually got up pumping machinery from Bandar Abbas, but the wisest man in Kirman could not erect it, and it was treasured up somewhere. The Khan had been "bitten" once in the matter of windmills, and one of my expeditions was to visit a huge structure which an engineering genius from Khorasan had induced him to erect at considerable expense. The axis of the sails was vertical, about twenty feet high, and the sails were made of mats, while side walls were built to guide currents of air on to them. It appears that the friction was so great that no Kirman wind could work it, and it had remained stationary ever since its erection. The chief export of Kirman worth mentioning is "kurk," previously described as being the long silky under down growing between the wool of certain sheep and goats commonly called Kashmir goats. It is made into good gloves, socks, felt carpets, and "Kashmir shawls." The Khan exhibited specimens of all these, and we made arrangements to inspect his factories. He is, like most governors in Persia, the principal manufacturer, camel and mule-owner, and general merchant. The Khan's agricultural arrangements seemed simple. He had a minister of agriculture, a stout farmerly looking man, who kept the government granaries, gave out seed, lent ploughs, oxen, etc., and took care at harvest time that he got a fair return on his outlay.

My walks through the bazaars were interesting, and made under unusually propitious circumstances. The bazaars are lofty, well built of burnt bricks, and fairly clean. I was preceded by one man, well known to be of the Khan's followers, who cleared the way, and another man followed to prevent mounted men or laden donkeys running over me. Thus I could always make my inquiries leisurely and without being crowded, while the answers I received were invariably respectful and as far as possible true. The foremost man handed down any article I wanted to look at, and if necessary purchased it at a reasonable price. There was every appearance of a wealthy town. We passed many well mounted cavaliers, handsomely dressed in rich velvets, silks, and Kashmir shawl or European broadcloth coats. There were very good saddles and bridles, black patent leather slippers that could be worn in England without exciting comment, and the brass and copper working was very good. I frequently passed my men in the street. They had been given a portion of their wages, and purchased the least Persian-looking kit they could find, but still excited considerable astonishment. The Khan had wanted to disarm them, but I undertook the responsibility should they be allowed to keep their weapons. The Khan yielded this privilege graciously, and I was glad of it, for the alternative would have been to the men an eternal disgrace before the "Gagar," or Persian.

One day I visited the Mint, a fine dome-shaped brick building; but the grubby, ragged appearance of the trusty men in charge was curious.

The Khan buys up dollars and old krans of other mints than his own, and melts and restamps them. The Mint was in full blast when I saw it. On one side the silver was being drawn out into a thick wire by a clumsy wooden apparatus. On another, a man was chopping it up into short lengths, with a rapidity and exactness that could only have been acquired by very long practice. The next process was weighing the lengths (and nearly all were right). They were then thrown into a charcoal brazier near the die cutting anvil, and here was the smartest operation of all. The anvil itself was a hard steel spike bearing one face of the die. One man stood by with a pair of tongs, a second with a small hammer bearing the second face of the die, and a third with a huge hammer. The first man seized a "dab" of silver from the brazier, and with unerring certainty placed it on the centre of the narrow anvil. Almost at the same instant man number two placed his hammer exactly on it, and thump came number three with a blow which flattened it and imprinted the die on both sides. They struck thirty-three or thirty-eight per minute, I am not sure which, as the second figure has become blurred in my note-book.*

A very interesting visit was to the Khan's shawl manufactory, and to many other private manufactories, which, however, differed only from the first by being smaller, darker, and dirtier.

The first thing that strikes one is that the actual workshops where the shawls are made are without doors or windows. The entrance is effected through a small square hole in the wall, about three feet from the ground, and light is very sparingly admitted through small holes in the roof. When you have once scrambled inside (a process involving loss of dignity), and when your eyes have become accustomed to the darkness, and your nose to the smell of a number of filthy little saucers of stinking oil with burning wicks in them, three or four of which hang about each loom, then you see before you the sort of Black Hole in which Kashmir shawls are made.

There were eighteen looms in the first "workshop" I entered, and at each one stooped two or three miserable, sallow, half-naked children, their preter-

---

* In the quarterly statement of the Palestine Exploration Fund, July, 1880, I find quoted from the Zeitschrift of the German Palestine Association, an account of some coins discovered in 1872 in Jerusalem, among which is one struck in Kirman in 311 of the Hegira; *i.e.*, about 947 years ago.

naturally thin hard fingers going nervously, and their noses almost touching their work even while I engaged them in conversation.

At first the interest of actually seeing Kashmir shawls woven overpowered all others, and I worked slowly down each loom. All were the same in principle, but there were only about six distinct patterns among all, there being many variations of the same pattern. A wan skeleton of a man, who only seemed galvanized into energy by my foremost servant's presence, showed us round. He was the head pattern maker, and explained all we asked. Some of the children were working by memory, others were nearly perfect, but had to have small grimy patterns tacked up on the loom in front of them, which to my eye were most difficult to understand. Our guide made the patterns and submitted them for approval to the owner or director of the loom. Then children were hired to learn them. Some can only recollect one pattern at a time (and quite enough I thought), and when that pattern was no longer in demand, were out of employment and off pay until they learnt another. Some clever boys could recollect two at a time. I asked why there were no windows to the place, and the skeleton replied that it would be too cold. I said, "Not if the children were decently clothed; the place would be warm enough with all these human creatures packed together like this, even if you took the roof off." But he said with these lamps the place was warm enough without clothing. It was just this: glazed windows and clothing were dearer than lamps without either. The last answers this poor man gave me were: "Yes, they are beaten often, for mistakes in the pattern," and, "they die soon." It seemed incredible that any one could strike these sallow, half-naked children; and yet, I suppose, should any one wearing one of these shawls examine it closely, he might safely infer, that for every fault in the pattern some defenceless creature has been beaten. I went through several of these shops. Some were a little lighter and some a little less light, but the main points of all were the same. I afterwards went to a sale shop, and found here a totally different scene. We were ushered into a well-furnished saloon in a fine large house, lounged on carpets, while shawl after shawl was spread out for our inspection, and we drank coffee, and rolled in our palms the fragrant quince,* and ignored how the beautiful fabrics were made. I was given a full account of the number of stretchings, moistenings, rollings, etc., that a shawl has to go through after leaving the loom before being fit for sale, but they were only what all woollen manufactures require.

The felt cap and felt carpet manufacture is simple but interesting. The workman has a wooden block, like a wig block, the shape and size of the cap he proposes to make. On his right sits a boy "twanging" wool with a bow, and reducing it to a coarse fluff. Next sits a boy with a bowl of soapsuds before him. This latter takes up handfuls of the wool as it is ready and kneads it and soaks it in the soap and water until it holds as much soap as it can retain. It is then handed to the workman, who pulls and hammers it out

---

* A pleasant Persian custom is to give a visitor a fragrant quince to hold in his hand.

into a flat flake, as large as the palm of a man's hand. This he sticks on the block and pats and smooths it down tight. When a complete layer has been put on the block is set to dry, and another block proceeded with meanwhile.

The carpets are made in much the same way, the patterns being produced thus: a mat of hard unabsorbent reed is laid out flat, and the various coloured patterns arranged in their proper respective positions upon it; over this a prepared flake of the brown felt is placed. The whole is then rolled tightly up round a thick stick, and three or four men stand on it, rolling it backwards and forwards until the patterns adhere to the ground flake. Then more flakes are added, and each tightly rolled by men standing on it until a sufficient thickness has been attained.

In the Wakil's workshops I saw some absurd patterns laid out on mats ready to receive their grounds,—among others, grotesque copies (?) of pictures in the *Illustrated London News*.

A visit to the great Madrasa, or school, was interesting; I had previously made the acquaintance of the great Sheikh in the Khan's society, and he kindly allowed me the privilege of walking about as I liked, and questioning the students. The school is a fine building of burnt brick, and its tall minaret carried—of all out of the way things to find—a large blue figured turret clock. It was more than an hour and a half slow on apparent time; but I was assured that it was going and never stopped.

Many of the students were really intelligent, and, had the curriculum provided for them been of any practical value, and had a fraction of the industry and patience they now bestowed on finding out subtle meanings in words probably written at random, been expended on practical science, Kirman would, under the present ruler, give birth to a second French revolution. The tafsīrs on the Kurān are, however, as reasonable as the English commentaries on Shakespeare, where a page is written to explain the hidden meanings of some word which was probably used merely to fill in the jingle of the rhythm. I put one or two of the most forward pupils through a chapter in the Kurān, which they read well enough, excepting always the effeminate Persian pronunciation of the Arabic, but—the old story—with utter indifference as to the meaning of what they read. I tried the old argument, that if this was the word of God it should be understood and acted upon; but they prefer to use it as a charm, as it is given them by their teachers, and as the Bible was given to us in Latin formerly by ours. For general rules of life the Persian is provided by custom, and the Kurān is only quoted by the learned as a law book is quoted by a lawyer, to bring in some old precedent in order to, generally, defeat the end of justice.

One day I visited the dungeon, for such really it is, an underground prison. We entered first the barracks, and then a heavy door was unlocked for us and we entered an enclosure of thick mud-built walls, where lay or sat four middle-aged prisoners, wearing light irons on their legs only. The place was simply a courtyard where the prisoners passed the day, and in the corner was a hole in the floor which I peered into. A short ladder led down into a sort of cellar, in which the men were confined at night. There was absolutely no light, and I could see nothing, but as the men spent the day in the open, and a jailer gave one a half-handful of tobacco as if it was a most ordinary matter, I conclude the imprisonment to be pretty merciful.* They were all "in" for highway robbery, the only thing that in Persia requires serious punishment. Highway robbery can be committed with such impunity, and the escape of the robbers to the mountain fastnesses is so easy, that when an offender is caught the most terrible punishment has to be inflicted, to have the due deterrent effect on his comrades. And I found afterwards cases of robbers being plastered up alive in mortar on the side of the road where their plunder had been made. The men were very apathetic, and I could elicit no response to my inquiries.

A day after this visit, I saw one of the prisoners being released. He had been dressed entirely in white and mounted on a camel, also caparisoned in white with bells and large tassels. He was thus led through the town, accompanied by some ragged minstrels and little boys, and (I was told) set free outside the city gate. He had a fixed sullen look, and appeared to feel his position a good deal, being probably a chief in his own district. I one day made a visit to the colony of Hindus, who being Her Majesty's subjects and thankful for it, and who having heard that I was a sahib from India who spoke Hindustani, kindly

---

* I have seen prisons of a different kind in Persia, witness in Abu Shihr (*Anglice* Bushire), men kept bareheaded in the broiling sun day after day, with their feet beaten to a jelly. Also a long log with sockets cut in it, into which men's legs were placed and kept there by a long iron bar, while chains kept their heads down to their knees.

sent to say that they would be glad to see me. They are a thriving and numerous colony, thanks to the liberal-mindedness of the Khan, and all the import trade from the coast is in their hands. They live, or rather the business places of a great number of them are, in a large caravanserai. They are most of them half Persianized and have been here a very long time.

I have yet to introduce to the reader our social circle at the dinner table. The nawab was the host, and the two young princes and myself made up the guests, supplemented once or twice by some young fellow of sufficient rank to dine with us. Every evening the nawab used to send round his servant, a handsome young fellow as dapper as himself, with a message that the "high in place" his master had discovered an unusually good thing (*i.e.*, some capital wine), and that he begged that my magnificence would illuminate his quarters about an hour after sunset. Thither I would duly repair, and probably be the first arrival. We would while away the time until the other guests arrived, in trying to put together an enormous and most expensive microscope, which the *ci-devant* doctor had brought from Paris, and never yet succeeded in using. From this we would be aroused either by a barbarous love-song chaunted by the two brothers, who would swagger in arm in arm and threaten to break the machinery, unless we immediately came and commenced drinking; or the doctor's servant would come quietly in, and say, "They've come, and are finishing the pickles;" when in self-defence we would adjourn to the doctor's snug dining-room, and commence the business of the night.

The two princes, younger brothers of the Wakil, were much of an age, "young bloods," and of great wealth. There was an English dining table, plates, dishes, knives and forks, etc., but the food and manner of dining was essentially Persian. We began with minute wine-glasses of raki, red wine, purple wine, white wine, and other wines, interspersed with morsels of pickle, sweetmeats, fried melon pips, etc., and had I not been pretty well seasoned, Mr. W. Ellis, of the Greenwich Observatory, would have found some of my observations of Polaris after midnight more difficult to work out than he did. After a sufficiency of small trifles, the real substantial dinner was brought in from the Khan's kitchen. None of the officers of the household were allowed to dine until the Khan had commenced. I have read of some famous ancient king, who caused a trumpet to be blown when his dinner was served, and this trumpet was the signal that his staff might commence. This was our case, and there was a good sound reason for it too, for if we had got only five minutes' start in our mess, we should have got the pick of the whole kitchen, and the Khan would have gone supperless to bed. This the Khan and the ancient monarch above mentioned probably fully understood. It was almost like dining on the stage of Drury Lane Theatre. The two princes came in new dresses every night; crimson velvet and satin were the least expensive articles of their costume, while they wore richly mounted daggers at their belts, and heavy gold chains round their necks.

We had occasionally a devotional element introduced: young Prince Hassan had something on his mind one night, and before touching wine must needs say his prayers. So he put his tasbiah or string of beads on the carpet before him, and knelt down and made the necessary rekaats or obeisances, though his brother was stuffing pistachio nuts down his neck; and he also managed during his devotions to return with interest a considerable amount of chaff from the doctor.

In sooth it was a goodly time,
For it was in the golden prime
Of good Harūn Arrashīd.

I have omitted to mention that the Khan, unasked, sent his cashier over to me to know if I would wish for any money. He brought with him a small sack of silver, of which I took 1,000 krans (£40), and gave him a cheque on Teheran. I do not know whether he does this for every visitor, but am inclined to put it down to respect for the Englishman, as inspired by Sir F. Goldsmid and his mission of '72, who spent some time here and left golden reputations.

I had been now a week at Kirman, and enjoyable as it was after the somewhat hard journey from the coast, I began to feel the traveller's restlessness to get on. The observations had been satisfactory, the men had made what small purchases they wanted to make, and I only waited for a convenient moment to ask the Khan to help me to find transport to Yezd. But he forestalled my wishes as usual, and I found he had a capital caravan of several mules and two stout travelling ponies all ready to start.

I had left a considerable balance of money with my old friend George White Sealy, at Jask, for the payment of the men's wages, and I made out a pay-sheet which they took with them. They picked the best of the camels, which they bought at their own price, and I provided them with a firman from the Khan to ensure their being unmolested. One very cold morning I bade them a rather sorrowful adieu. They were not sanguine about getting safe back home, and begged me earnestly to come back with them, which was of course out of the question. Ghulamshah, who remained with me, was much affected at the parting, and his voice faltered as he urged them not to forget to give his best love to his father, mother, brother, sister, and in fact everybody in Jask. The men swung themselves on to their camels, and got on march, disappearing like spectres in the grey morning light. I had to clap Ghulamshah on the back, and cheer him up a little; and we agreed that we should get along very well together.

Our future travels, however, were of a very different nature to those we had been enjoying: no more leading a band of good-natured, hardy companions through new and wonderful countries, picking out our camping places, going fast or slow as we liked, lunching *en route* in picturesque nooks, at night joking and chaffing, chatting over camp fire, etc. No more self-dependence or judgment required. Here we had a coarse boor of a mule-driver, who would go long or short stages according as he was paid, and would be rude if you were civil to him, and a straight uninteresting hackneyed track along a flat shingly desert between two barren ranges of hills, and fixed halting places at pretty regular intervals.

In the afternoon, I took leave of the Khan with much gratitude. He gave me a small but exquisitely fine Kirman carpet (not to be confounded with the Karmani or Syrian carpets) and accepted a pair of hurricane lamps and a tin of kerosine oil which I frankly assured him was, excepting scientific instruments, the only thing worthy of presentation. In the evening we had a farewell banquet at the mess, when a gallant Circassian captain of troops became so uproarious, that we were in fear of a message from His Highness, but I slipped away about midnight for a last observation of Polaris, and to see that nothing had been omitted in the packing up.

CHAPTER XIV.

En Route for Yezd.

Our new caravan.—Muleteers and mules.—Ghulāmshah's introduction to a horse.—Our garrulous friend.—He is pounced upon by the Charvadār.—Extraordinary affection of mules for leading pony.—Night in a caravanserai.—" Kum Karda."—The Kāshuwelli.—Value of bells on the march.—Commissariat arrangements.—Our soldier escort and his steed.—Night marches.—A dwarf camel.—Persian way of "bitting" a camel.—Bahramabad.—Designs on my Westley-Richards.—A pun in Persian.—Feeding camels.—The wall and the masjid, or two strings to the bow.—Anar Fort, and the deputation of distressed agriculturists.—Annoying curiosity of natives.—The sextant capsized.—We reach Yezd.—Neglected by the authorities.—Our fanatic friends.—Syeds.—Their gold mine discoveries.—Their murders.—Trade and silk manufactures.—The gabrs.—Brobdingnagian beet-root.—The present city getting gradually buried as the former one has been.—The soldier gets my gun for his horse.—We leave Yezd.

NEXT morning very early we started on our way for Yezd, with a hearty farewell from the nawab and the princes. Our cavalcade consisted of a very strong useful white pony, which was my mount, and which I often wished afterwards I had bought. A good chestnut was provided for Ghulamshah, so covered with trappings and large brass bells as to make a noise like an ambulatory battle of Prague. This animal was the leader of the caravan, and it was quite extraordinary to observe the affection the mules all had for him. Our muleteer Meshedi was a tall powerful fellow, with his feet swathed in endless woollen rags, and who used six feet of an iron chain as a whip for his six mules, whom he drove before him with incessant oaths and cursing. Last but not least, was a mounted soldier sent by the Khan, whom from the magnificence of his moustache I dubbed the Padishah.

The road from Kirman to Yezd is about 220 miles of uninteresting desert, with an occasional clump of mud houses surrounded by mud-walled gardens of at this time leafless mulberry trees.

At the villages marked on the map are good caravanserais for freight caravans, and chapar khanas for people riding post. It was very cold, the thermometer at 8 a.m. ranging from 29° to 33° Fahr. We started at 7.30 a.m. over a barren slightly undulating plain, with barren hills on either side of us. That sentence might be stereotyped as describing our proceedings for the next few days.*

* I was often surprised at the long distances old decrepit men would undertake in this country. They think no more of riding 200 miles across desert on a lame donkey, than an English farmer of going from London to Edinburgh by the express train. On one occasion thirteen donkeys, laden with beet-root covered carefully with sacks, accompanied us for four days, and on the fourth day what was my surprise to find one of the loads of beet-root sit up, and after a violent fit of coughing and spitting blood, call in a querulous voice for a drink of water. I asked his friends what was the matter with him, and found that he was suffering from an intermittent fever, which always came on at the time when they loaded up. So they used to put him on a donkey's back, put a leg in each saddle-bag stuffed full of chopped straw for warmth, lay him prone on his face, along his donkey's neck, and then cover him with sacks. I may add, that this coughing fit was the only sign of life the old man made while I knew him, and but for that, I should up to this day have regarded him as beet-root.

I was amused at Ghulamshah, who had not had much acquaintance with horses, spurring his jangling steed up alongside of mine, and exclaiming with joyful surprise, "Sahib, this is a horse." "Ah!" said I, "how did you find that out, butcha?" "Oh," said he naïvely, "I asked the muleteer." It was great glory to him to be on a horse, an animal reserved for ameers in his country.

Not long after starting, we were overtaken by a chatty old gentleman, who had heard of our intended departure for Yezd, and resolved to accompany us. But as we came from the Khan's palace, we were such great people that he could not ask leave to start with us, and so prepared to overtake us after we had left. He had, however, waited at the wrong gate of the city, and thus nearly missed us, and being a choleric old gentleman was actually indignant with us for "going out of the wrong gate."

He asked many questions about my religion and general habits, settled for himself that Ghulamshah was a eunuch presented to me by the Khan,* and finding that we were of much the same stamp, proposed eternal "sohbat" or friendship. His garrulity, however, received a sudden check. Meshedi the muleteer had been on ahead, but as we were talking dropped behind to see after the rearward mules, and detected the old man. Now it seems that recently the old man had hired one of Meshedi's "yaboos" or large ponies, and ridden it most unmercifully, and Meshedi

* There were some grounds for this idea, as I had had the good fortune by a timely surgical operation to save the life of one of his harem guardians. The cure made me rather a reputation, and in his gratitude the Khan had offered me the patient as a gift.

was very prompt to tax him with the matter. The row that ensued lasted some miles, and relieved the monotony of a considerable part of that day's march. We spent a comfortable night at the large village of Baghin, and started early the next morning with the thermometer at 33° Fahr.

This being the commencement of our mule travelling, I must say a few words about it. The charvadār (charwardar, *quadruped owner*) or muleteer is the locomotive of Persia, and I think must be about the hardiest of the human race. Not only gifted with extraordinary powers of walking on the most meagre food, he has such strength, that unaided he can reload a mule whose burden has gone crooked, and though the day's march may be only thirty miles, he often has to double the distance running after this or that mule, which has deviated from the path. He is a stalwart brute, with a keen eye to the main chance, and his language to his mules beggars description.

The Persian mule too is a unique thing. They are always led by a yaboo, or large sized pony, which is covered with as many bells as his owner can muster. They will follow that pony in the most docile manner, as long as he has all his bells on, and show a ludicrous affection for him.

There are some great strong mules and some small ones, but all seem to carry equal burdens, and though in some cases the small ones were badly lame at starting they always made the distance.

Camping at night too, in the caravanserais, was a new experience for us. We slept in close proximity to the mules, and though they were not my own property, as the camels had been in the first part of this journey, I took a keen interest in their loading, feeding, state of their backs, and general welfare, as indeed every traveller must do in his transport.

On first arrival, the dalan-dar, or door-keeper is hunted up, and firewood, eggs, and sometimes a fowl, are purchased at not exorbitant rates. In some caravanserais there are rooms for the traveller, but in some he accommodates himself on a raised dais in the stable—the most convivial place unless he has mapping or writing to do.

The mules on arrival are at once given their nose-bags, containing whatever was left from last meal, stirred up to prevent them from finding out that they have smelt it before. They are then unloaded, and their saddles taken off, and then ensues a babel of sounds. All the mules wear a few bells, and immediately set to work scratching themselves vigorously. Ghulamshah's yaboo was accustomed to be scratched by a very strong young white mule, whom we had named Kerimdad, after one of my servants in Jask, famous for great strength, stupidity, and exuberance of spirits. It may sound absurd, but on more than one occasion when Kerimdad was delayed in any way, I have heard the yaboo impatiently call him.

The barley is next doled out accurately proportioned by the muleteer. Some mules require very little barley, and their price is accordingly high, as the same amount of work is done by all.

The muleteer is very careful to give all the mules their corn at the same time, but I did not notice this until several weeks afterwards, when at a caravanserai in Kurdistan I saw the charvadār stabbing the palate of one of the mules with a large "jul duz" or packing needle, and squeezing out quantities of blood with his hand. On inquiring what this was for, he commenced abusing his assistant, a younger brother, for carelessness in having omitted to give this mule his corn at the same time as all the others, in consequence of which it had "kum karda," *i.e.*, got a swelling full of blood in the roof of its mouth, which rendered it incapable of eating. I found this actually to be the case, and it constantly occurred *en route*; every native whom I consulted, and I made exhaustive inquiries on this interesting subject, told me, and implicitly believed what he said, that it was simply owing to a watering at the mouth, and could be produced at any time by delaying the barley of one mule or horse while others all round him are feeding. This theory has met with a good deal of disbelief, but I believe that a Persian muleteer knows as much about mules as any one, and that there must be some truth in it.

The swelling is, on the march, lanced with a packing needle, and while stationary the animal is fed upon hard dry beans, which burst the swelling.

The muleteer takes a hurried snack of very hard dry bread, often six months old, and then sets to work with the curry-comb, or kāshuwelli. This is a simple but effective instrument, and could be made as follows: Take six inches of an iron pipe, say three inches in diameter, and cut it longitudinally down the middle. Serrate the sides, and stretch across the arch at intervals in its length two or three stout wires, on which string loosely a number of iron disks, like halfpennies. These, when the curry-comb is used, jingle and add to the music of the mules' bells, and also, by the persistency with which they are heard, tell the muleteer whether his assistants are scrubbing their animals down properly or not.

Travelling with mules in Persia is inseparably associated with the jangling of bells, and the traveller's are soon teaches him to attach a meaning to the various kinds of jangling. There is the steady jogging of the march, the violent irregular jangling of the scratching when the saddles are taken off, and the steady business-like quiet jangle when the noses are deep in the barley. These bells are of infinite use. They cheer the animals up on the march, and at night enable the mules to follow the leading yaboo without any trouble. They are of all sizes from a walnut to an English bucket. The largest size are generally used on camels, and are not fastened round the neck, but outside the load, one on either side, and their solemn tolling as you pass a large caravan on a pitch-dark night is most impressive.

We got on very well for food on this section of the route between Kirman and Yezd, and never had any of the starvation times that we had experienced in Bashakard. We carried pieces of raw mutton with us, and this boiled with onions, and pepper and salt, formed our almost invariable food. Ghulamshah commenced cooking as soon as the "cookhouse," or large box containing the cooking implements, could be unpacked. I had purchased in Kirman a copper basin with a very tight fitting lid, called a Kābulimā, and in this such a quantity of the meat and onions as was left from our dinner, without the soup, was enclosed for my morning meal, which I usually took on horseback, there being no trees or sheltered nooks in this barren part of the route. Our soldier escort the Padishah, was a cheerful conversational fellow. He generally rode by my side, and gave me much untrustworthy information respecting the government, trade, and wealth of the country. I thought he had been sent with me as a sort of guard of honour, but found afterwards, that he had a mission to obtain, on behalf of his master, my sole remaining gun, a much cherished Westley-Richards of the most perfect workmanship. He was mounted on a spare wiry white horse, which, in spite of a pensive or thoughtful aspect, could always muster up a canter at the end of the march, when his master, with his rifle banging about his back, rode forward to announce our coming.

Meshedi, our tall muleteer, very soon evinced an anxiety to travel at night. This however did not suit me, as I wanted to survey the country. The animals certainly travel better at night, and both they and their masters do go fast asleep while on the march. Meshedi's idea of enjoying a journey, was to start between one and two in the morning, and finish the stage at about ten, when he would spend the whole day bargaining for fodder, trying to "swap" mules, etc. I made a few journeys like this, when I was assured that the country was absolutely without a single point of interest, and we certainly got over the ground wonderfully, and had more time to spend in the halting places, where lay the only interest that existed. I also learnt to sleep on horseback, but on more than one occasion the cold was so intense that I had to get off and walk at frequent intervals to restore circulation, and it is hard work to go twenty-eight to thirty-five miles night after night through bitter cold and darkness.

We passed several caravans on these night marches, and the men of two of them at least were all utterly sound asleep, for though we all shouted to know when they had left their last camp, in order to form an idea as to how much farther we had to go, we could get no reply. As far as could be seen in the darkness, all had their feet in their saddle-bags, and were lying flat on their mules' necks.

Once we ourselves got off the track, and I was rudely awakened by Meshedi seizing my horse's head, and turning him round so suddenly that I nearly fell off. We had got on to a side path leading to a village off the road, and spent a weary hour and a half stumbling over loose shingly mounds full of holes until we recovered the main route.

Two days' good travelling brought us to Bahramabad, after having passed through the small village of Baghin, the larger village of Ruban containing 300 houses, and the caravanserai of Kaftar Khan.

Between these places we had crossed nothing but shingly desert. We had daily passed and been passed by a caravan of thirty large camels carrying henna to Yezd, each camel carrying about 320 pounds. They were colossal shaggy brutes, and realized the camel of my early picture books. Among them they had an extraordinary dwarf camel, who though only the size of a horse had the strength and temper of a demon. It objected equally savagely to being unloaded or loaded, and would bite any one or anything within its reach like lightning, darting out its head like a snake. In this country they do not attach the rein to a wooden stud fixed in a hole bored through the nose, as in Balūchistan. They have a worsted band about four inches long, which passes over the nose, being kept in place by a halter; at each end are attached strips of iron, one strip has a chain attached to it, and the other a ring through which the chain is passed, so that by pulling the chain the iron sides are pressed together and form two sides of an acute-angled triangle with the woollen band for a base. By shortening the base and sharpening the side-irons, you can almost cut a camel's nose off by pulling at the rein, and this wild camel, who was called mad by the men, had, judging from his scars, been often rather near suffering this amputation. I believe the nature of camels differs more widely than that of any other animals. One may see any day a small boy doing what he likes with a string of twenty huge camels, but it took five skilled and plucky men to load this little roaring brute.

Bahramabad is a considerable town of 4,000 houses, fairly clean, and evidently thriving. The caravanserai was a good one, the rooms having for the first time, if I remember rightly, doors and windows; but it was quite filled up by a large caravan of more than a hundred camels, with their burdens and attendants, and I was about reluctantly to seek the dignified solitude of the chapar khana, or post house, when, by some occult means or other, our gallant surbaz arranged the evacuation of one of the best rooms, and I took possession. Once installed here we were promptly called upon by the governor, who had evidently been instructed by the wakil, that my old Westley-Richards was to be got from me by any fair means available. I began to realize that the good old weapon must go, but for the present staved off

RUSH HILLS.

matters with profuse politeness. We then received the sarhang, or commander of the detachment of troops placed here. He was a fine handsome energetic Circassian, and said he was a slave of the Shah's, and had been educated in the college in Teheran.

From the moment of our arrival it had rained incessantly; so much so that Ghulamshah, with the diffidence of a boy offering his first pun, asked with an ill-concealed smile, " Is this Bahramabad (*the village of Bahram*), or Bairamabad (*the village of rain*)?"

After dinner I wandered about among the camel-men. The fact of my having been a camel-owner, and knowing something of camels, was always a passport to the sympathies of these rough fellows, and they would chat freely about routes, trade, etc. In spite, however, of their goodwill (sometimes propitiated by a stick of pitch plaster for a sore back, with instructions how to apply it), it took many questions and answers before one could get enough information on which to base a definite truthful statement.

I was up early the next morning, and it was interesting to watch all the camels get their morning feed. They quite filled the square enclosure, and were divided into messes of from five to eight members. Their attendant spread out his māshūk, or woollen cloak, and then poured on it their rations of chopped straw and cotton seed, which latter made a peculiar crumbling sound as it was munched up. Some messes were very harmonious, and merely munched their food up as fast as they could, but one ill-tempered camel would spoil a whole party, and one brute close under where I stood, would abandon his whole breakfast sooner than lose a chance of biting his neighbour in the back of the neck.

I found that the horse I had been riding was not to go any farther, he in fact belonged to the governor here and was only on his return trip. I had then three choices, the gallant soldier's white horse, Ghulamshah's yaboo, or the muleteer's pet riding mule.

The gallant soldier's horse was out of the question, as the Padishah's only value lay in the effect he produced, and that would be reduced to nil were he mounted on a humble mule. It was a shame to take Ghulamshah's horse from him, and the muleteer's mule seemed a very willing locomotive-engine kind of animal, admirably adapted for going mechanically over long dreary distances. So I took the mule, and was very sorry for it afterwards. For I could not bear the number of bells on it, and had them taken off, in consequence of which the mule sulked all the way to Yezd. This resulted on one occasion in my getting off and abandoning him in the desert, to the dismay of his owner, who spent the whole night in search of him.

The next place of importance was Anar, two marches farther on.

The country became a little less sterile, and we passed one or two small villages of one-storey mud houses and a little meagre corn. It will be seen on the map that there is a slight depression in the level here.

Near Hurmuzibad a lofty mud wall ran a considerable distance at right-angles to the path, and without any apparent design. Close by it was a small masjid, and I asked what they were for. Meshedi explained that the village was exposed to the danger of being buried in the sand, so the wall was built to keep this off. "But," I asked, "what is the masjid for?" "Oh," said Meshedi, who had a cheerful kind of cynicism, "that's for them to pray that the sand shall not be blown over them; you see, they're sure to manage it one way or another."

We had rain every day, and the fine caravanserai of Biath was approached in a slough of mud. Leaving Biath we crossed a belt of shingle, then one of sand, and then one of mud, there being about two miles of each. Here we met a cafila, or caravan, of fifty camels carrying opium and asafœtida, and after a tedious struggle through mud, reached Anar on the sixth January.

Anar consists of a fort and sixty houses. It is important as being the place where the trade route from Bandar Abbas to Yezd joins the Kirman route. This route, called the Sinjan or Rapsinjan route, was described as being all hilly, the road running along the beds of streams about twenty days' march, and provided with camel fodder along its whole length.

Here I was waited on by a deputation of distressed tradesmen and agriculturists, who deposed that they had been driven from their native homes in Shahri-Babeg* by the rapacity of the governor there. I do not know what idea they had of my power to help them, but they begged me to represent the matter to the governor of Yezd. I pointed out that it was none of his business, Shahri-Babeg belonging to the province of Shiraz, but I undertook to deliver any

* Corruption of Shahr-i-Baghi, "garden city."

letter they might write, which I duly performed, with the results one usually gets for meddling in other people's business.

Both from inquiries and from personal observation I think they were a shiftless, idle people. Their irrepressible curiosity annoyed me exceedingly while I was taking observations, but they got a ridiculous fright once. The sun was very low, and I had almost to lie on my back to see its reflection in the mercury. I was in this position waiting for the sun to come from behind the clouds. When it did emerge, I quickly seized the sextant and presented it, as they thought, straight at them, on which they dispersed in horror. We had a laugh, too, at an impetuous youth, the son of the dalan-dar who sold us firewood, eggs, etc. He commenced worrying Ghulamshah for payment. Ghulamshah was unpacking the instruments, and the youth's observations ran something as follows: "Now then, pay me what you owe me. I'm in a great hurry! Oh! but there is neither strength nor power except in God!"—this on his eye catching the sextant. "You owe me three krans, and this is only two and a half. Oh! merciful Lord!"—this as a large map was unrolled.

Next day it snowed hard, but after twelve hours in the saddle we reached Kirmanshahan, where a few soldiers levied black mail on caravans for protecting the route. We were exempt, our mules being known to belong to the Zabit of Bahramabad. Here the muleteer carelessly capsized the box containing the sextant, artificial horizon, etc., and I was much dismayed at finding them all in a chaotic heap. No harm was done except to two plates which we carried, more as a guarantee of our respectability than for use. The road here is a steady descent to Yezd; another twelve hours brought us to the village of Sar-i-Yezd, and villages began to thicken along the route. We stayed here at the chapar khana, and had a pleasant evening with the host, who was a most intelligent fellow, asked innumerable questions, and finally, posing with his head one side and looking fixedly at me, said, "Now your loftiness in place has made many journeys, and seen many countries. Have you ever seen any country like Persia?" A murmur of gratification went round our little circle, as I assured him with fervour that I never had.

Next morning, soon after starting, we saw our destination. The very large and important city of Yezd lay in the far distance, stretching right across the horizon. Its lofty minarets seemed innumerable, and it was years since we had seen a city nearly so large and important. Without any exaggeration the approach to Yezd is very fine and impressive. You see its whole size spread out over the flat plain, and nothing interrupts the view.

I had procured from the chapar khana a showy but incurably vicious horse, and Ghulamshah, Meshedi, and myself rode cheerily on ahead through apparently interminable winding streets, and finally landed in a large caravanserai, which led off from one of the main bazaars.

I was not at all well treated by the authorities of Yezd, in spite of a letter of introduction from the Wakil-al-Mulk which the surbaz duly delivered, but the effect of which was I suspect counteracted by the letter from the distressed people of Anar.

The governor sent for me the next day, and I went and waited in an ante-chamber for an hour or more; but he had just gone into his ante-room or private apartment, and I had to leave without seeing him. He sent after me then, begging me to come the next day. I went again, but after waiting half an hour I sent him an angry message, which I do not suppose he ever got, and made up my mind to see all there was to be seen by my own resources.

I missed very much the courtesy of the governor of Kirman and his genial associates, but though I was often hooted at in the streets, and more than once had stones thrown at me, I managed to see all there was to be seen. Not being able to get into polite society, I fraternised with such as I could get, and found much edification in the society of an intelligent drug-seller, whose stock-in-trade consisted in an extraordinary assortment of broken-up leaves of unrecognisable plants and various strong smelling powders. I was much annoyed by the fanatical nature of the people. Young students would come and argue and declaim for hours at a time on nice theological points, and quantities of little boys would at one moment be begging for money with outstretched arms, and the next shouting at the top of their voices the "izan," or call to prayer. Every second man or boy was a Syed, and I never was so tired of Muhammad's family in my life. Again, mysterious men would wake me up in the dead of night, and, after exasperating me to the utmost by interminable pledges to secrecy, would produce a bag full of pebbles, bits of copper ore, lead, etc., and say they had found them, and ask what they were worth, they being always under the impression that they were gold ore. Sometimes one of the party would beckon me out of the room, and point through the crack in the door at one of my self-invited guests, and inform me in a significant whisper that he had found a gold mine of immense value.

One man, who never appeared in person, sent numbers of urgent messages for me to come and dine with him, always stipulating that I should go at night-time lest the people should see me. This invitation I invariably refused, and have no doubt that I should have been murdered had I accepted. Just before I arrived, the leading Gabr merchant had been riddled with bullets and hacked to pieces for nothing else than not being a muslim. This the people related with a sort of pride, as exhibiting how religious they were. The governor, however, took some slight measures to stop this; for though in the case just mentioned no punishment had been inflicted, seven men had recently been beheaded for a riot in which several similar murders had been committed.

Yezd bears every mark of a thriving business place, and might I think be called the Manchester of Persia. Its chief industry is silk weaving, and next, perhaps, in importance is opium growing.

Yezd is surrounded by villages, the main part of whose industry is growing tut or mulberry trees for feeding silkworms, and in addition to this, large quantities of silk are brought here from Meshed and Herat to be woven. I went into many of the manufactories, the finest of which, as at Kirman, belonged to the governor. They were fine, clean, spacious rooms, some containing seventy looms all busily working. The chief patterns were broad striped sheets for the ladies to wear, and black-and-white silk handkerchiefs.

Some smaller workshops made a special kind of head-dress for export to Arabia *viâ* Charbar and Maskat. The silk looked to me poor in quality, and not much better than alpaca; but the weaving was undeniably close, regular, and good, and the colours brilliant. The trade is mostly in the hands of from six to seven thousand Gabrs or Persians who have not adopted Islam. One man, a frequent visitor and who always brought his poor idiot brother, pathetically imploring me to cure him, owned more than a thousand camels, who carried goods between here and Bandar Abbas, twenty-four days' march. Three or four of the Gabrs are British subjects, and I was assured that they had a school in the ancient Zand and Pazand language. I noticed here some enormous globular beet-root. The diameter of one was just the breadth of a page of the *Illustrated London News*, and I procured a quantity of the seed.*

A peculiar feature about Yezd is the number of large tanks far below the surface of the ground. They are neatly domed in, and approached by long flights of steps. Also many of the houses are far below the level of the street, and are approached by similar long flights of steps. After leaving Yezd, I crossed at about ten miles north the very extensive remains of ancient Yezd, buried in sand; and it appeared reasonable to think that present Yezd was gradually being buried, but the process was so slow, if indeed it was going on,

---

* It came up a fine *shrub* in England, all top and no root to speak of.

that no one could give me any information on the subject, though they seemed interested in my conjecture.

On the 14th our gallant soldier took his leave, with a good present *and* my last gun. He gave me in exchange his wiry white horse, thus gaining the only end with which he had accompanied me. The "Padishah," as we named the horse, was a good willing beast, and came into Baghdad as fresh as he left Kirman. Also to-day, to our great satisfaction, we found mules to take us to Ispahan, and joyfully commenced packing up. Yezd is a very thriving money-making place, but far from pleasant for a solitary European, whose presence the local authorities ignore. In our new caravan were not only good mules and companionable muleteers, but we had for our travelling companion the celebrated Hāji Katirchee, or Hāji the muleteer, who, together with his horse, merits a fresh chapter.

CHAPTER XV.

YEZD TO ISPAHAN.

The Hāji and his horse.—Our new caravan.—A stirring gallop.—Desertion by the muleteer.—Disaster to the chronometer.—Worst fears confirmed.—Night march back to Yezd.—The Hāji at home.—Maibut.—The weaver's beam of the Bible explained.—Minimum thermometers at night.—More Syeds.—Warmer weather.—We part company with the Hāji.—Difficulties ahead.—Snowed up.—Mulberries and vinegar as a diet.—Thermometer 18° Fahrenheit and no roof.—Fishark.—Attempt to deceive.—Its consequences.—Triumph on my part.—View across the Ispahan valley.—More night marching.—"Hinges" upsets the butcha.—Wild fowl on the Ispahan river.—A tiresome finish.—Ispahan at last.—Meet a white man.—Bass' beer.

NO one could see the Hāji's burly figure and round jovial face without at once taking a liking to him. Bustling, hearty, and an indefatigable traveller, he was one of the honest men in Persia, that is, of the English standard of honesty. He had a horse, too, on which he had seven times ridden to Mekka and back, a great bony, vicious animal that could walk 6½ to 7 miles an hour from sunrise to sunset. He made the arrangements for me, and though from the first day's experience I argued the worst possible results, we all, with the exception of an occasional "swap," landed safely in Baghdad. We had five mules, and a lame donkey, a horse for Ghulamshah, which afterwards became celebrated under the name of "Hinges," while I rode the "Padishah."

On the morning of the fifteenth we got *en route* for Ispahan, and splashed down the muddy streets of Yezd for as we hoped the last time, headed by the Hāji enveloped in an incredible number of coats and seated on such a pile of baggage as almost eclipsed his big horse.

On leaving Yezd we passed through sandy cultivated ground and numerous villages. I had been laughing at the Hāji's multifarious saddle-bags and garments, and asking him how he proposed to get on if he wanted to canter, when he gave a tremendous bellow and set off at full gallop; I of course followed suit, and we had a stirring gallop of about a mile. How the Hāji ever kept all his goods together, I could never imagine. He was the most ludicrous sight, sometimes on one part of his horse, sometimes on another, arms and legs, coatskirts and bundles all flying about and banging about him in all directions, while the old horse pounded along in a way that can only be likened to Smiley's fourteen-minute mare, in Mark Twain's "Jumping Frog."

And now an accident occurred which gave me more annoyance at the time than it need have done, had I known how really unimportant it was. We waited after our gallop to allow the mules to come up, and when they arrived found the muleteer absent and the baggage in charge of a young boy only about the size of Ghulamshah. I was told that the muleteer was only just behind, but we never saw him again.

Now Muhammad was a ruddy-faced, broad-shouldered, sturdy young fellow, very willing, good-natured, and anxious to be of any use he could. But he was not strong enough to put a crooked load straight, and the mules were fresh, continually stampeding and shifting their loads. The result was what I might have foreseen. The mule with the chronometer bolted, shifted his load, got frightened, and eventually came heavily to the ground. I was furious, but that was no use; we all jumped off our horses, and after about half an hour got things straight. So many passers-by had collected that I did not like to open the box, which contained also my bag of money, and I hoped for the best, knowing how carefully it was padded up, but I could think of nothing else all the rest of the journey. It seemed miserable, after hundreds of miles of really difficult travelling, to come to grief in this way.

When we arrived at Himmetabad I eagerly opened the box, and my heart really seemed to sink down when I found the faithful old chronometer stopped.

The Hāji sympathised with my distress in the kindest manner, and when I proposed to go back to Yezd that night to take a fresh set of observations in the same place as I had observed before, he volunteered to accompany me.

It was piercing cold, pitch dark, and the hail drove in our faces, and I was tired and dispirited. We got to Yezd by daylight, however, to the surprise of our friend the druggist, and I re-started the chronometer and took a long and very careful series of sights, and we started back again hopeful, and reached Himmetabad for the second time, after nearly thirty-six hours' consecutive travelling under very difficult circumstances.

I often wondered how Ghulamshah, who was only a youngster, stood such marches as this, and many others still longer we had to make afterwards, but I never saw him tired, and after the longest, coldest march he would unpack the instruments, cook the dinner, etc., and never omit anything.

The next day was only four hours to Maibut, for the Hāji's horse at a walk kept ours in a shambling canter. Here he was enthusiastically received into the bosom of his family, after a long journey, and half the inhabitants crowded round him, while he good-humouredly shouted at them to get away and not make a fuss. He left me snugly installed in the chapar khana, and went off to his own house, having extorted a promise that I would remain one day, and come and dine with him.

Maibut is a large thriving village of one thousand houses, a considerable acreage of mulberry trees, and a manufactory of "zeylis," or strong cotton carpets, and coarse pottery. The mail arrived from Teheran while we were here, being carried by two men in two bulky pairs of saddle-bags.

Maibut is best described as having been hewn out of solid mud. Everything is a friable mud—houses, walls, ground, and roads all of the same material. I noticed that the walls of the gardens, which were very high, got thinner and thinner towards the top, and found this was done on the same principle as loose bricks are placed on the tops of our prison walls, *i.e.*, to make it impossible to scale them. In watching the manufacture of the zeylis, or cotton carpets, we saw a good illustration of the biblical weaver's beam. The large bole of wood round which the carpet is wound by a capstan-bar-like arrangement as fast as it is woven, is made of the largest trees in the country; and I saw very few capable of supplying such timber except the plane trees, which are few and far between.

Ghulamshah was amused at the keeper of the chapar khana asking him naïvely where I had bought him. His being so very dark, combined with his more than regulation enormous Balūch nose, invariably led to his being mistaken for my slave. The thermometer here was 108° in the sun, and 35° at night, with a slight frost. With reference to the taking the minimum thermometer at night, I may mention an absurd incident that took place about a fortnight after this. It was always necessary to select a place for the thermometer which should fairly expose it to the air, be safe from prowling cats, and also from curious natives. And on this occasion I had put it in such a singularly safe place, that in the morning I could not find it at all, and eventually had to leave without it.

We went and had a bountiful lunch with the Hāji, who treated us with boisterous hospitality. I should think his house, which corresponded in some way to that of a country farmer, was always well filled with good things; but now, on the return of the master, the fatted calf was killed, and great were the rejoicings.

The people seemed a peaceful, contented community; old men sitting out in the sun in batches picking cotton, others better off appeared to spend their time in smoking outside the masjid, while the able-bodied made carpets and pots, cultivated their mulberries, and the women cooked the dinner, ground the corn, etc.

We were not yet free of the Syeds. One old man forced himself into my room three times, in spite of being put out forcibly by Ghulamshah, and would seize me by the coat and grin in my face, saying simply "Money, money." When remonstrated with, he said indignantly, "But I'm a Syed!"

When I mounted next morning I found fourteen old men calmly seated outside, each confidently expecting a considerable present. I lost all patience, and abused them roundly, saying I had not come all this way to throw away money on idle Jews who dressed themselves up in green turbans, and profaned the holy name of Syed.

I have forgotten to mention the fat little son of the Hāji, who sat for hours decanting chopped straw from one of his little boots into the other, with a supernatural gravity and importance of manner. He thought he was winnowing barley, as he had often seen his father do.

After leaving Maibut the range of snow-covered hills which had fringed our route so far ended, and the temperature became much warmer.

The next stage to the good caravanserai of Arjanun was without interest, save that the underground canal, which supplied the water, contained fine fish ten inches long. We passed over shingly plains past the small villages of Syed Muhammad, Zearat, and Shumsabad, and put up at the chapar khana of Aghd, where was an immensely polite dalan-dar. The Hāji had stayed behind at Maibut to complete his domestic arrangements, but caught us up here, and was joyfully welcomed by the people. He was a most generous fellow, and had always his capacious pockets full of bread, sweetmeats, and small coin for any one who wanted them on the road. The weather now became bright and sunny. We had as a result flies and musquitoes, and there were a few small date-trees and patches of wheat in ear.

Next day we went on to Nou Gumbaz. Here was a very large caravan of camels from Tabriz, if the men told me truly. They were still shaggier than those we had seen before. They were worked nine months a year, and were shorn once a year, and then greased. They were all fed on cotton seed, and the "crunkling" noise of so many feeding together sounded curiously on the still night air.

There was also an old watch-tower built before the caravanserai. In old times watchmen used to keep guard against marauding hordes of Balūchis, who came from beyond the, to other people, impassable deserts on the east. Ghulamshah was grimly pleased at the continual evidences of the fear his fellow-countrymen had created among the Persians.

The Hāji to-night was very strong on the very heavy taxes he had to pay—six tomāns per annum per mule—and had made up his mind next time he went to Tiflis to become a Russian subject. We parted with him here, as he went on due north to Teheran, and I branched to the west for Ispahan.

We bid the good Hāji God-speed next day, and started on our comparatively lonely march. We felt the loss of his cheery conversation very much. Moreover, there was no defined track on our route, nor any caravanserais, and I felt certain misgivings about taking the caravan (for it was evidently all on my shoulders) across, as I had heard much of people being lost in snowdrifts.

The first day was very uncomfortable; it rained hard the whole march, and the mules continually scattered all over the country. However, we reached Pudaz at last, persuaded some people to turn out of their house for a consideration, and made ourselves snug over a good fire. I may mention that I was taken in by a man who sold me a mān of green mulberry wood, which gives no heat, splits, bursts, and flies out of the fireplace with astounding reports.

The next morning, January 23rd, we were snowed up, and could with difficulty open the door. We got out, however, but any observations were out of the question. I never saw snow come down so thick. Pudaz was a small village of mulberry gardens, and the people were covered with white sores, which they attributed to their living in the winter on mulberries and vinegar, with a few dates. They brought round the stuffed skin of a remarkably fine white and brown wolf, for the exhibition of which the shooter asked for bakshish, which I willingly gave, for the poor fellow must have sat in the cold a good many nights before he made the successful shot. The people seemed comfortable enough. The cattle were all warmly stabled, and had plenty of fodder; while the general occupation was spinning wool or weaving woollen garments.

We got on march at half-past nine, but I could not help feeling in rather a ridiculous position. Here I was with five mules—one badly lame—and a lame donkey, and for my companions two boys, neither over eighteen, if as much. Muhammad certainly professed to know the road, but it appeared that he had only been over it twice. I knew nothing of it, except that it seemed to be a winding valley, that we were six thousand feet above the sea, and had made two thousand of that in the last stage; and that if we continued rising two thousand feet per day, and it continued snowing, we should find some difficulty in getting through.

We stumbled on to Todeshk, though the snow increased hourly. On either side were hills about three hundred feet high, and the valley we were going up contained every few miles a snowed-up village, with its accompanying walled enclosures of leafless mulberry-trees. All the villages were called "lāghari," and I did not at first realize that the word meant thin or in needy circumstances. At 4.15 p.m. the snow mercifully stopped. We crossed a level plain studded with walled mulberry gardens, and at 6.7 p.m. camped in a deserted and roofless stable, at an apparently deserted village called Todeshk. The thermometer was 38° when we camped, but went down to 18° in the night, and everything in the cooking pots was frozen as hard as stone. I got good, clear observations of Polaris, and the barometer showed that we had only risen two hundred feet that day, so I began to hope we were as high as was necessary.

We found in the morning that there were forty houses, and that two of the men could read.

Our troubles were over for the present; the weather was milder, and we marched over a shingly plain studded with plantations.

We began ascending the slopes of a lofty range of mountains. Villages were numerous, always dead and buried in snow, and only inhabited, as far as one could see, by numerous pert and incongruous magpies, and a few solemn hooded crows, while the everlasting square mud-walled enclosures of mulberry-trees became exasperating from their continual iteration. It was late that night before we got into camp, and in the darkness we missed one another, and lost our way more than once, and we were glad to get into the large thriving village of Fishark. I noticed that we rode through a large masjid, and was surprised to find myself welcomed most cordially, and provided with a large house, swept and garnished, a good fire, and all necessaries. Muhammad the ruddy-faced came forward and bashfully explained that this was his house, that his foot was now upon his native heath, and that he hoped I should be comfortable, and forgive any faults he had committed on march. Fifty willing friends helped to unload the kit. I thanked Muhammad, told him to be sure to load up early, and went sound asleep without any dinner.

Next day I took my morning sights, packed up the kit, and sat expectant for my muleteer.

After waiting some time I went out into the street, and meeting a man whom I recognised as having seen the previous night, I asked where was my muleteer. He answered, "Oh, he's gone to his uncle's."

"Well," I said naturally, "when is he going to load up?"

"Oh," said he coolly, "you're not going to load up for two or three days. Don't you know it's the Ashra, or feast of ten days?"

I was intensely disgusted; all this civility had been shown simply to trick me into halting. Had I been asked, I would willingly have halted a day or so, but to be cheated into it was unbearable. I inquired where the uncle lived, and sent a man to call the boy at once. Then I inquired where the mules were, and found them locked up in a stable at the other end of the village. I procured a guide to the house of the muleteer, Muhammad's elder brother, and I walked in, and after a tremendous row with all the members of the household, got the key, a thing like a wooden tooth-brush, and got into the stable. While I was saddling my horse, the people locked me in. But I took off the top door socket, and emerged, still triumphant. Then the mule-owner arrived, Ali Akber, Muhammad's elder brother, and he had a stock of indignation to express on his violated household and dismantled stable door. I stuck to my point that the contract expressly provided that no halts were to be made without my express consent. The row became general, and the whole village assisted. The aged mother was set on as a last resource, but in vain. I would give them a week if asked, sooner than they should cheat me out of one hour. We were on the march at 2.15 p.m., and did the forty-three miles into Ispahan by 2 p.m. next day.

Fishark is a healthy little village perched up among fine rocky scenery on the side of a lofty mountain overlooking the broad plain in which Ispahan lies. The view was grand from the immense region which the eye took in, but it had no peculiar features. The ground sloped down to a broad brown green plain dotted with many villages, the smoke from the houses of which going straight up in the still air reminded me of so many "latūrs" or sand-spouts, and pleasantly contrasted the air we were now breathing with the recollections of the burning fiery climate of Mekran.

Across the broad valley rose another high range of

mountains, and far up the valley to the right we saw a shimmer of water, which turned out to be the shallow lakes caused by the Ispahan river losing itself. We picked our way down the mountain, and started along the level plain at a good pace. We cheered up Muhammad, who had been reduced to tears by the abusing I had given him, and Ali Akber bore no malice.

We stopped for a smoke at a village called Wartūn, at some time in the night, and starting again we lost our way in the pitch darkness, until day dawned and showed us that we had not made a very bad hit. Ispahan lay before us, and leaving the baggage, Ghulamshah and I cantered on ahead, knowing that our horses would have a good rest for a week at the end of two days' march. There is nothing fine in the approach to Ispahan from the east, as the traveller has to go through at least ten miles of ruined mud houses, which are on slightly higher ground than the inhabited part of the town.

We had special interest in getting to Ispahan, for from there we could telegraph to know how our Balūchis had got on, and we could also telegraph to London for the sinews of war. While cantering along the muddy plain, Ghulamshah had the most pronounced and undeniable spill I ever saw. He was, as I have said, riding "Hinges," a horse so called from his having apparently an extra joint in the right foreleg, which caused him to stumble. When he caught his foot, he had a way of hurriedly recovering it with a loud stamp, like a sailor marking time in a hornpipe. We liked him though, as he was an untiring brute and never actually fell. But to-day, perhaps reflecting that it was rather hard to canter a horse who had been on his legs so long, he came down. I was cantering a little ahead when I heard a scramble and a thump, and looking round saw the butcha describe a complete somersault in the air, and Hinges, after ploughing up the ground with his nose for a minute, fall heavily on his side. No one was hurt, and we rode on through swampy lakes which swarmed with wild fowl.

Soon we began to enter fields, each field containing a large turreted tower, round or square, and painted in many cases in gaudy colours. These were pigeon houses. After that we got among a network of deep canals, with some awkward plank bridges to cross.

Then came a most disappointing and vexatious part of the ride. When we found the first houses were ruined, we made up our minds for a mile or so, as we had found this at Kirman. But who could be prepared for eleven miles? Again our goal was the English telegraph office; and we did not know that this was not in Ispahan at all, but in the Armenian suburb of Julfa, right the other side of the town and across the river. However we rode on and on. At last, just as I was beginning to despair, and Ghulamshah had handed me my Kabulima * full of cold meat and onion, I saw an Englishman in riding boots, swinging a big hunting-crop, and followed by four dogs. I need not detail the interview, it is enough to say, that in about ten minutes the tired horses were stabled, Ghulamshah installed in the kitchen, and myself seated at a table with a hearty English lunch and a bottle of Bass' beer, sent for in honour of the occasion by my new friend Fillingham.

* Kabulima, a covered copper vessel.

TWO OF THE EXPEDITION WHO NEVER RETURNED.

CHAPTER XVI.

ISPAHAN.

Sad news of our Balūchis.—Defeat of the Customs authorities.—Ispahan and Yezd.—Destruction by the Affghans.—Chehil Sitūn.—The shaking minarets.—The governor.—The Ispahan river and bridges.—Persian carpets.—Julfa.—Its cheapness of living, etc.—The Armenians.—Starting for Baghdad.—I buy a new horse.—Get a new groom.—Start for Kirmanshahan.—Ali Akber.—Curious device of caravanserai doors.—Attempt to levy black mail.—Muhammad the ruddy-faced deserts us and returns home.—An old shepherd.—Nearly a row at the village of Husseini.—Deh Hak and the cold.—Slate doors.—Ungrateful ophthalmic patients.—Terrible cold, thermometers below zero.—Durr Kokah.—Heavy snow.—Kokah and the magpies' parliament.—Caravan of wheat from Kirmanshahan.—A miserable march to Khomain.—Hādi turns out a trump.—Difficulties as an amateur charvadar.—Narrow escape of falling into river.—We reach Khomain.

AFTER a hearty lunch, during which to my great surprise a tall gentleman in the accurate black coat of an English clergyman dropped in as if it was the most ordinary matter in the world, we went over to the telegraph office, where by the courtesy of Mr. Hoeltzer, the superintendent, I was enabled to speak to George Sealy at Jask, and learnt the sad story of my Balūchis. Exhausted by fatigue, privation and exposure, the men fell easy victims to small-pox. Brahim was dead, Dād Arrahīm was dead, and three others (who eventually recovered) were very ill at about sixty miles from Jask, and almost within reach of their homes. Every care was taken of them by my friends at Jask, and the tent was burnt where it lay so as not to bring infection into the station.

On returning to the house at half-past four we found the baggage had arrived, Ali Akber and Muhammad being in a furious temper owing to an attempt at the Custom House to exact dues for the baggage. In order to settle the matter, they had taken the somewhat original method of bringing the customs officer with them. After they had taken so much trouble on my behalf it would have been cruel to have paid anything, and I pointed out to the officer that an English traveller could not be supposed to pay for his luggage as if it was merchandise, and after a feeble resistance he went away. He was an absurd person. He had been dragged nearly five miles, arguing incessantly, I imagine, the whole time, and now he had to go back five miles empty-handed.

I was glad to get off my heavy riding boots and moleskins, and appear once more in a clean shirt and collar and decent clothes.

Life in Ispahan, or rather in the Armenian suburb Julfa, was very pleasant. Although I had a bad attack of my old enemy dysentery, I rode out every day with one or more of the Europeans, who showed me all the sights, and were most hospitable. There were an English clergyman and his wife, three sergeants of the Royal Engineers, who worked the telegraph, and a German superintendent.

Just as Yezd gave me the idea of being a thriving go-ahead place, so Ispahan left the impression of being a crumbling rich old town. I have already spoken of the great number of ruined houses, and the next thing worthy of note was the number of lofty well-built bazaars now deserted and partly in ruins. They were two storeys high, and of well-made, well-burnt brick, which looked so new that I was puzzled to know whether the buildings had been arrested in course of construction or thrown down after completion. In answer to my inquiries I was invariably told that they were destroyed by the Affghans, who must have indeed cost Persia dear, for in most of the towns I afterwards passed through were examples of the same thing. There are many old ruined "palaces," remnants of the time when Ispahan was the capital, and the court resided here. Chehil Situn is the palace generally visited by travellers, and we rode there one day to see it. It is on the same plan as that already described at Kirman, an oblong enclosure with a tank in the middle and the royal quarters at either end. Near the tank was a lofty reception-hall; and over the water, so that their reflections could be seen, were twenty tall pillars, which with their shadows made the forty indicated by the name Chehil Situn (*forty pillars*). The hall was carpeted with the remains of a very ragged carpet, which I was told was 300 years old. Such of the pattern as could be made out showed it to be the design of Venetian artists, whom the nobles of old time imported to decorate their houses with mirrors. The walls were covered with pictures, painted, I believe, on the plaster of the wall,—hunting scenes, banqueting scenes, and court scenes. The colours were very rich, but the attitudes and the expressions were very quaint. Some of the side pieces were unmistakably Venetian: Cupids riding on golden cars and guiding furious horses with strips of blue ribbon, which served at once for traces and reins.

On leaving the palace we went to see the two shaking minarets, which are curiosities of almost world-wide celebrity. They are two tall brick towers. A man may ascend to the top of one, and on his rocking himself to and fro both pillars rock to and fro with him. It was proposed that I should go up and rock, but I did not. I had come on an exploring expedition to recruit my health and survey the country; this seemed a feat of hardihood by which nothing could be gained. Moreover, if one did go up a tower to take bearings or for any other useful purpose, it seemed reasonable to choose a solid one, not one admittedly shaky. I suppose some one will break his neck some day on these shaking minarets. The governor here is the "Prince, the Shadow of the Sultan." He keeps considerable state, and stains his horses' tails red, an appearance which at first sight is ridiculous enough, but with time loses its absurdity. He is a violent atheist, and sometimes horrifies the worthy padre here. A fine broad river runs between Julfa and Ispahan, which is crossed by four or five good stone bridges. One new bridge is an especially fine structure; and would be considered a well-built bridge in England. The river bed is occupied by colonies of dyers, and anchored out in the running stream are carpets being washed. This system of washing will soon be no longer in use in Persia. The two things that caused Persian carpets to be esteemed were the lasting quality of their dyes and the intricate and unique nature of their patterns. Now cheap European dyes are carried into the remotest villages of the country, and European patterns are being everywhere introduced, witness the coach and four at Kirman. The red and yellow colours of all Persian carpets should nowadays be tested by wetting the handkerchief and rubbing the colour hard. The old-fashioned "runashk" red, the "zarili"[1] yellow, and the duller yellow made from pomegranate skins, will never leave a trace on the handkerchief, while the European dyes, though more brilliant, come off freely. The chief exports from Ispahan are opium and tobacco, and I noticed nothing new in its manufactories. Still, however, I believe it is the only place where calico is printed in colours, this being very coarsely done. I spent fourteen very pleasant days here, repairing every morning to the site of the Venus transit expedition, which was marked by a large stone, and taking careful observations to rate the chronometer. Julfa is a quiet orderly little village of neat houses and straight streets, with a row of trees down either side of the road.

The cheapness of everything—house-rent, meat, bread, wine, etc., is marvellous, and they are very good.

Mr. and Mrs. Bruce had a large school of chubby, rosy-cheeked boys and girls, and there were also smaller schools of various other sects, none of whom seemed to agree very well together. Mr. Bruce was endeavouring to get a bell-tower on his church, and had been fighting for months against the most determined opposition, instituted on the same ground as I have known consuls quarrel about their flag-staffs, viz., that his church would then be higher than the churches of other denominations. The Armenian girls are pretty and rosy-cheeked while young, but rapidly become fat and ungainly when married. Many families

[1] "The Golden," a yellow flower from Khorasan.

have a son or two employed as clerks in a bank or merchant's house in India, who, such is the cheapness of living, can keep the family by remitting a portion of their pay.

Here were abnormally large sheep, also cabbages of which it was common to see only two forming a donkey-load, and of which I took seed to England. We took one cabbage with us, and ate of it for ten days, when my horse got at it in the night and spoilt our enjoyment of it.

I had been doubtful which way to turn my steps from Ispahan. The road to Teheran was out of the question, as being utterly hackneyed. But to go through Kurdistan *viâ* Kirmanshahan, and thence to Baghdad, was new, and I decided on that route. I was glad to find Ali and Muhammad willing to come with me, and by the help of the British agent, an influential Armenian gentleman, I got a very good contract drawn out and signed.

These fellows, however, gave a lot of trouble at starting. Ali Akber had picked up three or four more of his mules, and calculating that he could load and look after ten as well as five, he decided that I must wait until he had got a freight for his empty mules. This was very reasonable if he had only told me of it, but he did not, and kept promising to start day after day, causing me to sit some time with my boxes all packed up, and to say good-bye to all my friends three times over.

Just at the last I bought from Mr. Bruce, for the extremely small sum of seven Napoleons, a beautiful little chestnut horse of indomitable pluck and great sinew. His coat was like satin, and his legs as hard as iron. Only one fault he had, a big thick neck and large obstinate head that showed him, what he was admitted to be, an incorrigible bolter. He had recently thrown a worthy gentleman head first into a tobacconist's shop, and several people told me such desperate stories about him, that I half fought shy of buying him. But I reflected that the journey I was about to undertake was sure to tame him, and even if he did bolt in the open, it did not so much matter where there was plenty of room as it did in streets full of archways. We called this little horse (*pace* Mr. Bruce) the Padre. I intended to have him led out of the town, and mount him after a day or two, but Ghulamshah begged so hard to be allowed to ride him that I reluctantly assented.

I owe eternal gratitude to Mr. Hoeltzer who recommended me a groom, Hādi by name, who was worth his weight in gold.

It was February the 3rd when I got the caravan on march, and about 10 p.m., after a hearty dinner at the house of the kind missionary * and his wife, I mounted

---

* Mr. Bruce is among other things an accomplished Hebrew scholar, but I could not persuade him to adopt my pronunciation of the sacred words "Êli, Êli, lāmă săbăcthānĭ." A modern Arab would use just the same words, but would pronounce them as follows: "Illāhi, Illāhi, lĭmā săbāktănī." "Oh Allah! oh Allah! for what cause have you abandoned me"; or, more literally, "have you gone on before and left me behind?" Nor would he accept my theory that Elijah was fed in the desert by the Bedawin, and not by ravens.

In Arabic there is only the difference of a dot between "'urban,'" Bedawin Arabs, and "ghurban," crows or ravens, and the dots are often missed out or misplaced. In Hebrew the words are almost exactly alike.

to catch up the baggage, which had gone on ahead to a caravanserai called Robat (a generic term for walled enclosures in this part of Persia). I was glad it was only a short march, as the night was dark and cold, and my dysentery troubled me very much.

The next morning Ali was nowhere to be found, having gone back to Ispahan to get some more freight. I found that a hundred mule-loads of tobacco were leaving for Baghdad, and it was part of this that he was anxious to secure, and it was with this caravan he privately intended I should march, which meant marching all night, and resting all day; but of course his attempt failed.

By the help of Hādi we loaded up, and made a short three hours' march to Ain Shirwan, a fine, large caravanserai of hard black stone.

We were now fairly embarked on our arduous journey to Kirmanshahan. I had taken a tracing on a thin half-sheet of note paper of this part of the country from a map of the world in the Ispahan telegraph office, but it naturally gave but little information. What was of more use was a list in Persian of the halting stations, and the approximate number of farsakhs between them. But a farsakh or parasang varies in length from three to four and a half and even five miles in different parts of Persia, and our calculations were often very much out. When prepared for a short stage we found a long one, and *vice-versâ*. Nor could we halt when we liked, as we did in Balūchistan; it was a caravanserai or nothing, or at most a village hut, for we had no tent, and the cold was extreme. We were constantly warned that "Yakh mīkunī," (*you will freeze*) and we very nearly did once or twice when the thermometers went below zero, and the mercury retired altogether into the cistern.

Ali Akber got himself up like Bill Sikes. He was a coarse, powerful fellow, with a long black curl down each cheek. He had two or three red and white handkerchiefs round his neck, and over many other garments a drab coat of very thick cloth and voluminous skirts. He carried a thick stick seven feet long to beat the mules and defend himself from village dogs, and this stick he generally stuck through his waistbelt, whence it projected from under his coat tails and as he walked wriggled in a most absurd manner.

His favourite oath to his mules was, "Oh may the grave of your owner's father be defiled," and when I said that he was abusing his own father's grave, he coolly said : "Yes, but as he isn't dead yet I don't see that it matters either to him or any one else."

The caravanserai at Ain Shirwan was well built of huge stones, and I noticed a curious and ingenious device for keeping the massive doors either wide open or close shut, the only positions it was necessary they should assume. The upright beam on which the door swung, pivoted at top and bottom in stone sockets, instead of being placed exactly vertical, was slanting, the base being brought out about a foot from the wall. The door had thus a tendency to swing towards the stable. When open it was stopped by the wall, and when shut by a stone, placed for the purpose in the middle of the doorway. There were half a dozen mounted soldiers, and about sunset one of them started the "izān," or call to prayer, in a style most unorthodox, and I should think peculiarly his own. It lasted nearly an hour, and contained injurious reflections on the character of his comrades.

Our road hence wound along under the foot of Koh Salah, while on our right was a broad plain studded with numerous villages.

The country for the next five marches, *i.e.* to Khurumabad, may be described in a few words thus: Perfectly flat plains studded with villages, and broken up by irregular masses of mountains, or like a calm sea full of irregular rocks and small islands, which have to be crossed or gone round to get from one plain to the other. The numerous villages argue of course considerable cultivation, but at this time of the year not a blade can be seen.

Some goats here produced an inferior kind of "kurk," and I can see no reason why the goats bearing this very valuable wool could not be reared all over Persia.

The caravanserai at Chal-i-siah was built out of blocks of a hard black stone, many of which were 7 feet long by 1½ thick. Here some soldiers attempted to exact black mail, which, in spite of Ali Akber, who sided with them, I not only successfully resisted, but by ostentatiously taking down their names, I extorted from them humble apologies. Now here we were in the region of a British agent, and I noticed that, while along the route from the coast to Ispahan a man was only so much a man as his own individual pluck and energy made him, here he was a Feringi, and the title properly used means a great deal.

The affair resulted in my giving the men a small present of tea, and the charvadar paying about a penny each for his mules, which must have been a just charge or he would have remained haggling over it till now.

Here for once the muleteer successfully deceived me. Muhammad of the ruddy face was to return, being too young for the severe journey we had undertaken. It was probably true, and a sick man would have been a heavy encumbrance on the long marches before us. But I venture to think that Ali would have made his young brother come, had he not found in my new groom a willing, strong-armed, good-natured fellow, who would help him to load his mules; and after all, who knows Hādi did not profit by the arrangement?

However, we will suppose that Ali Akber's rugged heart was touched at the idea of taking his young brother this long journey. It is at all events a likely version of the matter, and the kindest. At Chal-i-siah we were in the middle of a wide shingly plain, dotted with small shrubs, which supported small and widely-scattered flocks of sheep. This plain appeared to be nearly circular, and about forty miles in diameter.

Having succeeded in sending home his brother, Ali proceeded to expatiate on various robberies and murders that had recently taken place on this route, and to insist upon our travelling with the large tobacco caravan I have before mentioned; but I had secretly taken Hādi into my confidence, and made it worth his while to tell me the truth. The result was that I travelled independently, starting when I felt inclined, and not obliged to pass through the country in pitch darkness, and half asleep on my horse.

Next day we were crossing low broken hills, partly covered with snow and scattered with tussocks of grass, and we passed during the day about 3,000 sheep. I stopped once and "interviewed" one old shepherd, about the ruggedest specimen nature ever produced. He spent his whole life out in the air, winter and summer, snow and sunshine, with half a dozen very savage but intelligent dogs, and enveloped in a perfect husk of woollen rags. I could get no information out of him, but he ate greedily of some bread I gave him, and never stopped spinning yarn the whole time I was talking to him, though I must have been the most extraordinary spectacle he had ever seen, and I seemed to get the impression that if he stopped spinning he would disappear, together with sheep, mountains, and everything.

Our stage to-day was to Deh Hak, and at 2.45 p.m. we arrived at a large village, with a fine-looking but ruinous caravanserai. Ghulamshah and I took it for granted that this was Deh Hak, and dismounting prowled about the ruined caravanserai for a part with a sound roof. Ruins in this country never look venerable, and there was the same difficulty in deciding whether this place was unfinished or ruined as we had experienced in the ruined bazaars of Ispahan. The villagers, a truculent-looking set, thronged round and were eagerly civil, would kill a sheep, give us warm stables, and do other hospitable things. Ghulamshah went off to see the warm stabling, etc., and soon came running back rather horrified. They had been deceived by his wearing Bedford cord riding trowsers and huge boots, and had spoken freely before him. Here were two lone travellers, who must have money in their pockets, and rode good horses. They would kill a sheep and be hospitable, but the next morning the horses could be removed, and so on. I was intensely indignant, for I had been thanking in my mind their kind hospitality, and I took my heavy "chapar" whip, and went down to the "warm stabling," and demanded fiercely the "Katkhuda," or chief of the village. A row was imminent, but I was too savage for them. A crowd got round us with big sticks and "shispars," or sticks with iron maces at the end. I cursed every mother's son of them, asking them if they thought sons of dogs like they could deceive Feringis with impunity, and after an anxious moment the Katkhuda (or somebody representing him) arrived. I believe the real Simon pure had been in the crowd all the time, but just now I heard the jangling of the mules' bells, and immediately afterwards Ali's hoarse voice, "Chi mikuni inja Sahib. In bad jai hust." (*What are you doing here, sir? This is a bad place.*) At the same time Hādi rammed his horse through the crowd up to us, crying hastily, "Where are your horses?" The crowd fell back, and we mounted our horses. The village was not Deh Hak at all, but Husseini, and I warn any future traveller against going to Husseini with any appearance of being solitary and unprotected.

Our road from here was a steady ascent; to our right close by hills about 500 feet, and on our left about twenty miles distant a snowy range 2,000 feet high. We went on getting higher and higher, until at 4 p.m. we entered the cultivation and suburbs of Deh Hak, a village appropriately named as far as we were concerned, for it meant "the real village," and we had had a narrow escape of the false one Husseini. We passed a very extensive graveyard—one always enters a Persian village through a graveyard—and noticed all the headstones were slabs of fine slate. As we entered Deh Hak itself, the main street was simply the outcrop of a thick vertical stratum of slate. All the doors of the mudwalled gardens were solid blocks of slate. One I measured was nine feet high, seven feet broad, and about ten inches thick; yet it was so admirably balanced that one man alone could open and shut it. The cold was intense, the village snowed up, and we could arouse no inhabitant, so had to wait about in the cold dark evening till the mules came up, and Ali inducted us into a miserable stable, where we spent the night. We rose early, being unable to sleep for the cold, and found ourselves in a village of about 1,000 houses, with a shahzāda or descendant of the Shah for a governor, called Rahim Khan. A lot of people crowded round wanting medicine, mostly for ophthalmia. I had treated one man, and was mixing a stronger solution of nitrate of silver for a second, when I overheard the first cursing "those d—d unbelievers who had all the good medicines," and so I sent the whole lot to the right about. The maximum and minimum thermometers here became useless for showing the temperature at night, as the quicksilver descended altogether into the bulb. But at 8 a.m. this morning the dry bulb marked 2° Fahrenheit.* Taking observations of the stars at night, when the thermometers actually will not mark, is terrible work; and had not Ghulamshah been always ready to prepare the

* The verification of my thermometers at Kew Observatory will be found in the meteorological appendix.

artificial, sextant, etc., I should simply have omitted them. But he never failed, and would get the instruments ready, and if the sky was cloudy would sit out and watch, and call me when there was a chance of a sight. He knew all the chief stars, and I can only wish the traveller an assistant such as he was.

Next day was an eight hours' bitterly cold ride to Durr. The road led over small level plains, frequently intersected by low ridges of vertical strata of slate. About half way we passed a deserted caravanserai, the walls of which were riddled with bullet holes. I have often seen a party of travellers while away the time in a caravanserai by practising at a mark, and believe this to be the case here, though the three or four men living here said they had been plundered, and that the bullets had been fired at their families. The bullets were all directed at some three or four definite centres, and there was no evidence of any random firing.

At Durr we had much the same cold as the previous morning. Therm. 2° at 8 a.m., 15° at 9 a.m., and 35° in the sun. Though we were four men, six mules, and two horses in a hermetically closed up small stable, everything liquid overnight was solid ice in the morning. On our next march to Kokah the ground was covered with snow frozen hard. The tracks too had been spoilt by a caravan of forty donkeys, who had made a narrow path about a foot deep, against the icy edges of which our mules and horses cut their legs. To walk out of the track was even more difficult, as the animals continually plunged into deep snowdrifts. There is great danger in a terrified horse plunging wildly about out of his depth in snow, and it was much heightened by the knowledge that the ground was full of kahns or deep pits now snowed over.

We were now entering the fertile plain of Julfugān, of which we had heard much. We met a caravan of fifty camels and about fifty donkeys carrying wheat from there to Ispahan.

Kokah is a large village of 1,000 houses ruled by Yahia Khan, a shahzāda. We put up here in a fine warm stable; and so entirely do the people shut themselves up in the winter, that the two men who brought us fodder and firewood were the only inhabitants we saw. I must have seen over a thousand magpies here. They were in noisy flocks on the roof of every other house. They seemed determined to keep the place alive, and all day held an endless series of animated public meetings, now on the roof of this house, now on that, and it did not require much imagination to fancy that they were passing resolutions of indignation at the slothful conduct of the inhabitants in persistently remaining indoors. They were bright cheery fellows, and by far the most amusing things on this part of the journey. It snowed heavily all night, and I was awakened, or rather aroused, for I hardly ever slept in the proper sense of the word, by the solemn booming of large bells, and looking out I counted in the blinding snow more than a hundred huge camels stalking past in the darkness. I called out several times, but could get no reply. I think the only man awake must have been at the head of the caravan, which had passed before I got up.

There was something grand in the resistless way these great brutes stalked doggedly on through darkness, blinding snow, and cold, with unchanging swing of leg, and each carrying his 350 lbs. of burden.

The next march, to Khomain, was one which none of those who made it will ever forget, and I did in a fit of passion what I hope is the cruellest thing I have ever done.

To a small caravan like ours there was considerable danger from robbers in the next march, and that it was not exaggerated was evident, for Ali, whose one idea was to get on, here wished to halt until another caravan came up, in company with which we might travel in safety.

But the morning was so exceptionally fine, therm. 55° at 9 a.m., that I persuaded him to start.

We passed through about five miles of cultivation, nearly every field containing an oblong well-built pigeon house for collecting pigeon's dung. The water here was plentiful, and on the surface, and we crossed a rapid stream running north-east, the bed of which was one hundred and fifty feet broad, by five deep, and the stream twenty feet by three. The bridge was a good brick and stone structure of five arches, and evidently built to resist great floods.

At 11 a.m. we commenced a laborious ascent up the Hassan Falak mountain, and an icy west wind blew into our faces. Then it began to snow harder and harder. At 2 p.m. it was hail driving in our faces, and the pleasant morning turned to freezing. The cold became fearfully intense. We were each wearing heavy riding boots over two pairs of English woollen socks, and one pair of Persian socks as thick as a double blanket, but it was impossible to remain on horseback, and we had to walk a bit and ride a bit.

Thus we struggled on against the driving hail, with our heads down, and in a grim silence until the evening began to draw in. Ali was evidently uneasy about the track, which was simply a blank waste of snow sprinkled with boulders of rock. Ghulamshah was riding the Padre, not a whit tamed by his journey, but as ready to break away as ever. He rode or walked close behind me, and when I mounted I generally looked round to see that he was safe up, for the Padre sometimes gave him some trouble, encumbered as he was in heavy clothing.

On one memorable occasion towards evening I mounted as usual, but on turning round and looking back I could see nothing of Ghulamshah. I shouted into the storm, but no reply. With an undefined dread I rode back to the top of the nearest hill. Here my worst fears were realized. There, already far distant, and but just visible through the sleet, was the boy galloping at frightful speed back to Kokah.

I put spurs to the old white horse, and in a kind of despair galloped after him, crossing at full speed many dangerous places, which on coming I had led my horse over.

Nothing could exceed the misery of that ride. At every corner, and at every dangerous place, I expected to find this faithful fellow either dead or maimed. I thought of all sorts of things—all he had done for me; what I should do if he were dead, what if a leg broken; whether the doctor would come from Shiraz, and how soon he could arrive; what I should say to his father and mother, against whose wish I had brought him with me. Thought after thought of this crowded into my mind, and I felt wretched. After about an hour's riding the old horse began to show signs of exhaustion, and I felt that I must husband his strength or I should have to camp where I was, and probably get frozen to death.

Soon after this, what was my intense relief on mounting a slight hill to see the boy quietly trotting towards me.

"Thank God," I cried out. "Are you all right, butcha? How did you stop him? Didn't you fall off?"

"No," he answered simply. "He did not bolt with me; I rode back after that rug you lent me, and which I dropped somewhere on the road."

The reaction of feeling made me almost beside myself.

"Good heavens," I said. "Why couldn't you have said so? Here I've ridden all this way back after you, dreading at each turn to find you dead or maimed;" and I added, "now you've gone back so far, you may go back until you do find it."

He said: "Very well, sir," and turned his horse's head and rode off.

He had hardly been out of sight a minute, when I realized what a hard thing I had done. It was getting dark; the icy wind and driving sleet were unabated; there was little or no track over the mountain; and the place was infested by robbers, who would probably note his leaving Kokah alone; also he had already ridden about 38 miles.

I turned round and rode gloomily back, having to go through the tedious operation of mounting and dismounting every two or three hundred yards, and picking out the way with difficulty. After an hour or so of this wearisome travelling, my horse suddenly pricked up his ears and gave a low whinny. I could see no one, but not knowing whether it was friend or foe I drew him away from the road, held his nose, and anxiously waited. I revolved in my mind dozens of stratagems in case of robbers coming,—I was unarmed,—but fortunately had not long to wait. In the distance I heard the tinkle of a bell, which reassured me, for I reflected that a dishonest man would hardly go about with bells on his horse. Soon, to my inexpressible relief, I found it was Hādi, who after seeing the baggage safe to Khomain, had become anxious about us, and set off to see what delayed us. Not only had he come back, but with extraordinary forethought he brought with him a bottle of raki, six bottles of which I had brought from Ispahan, and a long pull at which revived me immensely. I told him what I had done to Ghulamshah, and he proposed to go after him. I offered him my horse, which though tired was better than the pony, and he mounted and disappeared into the darkness.

I with some difficulty got myself on the back of the pony, which was loaded with saddle-bags containing various things. These same saddle-bags were destined to form part of my punishment for my fit of passion, and as will be seen formed no slight addition to the miseries of this miserable day.

I had not ridden far before my feet as usual got frozen, and it was imperative to get off and walk. But the detestable animal would not be led. In the most exasperating manner he backed and backed with his stupid head straight out and his tail between his legs. Then I tried to drive him before me, and he kicked me and very nearly broke away. Then his load got awry—I tried to put it right, but it was too heavy. The fall was inevitable, and in another hundred yards down came everything in the snow. I had to take out every single thing *seriatim*, put the saddle-bags on his back, and then put back each article one after another. There were some twenty things—a bag of blacksmiths' tools, bags of barley, bags of flour, spare bits of bridles and bells, Ali's "store clothes," etc., etc.

I take credit to myself for considerable patience and determination when I say that three separate times I went through this operation without omitting a single detail. The fourth time they fell off, I gave them a kick, got on the pony's bare back, and abandoned them in the snow.

It is a long lane that has no turning, and looming ahead I was pleased to recognise the mountain for which we had been heading when I turned back after Ghulamshah. I could make out that I was descending into a plain, for the rocky ground stopped, and we were evidently near cultivation, for I as nearly as possible rode into a kahn. This gave me great uneasiness, for when all is snow it is impossible to distinguish these deep holes from firm ground. I was wandering about trying everywhere for some vestige of a track, when the pony neighed, and to my joy and surprise I heard Ghulamshah talking to Hādi considerably to my left and *ahead* of me. If it had not been for the pony they would probably have passed me.*

* Even camels have the sense of hearing in the dark very acutely developed. I have often seen my camels stop feeding and listen

The invaluable Hādi had picked up the saddle-bags which had been so troublesome to me, and all three united we went on happily once more. But our troubles were not yet at an end. It appears that Hādi had not gone all the way to Khomain, and this piece of the road was new to him as to us. At last we struck a rapid swirling stream, and went up its bank expecting to find a bridge. We did find a bridge, a steep massive masonry structure with no parapet. I was riding foremost when suddenly the bridge stopped abruptly; it had been carried away by the stream. I was so close and so horrified that I pulled the horse violently on his haunches. He backed to the side where there was no parapet, and when close there made a bad slip on the icy stones. By some instinctive presence of mind I sprang off, and he recovered himself just on the edge. It would have have been a fitting finish to this day's work to have fallen into an icy cold stream, even if it had not been deep enough to drown us.

Our case now seemed rather hopeless. I made a solemn vow never to travel at night again, and we were discussing the possibility of walking about till morning, when we heard a dog bark on our side of the river. Hādi immediately set off in the direction indicated, with instructions to offer even 100 krans to a man to come and show us the way over this accursed river.

He returned after, to us, a weary time, bringing no guide but instructions for the route. He said 100

---

attentively, when even by putting the ear to the ground I could hear nothing. Balūchis have a peculiar word "Bramshi." When they see the camels stop feeding, they say, "Bramshi akait:" "bramshi" being, a sound inaudible to them but audible to the camels.

krans would not induce a man to stir out in such a night, but that we were close to the stables. A small temporary bridge of logs had been made just under the broken one, and there it was, within twenty yards of where we were standing. We crossed with some difficulty, and soon afterwards found the caravan. Never in my life have I been so thankful for a warm stable (though crowded with mules) and a fire. Ghulamshah made some soup, and we turned in for the best-earned sleep we had had for some days. It was not the distance that told so much as the intense, pitiless cold and the anxiety—anxiety about Ghulamshah, about the robbers, about the road, and about falling into kahns.

CHAPTER XVII.

The charvadar and his best clothes.—We halt.—Deputations from the natives.—Discovery of America.—The house on fire.—Bakhtiaris.—Haft Lang and Chahar Lang.—March to Khurumabad.—Terrible snow pass.—A real hardship.—Icy cold west wind always dead in our teeth.—No caravanserai.—The Kursi.—Difficulties in engaging house room.—The village system.—Persians essentially nomads.—"Please God, we shall capture Baghdad this time."—March to Imaret.—Delightful village.—Our hard times past.—The lake.—The "Ab bazi" and the fish shooter.—A new kind of wall.—Capons.—A new epoch in the journey.—Mysterious horsemen.—We strike the telegraph line.—Dowletabad.

NEXT morning Ali roundly declared that his bundle of best clothes was missing from the saddle-bags. He got out those, to me, hateful things, and placed them before him. Then he got a bundle and accompanied his harangue by a practical demonstration, at each period seizing the bundle and packing it firmly into a safe corner of the saddle-bags. He thus gave me to understand that there was not the least doubt that he was speaking the truth, as he could describe in detail the way in which the bundle was stowed.

I was induced to give a man a kran to go and look for this bundle; but he never found it, or, if he did, he wisely kept it—and the kran.

The Persians are judicious in such matters.

By reason of this delay, the tired condition of the horses, the reported fact that the next stage was a very long one; as moreover the villagers were fairly intelligent, and it was possible to secure a private room for myself, I decided on making here a "lang" or halt of one day.

Accordingly Hādi arranged for my exclusive possession of the room over the stables where we had spent the night, made a small fire in it, and I took possession. Ghulamshah set to work washing our flannel shirts, and I to writing up the road-book, calculating bearings, etc.

Our room was of good size, of sundried brick and a mud floor, while the roof, as usual in Persian houses, was constructed of beams close together, covered with strong mats, over which came a layer of mud a foot in thickness. Two iron door-bolts, of which the proprietor, a carpenter named Joseph, was very proud, were evidently of Russian manufacture. But the most noticeable feature of the room was that walls and roof were studded thickly with wooden pegs about five inches long. These I found were for drying bunches of grapes, which thus prepared retained the flavour of fresh grapes throughout the year. In a small side-room were stored about twenty wooden casks, just the shape of, but smaller than, London milk-cans. These contained swarms of bees hibernating, and this was the first instance of bee-culture I had seen in Persia.

Numerous visitors were announced, but after receiving very courteously three or four of very mixed rank, and finding many more waiting, I saw the thing must be done by method; and appointing Hādi master of ceremonies, instructed him to sort the people out and introduce them in batches.

First came the Akhoonds, or learned men of the

village. They were five intelligent, well-mannered old men, and gave me much information. The American nation will be interested to learn that the discovery of America was just at this time commencing to excite the attention of these worthies. They puzzled me at first by asking questions about some "yeng-i-dunea," and it was not until after some cross-questioning I found it to be a corruption of Yeni Dunea, or new world.

The people here are fair-haired and light-bearded, and they speak with the tips of their tongues, and cannot pronounce any gutturals except the ع (âin). I attach a note of a few words which I think peculiar to this district, which is just on the border of the Bakhtiari country, which commenced one farsakh to the west. The list is not long enough to trouble the unphilological reader, and the terms belong peculiarly to this place.

Ja'ada : a road.
Tahnāf : rope for tying mule-loads.
Wasut : corruption of biūst (Balūchi, Būsht), stand still.
Tīgh : beam.
Sirr : stony, gravelly ground.
Su : the Turkoman word for water, here meant the earthenware vessel containing it.
Wakhīn : make haste.

The river we had crossed the previous night and that of Kokah have their origin in the Ashnar Kur (? Koh), and join together and go to the holy city of Kum. The huge snow mountain we saw in the distance, bearing 131 (south-east), was Elwind. The chief cultivation was wheat, holur (not known), lentils, marsh (? galium), cotton. A little opium was grown, it having been introduced about twenty-seven years ago by planters from Ispahan. They had water-mills to grind their corn, but no other mechanical contrivances. Snow here lay three months on the ground; but in three more stages we should get into the "garmsil" (garm sīr) or warm region around Dowletabad.

The conversation was interrupted by a very energetic deputation from downstairs, who discovered that our fire was burning their roof; so we contented ourselves with a small blaze in a baked earthenware jar. We gave our friends coffee and kaliāns, which purely Persian form of entertainment confirmed their suspicions that I was an enterprising agriculturist of Ispahan, anxious to spread the cultivation of opium, and we then received another deputation—this time of Bakhtiaris.

These were wild-looking, freespoken fellows, more like Balūchis or Affghans than courteous, cunning Persians, but I could not draw them out about any of their grand forays, of which the Persians complained so much. They had, at all events, adopted a quiet agricultural life, and were living side by side with the Persians, a dangerous enemy for the latter to nurse in their midst, I should fancy, in case of their friends over the border planning a raid.

They were very proud of belonging to the "Haft Lang," and explained that their race had in olden times split into two factions, one party of seven brothers taking the country of the Haft Lang, or seven streams, the other of four brothers, that of the Chahar Lang or four streams. We had other deputations, but uninteresting. The houses at Khomain are of the Basreh pattern, square with a courtyard in the centre; the women are short, ugly, and very fat-legged.

It was annoying to find that the day we had chosen to halt and remain indoors was comparatively fine and warm. To-day the thermometers stand as follows :—

	WET.	DRY.	MAX. IN SUN.	BAR.
9 a.m.	36	40		
11 "	40	—		23·8
Noon	38	43	69	
1 p.m.	40	45	83	
3 "	36	42		
4 "	36	40		23·8
4.50 "	36	39		23·81
6 "	35·5	37·8		23·84
7 "	35	36		23·85
8 "	35	36		23·85

I got capital observations, both of sun for longitude, and Polaris for latitude.

We left next morning for Khurumabad, and perhaps I may be allowed, at the commencement of this eventful march, to extract a few notes *verbatim* from my note-book :—

8·41 40 68 9 40
w 7·17 14·5 Ch. 12 56 0
Feb. 11th, 8 a.m., d 18 w frozen. Bar. 23·78
b C. W., very cold.
8.30 a.m., left Khomain.*

course 270 (west), through fine ruined bazaar built by Hāji Khan fifty years ago, after two or three forays by the Bakhtiaris, eventually destroyed about fifteen years ago. This everlasting west wind, cold as ice, makes fearfully bitter travelling, while, if it came from the east, weather would be delightful. 9 a.m. course 300, aiming for

* At 8 hrs. 41 min. 40 sec. p.m. by the watch, the altitude of Polaris was 68° 9′ 40″. In the morning the watch showed 7 hrs. 17 min. 14·5 sec. as compared with chronometer 12 hrs. 56 min. 0 sec.; at 8 a.m. dry bulb thermometer was 18, the wet frozen, sky blue, rather cloudy, wind from west very strong and very cold.

north face of Elwind mountain. 9.20 a.m., back bearing to Khomain, 115.

Elwind	119
Mushroom-shaped hill	200
Peak of huge hill /\	80
* ∠ Huge hill	5° 38′
∠ Mushroom hill	6° 20′
Thermometer exposed to wind . .	25°

At 3.15 we entered a snow pass. On either side were lofty perpendicular hills covered with snow, which was drifted off like spray into our faces by an icy cold hurricane of wind. The lofty snow mountain Elwind towered over us on our left, and as we entered the pass, about a mile wide, the snow got deeper and deeper, the icy wind cut us to the bone, and the blasts of snow dust filled every interstice in our clothing. It was like wading up a broad river of snow of uncertain depth, and progress would have been impossible but for the recent passage of two or three very large caravans. These, however, had abandoned their loads, and we passed half buried in the snow heap after heap of bales and boxes which they would return and recover when the weather moderated. I being best mounted (on the Padre) went first, and narrowly escaped some bad falls from the plunging little horse, who over and over again found himself over his head in snow crossing some nullah or another, and made the most frantic efforts to get on to *terra firma*. I remarked that he never wanted to turn back, but the deeper he got the more tremendous efforts he would make to get through. The mules constantly fell, as,

* ∠ = angle taken by pocket sextant for purpose of obtaining approximate height.

owing to the nature of the track, they naturally would. Our endeavour was to follow the almost entirely obliterated track of the preceding caravans. On this track, which, when visible, was about a foot wide and three feet deep, the snow had been trodden hard; but it was like walking on the top of a wall, and when a mule put a foot a little on one side he went down into soft snow from eight to fifteen feet deep. It was an exhausting march, and it was not till 5.30 p.m. that we reached Khurumabad, a small and dirty village of about forty houses. Here there was no caravanserai, but the inhabitants came out to meet us, begging us to hire their houses, and assuring us of warm stabling. I referred them to Hādi, and was soon installed in a warm but dirty house, vacated for the time by the family.

Here was the commencement of a real hardship, perhaps the only real one we suffered: it was *lice.* The chief feature of the houses here was the "Kursi," which needs a full explanation as connected with those loathsome parasites. In the centre of the chief room a hole is dug three feet in depth and two in diameter. This is clayed round and a fire of wooden logs kept constantly smouldering in it. Over it is a wooden framework three feet high and six or seven feet square. On this are piled all the rugs, carpets, and clothes, rags, etc., that the family can muster, and round it they squat all day long with the overlapping edges of the carpets drawn over their knees and arms. When they sleep, they simply turn round and lie down where they were sitting, getting as much of the rugs over them as possible. Such is their winter life, and their conversation is mostly squabbling as to who shall get up to do such trifling domestic work as feeding the mules, getting eggs, etc.

It is as difficult for one who has not endured the misery of these kursis to imagine it, as for one who has endured it to describe them fairly and impartially and without breaking into open vituperation.

The family consists, perhaps, of twelve people, who have inherited the rags they wear without change year after year. These all crowd into the one small room where the kursi is, and there they eat, drink, and sleep under a mass of filthy blankets so swarming with vermin that once, when Ghulamshah showed me the pot in which he had boiled our two shirts after one night under a kursi, I could easily have believed he had been cooking some small white grain.

We had another annoyance on entering this part of the country where there were no caravanserais and we had to hire people's houses. The real owner of the house could never be found. As a rule some wretched child was produced, generally diseased, and always repulsive. It was invariably an orphan, whose sole possession in the world was the house you had occupied, and you were given to understand that whatever extortionate charge you paid was simply banked to your account in heaven. If the establishment could not raise a sufficiently wretched child, you had to succumb to a lone female with a pathetic cry of "Mard na dāram" (*I have no man*—to speak for me).

Khurumabad is the property of Hāji Ahmed Husni, of Sultanabad, a considerable town near here. Hāji Ahmed owns about a hundred and fifty villages, and a slight sketch of the system of village farming may be appropriate here.

Villages are created and abandoned as follows. A wealthy Persian commences by building in some place where there is good soil and plenty of water a "Robāt," or large walled enclosure, with cells all round and a pair of large folding doors. He builds very slowly, employing, perhaps, only three or four men at a time for a few months in the year. As soon as the outer wall, doors, and a few cells are finished, he establishes there a family, and charges no taxes. Other families are attracted, and as the village grows he appoints a Katkhuda, or head man, and gradually commences taxation. If he is a wise man, or, what is more important, if he is accurately informed as to the resources of the village, he waits until they have got a "strong haunt" before taxing much. I say, if he is accurately informed, for it is manifest that over-taxation means cutting his own throat. A rival speculator will at once commence a robāt near the village and attract away the inhabitants. It is not from tyranny that over-taxation occurs; it is from want of system and inaccurate information. A village properly managed soon becomes large enough to emancipate itself from the protection of the robāt, which then falls into decay.

I venture to make another statement, founded on long personal knowledge and intimate acquaintance with the people. The Persians are essentially nomads. Their houses are simply storehouses, and they live in the open air. Rich Persians, such as the Wakil-al-Mulk, governor of Kirman, will sit in the depth of winter with every window wide open, and practically in the open air. Their furniture consists simply of carpets, mattresses, pillows, and cooking pots, all equally adapted for the march, the open air, a cottage, or a palace. They have no idea of home,* and hence have the remedy against over-taxation in their own hands. I have several times seen whole villages deserted, and villages just being deserted; and had I not inquired carefully into the matter, I should have come home with graphic descriptions of grinding oppression, a long-suffering peasantry driven from their hearths, their poor remnant of property strapped on the back of the remaining cow, the mother with toddling babe, etc., etc. On inquiry, I invariably found that the taxes demanded were very light,—that they were going to virgin soil somewhere close by where was water, no taxes for a time, and a robāt built by some opposition village owner to shelter them and their cattle at nights. When a Persian villager has worked three months in a year, he can generally sit the remainder in the sun or shade spinning and smoking, while his harem weave carpets. This, however, is a long digression, and I would go back to Khurumabad.

After dinner I joined the extremely dirty family circle in the next room to mine, and excited discussion. It was an odd sight, so many blank round faces with chins resting on the kursi edge and their bodies hunched up as near to the side as possible.

We had, for a wonder, a topic of conversation. This day a sultan, or lieutenant, had passed through on his way to assist in the capture of Baghdad. The reader probably knows that Baghdad contains the Persians' most revered shrine, and it is always a sore

* They have a strong love for their country.

point with them that it should be in the hands of those accursed Sunnis, the Turks. Now, while Russia was engaging Turkey on the north, was the time to slip across the frontier and capture the much-coveted shrine. Such was the crafty scheme, and I, in my involuntary character of an Armenian from Ispahan, gained great popularity (which did not, however, reduce the bill) by a fervent "Inshallah īn daf' Baghdad mīgīrīm," (*Please God, this time we shall get Baghdad*), which produced a chorus of "Inshallah" all round. The reader will hear more of this army further on. The soldiers had left their mark on the place, a man and a boy, in some quarrel about payment, having been severely cut about the head and arm by the short broadsword the Persian soldier wears as a side arm.

No trees would grow here, there being only about two feet of soil over a stratum of gravel. They all died after reaching this, which they did in about two years. The cold this year had been slight, as in other years caravans often were detained ten or fifteen days. There were three hammams here, and I found all these villages had them, and that their number formed a good guide to the number and importance of the population.

On the 12th February we left Khurumabad much disgusted with the harpies there, and in the teeth of the everlasting icy west wind before mentioned. We followed up a broad snow-bound valley. To our right snowy hills six hundred feet high, and to our left snowy hills twelve hundred feet high, the valley being about a mile wide, gradually decreasing in width.

We passed a caravan of dates and fifteen bales of Manchester goods from Baghdad, and, after a short four hours' march, we reached the delightful village of Imaret. Here the snow was only a foot deep, the sun came out, the west wind moderated; there were trees, running brooks innumerable, and two or three decent-looking two-storeyed houses, with walled gardens, full, as usual, of our cheery friends the magpies.

Here we got capital quarters with the Katkhuda, a mild-mannered, unassuming young fellow, who was full of the Shah's recent passage through here on his way to Kerbela, and who proposed to treat me as a second Shah, *and*, as I afterwards found, that I should pay like one.*

Imaret will always bear our most grateful remembrances. Situated in the throat of the pass, at an altitude of 6,440 feet, it is the pleasant finish of excessive cold, and the commencement of warm sunny weather, the line between barren, shingly plains and fertile valleys, between ignorant boors and intelligent people.

Our affable young Katkhuda, with a smile somewhat of the "Heathen Chinee" order, led us into a nice, clean, white-plastered upper room, with luxurious carpets and glazed windows, looking over a mud-walled garden on one side, and a courtyard on the other. He made us hot sweet tea in a Russian samovar, and served it in Russian glasses like custard glasses.

He then courteously withdrew, promising to return in half an hour, and show us round the village. I

---

* N.B.—I did not.

had a welcome change of kit, and was ready for him when he returned, and we sallied out together. The first thing to be seen was the "daria," or sea, a name given to a deep, rocky margined pool, 300 yards long by 60 broad. It was a most picturesque pool, full of bright green water-weeds and cresses. There were numerous springs bubbling up all over its surface, and also pouring into it from a rocky granitic hill on one side. At one end, built right over the water, was a masjid, and at the other the water escaped by a natural waterfall, and supplied the irrigation of the whole district, for it was some feet above the level of the surrounding land. Waiting for us on the borders of this beautiful pool was an "Āb bāzi," or "player in the water," who had exhibited his feats before the Shah, and who, without more ado, stripped off his clothes and plunged in. He performed the ordinary acts of swimming on his chest, on his back, etc., and was regarded as a wonder, being the only man they knew who could swim; and seeing that the temperature was dry bulb 41°, wet 37°, I thought the man deserved something for his pluck. But the refreshing greenness of the water-reeds seemed incompatible with the temperature and I found by experiment that of the water was 61° Fahr.!

At the sluice or waterfall end was another performer anxious to display, and who had also exhibited before the Shah. He was armed with a long old "Tower" musket, and, stationing himself over a deep part of the pool, he shot at the fish which came near the surface. They were so numerous that at each discharge he killed two or three. The stunned fish were always carried down the waterfall, and the performance was as follows: The "shikarri" would poise himself, with gun at the "present," for as much as ten minutes, until three or four fish came near the surface close together. Then he would fire, and watch anxiously for the result. If one turned belly upwards, down went his gun, off went his boots and stockings, and helter-skelter down the waterfall went he to secure his prize.

I made a careful sketch of the fish, which, owing probably to some fault in my drawing, could not be identified.

Our youthful Katkhuda related that this pool was in olden time inhabited by "Asp-ābi" or water-horses, but I could form no conjecture as to what they were. It was more easy to understand the existence of "Sag-ābi" or water-dogs, which, being said to live upon fish, and make burrows under the roots of willow-trees by the water side, I put down as otters.

We strolled about over "the farm," and saw many acres of young wheat. A curious thing was the tops of the walls round the gardens. At Maibut we had seen the walls so thin at the top that any attempt to get over them must have resulted in a breakage and consequent detection. Here a different device was used. Across the top of the wall, which was of stone, was placed a row of sticks close together, and projecting about a foot on either side. They were kept in their places by a line of clay down the centre. No one could get over this wall without disturbing the sticks, and the device was effectual; for when I asked if people ever did get over, the reply was, "No, they would at once be discovered."

There were many acres of young wheat, opium was

grown, runask* (madder), the red dye, and cotton and grapes. Many carpets were woven here, some of the women and children of every family being experts. They bring indigo from Shuster (probably from India, *viâ* the Karūn river), and make a yellow dye from vine leaves. There was one family who could weave a carpet two yards by one in from fifteen to twenty days, but the general time was two months.

The Armenians had a small trade in fox-skins, which they bought from the villagers at two and a half krans each.

There were rumours of two Europeans travelling about the country, buying up old carpets of antique pattern, and having new ones woven like them, and the Katkhuda was very anxious that they should come his way.

We had tea in Russian teacups, bread and cream, and capital fowls, which I found were caponised by the Katkhuda, who professed to have originally discovered the operation, and was the only man I met who knew of it.

We left next morning for Hissar, and, as I have said before, from here dates our third epoch of travel. The first from the coast, with Balūchis, camels and tents, across the landstrip of Mekran, the hundred-mile belt of rocky crags and steep watercourses and wild scenery of Balūchistan, the gradually rising plains to the huge Jamal Bariz range, and arrival on the high plateau of Persia. The second, with Persians, horses and mules, across the barren shingly plains and snow-

* I found this word always pronounced "Runask," but Johnstone gives it "runas."

covered mountains of Persia proper. And now through fertile valleys, studded with small towns and villages with semi-civilized inhabitants. We passed down a valley about five miles broad, all good wheat-bearing soil, though now a quagmire of mud and half-thawed snow, and heavy travelling for the cattle.

As evening drew on, a mysterious horseman appeared stationary on a hill to our right. Soon after another was observed, then another. They watched us carefully, and seemed to be estimating our forces with a view to plunder, but I had had so many scares of robbers that we passed on unconcerned, though Ali explained that it was all very well for me to feel secure when I was not the owner of the mules, the only part of the caravan which he regarded as of any value. To-night was the end of our monster cabbage, and the charvadar bought forty eggs for half a kran (fivepence), and, I believe, finished them all at a sitting.

The next day's march was to Parri, over a blank plain of snow and mud, studded with snowed-up villages, and flanked by waste snowy hills, without a shrub or blade of grass. On this march we struck, to my profound astonishment, a telegraph line. I saw it in the far distance, the poles being little black dots, half buried in the snow, but at such regular intervals, that, though the charvadar positively denied it, I could not be mistaken.

It was the Persian Government line between Teheran and Baghdad, built by English engineers but worked by Persians.

Following this, and passing numerous villages and hourly increasing signs of population, we arrived at the fine town of Dowletabad, which must be given a chapter to itself, not only from its being at the cross-roads from Hamadan to Shuster and Teheran to Baghdad, but also for the incidents that occurred there.

CHAPTER XVIII.

Dowletabad.

Dowletabad.—" Sweep your steps, sir?"—Shuster and Dizful.—Attempted expedition there.—Difficulties.—Hādi and the cork-screw.—The charvadar and the popguns.—The post from Teheran.—The most mendacious man in the country.—The Telegraph office.—Muhammad of the ruddy face once more turns up.—The Shahzada arrives.—Grand reception, illuminations and band.—Load up for Kirmanshahan.—Parrispar.—A useful bridge.—Grinding oppression.—Pilgrims from Karbala.—Summer weather at last.—Mistaken for the post.—A courteous Frenchman (?) in disguise.—" How shall I go outside? Am I not a Darwish?"—A rainy march to Sahna.—Commencement of Kurdistan.—More soldiers going to capture Baghdad.—The little boy whose father was sick.—Bisitun.—Shah Abbas and his 999 caravanserais.—Musuks.—Dogs.—The Kurdi women.—We arrive at Kirmanshahan.

DOWLETABAD is a large and pleasant civilized town. It contains a public square planted with trees, a telegraph office, and a well-built bazaar.

It is situated in a fertile valley, with a high hill about three miles to the south-east. Water is plentiful about six feet below the surface. The people used no windlass, but let themselves down into the wells, and it was odd to see in the middle of streets heads of men engaged in drawing water bobbing up and down on a level with the ground. The water was deep enough down to remain unfrozen throughout the winter. Gangs of boys paraded the streets with wooden shovels and baskets to dig away the snow from doorways and courtyards. Jews brought huge ancient coins for sale, and were much disappointed at our indifference. I had half lost my sight from snow-blindness, and four days before would have given much for a pair of dark spectacles, or even for some means of making my old ones (which had been trodden on) serviceable, and here when the snow was finished I found them plentiful in the bazaar at one kran each.

We got a room in a fairly comfortable mud-built chapar khana, and had a good fireplace which did not smoke. But there certainly was what Carlyle calls the "oldest smell in the world" in it somewhere, but where we could never find out, and the lice were fearful. I remember Ghulamshah one night—he had huddled himself into his "abba," or cloak he wore at night, and after taking off all his clothes (he *would* do this, however cold), and going through the usual investigation, he put them on one side, and then looking pensively at his "abba," said with a heavy sigh, "Now I wonder if there are any in that."

These loathsome pests, against which there is no remedy, were the only things we grumbled at on the march, though, among other things, we had fever, ague, sunstroke, and small-pox.

The chief thing that gave an interest to Dowletabad was its being the starting-place for caravans to Shuster and Dizful.* These two places are here always mentioned together as one. They are the halfway-house for trade between Basreh *viâ* the Karūn river and Ispahan and Hamadan. This trade is mostly in the

---

* Diz, a fort; ful, a bridge. A place on a river large enough to have a fort and a bridge over the river.

hands of the famous Hāji Jabr, who lives in a mud fort at Muhammerah, the farthest point to which our troops went in the Persian war in 1856–57.

Shuster and Dizful had always had a great interest for me ever since an adventurous journey made there from Ispahan by Mr. George Mackenzie with six good horses and very light baggage; and finding there was a route, I determined, if by any means possible, to leave my baggage here with Hādi, and taking only Ghulamshah and a prismatic compass and an aneroid, to make a careful dead reckoning survey, at which I was now pretty skilful. So I proposed this to Ali Akber, and it is not easy to imagine the storm of indignation.

"Verily, there is no God but one God. You have arrived here by the hand of God only. My mules are dead beat. You have got to go through Kurdistan and through Turkey, and now you want to go into this fearful country, where the snow is such that elephants could not pierce it, where there are no houses nor fodder, and the inhabitants are so savage that no caravan ever dreamt of passing except two hundred strong, with an escort and mules to carry fodder."

I expected this, and argued the case the whole day. Ali brought the naib, a little dried-up sub-lieutenant with the lining of a uniform coat on, who was in charge of the chapar khana. The naib doubled the horrors of the country, and brought all sorts of people to corroborate his statements. I sat on one side of the fireplace, and they all squatted in a row on a carpet I spread for them on the other side. They all declared that once a year in the summer a number of caravans collected and travelled in company and with soldiers as far as a town called Khurumabad (not the village we had passed through). There they waited until another caravan was collected at a place called Dastfil, on the opposite side of some very robber-infested desert, and crossed at the same time. I offered double fare, even treble, but without result. However, I had time to argue, so dismissed the subject for the night.

The next day, February the 16th, was very cold, and I lay under my rugs till late. I was amused at hearing the following dialogue.

Hādi, who has become carpenter to the expedition, calls out from the far end of the room, where he is mending some of our boxes: "Throw me over the corkscrew, my child."

Ghulamshah, busy with his cooking, throws it over. He appears afterwards to consider the matter, and on reflection says: "What do you want to do with the corkscrew, O Hādi?"

Hādi: "I am mending the black box."

Ghulamshah becoming interested: "But what have you to do with the corkscrew when you are mending the black box?"

Hādi: "Oh, the Sahib told me so."

Ghulamshah, *sotto voce:* "Now what *does* this idiot want with the corkscrew, and it is the last one." Aloud, contemptuously: "*What* did the Sahib tell you?"

Hādi: "Oh, I must not use nails, but always screws, and I must always bore holes for them."

Ghulamshah hastily: "But you can't bore holes with a ——"

Explanations follow, and Ghulamshah rescues his corkscrew.

Ali Akber seemed at his wit's end to know what to do with himself during this halt. He sat for hours in the sun in the porch, bullying little boys, enticing dogs to come within reach by offers of bread, and then chopping at them with his sword, and bargaining for wooden popguns, a new sign of civilization which he had never seen before, and which amused him immensely.

We had several visitors, and a chief topic of conversation was the magnificence of Shah Abbas (a former ruler), and the number of caravanserais he had built.

I found that the regular road for caravans to Shuster crossed mine at Khurumabad, the small village before described, and that most European goods came from the north *viâ* Tabriz, not from the shorter but more difficult route from the south *viâ* Shuster.

The carpets made here were the best we had yet seen. The woof was of cotton, not, as in former carpets, of wool. The cotton woof carpets are not so suitable for travelling as the others, but lie flatter on the floor, and the pattern can be made more regular. During the afternoon I noticed a man deliberately taking away portions of the mud roof in bags. On inquiry I found that he proposed to mend his own roof, which had suffered from the weather, and that he was related to the "naib," who probably considered the Government roof fair plunder.

There is a superstition here that lice produce a sore in the nose. This was so generally insisted upon by my visitors that I think there may be some connection between the two things, but they could not produce a man afflicted as described.

The whole day was spent in receiving people, acquiring information about the Shuster route, bargaining for carpets, writing down Balūchi and Persian folklore stories, and last, but not least, taking incessant observations on the roof, where I established a regular observatory.

On the 17th a chapar of five horsemen arrived from Teheran, and to my triumph and Ali's discomfiture were going to Shuster. They were such mountains of sheepskins, wolfskins, felts, and blankets, that they evidently expected a cold trip, and they laughed good-humouredly when I suggested that, in case of an attack, they would have to take off most of their clothes before being able to get at their weapons. They said that the road was very bad, but that they were safe, as it was known that they had nothing but the king's mails, and that the chief would be heavily fined should anything happen to them. They called the country Arabistan, or land of wanderers. The road leads by Orojet (same as Burujird), there are chapar khanas for five stages, after which only chadar nisheens or dwellers in tents. I tried to get these fellows to let me go with them, but they would not hear of it. I offered all the money I could afford, but it was no use. They said they rode eighty miles a day, and this I could not do; that they had been trained for it, I had not; that I should fall ill and have to be left behind; that the dwellers in tents would not shelter me for love, and if I showed money would murder me and plunder me, and the responsibility would fall on them. These men were from Teheran, were familiar with Englishmen, and knew me for one, and feared the difficulties with our ambassador should anything befall me.

I argued hard and produced some result, for I overheard an animated discussion on the subject, but it was no use. What weighed with most of them was that I was so thin and small, for I was much pulled down by constant recurrence of dysentery.

I went to see the governor about it, but he was a crabbed, uncivil old fellow, and I believe the most mendacious man in a very mendacious country, and after some time, when question after question had been answered by a palpable untruth, I got up in a huff and left him, saying that I had done nothing yet to show I was such a fool as to believe the things he said, but was not sure whether he was not a fool to say them. His was the only house glazed in the town, the glass being said to have been made at Hamadan.

On going home after this, I decided to call at the telegraph office, hoping that I might get some truth from a brother of the craft.

The office was a nice clean upstairs room, and the telegraphist, a portly old gentleman, was seated majestically on the floor, writing a message which was read out to him by a wretched little mirza or clerk, who wound up the instrument (an old Morse embosser on its last legs) and gave the reply.

To my disappointment the old gentleman had but recently been sent here,—considered himself banished, and would admit no knowledge of the people or the country. He told me that a general officer was shortly arriving to make a conscription, and that there would be grand illuminations, and I left after the ordinary civilities of tea and kaliāns.

I went home, and again attacked Ali about the Shuster route, and after much argument he consented to go; but at what a price—six pounds a day! and this after all the money I had already spent and should have to spend before getting to England. It was most disappointing, and I took a night to sleep on it. I suppose it was under the influence of this disappointment that I made the following observation in my note-book—a general summing up of Persia in one sentence!

"Persia, a barren country;—a country of mud-walled plantations of mulberry-trees, willows, and poplars;—a country of mud-domed houses;—of chopped straw, barley, and brown bread."

It rained heavily in the night, and a large portion of the roof fell in, but fortunately no one was injured. It was with a heavy heart that I resigned the trip to Shuster. I had the barren honour of having, to a certain extent, made my point, for I believe that Ali's offer was genuine, and that he would have seen me through, and that even in mid-winter a caravan could go to Shuster. I resolved, however, not to announce my decision until the very last moment, but an incident occurred to-day which reduced my chances to zero. The caravan of 100 mule-loads of tobacco arrived, and five of the mules were the five of Ali's that we had left behind, and of whom should they be in charge but that ruddy-faced scamp Muhammad? So much for Ali's tenderness to his poor younger brother.

I had been determined to go to Shuster, but the difficulties were too tremendous. Robbers who shot from behind bushes, impassable snowdrifts, etc., could be dealt with, but alas! the sinews of war were wanting. The young pidar sukhta (son of a burnt father) Muhammad had managed to get his five mule-loads as far as here, the other muleteers having helped him on the condition that Ali Akber should join them at Dowletabad, and thence help them in turn. This made Ali's prices still more exorbitant. I could not, however, bear to be controlled in this way, and ordered a halt until further orders, so that Muhammad and the tobacco caravan should get so far ahead that Ali could not hope to join them.

On the 19th a great stir appeared in this always busy little town. The general was hourly expected, and an "istikbal," or reception, was to be immediately prepared. The poor little naib was galvanised into activity, and was hunting for his uniform trousers, and the remainder of his uniform coat, and abusing his family for their loss, when an excited crowd rushed in and demanded all his post horses *instanter*. This finished him, and he came to me imploring advice. "What can I do? There's a chapar coming in from Kirmanshahan, and there will be no horses, and then they will report me." But I had enough to do to look after my own horses, as Hādi and Ali were in the town, and could give him no assistance. They captured the naib's horses, which soon appeared in a garb very different from that in which they went out, cashmere shawl saddle cloths and bright saddle carpets having been put over their rough but serviceable leather saddles.

The chapar khana was at the extreme edge of the town, and from the roof I overlooked a long stretch of the Hamadan road, while beneath me collected the istikbal, or reception. Soon the party came in sight, a broad line of horsemen with a nucleus in the centre. At a given sign off started our party full gallop, with left hand outstretched and head almost level with the horse's head. They did some graceful evolutions by the help of a very cruel bit and a big pommel to hold on by, and after shooting rapidly two or three times across and across the path of the advancing cavalcade they quietly joined its ranks. But every half-minute one horseman on either side of the nucleus, which I could not yet clearly distinguish, shot rapidly from the rank, and crossed over to the opposite flank.

At last the servants and baggage began dropping in in twos and threes. The baggage consisted of twelve mules loaded with fine large carpet saddle-bags, eight more with large white leather-covered boxes, and eight more with large gaudy japanned boxes. Then came the horsemen scampering along, and all endeavouring to avoid a huge puddle just in front of the chapar khana, and jostling one another in the most undignified manner. Then his Serene Highness himself on his war-horse, while his palfrey was led by him with a blue and white satin pad on its back. One great feature of the procession was the bobtailedness of the horses. The long flowing tail is much prized in Persia, and when the road is very muddy the grooms tie them up into a tight bob which looks most grotesque.

There was not much excitement among the populace. I saw one old woman on a neighbouring house-top and a few old men sitting on the sunny side of a wall, but the dogs in enormous numbers barked themselves hoarse. In the evening the bazaar was "illuminated," and a deafening band of drums and bagpipes played in it. I put on a Persian cloak and strolled through it, but it was an ordinary Persian crowd, and the noise and jostling were so great that I soon came away. There were no games or fun of any kind. The deafening noise, and, to them, unusual light seemed to be all their senses required.

It was a good, clean bazaar, half a mile long, about one-third newly built of brick, and the illumination was well done so far as wicks in cups of oil can do it. I was told that any one lighting less than one hundred lamps would receive two thousand sticks and pay forty-five tomāns fine. This might be a hint for our corporations. The Manchester goods men had the best of it, for they had but to hang out some gaudy handkerchiefs to assume a most festive aspect.

Long after we had turned in, Ali came in exulting greatly at having outstayed us and seen the shahzāda go through the bazaar in procession with three troops of soldiers.

That evening, to the intense delight of all, I gave orders to load up for Kirmanshahan, thus removing the greatest anxiety from all minds. I never appreciated the comfort of a good servant so much as when loading up early on cold mornings. You wake up early under warm rugs and hear a whispering. You ask the time. "Seven o'clock, sahib, and tea ready." You find a good fire, and everything packed up and half-loaded, and have nothing to do but eat your breakfast and get on your horse.

Our stage to Parrispar was twelve hours, and we did not arrive till 8.30 p.m., when it was dark and dangerous travelling.

The country was little changed from that already described,—level mud and snow plains interspersed by islands of rocky hills, while all around in the far distance were snow-covered mountains which were difficult to distinguish from the clouds.

In all the hills were outcrops of an iron-hard brown clay, strike north-west and south-east, and dip about forty-five degrees. The dust of the watercourses was sometimes coaly and sometimes slaty. We crossed fertile plains with many villages, and at about fifteen miles we crossed a level inundated plain ten miles broad, in the middle of which were massive stone causeways, each about two hundred yards long, and placed about one hundred yards apart. I suppose in the dry season the existing inundation would be confined to a channel somewhere about here; but at present the place was no deeper than anywhere else, excepting some dangerous eddies near the abutments. The rest of the march was a struggle through deep mud and numberless muddy creeks. After getting across this plain I stopped for breakfast at a large caravanserai called Dumb-i-Shatir (the clever man's tail). This was intended to be the commencement of a village, but as yet only one family were there, and a very miserable condition they were in. There was the inevitable agriculturist, with his long-handled spade and greasy felt cap, enveloped in strips and bandages of home-made woollen stuff which would appear to defy any attempt at classification, but to each of which he gave a name with confidence. There were three or four ragged women, and a few sheep and fowls.

At 4.30 we were still drudging on past the large village of Halimabad, and found a little "bahar," or spring vegetation, growing through the snow. Then we had a steady pull up an apparently interminable hill.

Then an anxious time wandering about in the dark among steep ravines and watercourses, and at 8.20 p.m.

we crossed a good bridge, of five arches, over a rapid stream, twenty feet wide, called the river Helwind, and soon after reached the village of Parrispar, where we got stabling and a room in the house of a "lone woman." I was struck here with the curious meanings of the word "haft" or "seven." A Balūch, speaking of the antiquity of his chief's family, will say that he is "haft pusht," *i.e.*, has "seven at his back," or an indefinite number of ancestors. Also if you ask for anything from your box or saddle-bags which is down at the bottom, and difficult to get at, he will say it is "haft pusht," and will ūse the same expression if you ask if anything is securely tied on a camel.

To-night I made Hādi insist on a tremendous sweeping out of the room I was to occupy, but he said pathetically, "Īn sheppishha haftbāla mīgirdand." (*These lice wander seven upstairs*, or, *wander everywhere.*)

Parrispar was an ordinary village of 150 thick, mud-walled, square flat-roofed houses, with small court-yards in the centre containing firewood heaped up for the winter. Inside the houses are one or two round half-baked cylinders of clay full of wheat, a spinning-wheel or two, and a hand mill, with the inevitable vermin-breeding kursi in the middle.

Parrispar is situate at the foot of a high slate hill, crowned by the remains of the robāt or fort which had been the origin of its existence. To the north and south-east stretched a fertile wheat plain for about seven miles, and near the village itself were many acres of grapes. In the morning I went up to the top of the hill, and took a round of bearings, and made a sketch map of the country, while the principal inhabitants thronged round me and fully answered all my questions.

They, it appeared, lived in one of the unfortunate villages ground down by taxes, and were shortly going to abandon their homes and go elsewhere.

I inquired closely and at length into this matter. The taxes here were (please read francs for krans) five krans per head, six krans per house, and six krans per jīvar (jerīb) shahi of land. A jerīb here is one hundred yards long and fifty yards broad. So that a man with three wives, three children, a house, and a jerīb of land, would pay forty-seven francs per annum. His women would make in two months a carpet worth thirty krans, of which I think it fair to say fifteen would be net profit, and his jerīb grows enough wheat to feed him.

These people were not quite brought to despair. They were going to wait quietly, and get in their wheat and grape crops, and leave in the nou rōz, or new year, for a new robāt, not far off, where was virgin soil and no taxes. Some of the land here was "Khālisa," or belonging to the Shah, and some "raiāti," held from farmers.

Next morning we left for Kangiwar at 9.30 a.m. The huge mountain Khangir Marz was in sight all day, and I was told that it was almost inaccessible, that its summit was frequented by lions, and that murderers took refuge there; and that when the Shah passed here on his pilgrimage, he halted, and had two days' unsuccessful hunting there.

We met a large party of pilgrims, all with white turbans, who were returning from the sacred shrine of Kerbela. I noticed here a practice I have already alluded to in my account of Balūchistan. Those of the pilgrims on foot continually picked up big stones in the road and threw them on one side, and it was acknowledged here to be merely a primitive system of road making, and a "sowab" as easing the weary pilgrims' feet.

There are two pages of bearings and other scientific observations in my note-book, but they will be found in the appendix. The great feature of to-day's march was that here we actually entered the garm sīr, or warm region. First crocuses began peeping through the snow, then dwarf irises, and at 1.30 p.m., on the 21st of February, we came on a considerable expanse of genuine English greensward, the first of the kind I had seen for four years, and shortly afterwards a herd of English-looking cows peacefully cropping it, as if it were the most ordinary thing in the world. At first I wanted to dismount and pick each new flower I saw. This was impossible, but we did sit down and have a glorious lunch in the middle of the meadow until the "bār" came up, when we had to resume business.

The approach to Kangiwar was absolutely park-like compared to the country we had been travelling through for so long. We crossed a low range through a pass, and on rounding a corner found ourselves in a green valley, with plenty of water, and no snow, while at the extreme end, nestled under a huge hill, lay our destination. I cantered on ahead with Ghulamshah, we saw larks and other birds, herds of cattle, and at last drew rein at the caravanserai. This, however, was full, and the people, who mistook us for the "chapar," as was very natural, seeing only two horsemen, one with two large bundles slung across his saddle,* kindly and even eagerly directed us to the chapar khana. This also was quite full of Georgian pilgrims, in their tall black sheep-skin caps, returning from Kerbela. But the pilgrim who occupied the best room, and whom I strongly suspect to have been a Frenchman in disguise, most courteously made us some tea and evacuated his quarters for us.

This gentleman certainly was not a Georgian. Although all the separate items of his dress were Georgian, they were not such as a genuine one would wear all together. He made one or two short and uneasy visits during the evening, and seeing him looking at my books, I handed him "Maunder's Treasury of Botany," but without result. If, as I suspect was the case, he was an European who had been to Kerbela in disguise, it was very wise of him to hold his tongue, for here at a chapar khana, with constant communication with Teheran, I was of course an acknowledged Feringi.

Kangiwar was a most pleasant little town, the air mild, and the people very civil, though a little disappointed at our not being the post, as there was great excitement about the war between Turkey and Russia. The chaparchi, or post-house-keeper of Sahna, our next stage, was here, and promised to go on ahead and prepare everything for us. I have a note here, connected I suppose with the civility I received, that "Feringis command respect here because they have money, are accustomed to use it, and are not afraid to own possession of it."

* These were our clothes of the previous day, which we always carried ahead with us to have them boiled and dried in time for next day's wear, so great was the plague of lice.

At 7 p.m. the barometer showed 6,020 feet. Thermometer: dry, 46; wet, 42; rather misty and very cloudy, and on the morrow we got the benefit of those clouds. I was amused here at a little ragged boy who had somehow climbed upstairs and invited himself to assist in Ghulamshah's cooking. Ghulamshah had "shu'd" him twice, but he always returned, oozing slowly into the room rather than walking in. The third time, on being told to go outside, he said in his childish voice, but with great indignation: "How shall I go outside? Am I not a Darwish?"

Kangiwar is situate under a lofty snow-topped mountain at the west-south-west corner of a fertile plain about ten miles square.

The next stage to Sahna was over a mountain range by a well-engineered zigzag road made to enable the Shah to drive all the way to Kerbela in carriages. Along the left side ran the telegraph line, and if one only disregarded the somewhat outlandish garb of himself and companions he might easily imagine himself in Scotland. We wound up and up through incessant torrents of rain, which, however, well protected as we were by mackintoshes, we thought a welcome change from the terrible icy west wind and driving snow we had battled with so long. The highest point we reached was 6,760 feet, though it seemed much more, and at 12.45 commenced a winding descent. The scenery was grand; for though the actual heights were under 2,000 feet, yet half hidden in rain and magnified by mist, which lifted at times, now here and now there, and showed unexpected mountains whose tops were snow clad and indistinguishable from the clouds, it was a very striking picture. On getting to the foot of the hills we had a most muddy ride, still in incessant rain, to the comfortable chapar khana of Sahna, where we found everything ready for us, thanks to the proprietor, whom we had met at Kangiwar. We had now reached a pleasant land indeed. Incessant rain, though disagreeable, was at least a change from the burning heat of Mekran and the freezing cold of the Khurumabad pass.

Here we found much to interest us. There was an old mulla, or schoolmaster, keeping school in one room, I suppose the most ignorant of his tribe, and that is a strong assertion. I attended school after dinner, and observing me listening critically, he put on an extraordinary amount of self-complacent superiority. He was teaching five or six children a verse of the Kurān, and not knowing anything of its meaning, ran over the stops and put a pathetic emphasis on any good-sounding word that seemed able to bear it. Here also was a new type of face—big nose and overhanging eyebrows, and a stiff, bristly moustache and slight beard being the main features. All here spoke Kurdi in preference to Persian, though they knew the latter language well, always, however, avoiding the letter "w;" *e.g.*, "birraīd" (*you will go*), for "birawīd." There were also here two distinct kinds of dogs, both good and intelligent, and not at all parias. One kind, long-bodied, long-nosed and bow-legged, I can only call "Boonders," from Bret Harte's famous "Boonder." The other was a good specimen of a long-haired wiry Scotch terrier. Though the breeding of these dogs was never attended to in any way, they never intercrossed, nor was there any medium between the two distinct varieties. The same thing was seen more markedly further on. Here the houses showed evident preparations for much rain. They were still mud, but the rafters projected beyond the walls three or four feet, making a verandah, and each house had a porch, so that the proprietor could enjoy the open air without being rained upon. Here also the reign of the kaliān was at an end, the pipe being invariably a small red bowl and thick wooden stem a foot and a half long. The people here had bare legs and feet, and their drawers were tucked high up to keep them out of the mud. They make here woollen carpets, but only woven and in zigzag patterns of two or three colours only. Here it is a great mark of respectability to give a guest white crystallized sugar, which, from its rareness, has acquired medicinal virtues in the eyes of the inhabitants.

Some visitors came and sat with us in the evening; and I noticed a curious transmutation of letters in a story one of them told of getting lost in the mist on the mountain. After two days' wandering he had only one small piece of bread. His expression was, "Bas yek galantam bīta" (*It was only one mouthful for me*). In the Bampūri dialect of Balūchi that would be "Bas yek galampam bīta," showing a transposition of "mp" and "nt."

Next morning an intelligent son of the chaparchi took me on to the roof and named all the hills as I took their bearings.

I got capital sights, and at 9.30 a.m. we were on march to Bīsitūn.

We were making a gradual descent, the barometer showing 5,580 feet; thermometer: dry, 49·5; wet, 45·5; blue sky, misty, cloudy, and variable moderately strong west wind. I was interested at starting to see the chaparchi's married daughter come out in the rain with her baby to meet her husband, who just then arrived from Kirmanshahan. The village of Sahna was a thriving one of about 150 houses. Hādi had fortunately bobtailed our horses, and we crossed without inconvenience a brawling torrent which ran through the middle of it. The streets, however, were knee-deep in slush, and we were glad to get out into the open. We passed several dyers' shops where the wool for carpets was dyed, and a magnificent caravanserai in process of construction at the sole expense of a certain Hāji of Nerwan. It had already been two years building, forty or fifty men working at it for about two months a year at the rate of fivepence a day each. The brickkiln was two miles away from the site.

We overtook three or four scattered detachments of horse soldiers "going to the front," and I tackled them about their proposed capture of Baghdad. They were from Khurassān, and to my inquiries replied indignantly, "Do you think we won't go to Baghdad? Here are the Turks being tyrannical; and now that the shahzāda has twenty regiments and cannon, who is going to fight against him?"

Green tender grass was springing up on all sides, and was in itself a luxury to our unaccustomed eyes. We trudged on over a muddy and uneventful march until we got close to the huge bluff of Bīsitūn, which had been our landmark all day. Here we crossed a rapid stream sixty feet wide; and as our horses had at times to swim, it may be imagined that our loads got somewhat wet. How the charvadar got the lame donkey across I cannot say, and I suppose no one but himself with his long pole and extraordinary powers of vituperation could have done it.

I have forgotten to mention a very little fellow we overtook on the way much overweighted with a large earthenware pot of sour milk which he was carrying to Bīsitūn to his father, who had been very sick for a long time. I was struck with his childish earnestness (he could not have been ten years old, and had walked by himself about twelve miles there and twelve back for this milk), and I offered to mount him on one of the mules. This he declined, so I gave him a kran, for which he thanked me with dignity, and begged me to make his father's house my own while I was at Bīsitūn and dine there to-night. He treated me throughout the conversation as his equal, I suppose because I did not speak loudly or bully him.

To-day I rode all day without my woollen gloves, the weather was so much warmer, and at 4 p.m. we crossed a good brick bridge, and arrived at the clean chapar khana of Bīsitūn. While things were being arranged I strolled over to a fine large caravanserai, close by which were some fifty huge camels being fed with large balls of barley, slightly bruised and soaked in water. I found the keeper of this place a chatty old gentleman, who had been in Kirman when our troops took Bushire, and who had plenty to say about the matter. I asked who built the caravanserai, and, as I expected, "Shah Abbas." "Shah Abbas," he resumed, "built 999 caravanserais." "And why," said I innocently, "didn't he make it a thousand while he was about it?" He was greatly pleased. "Because he wished people to ask just the question you ask!"

He was as proud of the Bīsitūn bluff as if he had

made it himself, and I believe that he had brought himself to believe that he was in some way responsible for it, and really the way the monstrous mass of hard blue stone towered over the village almost made one feel that if he made much noise it would fall down and crush everything.

Here was another sign that we were in a warm country. The people drew water from the well with a leather "dhole," and carried it away in musuks (*waterskins*). Ghulamshah was so charmed at this reminiscence that he immediately went and had a long pull from the mouth of a musuk. "No more melted snow, or making tea from junks of ice, now," said he delightedly. To him, that drink out of the musuk was the first real drink he had had since we had abandoned our camels at Kirman.

The dogs here were surprising; they were very numerous, but of four perfectly distinct varieties. There were little neat liver-coloured retrievers, with the silkiest ears, and long fringe behind the forearm. There were great black-and-white wolf dogs, with long fur. There were what any one would call genuine setters, long-backed, wavy-haired, and wavy-tailed fellows, with most sagacious-looking noses; and a kind of black, smooth-haired, shiny-coated terrier, with very small feet.

On returning home to the chapar khana, after a friendly farewell to my chatty friend, I found the chaparchi had provided me with a cook, and the dinner was in a state of active preparation. The said cook being a charming young Kurdi lady, I acquiesced in Ghulamshah's temporary abdication, and we had a very comfortable dinner.

I think the Kurdi women are some of the finest produced by nature. Of fine, upright stature, they have rosy cheeks and dimpled chins, while their manners are naïve to the last degree. They wear an akkāl like the Bedawin Arabs, with a diadem of beads across the forehead; a tight-fitting shirt and a short thick embroidered jacket, and from eight to fourteen petticoats, according to their wealth. Their arms are bare from the elbow, and their legs from the knee downwards, and they are of magnificent physique and of most sociable manners.

I stayed at Bīsitūn all the next day writing up journals, taking sights, etc., and on the 25th February left for Kirmanshahan, with lovely weather, and over a cheerful country of young growing wheat. Carved in the face of the bluff, were some huge stone figures; they were, however, so high up that I could not describe them. Lower down was a modern Arabic inscription, setting forth the terms on which the caravanserai was bequeathed to the people.

As we left the hill I noticed the extraordinary echoes produced by cows lowing or donkeys braying, and the effect of this was most singular. The warm air was delicious, and we rode without gloves and without overcoats. On the way we interviewed an old agriculturist, who was breaking up some new ground. He was working on, to me, a new principle, which he called "Sakko Kāli." He described it thus: He received the seed (wheat), and the land was of course free. He paid yearly one fowl, six eggs, seven donkey-loads of cut straw, five krans for each pair of bullocks he used, and one load of wood. After that he kept for himself two-thirds of the crop he raised.

At 12.50 p.m. we crossed a rapid stream one hundred yards broad, and entered the long-looked-for gate of Kirmanshahan, and were most hospitably received by Agha Hassan Khan, ex-governor of Kirmanshahan, and British agent.

CHAPTER XIX.

KIRMANSHAHAN.

The ivory binoculars.—Agha Hassan.—More languages than one.—Spirit rapping.—The little horse distinguishes himself.—Autumn manœuvres.—Water under the grass.—The Hissam as Sultana.—Drives in the Agha's carriages.—Muhammad Khan.—Hāji Mulla Hussein.—Kurind.—The graveyards of the Ali Allahi sect.—A Kurind interior.—Horse-hair veils for ladies.—An old man in difficulties.—From plateau to plain.—A sporting Turkoman telegraphist.—A herd of brood mares.—Toby and the cows.—Mahmud Bey, our new master of horse.—We cross the frontier into Turkey.—Difficulties with the Quarantine authorities.—Cavalry escort.—Sunstroke.—A puzzled stork.—The concert interrupted.—Death of the Bey's horse.—Baghdad.—The plague.—Basreh.—Marseilles.—London.

ON entering the narrow and muddy streets, Ghulamshah and myself, who were as usual far ahead of the "Bār," inquired as we had been instructed, for the "Wakil-al-Dowlat," for by such title was the hospitable Agha best known. After passing through many thronged bazaars we reached a tall house, at the door of which we dismounted, conscious all the while of an inspection through a pair of ivory binoculars from the upper storey. We mounted the steps and were ushered into a long room, where were seated three or four Persian young gentlemen, to whom I made the customary salaam, and by whom I was courteously received, but with a certain amount of indifference, as if it was a matter of ordinary routine.

When, however, after the usual salutations had been gone through, and coffee had been drunk, I began to explain that I was an Englishman, a traveller, and provided with a letter from the British agent at Ispahan, things assumed a different aspect. A young fellow who had resumed his gazing out of the window with the ivory binoculars, hastily turned round, and after inspecting me narrowly, sent for a certain Muhammad Agha, the eldest son as I found of the Agha, and a prince of good fellows. We had more coffee and kaliāns, and a young scribe who had been to India was sent for to read my letter of introduction, which was in English. While we were in conversation as to the journeys I had made and the countries I had seen, I heard Ali's hoarse voice shouting for me in the street below, and orders were immediately given for the admission of my baggage. Then Muhammad Agha turned up and ushered me into a spacious room, which was to be my own special apartment. He explained that his father was now absent, but would come soon, meanwhile I must be tired and want to rest, so sending in a copious supply of clean water he left me to myself, and I had a good tub and change of raiment. The room was well carpeted, but without any furniture save an iron bedstead, from which four of the nine bottom laths were missing. It was also over the stable and over another place, so that one had one's choice of smells. There was a capital fireplace which "drew" well, and shortly after my installation a roaring fire of oak logs.

I had hardly got myself into decent costume (I had just one good coat left, for, between Kangiwar and Sahna, a pint bottle of Warburg's fever-drops had broken over my black frock-coat) when Muhammad Agha begged to be admitted, and we had a cosey chat by the fireside. Later on, by invitation of the Agha, I went down to his majlis. He had a suite of apartments in a remote part of the house, and received me in the most cordial manner, and introduced me to numerous friends sitting round in a large well-painted saloon. He was rejoiced at my knowing Persian, but when I found him making side remarks about me in Arabic, and I felt bound to tell him I knew that language also, he was still more interested.

He was a tall fine man, of remarkably good presence, looking haughty, as if accustomed to command, but utterly kind and courteous in his manner. When he found that I knew also the Kurdi dialect, he elected me to sit next him and eat out of his dish, and even went to the length of secretly ordering some arrack, which was brought in an old Johann Farina bottle. The conversation was general, but the whole household were, at the time of my arrival, much exercised by a case of spirit rapping. Stones, as large as an orange, had for three nights running been pitched by supernatural hands into the Agha's inner courtyard, and though he had put soldiers on guard he had discovered nothing. I saw two of the stones, so, as Mark Twain might say, I am bound to believe it. We had a capital dinner, and I soon afterwards turned in for a well-earned sleep in the almost lathless bedstead, under which Ghulamshah arranged two of my boxes.

Kirmanshahan is a large city of about 40,000 people, containing houses of from one to three storeys, and situated near low hills on the north side of a broad undulating plain, which is to a great extent sown with corn.

From the window of the topmost room, our common drawing-room, one looked over a wide plain partly green with young corn and partly yellow with gravel, and three or four miles distant, in a large garden, was the huge but unsightly Imaret, a kind of fancy palace, uninhabited. In a long line in front of this were hundreds of white tents, the camp of the Hissam as Sultana, the uncle of the Shah, and known as the conqueror of Herat. Far away was the bold bluff of Bīsitūn, and the range of which it was the head, the upper half still being covered with snow.

We had a very pleasant time at Kirmans̓hahan * in spite of incessant rain, and a large party of us rode out almost every day.

On these occasions the Padre distinguished himself. The little horse, with plain, much-worn English saddle, did not show to advantage among the big showy horses and gorgeous trappings of our friends. The first time we went out their head groom was just breaking in a very fine young Kurdi horse, and wanting to show off, suggested a gallop. The little horse was wild with delight, and in less than a mile the whole party were hopelessly in the rear, puffing and blowing, and totally disordered as to their trappings. The Padre was quite uncontrollable, the slightest slackening of the reins being sufficient to start him off at full gallop at one bound, while his previous hard

---

* I was puzzled at first at hearing this place always spoken of as Kirmanshahan. I believe that this is correct for the town, and Kirmanshah for the district.

work had put him in such condition as the other horses could not hope to rival.

One day we went to the camp and had an interview with the commander-in-chief. On riding there our route took us over a muddy field of young wheat. On my remonstrating at the damage we were doing to the tenant's crops, Muhammad Agha replied with great naïveté, "What can he have to say, he's got plenty of it." The camp was well arranged, so far as details were concerned. Each subdivision of troops was well defined, and its head-quarters marked by a pole bearing a square of bright tin, which blazed in the sun most brilliantly, and was decidedly better than a flag, which would during the rains have drooped miserably.

But the conqueror of Herat was not happy in his choice of situation. He had pitched his camp on the banks of the river (the Kara Su or black water) which had overflowed its banks and inundated the surrounding country. The result was that the mud was knee deep, and that the soldiers had all taken off their trowsers and presented a most unmilitary aspect.

We sent an ambassador to the commander-in-chief, and, while waiting, left our horses in the charge of the grooms, and took coffee in the tent of the "sartip" or general. The water was here as everywhere, but the sartip had spread a quantity of chopped straw on the ground and put his carpets over that. The result was that though we were sitting on mud and water we were quite dry, and I thought to myself that this might be the origin of the saying, "like water under the grass"; the chopped straw being dry, hard, and springy, absorbed no moisture, and though water was running under us, we sat as if we were on the roof of a house. Our credentials having been presented, we ploughed through the mud from the sartip's tent to that of the commander-in-chief, which was gorgeous and well guarded, no others being allowed within forty yards of it.

The commander-in-chief was very courteous, and we had coffee in cups of silver studded with turquoises. He did not omit to remind me that he had been to England, and been presented to Her Majesty. He was dressed as an European, possibly in honour of my visit, and we conversed freely. Observing a prismatic compass sticking out of my pocket, he asked various questions as to its use, and sent for a "kibl-nama" of his own. This on arrival turned out to be an old French prismatic, with a clinometer included, for the use of which he begged me to write him out a paper of instructions, which I readily promised to do.

On another occasion we made an excursion to the Tāk-i-Bustān, a place made celebrated by Sir Henry Rawlinson, who has minutely described it. At the foot of the range, which terminates at Bīsitūn, are some huge clumsy carvings of ancient heroes, some on horseback, and some wrestling, cut into the live rock. Near them is a small summer-house, which looks over a large square pond surrounded by trees. This is a favourite summer resort for picnics, but the time of the year was against our enjoying it fully, and the incessant rain affected our spirits.

On our way back we visited the Imaret. We entered the long garden attached to it by a gate at the south end, and cantered down a long gravel walk bordered by shrubs and flowers until we came to the Imaret. Muhammad Agha's presence readily procured us admission. It was a large palace, the rooms of which were profusely ornamented by elaborate mouldings in plaster of Paris, the work of Italian artists. The interior is much more interesting than the exterior, the prominent feature of which is that the window frames have been "glazed," if I may use the expression, with plates of tin—some are natural and some painted red.

In sketching our life at Kirmanshahan, I must not forget sundry drives with the Agha in his carriages. These carriages had been part of the Shah's equipage on his pilgrimage, and had been left behind broken down. Of the seven or eight existing, the Agha, as became his rank, owned three.

Sometimes of an evening he would propose a drive, to which I, taking the compliment as it was meant to be taken, would readily respond. We would then at the appointed time wade down endless narrow streets ankle-deep in mud to the outskirts of the town, where the carriage awaited us. Our progress was always considerably retarded by the respect in which the Agha was held by all, great and small. It was one incessant series of polite salutations, and I can never sufficiently admire the tact my host exhibited. The amount of cordiality was dealt out to each in exact proportion to his position, and the humbler people formed themselves into procession after us to such an extent that we materially interfered with the traffic, and often had two or three hundred people collected to see us embark. The drive itself was not without its "discrepancies," for a road practicable for carriages led but a short distance from the town. After this came muddy lanes and fields saturated by rain. We generally went at a very slow pace, but the driver was a courageous fellow, and the horses but imperfectly broken to harness, so that at times we went much faster than was safe, and there arose in my mind the question, "On which side shall we fall when we upset?"

I must not leave Kirmanshahan without a short mention of the Agha's familiar friend, one Muhammad Khan.

This was an old gentleman who had formerly been the possessor of great estates. He had, however, lost his wits, and I believe the Agha had constituted himself Commissioner of Lunacy, and taken charge of the estates and the possessor. Muhammad Khan was installed in the house as a sort of tame rabbit, and great deference was shown to him by all. He was the most consummate and irritating bore I have ever met. He would come and sit with me for hours, asking over and over again the most impertinent and disgusting questions; and I once went straight to the Agha, begging that he should be placed under restraint. I may add that I had grave doubts whether or not he was the poor idiot he represented himself to be, and up to the present cannot help thinking him the original of Lever's famous Terry Driscoll in "Davenport Dunn."

It was a cold morning on the fifth of March when we left our kind host and, escorted by Muhammad Agha, commenced what proved to be the last section of our long journey. We were bound for Baghdad by the road which had been made practicable for carriages on the occasion of the Shah's pilgrimage to Kerbela We crossed the range beyond Kirmanshahan, and after an uninteresting march over bare plain, arrived at Mahi Dasht, a small village with a caravanserai.

The people here seemed poor and wretched. They had no flocks, and consequently the almost universal employment of spinning was wanting, and they sat listlessly about the muddy streets, doing nothing and waiting for the spring.

Many of the rooms in the caravanserai were plastered up with mud covered with various devices in whitewash, as a seal which would lead to the detection of any attempt at burglary. The caravanserai was built of small burnt bricks, but the spouts were prodigiously heavy stone troughs, five feet long and a foot thick, the result being that the wall in which they were set was in all places giving way.

We found here a very noisy Persian merchant, by name Hāji Mulla Hussein, who was in a great state of exasperation at what he called the unmanly conduct of our late host Agha Hassan.

The Hāji had, it appears, been for a considerable period the Agha's guest, and the latter had given him a letter to a friend in Baghdad. The bearer regarded this as sufficient to pass him across the Turkish frontier, but found on arrival at the first stage that it would do nothing of the sort, and that he would be arrested the moment he attempted to enter Turkey without the proper firman.

He took it for granted that I was in the same difficulty as himself, and detailed at length the manner in which my luggage would be confiscated, and I should be plundered and kept waiting for days in the open air. But I read him my firman, and showed him the seal of the great Hissam as Sultana, and this produced a marked change in his manner. He immediately proposed that we should be companions, but this I firmly refused, as I had taken a great dislike to him. After several attempts to gain over the groom to plead his cause, he begged to be allowed to accompany me as my head groom. This also I refused for many reasons, and left him to make his way as best he could by bakshish.

The next march, to Harunabad (the place of Harun), was alternately over barren rocky ridges and small plains of fertile silt. Here was a good caravanserai, and I noticed a decided change in the features of the people. The men had fine striking faces, hollow cheeks and eyes, and huge moustaches, but no beards. They formed a striking contrast to the sleek, rounded Persians, and impressed me with an idea of fierceness and manliness.

As we marched on to Kurind, the capital of Kurdistan, the scenery gradually got more rugged and mountainous. The hitherto barren rocks became covered with stunted oak scrub. We passed several small villages perched on the slopes of hills, and all showing signs of activity in the manufacture of woollen carpets of a zigzag pattern not very handsome. About noon the stunted oak scrub gave place to trees twenty feet high, and we travelled up a picturesque valley the sides of which were lichen-covered terraces of yellow limestone from six to even fifteen feet broad. Streams trickled and leapt down the crevices, the air was bright and sunny, and we ended our march by arriving at the most picturesquely situated town we had yet seen—Kurind.

The traveller approaches Kurind up a broad valley, now green here and there with young corn. The range on the north side has been cleft as with an axe, and in this gigantic cleft, hardly distinguishable from the rugged boulders of the mountain, nestle the houses of Kurind. Opposite the cleft and half down the valley is a low grassy hill of earth covered with gravestones. Near this some of the wealthier people have built their houses. The greater number of the inhabitants, however, seem to prefer the mountain gorge, a preference probably to be ascribed to its greater security from plundering parties, which, report says, were frequent not long ago. A full head of water tumbles and dashes itself down the gorge, and has such great natural wildness and vigour that it can be tamed and made to drive corn-mills without losing in dignity.

I was so interested in the rugged scenery and unique position of Kurind that I willingly agreed to stay there a whole day to examine it more closely. On the morning after our arrival I set out on foot to explore the place. I took a bird's-eye view from the top of the caravanserai, and noticed that the whole valley was more or less cultivated, even partly up the sides of the hills, where huge boulders of limestone well adapted for lithographic purposes, were so thick that before the land could be tilled they had to be piled up in miniature castles four feet in diameter about the same height, and twelve feet apart.

On leaving the caravanserai we were pestered by journeyman tinkers, ironmongers, etc., who manufacture all sorts of handy travelling implements for sale to the pilgrims who pass here on their way to Kerbela. I bought one or two small things, partly to encourage the idea that I was a pilgrim; but they were quite worthless. I was told that this year two thousand pilgrims had passed, all of them Russian subjects.

On the earthen mound or hill we found numerous gravestones, many of which bore gaudy pictures of horses, showing that the person buried there had been wealthy and owned horses, and all bore the Muslim Declaration of Faith—"There is no God but one God." Tall slender pillars marked the graves of very great men. Finding the inscriptions on the gravestones different from any I had seen before, I questioned one of the bystanders, a tall, fierce-looking Kurd. He proved an intelligent and civil fellow, and I willingly accepted his services as a guide. I give here, however, only such of his information as I had opportunity to verify.

Kurind contains about one thousand houses, and the inhabitants are mostly employed in agriculture. They belong to a sect called Ali Allahis, and are divided into four clans or tribes, viz., the Zarday, Shuar, Nou Darwan, and Nou Chem (*Cheshm*, fountain).

Chatting with our new friend, who was proud of his native place, keenly appreciative of the grand scenery, and pleased with our interest in it, we walked towards the gorge, and soon came within hearing of the plashing torrent and the hum of the numerous mills it condescended to turn. Very soon our walk became a climb, and the path difficult even for a pedestrian. On either side rose almost perpendicular cliffs of limestone, and before us was a steep narrow ravine choked with boulders of all sizes. The houses with their flat brown roofs looked like card houses, for the flat thin roof was the only thing that caught the eye. The back of the house was always the cliff, and the walls very often huge boulders. The inhabitants had, for the most part, merely roofed in a space between two rocks.

I peeped into one house and saw an odd juxtaposition of nature's grandeur and dirty domestic comfort. Three frouzy old women were baking bread, and two more sifting flour, while two dirty children rolled about on the mud floor, idly hitting at the women's hands every time the slow motion of the sieve brought them within reach. The back of their house was a sheer cliff with an unbroken front for 200 feet. One side was artificial, and the other a slope of live rock, while across the middle of the floor was a deep crevasse down which rushed a rapid stream which drove the mill. The mills deserve a slight description. A convenient spot is chosen whence to take the water, and a wall, the top of which is plane with the horizon and trough-shaped, built to lead it to the mill.*

A thick block of wood in the shape of a truncated cone is suspended underneath the fall of water. This cone is provided with flanges going diagonally down its side in such a way that the effect of the water is to make it revolve rapidly. Under this is a trough to catch the water after it has done its work. The bush is connected by strings to the upper grinding stone, which consequently revolves, and is so hung as to work lightly on the lower stone.

I examined several of these mills, but all were clumsily made, and involved great waste of power.

---

* On visiting Clovelly, in Devon, after my return to England, I was strongly inclined to describe it as a miniature and civilized Kurind.

At about the middle of the ascent we came to an almost level place, through which the stream ran slowly, producing dense rank grass and tall weedy shrubs. On the east cliff were narrow terraces cut in the rock, and planted with pomegranates, walnuts, plane-trees, lilacs, grapes, apples, almonds, figs, cherries, quinces, and other fruits. Nor must I forget a patriarchal old plane-tree, whose hollow trunk served for a firewood warehouse. A little above this level place is an enclosure said to be sacred, but no one could explain for what reason.

On returning to our quarters, which were just by a fine but ruinous caravanserai, built by Shah Abbas, we found the Hāji Mulla Hussein in a state of profound despair. He had had difficulties with his muleteers, and they had left him in a body with their beasts. This seemed to be entirely owing to his own violent and niggardly conduct, and I felt less inclined to help him than ever; nor did my men show him any sympathy, though he sat up a great part of the night trying to win them over.

On the 9th of March we left Kurind and travelled up the broad valley before mentioned, along a telegraph line belonging to the Persian Government. This line has since been placed under European superintendence, not a moment before it was necessary.

We constantly passed straggling parties of soldiers, all proceeding to a great "camp of exercise" or "demonstration" on the frontier. We had a bright warm sun and blue sky, and were in great spirits. I overheard an animated conversation between Hādi and Ali Akber, from which I gathered that the former had accumulated about three pounds weight of horse-hair from the manes and tails of my stud. This he had sold for four krans (or francs). I found on inquiry that it was used for the manufacture of women's veils.

On the way we met a very ragged old man driving four donkeys laden with salt. He was so ill that he could hardly walk, and seemed quite unequal to his task, which required considerable activity. We encountered the donkeys first, grazing on and about the track, and apparently quite unattended. Passing on we found the owner quite exhausted by fatigue, and seated, a chaotic heap of rags, on a boulder of limestone.

We roused him up, but his temper had quite given way under fatigue and exhaustion, and he abused us all roundly, but we talked to him kindly, and gave him some cheese and a piece of meat, which he greedily devoured. In answer to our questions he related that, as was his custom, he had gone to a salt mine in the neighbouring mountains to bring salt to Kurind.* His nephew had accompanied him, but, at the salt mines this nephew had accepted a freight more lucrative than salt, and gone off in some other direction, taking with him the best donkeys. He had not warned the poor old man, but had accompanied him one stage on his journey, and then abandoned him in the night, leaving him with bad donkeys and double loads.

The old man had now, however, not far to go, and we left him refreshed and good-tempered.

At half-past two we passed a village called Mian

---

* The salt exists at five days' journey from Kurind. It is worth 1*d.* a pound in the summer and 2*d.* in winter.

Jangal (middle of the scrub), which was composed half of stone huts and half of black tents. A few carpets were woven here, but none worth purchasing. Soon after this the stream which we had been following disappeared into a limestone cave. Then the prospect before us opened out, and we were at the edge of the great plateau of Persia. The great tableland on which we had mounted by ascending the Jamal Bariz range was now crossed. Far below us we looked down, not yet upon the flat alluvial plains of Mesopotamia, but upon the low hills formed by the detritus from the plateau on which we stood. After sufficiently admiring the grand panorama we began the steep descent down a rugged zigzag road.

Right down below us was a vivid green valley, and we saw the small village called Pai Takht (foot of the throne), which was to be our halting-place. The descent took us an hour and a quarter, and when we got to the bottom we found the village deserted. This desertion, however, was not occasioned by overtaxation, as the people only used the stone huts in the winter, and were now in tents, pasturing their flocks and horses on the sweet fresh grass. We made ourselves comfortable in a rough and ready caravanserai.

There is nothing to note in the next day's march to Sar-i-pūl-i-Zohab (head of the bridge of Zohab). We crossed through a gap in some low hills, and at last reached the alluvial plains that stretch away to the coast. We noticed to-day the change in the clothing of the natives. The ragged bundle of woollen rags necessitated by the cold of the plateau, gives way to calico garments and cotton turbans. Judging from the dress only of the two classes of natives, one would incline to think that he had arrived at a much wealthier and more civilized country than that which he had recently crossed. This is not altogether the case. It must be remembered that the coarse home-made woollen garments, loosely woven as they are, cannot look tidy, though they may be of more value than the calico shirt, which can be renewed at little cost when worn out.

At Sar-i-pūl-i-Zohab, where is a massive stone bridge over a rapid stream, we found so many soldiers that we could not get even an old outhouse to put up in, and were glad when the telegraph clerk sent and invited us to stay with him. He was a tall, fine Turkoman, much given to sporting. At dinner, which comprised trophies of his skill, such as snipe (?) and some godwits (?), his three dogs were brought in and made to sit in a row while fed. He was delighted at my sympathy with his tastes, and related with great enthusiasm numbers of anecdotes, in which one particular dog or another had shown especial sagacity. Two might be described as medium-sized liver-and-white English pointers, and the way they sat up on their haunches, side by side, just at the edge of the table-cloth, wagging the ends of their tails, looking earnestly first at the food and then at their master, reminded me forcibly of home. The third was an especial pet, and allowed great liberties. He might be described as a small, long-bodied, wavy-haired liver-and-white spaniel, and could not only find game, but could fetch and carry, which the two others could not, and he would take readily to water. His master called this one the English dog, and the two others Persians.

On the next march I nearly got into a difficulty. I was far on ahead, and encountered the camp of the Pai Takht villagers, scattered over a rich green expanse of grass. Here was a herd of about thirty brood mares and five or six stallions, and the Padre instantly prepared for battle. He commenced by planting his fore-feet well in front of him, raising his head, and sending forth a succession of the fiercest and most awe-inspiring neighs he could muster.

The challenge was instantly accepted, and in a moment we were the centre of a prancing, kicking, squealing crowd of glossy, beautiful, but half wild horses. Some got before us and kicked up just by the Padre's nose, while others reared and struck at him with their forefeet. It was rather an awkward predicament, but I had a very heavy thong seven feet long, and by lashing out at them, shouting, and double thonging the Padre, I got clear away from them without injury.

I believe that there was no danger, and that the horses only wanted to play with us, for I think they always bite when vicious. This, however, did not occur to me till afterwards. I was once in a similar predicament at Jask. I was coming home from a very hard day's ibex shooting, mounted on a tired donkey, encumbered by two rifles and accompanied by my small brown dog Toby, who had been taking care of the cook while I was away in the hills. Suddenly we came on a herd of half wild cows, who evidently mistook Toby for a jackal. In an instant they all charged furiously down upon him, heads down and tails high in air. Poor Toby came to me for help, and got between the donkey's legs. I shouted, brandished the rifles, and kicked the poor donkey into a sort of three-legged canter. It was the most exciting donkey ride I ever had in my life. Toby scampered here, there, and everywhere, but always as close to the donkey's legs as he could get. Rush would come one old bull from the right and just graze the donkey's tail, then another would just miss his nose, and I thought the climax was reached when head over heels went the donkey and we all rolled on the ground together. To my surprise this frightened the cows, and I had time to pick Toby up in my arms, after which they took no further interest in the matter.

But to return. I got through the horses safely, and soon afterwards I overtook a tall, well-dressed Turkoman, mounted on a big-boned brown horse, and armed to the teeth with long gun, pistols, knife, and cartridge cases, all plated with silver. He rode well with a military seat, and barely the tips of his toes in the stirrup. When I found him he had halted his horse in the middle of a stream, and to avoid getting off, which would be a work of time with all his arms and paraphernalia, he was letting down a small brass cup by a string and drawing up water. I saluted him, and received a courteous reply and the immediate offer of a drink of water. He was a handsome young man of about twenty-five, and of gentle manners, and I took a liking to him at once. His name was Mahmud Bey, and he was fifty-five days out from Erzevil, on his way to Kerbela, there to wash away the stain of some crime.

He was a Russian subject, but had lost his certificate to that effect, and was in great perplexity as to how he should pass the frontier. I said I would do anything I could for him, and after a consultation with Hādi he begged to be allowed to enter as my master of horse. I gladly assented, and he was so grateful that he got off his horse with all his harness to kiss my hand. Nor did he make a sinecure of his appointment, but scrupulously attended to everything connected with my horse, and Hādi was too good a fellow to resent the interference.

We jogged along together over flat plains, passing through occasional bright patches of crocus, cuckoo flower, anemone, dog daisies, narcissus, and dwarf iris, and at 5 p.m. came to the ruined fort of Kasr Shīrīn, where, according to some tradition, a lovely princess was walled up to keep her from a too importunate lover.

Kasr Shīrīn is a well-built stone village, and here was another considerable force of troops going through "Autumn manœuvres."

I went and had tea with the general of the forces, and arranged for Mahmud Bey's passing unmolested across the frontier.

We were now 1,048 feet above the level of the sea, and this evening we entered Turkish soil. The actual frontier is about four miles north of the town of Khanakin, and is marked by two neatly built round towers manned by soldiers, well armed, well dressed, fierce looking fellows, forming a striking contrast to the Persians we had seen. Khanakin is a large, busy, thickly populated village full of European goods. The letter of introduction from the Agha of Kirmanshahan procured us quarters in a good but noisy caravanserai. I called upon the governor, a most civilized man in a fine well-built "muderia" or governor's office, and attended by soldierly Kowasses (orderlies) in smart uniforms. I had to explain a little contretemps that had occurred at the entry to his village. Just as we approached a young man emerged from a hut by the roadside and asked for our certificates. I replied that I had never heard of any certificates, and that I had not got any. He then proposed to sell me some. I, regarding the matter as an attempt at extortion, told him indignantly that I was going to see the governor, to whom I would relate what had occurred, and to whom I would pay anything he decided to be legal.

When I related this to the governor, he explained that the man in question was the assistant quarantine doctor, who wanted to give me a bill of health. I said I was sorry that I had been rude to one of his officials, and suggested that they should either be put in uniform or labelled in some way, so that unwary travellers like myself should know that they were men in authority.

He proposed to send a Kowass with me to the Quarantine office, and to this, to prevent any unpleasantness, I acceded.

Here I found some very good-natured fellows, who laughed heartily over our misunderstanding. Among them was a doctor, Szymonski Lubicz, who readily drew out the necessary certificates. After this I went over to his house, and inspected some promising young colts in which he took great pride. Walking back I noticed wild tulips, and some "lords and ladies," the inside of the sheath of which was covered with the same black velvety powder as the stamen. I also observed that we had got into the land of date-trees again.

Returning to the caravanserai I found the Agha's agent had invited some friends to meet me, and we sat discussing agriculture, politics, etc., until dinner time.

The governor sent over an offer of an escort of twelve mounted soldiers, but these I refused with many thanks, saying that we had come safely through many wild countries, and trusted that no such precaution could be necessary in a country so well governed as his appeared to be.

His messenger returned in the evening, saying that there were Iliaut families in the road who were very dangerous. I considered that it was merely an attempt to obtain bakshish, and replied that I knew the Iliaut well, and spoke their language, and so the matter rested.

I had strong fever all night, and in the morning could hardly touch the hospitable doctor's breakfast, but I was anxious with a feverish anxiety to get on to Baghdad, where was an European surgeon, and insisted on pushing on while I could ride. I remember on leaving Khanakin we forded a rapid, shallow stream, and some hundred yards beyond crossed a lofty stone bridge under which it had formerly run.

As the sun got high I felt very ill, and Ghulamshah and Mahmud Bey rode close by me, one on either side. It was fortunate that I took this precaution, for I suddenly felt dizzy and helpless, and should have fallen heavily had they not cleverly caught me and taken me off my horse. I recollect little that followed. Ghulamshah squeezed an orange into my mouth, and twice my head was bathed with water. Mahmud Bey rode about twenty-eight miles for those two bowls of water. I next awoke to find myself lying on some grass. It was evening, and there were a little boy and girl tugging at some shrubs to make firewood. I thought I was all alone, but presently some one said: "He's dead." Then Ghulamshah's voice said: "Sahib! Sahib!" and I turned round and answered him. Then they carried me into an Iliaut tent. Some time afterwards they gave me some hot tea, and I roused up. We were in a large black tent and ten or a dozen swarthy Iliaut were sitting round the fire. Hādi was there, and Ghulamshah was boiling water for tea. I soon pulled myself together, and saluted the assembled company. The sheikh ordered a large bowl of milk and rice. He then called for a box, and this he very carefully unpacked. It contained two custard glasses, and one glass saucer. These he produced with immense gratification and pride for me to drink my tea in. Ghulamshah had made sweet weak tea for all parties, and overcome the sheikh's scruples against adding to our meal the meat we had brought for the day's journey. Mahmud Bey had galloped off to Kazrabad, the next station, for soldiers. I ate a little rice and milk, and then they wrapped me up and I fell asleep. I was awakened some time after by the noise of driving tent-pegs. This, however, was a familiar sound, and I slept again.

About midnight I was awakened by voices, and found Mahmud Bey had arrived with an escort of cavalry. On trying to rise I found that a wind had arisen in the night, and that the tent-pegs had been driven through my blanket, and that I was a prisoner. I was soon released, and after several attempts, was hoisted on to Ghulamshah's horse, which was quieter than mine, and we marched out into the night. We thanked our host as well as we could, and I gave him some present, but I do not remember what. We got to Kazrabad about sunrise, and I was put to bed on the roof of a caravanserai. Here I dozed away the whole day. I remember nothing about Kazrabad, but two incidents that occurred there are still very fresh in my memory. It is perhaps odd that they are more or less ludicrous.

On the same roof as that on which I was lying two storks were building a nest, and close by me were a number of sticks suitable for the purpose. The old stork was very tame, but still rather doubtful about coming close enough to get the sticks. After much caution he came and took an outside one; then another; then he seemed to me to reflect that as each journey was rather hazardous, he would do well to take two or three at a time. So he came, took up one, and gave it a jerk into the back part of his bill, and then clawed about for another. Of course his bill was wedged wide open, but he did not understand that, and he tried first one stick and then another, naturally without success. At last I involuntarily burst out laughing, and said out loud, "You stupid ass"! He gave one tremendous leap on to the low wall round the roof, looked sharply at me over his shoulder for a second, and then sidled along the wall to a safe distance and eyed me pensively. Soon he appeared to give the matter up, and looking round he found his wife catching frogs in a stagnant pool down below, instead of gathering sticks. So he flew off to the pond too, and was soon as busy fishing as if he had never wanted any sticks in his life.

Another thing that amused me while lying there on the roof was this. Two or three of the soldiers were talking down in the courtyard, and one of them began to sing. I could not see them, but I heard what follows. In the middle of the song one of the mules began to bray.

Singer angrily: "Are you going to take the very words out of my mouth?" All waited gravely until the mule had finished, when the singer resumed his song as if it had never been interrupted.

We were now eighty miles from Baghdad, and Mahmud Bey fearing I was getting worse, volunteered to ride straight there and tell the English surgeon how ill I was. He started, but, poor fellow, killed his beloved horse, and had to walk fourteen miles with all its heavy harness, saddle-bags, etc., and a heavy heart of his own into the bargain. At the end of that distance, however he hired a horse and arrived safely.

I picked up rapidly (this was my third sunstroke), and next day we marched slowly on to Shahr Reban. I have many notes here, but they are undecipherable excepting the figures of the meteorological readings, which I evidently spared no pains to make clear.

From Shahr Reban to Yakubabad was rich fertile ground. I remember a "sounder," of fourteen wild pig, and numbers of francolin, and that we were caught in a violent shower of rain, accompanied by heavy thunder and lightning. The mud was excessively heavy.

Here we looked out clean clothes in which to appear before our English friends. The less said on this head the better. The mackintoshes were all right, and covered a multitude of sins. From Yakubabad to

Baghdad is a long ride over a barren plain—barren because inundated entirely every year. But our spirits rose as we neared the place, and saw the tall minarets growing nearer, the fringe of the palm trees that marked the line of the Euphrates growing gradually clearer and clearer, and at last we fairly galloped up to the gate.

We rode through apparently endless streets, asking our way to the British Residency, where we eventually arrived, but only to find it deserted of Europeans. However, an old Hindoo servant showed me a room in which I might sleep, and made me an omelette, and I did what I could to eat it.

Next morning I sought the hospitality of Messrs. Gray Paul's agents, and at once found myself at home.

I think the general impression Baghdad gave me was that it was a place of great commercial activity and intelligent progress.

Midhat Pasha's work has not been thrown away. At Kirman you go to see a stifling hole in which Cashmere shawls are made, and a finely built richly endowed school of learning of doubtful utility. At Yezd you go and see fine airy workshops for weaving and dyeing silk. At Ispahan you go to see a tawdry old palace, or climb up pillars whose only apparent feature is that they are not so safe as it might be. At Kirmanshahan you go to see an army camped in a valley liable to perpetual inundation, and some rock sculptures, which are very old. At Baghdad you go to see a magnificent school of trades and arts. Here boys are taught carefully and well every trade that I can think of. They are made blacksmiths, coppersmiths, tinsmiths, carpenters, weavers, dyers, printers, bookbinders, and I believe every trade is represented.

This institution was so admirably established that it was self-supporting. At Baghdad also, is a fine large well-built and well-arranged custom house, where the goods are properly housed and can be got out without unnecessary delay.*

I spent eleven days in Baghdad very pleasantly indeed, thanks to my friends Messrs. Coupbara and Halliday. Still there were one or two difficulties. Poor Ghulamshah got cruelly beaten and robbed merely because he was an inoffensive youth, and was dressed in a strange costume, and the worst was that I could not get any redress, until I telegraphed to the Foreign Office, to whom I was grateful for a prompt reply.

From our start from Jask up to Baghdad not a man of mine had ever had a finger laid on him. And here, if there had not been a Residency, I would have bought the men who beat my boy the best bastinadoing I could get them, whatever it might cost me.

Mahmud Bey was pursued by ill luck, and now fell ill of small-pox. He had but a slight attack, however, and soon got over the worst. Rumours of plague were prevalent, and every day we were threatened with quarantine. We had, however, delightful rides out of the town among the country houses and orange gardens, the scent of which filled the air. The sanitary arrangements in this quarter were not, however, so good as in the crowded city, and when one drew in a long breath of fragrance of orange the last few inches of it were not unfrequently dead camel. This was disagreeable.

---

* Tobacco from Ispahan, pays here 75 per cent. customs duty.

We went to see the ex-king of Oudh (Oude), a rather well known character, who draws a large annuity from the British Government on condition he lives out of India, and who consequently has attained an immense age. In the parallels I have drawn in this chapter, he should be introduced into the sights of Baghdad as a set-off to the shaking minarets of Ispahan.

One day we rode out along the great dyke which is built all round Baghdad, to keep the water of the Euphrates from drowning the city during the inundation. I was not prepared for what was to come, and was astonished on mounting the bank to find the broad dusty plain over which we had ridden was one sea of muddy water as far as the eye could reach. Baghdad was an island. Along the embankment were soldiers' tents, and hundreds of men were hastily repairing breaches and strengthening places threatened.

I made inquiries as to whether any engineering works existed for controlling and using this grand fertilising stream, but could hear of none.

On the evening of the 28th the doctor came in after dinner and warned me that I had better depart as soon as possible if I wished to avoid being placed in quarantine for fifteen days. A boat was starting at midnight, and after consideration I decided to leave by that, more especially as the captain of it was a friend of mine. Hādi was already on his way back to Ispahan, taking the Padishah at his own price as part of his wages. Ali Akber had been paid up, and was now looking for a new freight. Mahmud Bey was nearly recovered, and ready to resume his pilgrimage to Kerbela, and I won his eternal gratitude by giving

THE TREE OF THE FRUIT OF GOOD AND EVIL.

him the Padre and a letter to show to any one he might meet who knew English.

We packed up in very short time, and by midnight were trudging down the deserted bazaars to the steamer. I said good-bye to my two kind hosts, and at daybreak we were rushing down the tide to Basreh (often spelt Bussorah). Sometimes during these inundations lions get stranded on islands and are shot from the steamer, but we saw none on this trip.

We passed Gurna, the reputed site of the garden of Eden, and two Effendis, with whom I had got into conversation pointed out a very lofty tree, enclosed in a fence, and gravely assured me it was the tree of the fruit of good and evil. They vowed that it was the only one of its species known, and I took a careful sketch of it.

Once arrived at Basreh I was among old friends, who counted in their number poor Captain Carter and Cadenhead, both of whom were afterwards killed in Central Africa.

Having now once made up my mind to go home, I was all anxiety to get there as quickly as possible. Fortunately the ill-fated Mesopotamia * was just starting, and we took our passages. After an uneventful voyage we landed at Marseilles, where I got a huge bundle of letters from home. Ghulamshah, who now for the first time saw railways, gas lamps, etc., was presented with a suit of European clothes, and we rushed off by express through Paris, Calais, Dover, and about 5 o'clock on the morning of the 12th of May we arrived at Charing Cross in one of the

* Afterwards wrecked off Lisbon.

densest fogs I had seen for years. As the porter slammed to the door of the hansom, he touched his cap, and said: "Going to be a fine day, sir," and we drove off home.

APPENDIX A.

OBSERVATIONS ON SOME DIALECTS OF WESTERN BALUCHISTAN AND OTHERS AKIN TO THEM.

In October, 1874, Mr. Edwin Pierce presented to the Royal Asiatic Society in Bombay, a paper in which for the first time the Mekran Balūchi dialect was reduced to writing, and which contained an admirable statement of the general laws governing it, and a useful vocabulary.

In this vocabulary he gave the derivations of nearly all the words, tracing them to Persian, a few to Sindhi, and some to Arabic. There were, however, a considerable number "undesignated." During two explorations in Western Balūchistan I collected several vocabularies, but recently having had an opportunity of getting north into Kurdistan, I was gratified to find nearly all the undesignated words in common use there. I soon afterwards had an opportunity of collecting Aughāni (Affghanee) vocabularies, and also some in the islands of the Persian Gulf.

The study of dialects is, I think, a much more interesting study than that of written language. Where there is a literature, and the grammarians of a country agree to refer to one standard, it is useful to keep up a standard, though that should be constantly altered to keep pace with the constantly changing language. I would suggest that the dialects in the following pages (and possibly all dialects) have been modified by two causes. The physical nature of the country and the occupations of the inhabitants decide what words are wanted, and the pliability and fineness of the muscles of the tongue and lips, and the shape of the former, decide the pronunciation.

The Mekran Balūchis have a separate name for a camel at each year of its age. At each village there are almost as many kinds of dates as there are trees, each with a separate name. Dates at each period of their ripeness are called by a different name; when packed up for transport they receive a different name. This is the same among such Bedawin as depend much upon their camels and dates, such as those in the Syrian desert. We have only the words "camel" and "date" to represent nearly one hundred words in Balūchi. The reverse is of course easy to find, as the number of words for "house" in English as compared with the Balūchis' one word.

In the matter of pronunciation I think proof is easy. Many Balūchis cannot pronounce the letter *f*. It is to them an unwonted contraction of the upper lip, the muscles of which are not accustomed to the particular direction of movement required. But he can learn, just as a man's fingers can be taught to write. It took me nearly six months to acquire full power over the Arabic guttural ḥ, and nearly the same time over the Devanagari four dotted "ra." But I found I acquired them gradually, showing that the muscles by degrees attained the necessary elasticity. The Persians never get over the ḍh sound, and the Egyptians the Arabic ḳāf, because they do not try; but they could be taught. I will merely add that each variety of man has his facilities and difficulties among the consonants. The Aughān may be said to find gutturals come natural to him, and labials almost impossible. To the Bakhtiari gutturals are impossible, labials difficult, and linguals and dentals seem to be his sole stock.

I will but offer one more suggestion before proceeding to the actual dialects under review, and this perhaps I should have mentioned before. It is that the study of languages and that of dialects should be held somewhat distinct. The language should be studied. It is the standard, or, as it were, the solidification of the various changes that language has undergone during past centuries. But the dialects are the coming race; they mean so much, and speak so much, especially if the people have no literature, and cannot tie themselves down to forms, whose application has very likely gone out of use. You are not troubled with synonyms. Useless words drop out of circulation, and only those remain which are necessary.

The copiousness of a vocabulary, the capacity of its verbs for expressing involved or abstract ideas, whether it is adopting new words or dropping old words, all afford an insight into whether a country is progressing or not, *i.e.* whether its wants and consequent supply are increasing or decreasing.

With reference to the vocabulary, I would mention that the Persian is merely inserted to give, as it were, the standard; and that the expressions in that language are not always idiomatic, though always grammatical. The idiom has been departed from in order to use the word used in the dialects, but it is always given in a note. The basis of the vocabulary is taken almost without alteration from Mr. Pierce's book.* I cannot sufficiently regret the destruction of much of my Bashakard manuscript. That dialect is a more extraordinary corruption than any of the others, and has the peculiarity of retaining some gutturals. Pers. *Kh*urma, for instance, they pronounce *Kh*um or Rum. One more example. The Persian root "bīn," to see. The Balūchis prefer *g* to *b*, and make it "gīn." But *n* is too light a letter to rest a long *ī* on without an effort. So they compromise by assisting the *n* with a *d*, thus making it easier to say, but leaving it the same preponderance of sound; they make it "gind." But the Bashakardi does not shrink from the "gīn." I remember Rais Ali's observation when trying to see through my microscope, "Man hīch nāgīnan"—"I can see nothing."

1.

Eng. Come here. — Bashakardi, Rrā ī mail.

Bal. Ingwa biā.

Kur. Rrā li men.
Bowa li men.

Pers. Injā biā.

Affgh. Rāsha.

2.

E. Come near.

B. Nazik biā.

K. Bowa nazik.

P. Nazdik bia.

A. Nazdi Rāsha.

3.

E. Come inside.

B. Thār bia. — Bash., Budu ba-dil: go to the heart of; also used thus: Are you going to Anguhran?—Ba-dil-i-anguhran arāi?"

K. Bowa na.

P. Dakhil bia.

A. Danana Rāsha.

---

* Mr. Pierce has since nearly completed a perfect grammar and dictionary. The first book, however, notwithstanding the extraordinary difficulties of putting into writing the language of a wild illiterate people, was so carefully done that it will always be valuable.

4.

E.	Don't make a noise.	The English "bang," onomatopœic, *b* becomes *gw*, and *d*.
B.	Gwanka majan.	
K.	Dang makan.	
P.	Bang mazan;	*id.* Jinjal makun. Bang zadan is a book expression.
A.	Chŭpkau;	*i.e.* Be silent; *conf.* Urdu chuprao.

5.

E.	Be careful.	
B.	Habardar bu.	خ becomes ه
K.	Hushyar bah;	*i.e.* Be active.
P.	Khabar dar.	
A.	Khabardar waussah.	

6.

E.	Don't forget.	
B.	Dila mabar.	Do not take from your heart.
	Behayal mabu.	Do not be without thought.
K.	Faramush makan.	
P.	Farāmūsh makun.	
A.	May ra ghwāra.	

7.

E.	Remember what I say;	or, whatever I say, remember.
B.	Mani habara haiyal bedar.	
	Har che man agweshin hayal bedar.	
K.	Owa ki man yeusham to yād bigīr.	Note *gw* of Bal. agweshin becomes *y*.
P.	Har chi man mīgūyam tū yād bakun.	
A.	Har chi zowāim yad-i-kowa.	*b* into *z*, and *g* omitted.

8.

E.	Do you remember?	West. Bal., Tura yad abī?—Is there to you remembrance?
B.	Turā haiyal in?	
K.	Hāla fikarat?	
P.	Yād mīkuni?	
A.	Yad-i-Kawa?	

9.

E.	I do not remember.	
B.	Man behaiyal un.	
K.	Balad nim.	Balad in Bal. is a guide. Balad nim *or* nīstam—I am not a guide, don't know.

P. Yad namikunam ; — *id.* yad nadāram.
A. Na yad a kunan. — As in Bal., the *m* of kunam becomes *n*.

10.
E. Come back.
B. Pada bia.
K. Bo dua.
P. Pas bia.
A. Rustar rāsha.
Pusta rāsha.

11.
E. Go home.
B. Loga boro. — Bashakardi, Rra lahar. "Jade" is homestead ; "lahar," a single hut. "Rra" means "come" or "go," according to context.
K. Bishua rummāl.
Bishū rummāl.
P. Biro khāna.
A. Warza kurta.

12.
E. Light the lamp.
B. Chiraga rok pekan.
K. Chiragh bar roshan bakan.
P. Chirāghra rūshan bakun.
A. Chiragh wala kowa. — Ar. ولع walʿ, *he lit.*

13.
E. Put out the lamp.
B. Chiraga pukush.
K. Piffkan li chiragh.
P. Chiraghra bukush.
A. Chiragh murakka.

14.
E. Turn to the right.
B. Rasta bitar.
K. Dast i rast bichú.
P. Dast i rast biro.
A. Khīl las warza. — *d* becomes *l*, and *t* of "dast" omitted.

15.
E. Give my compliments.
B. Mani salāma birasān.
K. Salāmi man birássan.
P. Salām i man birasān.
A. Az man salām wāĭă. — Pers. root "guy," *g* becomes *w*, and there is no prefix for imperative.

16.
E. Be silent.
B. Towar makan.
K.
P. Shūr makun.
A. Jung mukowa.

17.
E. As I say so, do.
B. Hanch ki man agweshin hancho pekan. — West. Bal., "chōsh pikan."
K. Owa ki man yeusham chīno bakan; — lit. That which I say.
P. Hamchunān ki mīgūyam chunan bukun. — Pers. root "guy" becomes "gwe," "yeu," and "zow."
A. Harchi zowaim to wukowa.

18.
E. Mind your own business.
B. Wati kara pekan. — The Pers. for "own" is *kh*ŭd, spelt خود khwud. Persians in pronouncing omit the *w*. Bal. omit the *kh* and make *d*, *t*. Kurd. retain both, open the *u* to *a* (like "fat"), and put *t* instead of *d*. They reject also the prenominal affixes "my own," "your own." Pers. khudum, khudut.
K. Kar i *kh*wat bakan.
P. Kar i *kh*udut bakun.
A. Khpŭl kar wukowa. — This seems improbable. I merely suggest *p* and *f* and *b* and *v* and *w* are always interchangeable, and, as in No. 14, *d* often becomes *l*, which makes khwud.

19.

E.	Bring drinking water.	
B.	Waragi apa biar.	Persian root "to eat," khwurdan, خوردن; same observations apply here as in No. 18, *re* omitting *kh*. Here is Bal. infin. term. on Pers. root.
K.	Yitki āba bār, bukhwum.	Bring a little water that I may drink it. Bukhwum = bukhurum, *r* omitted.
P.	Ab i-khw̄urdan biār.	
A.	Khougi oubou roura.	*Kh* retained and *r* omitted.

20.

E.	Bring water for washing hands.	
B.	Dast shodaga āpa biar.	"r" of Pers. root shur, "wash" becomes *d*.
K.	Yitki aba dam sho bashūram;	lit. That I may wash.
P.	Ab biar ki dast bishuiyam.	
A.	Oubou roura che las yinzim.	

21.

E.	Go slowly.	
B.	Wash washa biro.	Query from Pers. khwush, "pleasantly, gently."
K.	Yowashta bichu.	In the verb "to go" Bal. take some tenses from Pers. root "ro" and the rest from Kurdi "chi."
P.	Āhista, āhista biro.	
A.	Ro ro zā.	

22.

E.	Don't let him go.	
B.	Aira mäil roaga.	Root yele with Per. neg. prefix; lit. Don't allow him to go.
K.	Mäil bichut;	lit. Do not allow that he go.
P.	Maguzār ki birawad.	
A.	May prida chi zī.	

23.

E.	When are you starting?	
B.	To kadīn sark agīri?	When do you take the road?
K.	Kay towa bichit?	
P.	Kay rāh migīrī?	When do you take the road?
A.	Kala bat to zī?	"bat," corruption of wakt وقت Ar.; in Bal. wakt becomes wahdi and waht.

24.

E. We go to-morrow early.

B. Amā soba mahala 'roan.

K. Dami su chīmen. — Here the bḥ of subḥ disappears. Note the verb chimen and Affgh. azum.

P. Mā sūbḥ mīrawīm ; — pronounced suhb. Ar. صبح by metathesis. Many Arabic words in which a final guttural follows a jezmated consonant are unpronounceable except by metathesis. *conf.* naf' نفع pronounced na'f, "profit." daf', دفع pron. da'f, "repelling."

A. Subah sohr azum.

25.

E. Who are you?

B. To kai e.

K. To kai īt.

P. To kīsti.

A. To tsōkī.

26.

E. Where have you come from?

B. Ash kūjā ātkăgĕ? — West. Bal., Hāndăgi. See prelim. obs.

K. La ku hātĭtā?

P. Az kuja āmadī?

Bas. Katam mail wokho? — Pers. kudam, "which"; Ar. mail, "inclination."

A. Kum zana rāghali?

27.

E. Where have they gone?

B. Ā kuja āngu shutagan?

K. Rra kou towa bichīt?

P. Anha kuja rafta and?

A. Ā *kh*ulk chirta lāra?

28.

E. What do you want?

B. To che lōtĭ?

K. Che towait? — Note the *w* of Pers. root خواه "wish" not pronounced in Pers. Here *kh* is lost.

P. Chi mi*kh*w̄āhi? — towait—twait—khwait—khwahud.

A.

29.

E. Where do you live?

B. To kuja ninde?

K. La ku nīshīt?

P. Kuja nishasta ī? or, kuja minishini

A. To chīrta nasti?

(Kuja nishasta ī, kuja minishini, To chīrta nasti: All from Pers. root nishīn, "sit.")

30.

E. Where are you going?

B. Kujanga aröi (or arāī)?

K. Rra kou chīt?

P. Kuja mīrawī?

A. To chīrta zī?

31.

E. When will he return?

B. Ā Kadīn pada 'kait?

K. Kay galow akhwait?

P. Kay pas miāiud?

A. Agha ba kala rāshi? — The termination *gha* appears to be affixed to *ā* "this;" and *da*, "that," whenever those pronouns are subjects, or otherwise require emphasis.

32.

E. He will never return.

B. Ā izhbar pada na ait.

K. Hargiz galow nakhwait.

P. Izbar pas namīāud

A. Agha na rāshi.

33.

E. What is the use of that?

B. Ā che kar akait? — lit. That, what work does it come.

K. Yeh wa che kar atait?

P. Ān ba che kar miāiud?

A. Da shay du che kar day?

34.

E. Why do you do thus?

B. To parcha chosh akáni? — Parcha, "why" = Pers. barai che—"for the sake of what," "why."

K. Rra chino akait?

P. Chura hamchi mikuni?

A. To tsilora hay dassi?

35.

E. What is the matter?

B. Che buta? — lit., What was it? West. Bal., Che bīd, by common interchange of *ū* and *ī* and *ŭ* and *ĭ*, as, nusf, "half:" nisf.

K. Cha pīāt?

P. Che būd?

A. Tziddi; or, Tzo wushu?

36.

E. What do you call this?

B. To eshira chi 'gwashi?

K.

P. To īn chīz chi mēguyi?

A. Deday chīz to tso wāī?

37.

E. What is the name of this?

B. Eshi nām che?

K. Nāmi chi ast?

P. Nam-i-īn chīst?

A. Deday nŭm tsiddi?

38.

E. Do you {understand? / know?} No I don't.

B. To sarpad abi? Na man sarpad n'abain; — lit. Are you informed?

K. Zānīt? Na, nayazanum. — *Conf.* Bal., Azāni? Na nayazānun—Do you know? No, I don't know; and Pers., Mi dāni? Na namidānum.

P. Mifahmi? Na namifahmum.

A. Tātō ma'lum di? Na, nay payjanum. — *Conf.* Urdu, Nai pachanta.

39.

E.	Make him understand.	
B.	Aira sarpad kan.	West. Bal., Aira hali bukun.
K.	Hali bukun.	*Conf.* West. Bal., Hali bī—Do you understand?
P.	Hālush bukun	Vulgar.
A.	Da samjou wukowa.	*Conf.* Urdu Samjāna—to cause to understand.

40.

E.	Listen to me.	
B.	Mani habara gosh dar.	West. Bal., Mana gosha bikash—Pull to me your ear.
K.	Gosh biā ;	lit. Bring your ear.
P.	(Vulg.) Gōsham bidih.	
A.	Az ma khabara woura	

41.
E. What you say is true.
B. Hancho ki to agwashi rast an.
K. Owa ki to ayūshi rās an.
P. Hamchi (or ān) ki to migūyī rāst ast.
A. Da to che wāī tol rishtiā dī tol, Ar. طول, "length."

42.
E. Say it again.
B. Noka bagwash.
K. Hambūsh bezan.
P. Nō bugū.
A. Biā owāia.

43.
E. I will give you ten rupees a month.
B. Man tura maha dā kaldāra deīn.
K.
P. Man tura dah rupīa mīdahim mahi (or, ba mah).
A. Zŭ tāta lass rupīa dar miashti dar kōwuma.

44

E.	Very good, sir, I agree.	
B.	Sak shar Wāja kabul in ;	Sak for saḳt, "hard, vehemently."
K.	Khāsa kaboul deyrim.	
P.	Khūb khwāja kabul dāram.	
A.	Khădtha kabul dī.	

APPENDIX B.

BOTANY.

The following is a list of the plants collected *en route*. I owe my best thanks to Professor Oliver and Mr. Spencer Moore, of the Royal Gardens, Kew, for the great trouble they took in identifying my specimens collected in the desert island of Henjam.

Arnebia sp. ?
Anagallis ; English Pimpernel.
Astralagus corrugatus Bert.
Antirrhinum orontium, L.
Capparis spinosa, var. Leucophylla.
Æluropus lævis, Trin. ; Balūchi, Bān.
Helianthemum Lippii, Pers. ; Balūchi, Rukh.
Erucaria Aleppica G.
Picridium tingitanum, Desf.
Cuscuta globulosa ; English, Dodder ; Balūchi, Rōgānū.
Urospermum picroides, Desf.
Geranium, sp. not determinable.
Cometes Surattensis, B. M.
Gymnocarpus sp. ?
Farsetia Heliophila ? Bunge ; Balūchi, Darispeet.
Senecio gallicus ; English, Groundsell ; Balūchi, Sūrūwāhing.
Ononis, English Restharrow.
Caroxylon fœtidum, Moq'.
Herniaria Hirsuta, Lam.
Rumex vesicarius ; English, Sourgrass ; Balūchi, Turushuk.
Spergula pentandra ; English, Cornflower.
Abutilon denticulatum, Pl. ; English, Mallow.
Lericostoma Katschyi, Bth.
Iphiona scabra, D. C. ; compare Asphodelus.
Frankenia pulverulenta.
Senecio dubius, Led.
Boerhaavia plumbaginea, Car.
Crotalaria furfuracea, Bois. ; Balūchi, Yellow darispeet.

Kœlaria Phleoides; Balūchi, Kah-i-gandum-gia.
Andropagon foveolatus, Del.
Parietaria alsinœfolia; English Pellitory of the wall.
Erucaria linearifolia.
Mesembryanthemum nodiflerum; used in making powder.
Jygophyllum album, L.
Cleome trinervia; Balūchi, Rogardish, *i.e.*, revolving with the sun.
Reseda canescens, L.
Taverniera spartea, D.C.; Balūchi, Lorti, the famous camel-grass; Persian, Khurus.
Oligomeris glaucescens, Camb.
Lotus trigonelloides, Webb.
Acacia Nubica, Bth.
Abrua Javanica, L.; Balūchi, Gurmanuk.
Heliotropium rotundifolium; Sieb. vel. sp. aff.
Lavandula, a dwarf English lavender.
Microrhynchus nudicaulis, Less.
Anclusa Milleri, W. var.?
Ephedra campylopoda, C. A. Meq.
Stipa tortilis.
Polycarpæa spicata, Arn.
Triticum sp.?
Lotononis sp.?
Indigofera Arabica?
Pennisetum cenchroides, Rich.; Balūchi, Sivr.
Solanum sanctum, L.
Scrofularia marginata, Boiss? Balūchi, Mughīr; Arabic, Ghaubān.
Stipa pennata, a lovely grass like miniature ostrich feathers.
Blepharis edulis, Pers.
Crozophora tinctoria.
Salicornia sp.?; Balūchi, Trāt, the famous camel appetizer; Arabic, hamth (حمض), or sourness.
Heliotropium undulatum, Vahl.
Vincetoxicum sp.? Balūchi, Bīshdār.
Periploca aphylla.
Haplophyllum furfuraceum, Bge.
Reaumuria Floyeri. A new species; a small upright plant with a flower something like a convolvulus, and varying in colour from white to pink and purple. It has the power of condensing on its leaves large crystals of salt, which, on being removed, are rapidly reproduced.

Extracted from THE JOURNAL OF BOTANY *for October*, 1877.

"REAUMURIA FLOYERI, SP. NOV.

"Erecta, ramis ad angulum prope rectum divergentibus, folii planis sparsis spathulato-oblongis quasi subpetiolatis obtusissimis, anillaribus nullis, ramorum floralium reliquis subconformibus, bracteis erectis foliis subsimilibus (basi paullo latioribus) calyci subæquilongis margine minute undulatis, calycis pone ad basin partiti laciniis erectis oblongo-linearibus, petalis fere oblongis calycem æquantibus lobo altero obsoleto, filamentis basi integris, placentis circiter 7-ovulatis.

"*Habitat.*—Ad Henjam, prope Sinum Persicum.

"COLL. E. A. FLOYER."

"Planta quippiam misera. Folia 1·0–1·4 cm. long., sub apice 0·25 cm. lat. Petala foliis subæquilonga ob paucitatem materiei infaustam ovula exactius numerare non potui.

"Ex affinitate R. Stocksii Bons., et R. hypericoides, L. Ab illa abhorret inter alia equidem foliis planis sparsis majoribus basi manifeste angustatis, ab hac vero forma, foliorum diversa, calycis laciniis angustioribus et longioribus, petalis fere oblongis."

Polygala erioptera, D.C.
Arnebia hispidissima, D.C.
Euphorbia chamæ?
Ochrademus baccutus, D.C.
Pimpinella sp.
Filago Germanica.
Plantago villosa. var?
Spinacea; Balūchi, Gastak.
Malva.
Zizyphus vulgaris: Balūchi and Persian, Kunar; Arabic, Nabk. I have here taken the liberty to differ from Professor Oliver, who named this Capparis Spinosa. The plants are much alike, and possibly my specimens were not large enough for accurate identification.
Aizoon canariense.
Trifolium; English Clover.
Trianthema pentandra.
Trigonella.
Crotolaria Ægyptiaca.
Convolvolus glomeratus.
Ipomœa sescapræ.

Cressa cretica.
Eragrostis megaslachya.

The following were collected in Bashakard.

Astragalus.
Acacia.
Iphiona.
Forskahlia.
Chenopodiacea?
Potamogeton natans. Found at Manujan.
Zizyphus lotus.
Lycium; Balūchi, Dihīr.
Carthamus.
Ephedra; Balūchi, Majgūk.

The following from Persia and Kurdistan.

Caroxylon salicornicum. Persian Odalik poisoned my camels at Raiūn.
Muscari racemosum. Used for dyeing eggs.
Erodium, near E. cicutanium.
Iris reticulata.
Colchicum bulbocodioides.
Ceratocephalus falcatus.
Ranunculus calthæfolius.

I am indebted to the kindness of Dr. Dickie, of the British Museum, for identifying the following seaweeds collected at Henjam.

Gelidum corneum, Huds.
Acanthophora delilei, Lamour.
Champia Kotschyama, E. and D.
Laurencia obtusa. Huds.
Sargassum latifolium, Turner.
Dasya lallemandi, Mont.
Ulva reticulata, Forsh.
Chætomorpha Indica.
Cladophora albida, Huds.
Gracilaria corticata, Jaq.
Hypnea valentiæ, Turner.
Ulva latissima, L.
Cystoseira myrica, Grev.
Sargassum Acinaria, L.
Sargassum Boreanum, Jaq.?

APPENDIX C.

GEOGRAPHY.

The instruments used for the following observations, were artificial horizon and a large sextant; a large ship's chronometer by Frodsham and Kean, and a chronometer watch. For heights I had a large boiling-point thermometer and a five-inch aneroid barometer, made by Stanley, which gave very good results when tested at Kew Observatory on my return.

The astronomical observations were submitted for examination and discussion to William Ellis, F.R.A.S., of the Royal Observatory, Greenwich, who has furnished me with the following report thereon.

The astronomical observations made by Mr. Floyer consist of (1) meridian altitudes of the sun, and altitudes of Polaris out of the meridian, for determination of latitude; and (2) of observations of altitudes of the sun, before noon and after noon, for determination of local times, and differences of longitude.

As regards the results for latitude it will be seen that at some stations the latitude has been found, both by observations of the sun (south of Zenith) and of Polaris (north of Zenith), and the good agreement of the two results in all these cases shows that the observations are trustworthy.

No observations for absolute longitude were made, and in the absence of any good determination of chronometer rate, the observations for differences of longitude have been treated as follows:—

The whole journey between Jask and Baghdad was divided into three portions:—I. Jask to Kirman; II. Kirman to Ispahan; and III. Ispahan and Baghdad; and longitudes of Jask, Kirman, Ispahan and Baghdad assumed as follows:

	°	′	″	h.	m.	s.	
Jask . . .	57.	46.	2	3.	51.	4	East from Greenwich.
Kirman . .	56.	59.	0	3.	47.	56	
Ispahan . .	51.	40.	9	3.	26.	41	
Baghdad . .	44.	25.	0	2.	57.	40	

Then, for the stations included between Jask and Kirman, applying the difference of longitude between Jask and Kirman (3 m. 8 s.) to the chronometer error on local time as determined at Jask, the corresponding chronometer error on local time at Kirman is obtained. The difference between this result and that given by actual observation at Kirman was assumed to be due to chronometer rate; and this difference being divided by the number of days intervening between the observations at Jask and Kirman, the daily rate to be used in deducing the longitudes of all the stations included between Jask and Kirman was found. The longitudes of all stations in the first portion of the journey thus depend on the assumed longitudes of Jask and Kirman.

The longitudes of the stations in the second and third portions of the journey similarly depend on the longitudes of Kirman and Ispahan, and on those of Ispahan and Baghdad, respectively, the chronometer rate for these portions of the journey having been determined precisely in the same way as the first portion.

The method of reduction adopted assumes that the chronometer rate is uniform throughout each portion of the journey. The rates (gaining) actually found in the several portions were 1·37s., 5·77s., and 1·80s., respectively. If the assumed absolute longitudes of the terminal stations, above given, are to be depended upon, it would appear that the chronometer rate, in the second portion of the journey, was much larger than in the first and third portions. It may be mentioned that at Yezd, in the second portion of the journey, the chronometer error, through an accident, became altered, but observations obtained at Yezd, both before and after the change, gave the means of determining its amount.

For reduction of the time observations at places whose latitudes are not found in the annexed table, latitudes were adopted as follows:

	°	′	″	
Jask	25	38	0	North.
Aghd. ch. Kh.	32	28	0	„
Pishark or Fishark . . .	32	50	30	„
Ispahan	32	37	0	„
Kokah	33	30	0	„
Sahna	34	28	30	„
Baghdad	33	19	0	„

The whole of the results deduced from the observations are contained in the following table:—

Table of Concluded Latitudes and Longitudes.

Name of Station.	Latitudes as deduced from altitudes of — Sun.	Latitudes as deduced from altitudes of — Polaris.	Concluded Latitude North.	Concluded Longitude East from Greenwich.	Positions on which the Longitude depends.
	° ′ ″	° ′ ″	° ′ ″	° ′ ″	
Geigen Village	25 48 2		25 48 2	57 36 47	Jask and Kirman.
Geigen Valley	25 49 6		25 49 6	57 33 2	
Near Marrik	25 53 50		25 53 50	57 35 32	
Camp Rais Ali	26 26 10		26 26 10	57 38 2	
Sharifi River Head	26 26 20		26 26 20	57 36 32	
Bun Keram	26 34 34		26 34 34	57 30 2	
Dar Pahan	26 40 28		26 40 28	57 31 47	
Telling	26 54 33		26 54 33	57 9 47	
Manujan	27 23 43		27 23 43	57 24 2	
Bargah		27 38 21	27 38 21	57 35 2	
Kahnu	27 56 49		27 56 49	57 38 2	
Dosari		28 26 47	28 26 47	57 51 47	
Dasht-i-Kuch		28 40 50	28 40 50	57 47 47	
Maskun	28 57 0		28 57 0	57 47 17	
3¾ miles north of Diarbekri Caravan	29 5 15		29 5 15	57 52 2	
Bam Plain		29 12 16	29 12 16		
Sablistan or Sarvistan	29 16 36		29 16 36	57 49 47	
Tahrut River		29 25 44	29 25 44	57 39 47	
Fort Raiūn	29 35 56		29 35 56	57 21 17	
Kirman	30 17 39	30 18 7	30 17 53		
Ruban		30 19 42	30 19 42	56 11 0	Kirman and Ispahan.
Bairamabad	30 25 23	30 24 46	30 25 5	55 55 30	
Anar	30 53 22		30 53 22	55 16 30	
On road from Anar to Kirmanshah	31 2 5		31 2 5		
Kirmanshah		31 17 38	31 17 38		
Yezd	31 54 40	31 55 8	31 54 54	54 17 30	
Maibut	32 14 21	32 14 24	32 14 23	53 58 15	
Arjanun Caravans		32 20 39	32 20 39	53 45 45	
Aghd. ch. Kh.				53 36 0	
Todeshk		32 43 43	32 43 43	52 34 30	
Pishark or Fishark				52 15 45	

Name of Station.	Latitudes as deduced from altitudes of		Concluded Latitude North.	Concluded Longitude East from Greenwich.	Positions on which the Longitude depends.
	Sun.	Polaris.			
	° ′ ″	° ′ ″	° ′ ″	° ′ ″	
Ain Shirwan or Sharun . .		32 45 24	32 45 24	51 33 54	Ispahan and Baghdad.
Chali Siah Caravans . . .		32 52 22	32 52 22	51 23 39	
Dey Hak . . .		33 7 21	33 7 21	50 56 24	
Durr		33 18 29	33 18 29	50 37 54	
Kokah				50 20 54	
Khomain . . .	33 39 20		33 39 20	50 2 39	
Khurumabad. .		33 48 29	33 48 29	49 42 9	
Imaret		33 52 35	33 52 35	49 33 39	
Parri		34 7 45	34 7 45	48 57 39	
Dowletabad . .	34 18 23	34 18 25	34 18 24	48 47 39	
Kangiwar . . .		34 29 54	34 29 34		
Sahna				47 33 24	
Bis Situn*. . .		34 23 4	34 23 4	47 21 24	
Kirmanshahan .		34 19 14	34 19 14	46 59 24	
Garind or Kurind		34 16 56	34 16 56	46 11 9	
Pai-i-Takht . .		34 25 12	34 25 12	46 12 39	

The position of Jask was determined by officers of the late Indian navy. That of Kirman by Colonel St. John, Political Agent at Kandahar. In the work edited by Sir F. Goldsmid, "Eastern Persia, 1870–72," Colonel St. John, (then Major) has devoted a whole chapter, pp. 111–115, vol. i., to the position of this place, but by a mere printer's error it was given twice over as 59° 59′ 60″, instead of 56° 59′ 0″ as marked on the valuable map recently made by Colonel St. John for the Foreign Office. The position of Ispahan was determined by the German transit of Venus expedition, and the result kindly forwarded to me by the Astronomer Royal at Berlin. The position of Baghdad was determined by officers of the late Indian navy. The latitudes of Aghd, Pishark, Kokah, and Sahna are adopted from a very carefully plotted-out dead reckoning from the last place of observation.

Every precaution possible was taken in carrying the chronometer; I believe, without exaggeration, I could have taken two babies in arms with less anxiety. All sorts of methods were carefully experimented on before starting, and the one found best was that it should be placed on the same side of the same camel, and placed at such

* Bis Situn means twenty pillars; Bī Situn means without pillars. My informants differed as to the correct name of this place.

an angle in the box that when loaded it was horizontal, and that the number of marching and stationary hours should be noted. It was kept at a uniform temperature by being wrapped in my spare clothes.

After my return home I found Sir Frederic Goldsmid's book on Persia just published, also Major St. John's fine map, on which much of the country which I surveyed is marked "unexplored," and Anguhran placed, at a guess of course, about thirty miles from its true position. It was gratifying to find, during the short piece of country where our routes were identical, the results corresponded very closely. I believe I am wrong in putting the name of one place Diarbekri, and that Major St. John is right in writing it Deh Bakri, or the village of Bakri; but I believe I am right in putting "Kahnu" for "Khanu," "Dasht-i-Kuch" for "Dasht-i-Kushk," and "Sagdir" for "Sakht dar."

"Kahnu" is I think derived from "Kahn," the underground watercourses there. Dasht-i-Kuch means the plain in a corner or angle, which is just the situation of the place indicated. Sagdīr means a blackberry bush, which is particularly abundant at the place thus named, and nowhere else that I saw. Sir Frederic Goldsmid said in conversation that he thought I was right in my version of the last of these three places.

An interesting problem would be solved as to the disappearance of the Haḷīri and Bampūr rivers by a short journey from Fanōch through the Shahri district, and another following up to its source the Gabrig river.

The Bampūr river cannot I think be that of Bint, nor that of Maskhūtān, nor, as has occurred to me, does it split and form both. That of Bint comes from the Rimish country, and forms a perennial tributary to the Rapsh. That of Bampūr comes from the N.E., and the Halir from the N.W., and the two would probably meet in the fertile plain of Shahri. This plain receiving, as appears inevitable, two large perennial rivers, also the drainage from the northern side of the Band-i-Marz, must either contain such a lake or marsh as we must have heard of, or its water find an outlet southward. There are, I believe, three possible outlets:—

(1) The water may choose either of the huge torrent beds which meet at Anguhran, and go to Jagīn; or (2) It may be turned eastwards along the foot of the Band-i-Marz, until it reaches the Shimsani pass, whence I am assured the Sadaich river comes, and thus find its way to the sea; or, (3) It may form the western tributary of the Bint river at Fanōch, and come down with it.

To be considered with reference to these three possible routes are the following things :—

The Bampūr-i-Khaur, soon after leaving Bampūr, goes through a vast sandy desert. The effect of this may be illustrated by the Sadaich-i-Khaur, which in the hills is a huge river bed, with at all times a considerable stream equal to that of Bampūr at Bampūr, but which, when it emerges from the hills and passes into the sand-strip, is nearly lost, and nearly dry in the summer season. The Bampūr-i-Khaur might, in like manner, arrive at the northern mountain boundary, a very insignificant stream. The Haliri river would, however, arrive at the Shahri plain about as large as when I crossed it in Lat. N. 28, and Long. E. 57·40.

With reference to possible outlet No. 1, the torrent bed after the junction is nearly a mile wide. But from the number of date-trees planted in it, it has not been filled for at least thirty years. The bed, however, is very flat, and the channel on the south-west side could convey an enormous flood, but I could not gather from the natives, after repeated inquiries, that such floods did occur. On the whole, I think the third or Gabrig outlet to be the most probable. It is always spoken of as a very important river. No one has ever traced it up into the hills, and its size there cannot, as I have before explained, be conjectured from its size in the sand-strip.

APPENDIX D.

METEOROLOGY.

The following observations were made as regularly as consistent with incessant travelling.

Prefixed to them are the Kew certificates as to the condition ot the instruments after the journey.

The letters used to describe the weather are adopted from Inskip's navigation, and are as follows :—

B Blue sky, whether with clear or hazy atmosphere.
C Cloudy, but detached opening clouds.
D Drizzling rain.
F Foggy.
G Gloomy, dark weather.
H Hail.
L Lightning.
M Misty, hazy atmosphere.
O Overcast, the whole sky being covered with an impervious cloud.
P Passing temporary showers.
Q Squally.
R Rain, continued rain.
S Snow.
T Thunder.
U Ugly threatening appearance of weather.
V Visibility of objects, whether sky cloudy or not.
W Wet, dew.

The use of italics for any letter emphasizes the letter. Use of capital doubles it.

KEW OBSERVATORY.—Certificate of Examination.

Mountain thermometer (ranging from 190° to 212°), by Stanley, London.

Corrections to be applied to the scale readings, determined by comparison with the standard instruments at the Kew Observatory.

At 190°	. . . .	—1·7
195°	. . . .	—1·6
200°	. . . .	—1·0
205°	. . . .	—0·6
212°	. . . .	—0·2

KEW OBSERVATORY.—Certificate of Examination.

Mountain thermometer, (ranging from 170° to 190°), by Stanley, London.

Corrections to be applied to the scale readings, determined by comparison with the standard instruments at the Kew Observatory.

At 170°	. . . .	—0·2
175°	. . . .	—0·4
180°	. . . .	—0·7
185°	. . . .	—0·9
190°	. . . .	—1·1

KEW OBSERVATORY.—Certificate of Examination.

Thermometers, Sixes. Scale divided on boxwood, by Stanley London. (Verified unmounted and in a vertical position.)

Corrections to be applied to the scale readings, determined by comparison with the standard instruments at the Kew Observatory.

MAXIMUM.			MINIMUM.		
At 32°	. . . .	—0·2	At 32°	. . . .	—0·4
42°	. . . .	—0·2	42°	. . . .	—0·5
52°	. . . .	—0·2	52°	. . . .	—0·4
62°	. . . .	—0·1	62°	. . . .	—0·6
72°	. . . .	—0·1	72°	. . . .	—0·5
82°	. . . .	+0·1	82°	. . . .	—0·2
92°	. . . .	+0·1	92°	. . . .	—0·0

Note.—I. When the sign of the correction is +, the quantity is to be *added* to the observed reading, and when — to be *subtracted* from it.

II. Mercurial thermometers are liable, through age, to read too high; this instrument ought, therefore, at some future date, to be again tested at the melting point of ice, and if its reading at that point be found different from the one now given, an appropriate correction should be applied to all the above points.

G. M. WHIPPLE, Superintendent.

Kew Observatory, *June*, 1877.

KEW OBSERVATORY.—Certificate of Examination.

Aneroid barometer, by Stanley, London, No. 5,449.

Compared with the standard barometer of Kew Observatory (reduced to 32° Fah^r), with the following results :—

Pressure Inches.	Correction in English Feet.	Correction to Aneroid with a pressure diminishing.	Correction to Aneroid with a pressure increasing.	Correction in English Feet.
30	— 64	+ 0·07	+ 0·12 *	— 109
29	— 75	+ 0·09	+ 0·13	— 121
28	— 59	+ 0·06	+ 0·12	— 117
27	— 42	+ 0·04	+ 0·12	— 121
26	— 42	+ 0·04	+ 0·11	— 115
25	— 54	+ 0·05	+ 0·10	— 109
24	— 68	+ 0·06	+ 0·07	— 80
23	— 24	+ 0·02	+ 0·03	— 36
22	— 11	+ 0·01	+ 0·01	— 11

Note.—When the sign of the correction is +, the quantity is to be *added* to the observed scale reading, and when —, to be *subtracted* from it.

(Signed) G. M. WHIPPLE, Superintendent.

Kew Observatory, *June* 13*th*, 1877.

KEW OBSERVATORY.—Certificate of Examination.

Thermometer, Mason's Hygrometer. Scale divided on boxwood, by Stanley, London. (Verified unmounted and in a vertical position.)

Corrections to be applied to the scale readings, determined by comparison with the standard instruments at the Kew Observatory.

D.		W.	
At 32°	—3·0	At 32°	—3·8
42°	—3·0	42°	—3·2
52°	—3·0	52°	—2·7
62°	—2·8	62°	—2·5
72°	—2·7	72°	—2·3
82°	—2·6	82°	—2·2
92°	—2·5	92°	—2·1

* It is probable that this correction will have become reduced to that first obtained after the instrument has remained at the normal atmospheric pressure for a few days.

Note.—I. When the sign of the correction is +, the quantity is to be *added* to the observed reading, and when — to be *subtracted* from it.

II. Mercurial thermometers are liable, through age, to read too high; this instrument ought, therefore, at some future date, to be again tested at the melting point of ice, and if its reading at that point be found different from the one now given, an appropriate correction should be applied to all the above points.

G. M. WHIPPLE, Superintendent.

Kew Observatory, *June*, 1877.

1876, NOVEMBER.—GEIGEN TO KAHNU.

Place.	Date.	Time.	Dry bulb.	Wet bulb.	Aneroid Bar.	Max.	Min.	Sky.	Wind.		Remarks.
									Str.	Dir.	
Geigen	Nov. 1st	9.30 a.	93·5	80·5	29·95	...	...	m.	0		
		11 a.	100	...	...	...	...	...	3	S.E.	
		Noon	91·5	90·5	30·	...	...	m.	4	S.E.	
		3.30 p.	91	82·5	29·8	...	...	...	0		
		6 p.	84	76	·82	101	66	c.	0	...	Distant thunder and lightning to N.E.
		9 p.	78	73	·86	...	...	...	0		
		Mid.	73·5	71	·86	...	...	...	0		
	Nov. 2nd	9 a.	89	...	·9	...	...	...	1	S.E.	
		3.30 p.	91	82	·79	...	...	m.	3	S.E.	Distant thund., vivid lightning to N.E.
		6 p.	87	72	·82	101	65	m.	0		
		9 p.	80	72	·87	...	...	m.	0		
	Nov. 3rd	6 a.	70	63	·86	...	..	m.	0		
		Noon	101·5	80	·80	101	65	m.	1	S.E.	Solar-radiation; thermometer at 2 p. 106.
		3 p.	98	84	·77	...	...	m.	3	S.E.	
		6 p.	84	78	·79						
		9 p.	75	72	·82						
	Nov. 4th	9 a.	85·5	75	·84	...	65				
		3 p.	87	80	·74	...	...	gl.			Th. and ltng, squalls of rain and wind from all quarters, raging storm.
		5 p.	...	...	·75	...	...	...	...	...	
		6 p.	83	79							
		6.30 p.	...	...	...	...	...	...	...	...	Vivid lightning to W.
	Nov. 5th	6.30 a.	79	78	·91	...	...	...	4	...	Storm abt. 12 m. away, th. shakes ground.

1876, NOVEMBER.—GEIGEN TO KAHNU (*continued*).

Place.	Date.	Time.	Dry bulb.	Wet bulb.	Aneroid Bar.	Max.	Min.	Sky.	Wind. Str.	Wind. Dir.	Remarks.
Geigen	Nov. 5th	9.30 a.	75	72·5	29·92	...	...	gl.	...	...	Gloomy, th. to N.W.
		Noon	74	71	·88	...	...	gl.	...	...	Thunder to S.W.
3 miles N. of Geigen	Nov. 6th	7 a.	66	66	·66	...	...	gl.	o		
		9 a.	75	72·5	·68	...	...	b.	o		
		10 a.	76·8	74·5	·66	...	...	b.	o		
		10.30 a.	77·5	...	·64	...	...	c.			
		4 p.	78	70	·42	...	...	gl.	4	...	Thund. tremendous, raining irregular blocks of ice, 1 in. by ¾ in.
		4.20 p.	72	68	·45	...	...	gl.			
		6.40 p.	70	68	·42	...	...	gl.	o		
		8 p.	69	67·5	·46	...	...	o	o		
Oushdan-darri.	Nov. 7th	6 a.	67	60·5	·44	...	62	o	o	...	Stormy, rain all day.
		6 p.	73	69	·29	...	...	o	o		
		7.40 p.	71	68·5	·32	...	...	o	o		
	Nov. 8th	5.30 a.	63	61·5	·36	...	59	o	o		
		9 a.	73	70	·41						
Sharifi River		4 p.	82	75	28·9	...	...	b.	2		
		7 p.	79	66	·96						
		9 p.	70	66	·9						
Dāzakā	Nov. 9th	6.40 a.	68	60	29·	...	63	c.	2	N.	
		9 a.	68·5	73	·1						
		9 p.	68·5	63	27·26			c.	2	W.	
	Nov. 10th	6 a.	58	56	·25	...	55	c.	1	W.	
Rais Ali's Camp		9.30 a.	74·5	66	·26			b.	o	...	Streaky clouds.
		6 p.	66	62	·07						

1876, NOVEMBER.—GEIGEN TO KAHNU (*continued*).

Place.	Date.	Time.	Dry bulb.	Wet bulb.	Aneroid Bar.	Max.	Min.	Sky.	Wind. Str.	Wind. Dir.	Remarks.
Rais Ali's Camp.	Nov. 11th	6 a.	63	60	27·1	...	59				
Bir Buland	Nov. 12th	6 a.	...	...	...	...	55	...	...	...	Min. at night in open air.
	Nov. 13th	8 p.	69	65	·17						
Sharifi River	Nov. 14th	8 p.	70	61	·41						
		10 p.	62·5	60	·44	...	...	o			
	Nov. 15th	8 a.	70·5	60·5	·45	...	58	b.	0		
		9 a.	78·5	66	·44	...	...	b.	0		
		1 p.	82·5	64	·33	...	...	b.	1	N.E.	Solar radiation, 1 p.m., 108°.
		4 p.	78	dry	·32	...	...	b.	2	N.E.	
		6 p.	74	67	·4	...	...	c.	0		
		10 p.	65	59	·42	...	...	...	0		
	Nov. 16th	8 a.	71	59	·47	...	55	...	1	N.E.	
Barahing		6 p.	71	65	·7	...	...	b.	0		
	Nov. 17th	8 a.	69	61	·75	...	59	dull	0		
Gaz Shirai River.		3 p.	80	65	·8	...	...	b.	1	N.E.	
		6 p.	74	63	·84	...	...	b.	0		
	Nov. 18th	7 a.	65	61	·84	...	...	dull	0		
		9.15 a.	85	75	·84	...	...	b.	0	...	Slight streaky clds.
	Nov. 19th	9 a.	79	71·5	28·19	...	62	c.o.	0	...	Heavy clouds, thun., ltning, heavy rain, strong cold gusty wind from E. during night.
		6 p.	72	65	·14	...	...	o.			
	Nov. 20th	Noon	80	71·5	·2	...	60	c.	...	...	Strong mist till 9 a.m.

1876, NOVEMBER.—GEIGEN TO KAHNU (*continued*).

Place.	Date.	Time.	Dry bulb.	Wet bulb.	Aneroid Bar.	Max.	Min.	Sky.	Wind.		Remarks.
									Str.	Dir.	
Gaz Shirai	Nov. 20th	...	80	65	29·18	...	...	b.	0		
	Nov. 21st	7 a.	60	55	·26	...	55	m.	0	...	Heavy dew at night; morning cold.
Zamin Mulla		4.30 p.	84·5	70	·2	...	...	c.	0		
		6 p.	72	67	·25						
	Nov. 22nd	7 a.	68·5	60·5	·3	...	63	c.	1	S.E.	Mackerel sky.
Telling		6 p.	71	67·5	...	...	...	o.	1	S.E.	
		9 p.	72	66·5	·9						
	Nov. 23rd	6.30 a.	65	62·5	·92	...	57	m.	0		
		3.30 p.	82·5	70	·76	88	...	m.	3	S.E.	Gusty.
	Nov. 25th	6.20 a.	68	56	·68	...	65	m.	1	N.	
Jagin Fort		4 p.	80	63	·15	...	...	m.	2	N.	
		9 p.	63	57	·25						
	Nov. 26th	6 a.	52	48	·29	...	49	m.			
Manujan		4.30 p.	76	62·5	28·86	...	...	...	...	...	Streaky clouds.
	Nov. 27th	11 a.	85	78	·95	...	48				
Sar Kahur		8.30 p.	67	62	·87						
	Nov. 28th	6.40 a.	52	50	·91	...	50	m.	...	...	Heavy dew.
Bargah		3 p.	77	dry	27·84	...	...	c.			
		7 p.	...	...	·9	...	...	c.	2	E.	Gusty irregular cold clouds going to S.
		9.30 p.	66	...	·92	...	...	c.	0		
	Nov. 29th	6 a.	58	...	·9	...	47	c.			
Kahnu		5 p.	65	62	28·25	...	...	*o.*	...	...	Muggy & rny. all day.
	Nov. 30th	6.30 a.	59	58	·3	...	57	*c.*	2	S.	Cold damp raw mng.
		5.30 p.	73	64	·27	...	...	*o.c.*	3	S.	
		8.30 p.	70	63	·3	...	...	m.	4	S.	Cold wind.

1876, December.—Kahnu to Kaftar Khan.

Place.	Date.	Time.	Dry bulb.	Wet bulb.	Aneroid Bar.	Max.	Min.	Sky.	Wind.		Remarks.
									Str.	Dir.	
Kahnu	Dec. 1st	6.20 a.	63	59	28·4	...	60	c.	0	...	Mild morning.
Mahmudi		6 p.	65	62	27·99	...	...	o.	1	S.	
		8.40 p.	65	61	·99	...	...	o.	0		
		10.40 p.	65	61·5	28·	...	...	o.	0	...	Raining lightly, stdly.
	Dec. 2nd	6.30 a.	59	58	·1	...	55	o.	...	...	Steady rain for three hours.
		8 a.	63	61	·15						
Dosari		7.30 p.	60	58	27·82	...	...	c.	0		
	Dec. 3rd	7.30 a.	51	50	...	...	51				
		9.15 a.	65·5	62·5	·9	...	...	b.			
Jiruft		6 p.	59	55	·9	...	...	m.	0		
	Dec. 4th	7 a.	49	47	·97	...	40				
Dashti		4 p.	73	...	·51	...	...	...	...	...	Solar radiation, 82.
Kuch		7.30 p.	65	56	·57	...	45				
Sagdir	Dec. 5th	5 p.	56	51	24·45						
		7 p.	...	...	·47	...	...	o.	...	...	Heavy clouds.
	Dec. 6th	7.30 a.	46	43	·45	...	36	o.			
Deh Bakri		2.40 p.	51	46	22·65	...	...	o.	3	S.W.	
		6.30 p.	51	48	23·	...	...	o.	3	S.	
		9 p.	49	47	22·99	...	...	o.	1	S.	Light rain.
		10.15	50	48	...	...	...	o.	0	...	Light rain.
Sablistan	Dec. 8th	2.30 p.	60	53	24·13	...	...	c.	4	W.	
		6.30 p.	59	52	·18	...	...	c.	0		
Tahrut	Dec. 9th	3 p.	63	54	23·81	...	...	c.	2	N.E.	
		10 p.	47	43	·87	...	...	b.	1	N.E.	
	Dec. 10th	7 a.	...	...	...	...	29	...	...	...	All the 10th cloudy,
Raiun Village	Dec. 12th	9 a.	47	40	·12	...	...	b.	3	N.W.	strong cold wind.
		Noon.	56·5	45·5	·11	...	...	b.	2	N.W.	11th, cl. sun stg., cm.

1876, DECEMBER.—KAHNU TO KAFTAR KHAN (*continued*).

Place.	Date.	Time.	Dry bulb.	Wet bulb.	Aneroid Bar.	Max.	Min.	Sky.	Wind. Str.	Wind. Dir.	Remarks.
Raiun Vil.	Dec. 12th	3 p.	60	47	23·8	...	...	b.	o	...	Sun hot.
Raiun Fort	Dec. 14th	3 p.	52	42	22·84	...	...	b.	1	N.W.	Gusty.
		6 p.	51	43	·89	...	...	b.	o		
	Dec. 16th	9 a.	48	41	·95	...	29	c.	o		
		Noon	52	42·5	·87	...	...	...	o		
		3 p.	52·5	42·5	·83	...	...	*o.*	...	...	
	Dec. 17th	1 p.	48	42	·85	58*	21	...	...	...	* In sun.
	Dec. 18th	10 a.	43·5								
		Noon	48	39	·88						
		3 p.	50	42	·85	62*	...	b.	4	E.	* In sun.
Kirman	Dec. 23rd	Noon	46·5	45	24·12	...	...	*o.*	o	...	Raining all day.
		3 p.	44	43	·1	...	...	o.	3	W.	Stopped raining at 2 p.m.
		6.30 p.	44·5	42·5	·17	...	...	o.	o		
	Dec. 24th	9 a.	42	42	·24	...	34	b.	o		
		1 p.	48·8	42·8	·17	...	...	b.			
		3 p.	49	44	·14	...	...	b.	o		
		6 p.	46	42	·17	...	...	...	o		
	Dec. 25th	3 p.	50	45	·23	...	27	b.	o		
		9 p.	40	37	·3	...	...	b.	o		
	Dec. 26th	Noon	48	44	·32	...	28	b.	o		
	Dec. 27th	Noon	51	44	·3	...	25	b.	o		
		6 p.	48	41	·28	...	...	...	o		
	Dec. 28th	8 a.	35	32	·33	50	25	b.	o		
Ruban	Dec. 30th	6.30 a.	33	...	·30	...	...	*o.*			
		3 p.	57	...	·4	...	...	*o.*			
		5.30 p.	51	46·5	24·	...	...	*o.*			
	Dec. 31st	3 a.	39	...	...	...	...	*o.*			
KaftarKhan		8 a.	51	41	·45	...	...	*o.*	4	S.W.	Strong S.W. 4 p. to 6p.

1877, JANUARY.—BAIRAMABAD TO FISHARK.

Place.	Date.	Time.	Dry bulb.	Wet bulb.	Aneroid Bar.	Max.	Min.	Sky.	Wind.		Remarks.
									Str.	Dir.	
Bairam-abad.	Jan. 1st	8 a.	44·5	37·5	24·86	..	...	o			
		10.15 a.	60	48	·86						
		Noon	61	48·5	·83	...	...	...	...	...	Fitful breeze.
		6 p.	58	48	·86	...	...	o	1		
	Jan. 2nd	9 a.	48·5	45·5	25	...	43	o	o	...	Light steady rain in morn., stopped at 10 a.m., then b. sky, then overcast.
		Noon	53·5	49·5	24·91	...	...	o	o		
		3 p.	52	49·5	·90	...	...	o	...	...	Light rain at 2.15 p.
		6 p.	50	49	24·90	...	...	o	o	...	Small steady rain.
	Jan. 3rd	8 a.	42·1	41·9	25·1	...	...	o	o	...	Heavy rain all night, morn, thick mist.
		9 a.	44	43	·25	...	...	o	o		
		12.45 p.	52	50	24·95	...	...	o	...	...	Clearing.
		3 p.	56	53	·91	...	...	b	o		
		6 p.	55	52	·95						
	Jan. 4th	...	...	...	...	...	...	...	...	...	Rained heavily all night, and in morning snowed.
Kashku	Jan. 5th	7.20 a.	48	...	25·16	...	...	o			
Biath	Jan. 6th	7 a.	46	44	·3	...	...	o	4	N	Rain steadily.
Anar		4 p.	46	44	·34	...	...	o			
		6 p.	44	41·5	·37	...	...	o	o		
	Jan. 7th	3 a.	40	39·2	·39	...	...	...	...	...	Snowing.
		9 a.	42	40	·4	...	...	o			
		2 p.	42	39	·31	...	...	o			

1877, JANUARY.—BAIRAMABAD TO FISHARK (*continued*).

Place.	Date.	Time.	Dry bulb.	Wet bulb.	Aneroid Bar.	Max.	Min.	Sky.	Wind.		Remarks.
									Str.	Dir.	
Anar	Jan. 7th	3.15 p.	52	47	25·31	...	...	*o*	...	...	Cleared at 3 p. for few minutes, then rain.
		6.30 p.	42	40	·3						
Kirman-shahan	Jan. 9th	8 a.	35	...	24·98	..	31				
Sar Yezd	Jan. 10th	9 a.	35	...	25·43						
Yezd	Jan. 11th	Noon	46	41	·89	...	...	b c	o		
		3.30 p.	48	44	·81						
	Jan. 12th	Noon	51	46	·81	...	...	...	o	...	Dull lead-coloured sky, misty.
		3 p.	48	44	·76	...	...	...	o	...	Dull sky.
	Jan. 13th	3 p.	54	48	·54	...	...	b	...	...	Clear, no clouds.
		5 p.	50·5	43·8	·55	...	...	b	...	...	Few clouds.
	Jan. 14th	9 a.	...	...	·81	...	38	...	...	...	During night violent gusty wind, rain, and snow.
		Noon	52	49	·8	...	...	b	...	...	Constant clouds.
		3 p.	50	46	·78	...	...	b	...	...	Clouds.
	Jan. 15th	...	...	...	·94	...	33				Icy E. wind till sunrise, then hazy, increasing to overcast till 3 p., then clear, calm evening.
	Jan. 16th	...	...	...	...	...	...	...	...	...	
Maibut	Jan. 17th	2 p.	54·2	49·8	26·13	...	...	b	...	...	Thin clouds, sunny warm morning, light W. breeze, whispy clouds.
		4 p.	54·5	49·5	·15						
		7 p.	53	50	·18						

1877.—JANUARY.—BAIRAMABAD TO FISHARK (*continued*).

Place.	Date.	Time.	Dry bulb.	Wet bulb.	Aneroid Bar.	Max.	Min.	Sky.	Wind.		Remarks.
									Str.	Dir.	
Maibut	Jan. 18th	9 a.	50·8	47·8	26·26	...	...	b	o	...	Light clouds.
		Noon.	53	49	·24	108*	...	b	o	...	* In sun.
		4.30 p.	55	51	·2	...	35	...	...	...	Slight frost at night.
	Jan. 19th	8.15 a.	45	43	·3	...	...	...	...	...	Slight frost at night.
Arjanun		5 p.	59·2	50	25·85	...	...	b	1	W.	
		7 p.	56·5	50·5	·87						
		10.15 p.	54	51	·87						
	Jan. 20th	8 a.	49	dry	·83	...	42·5				
Aghd		4 p.	63	53·5	·92	...	...	b	1	N.W.	Thick passing clouds.
		5.30 p.	57	52	·94	...	...	o	1	N.W.	
	Jan. 21st	6 a.	55	53	·96	...	42				
Nau Gambaz		6.15 p.	55	50	26·5	...	...	*o*			
		7 a.	49	dry	25·42	...	46	*o*			
Pudaz	Jan. 23rd	8 a.	45	...	23·48						
Todeshk		8 p.	38	...	·27						
	Jan. 24th	7 a.	18								
		8 a.	21	23 frozen	·31						
Maskinun		Noon	56	...	·53						
Fishark	Jan. 25th	9 a.	34	...	·92						
		10.30 a.	39	37	·91						

1877, FEBRUARY.—AIN SHIRWAN TO BAGHDAD.

Place.	Date.	Time.	Dry bulb.	Wet bulb.	Aneroid Bar.	Max.	Min.	Sky.	Wind.		Remarks.
									Str.	Dir.	
Ain Shirwan	Feb. 4th	2.30 p.	46	39	24·28	...	...	m c	o		
		3.30 p.	48	40	·28	...	...	*o*	...	...	Light snow.
		5 p.	47	41	·31	...	...	*o*	o		
		5.30 p.	44	41	·32						
	Feb. 5th	7.30 a.	39	38	·37	...	34	b c	...	...	Frost.
Chāl-i-Siah		2.30 p.	54·5	45	23·86	...	...	v c	o		
		5 p.	47	dry	·89	...	...	v c	3	W.	
		6.30 p.	42	36	·92	...	...	b c	3	W.	
		7.30 p.	42	36	·93	...	...	b c	o		
	Feb. 6th	6.30 a.	33	31	·99	...	...	m	o		
Dey Hak	Feb. 7th	8 a.	34	32	·4						
Dūrr	Feb. 8th	7 a.	2	frozen	...	...	...	o			
		8 a.	2	...	·97	...	...	m			
		9 a.	15	...	...	35*	...	...	...	...	* In sun.
	Feb. 9th	9 a.	55	...	·75	...	...	m			
Khomain	Feb. 10th	11 a.	40	...	·8	...	...	b *c*	2	N.W.	
		Noon	43	38	·8	69*	...	b *c*	2	N.W.	* In sun.
		1 p.	45	40	·79	83*	...	b *c*	2	N.W.	* In sun.
		3 p.	42	36	·78	...	...	*c*	3	N.W.	
		4 p.	40	36	·8	...	...	*c*	4	N.W.	
		4.50 p.	39	36	·81	...	...	b c	1	N.W.	
		6 p.	37·8	35·5	·84	...	...	m	2	N.W.	
		7 p.	36	35	·85	...	...	m	2	N.W.	
		8 p.	36	35	·86	..	...	b *c*	1	N.W.	
	Feb. 11th	7 a.	...	...	...	...	25				
Road Khomain		Noon	...	...	...	35	...	c	6	W.	
to Khurumabad		3 p.	...	...	. .	25	...	*c*	6	W.	Temp. of wind.
Khurumabad	Feb. 12th	8 a.	25	...	...	...	18				

1877, February.—Ain Shirwan to Baghdad (*continued*).

Place.	Date.	Time.	Dry bulb.	Wet bulb.	Aneroid Bar.	Max.	Min.	Sky.	Wind.		Remarks.
									Str.	Dir.	
Khurum-abad	Feb. 12th	9 a.	26	...	23·01	...	...	m c	6	N.W.	Driving sleet 12 feet above ground.
Imaret		5 p.	41	37							
		6 p.	38	37	·4						
		8 p.	37	34	·42	...	...	b *v*	0		
		9 p.	35	33	·45	...	...	b *v*	0		
	Feb. 15th	8 a.	18	...	·45	...	5				
Dowlet-abad	Feb. 16th	9.30 a.	43	41	24·125	...	...	m	1	N.W.	Roof of chaparkhana.
		Noon	48·2	43	·08	77*	...	b v c	2	N.W.	* In sun.
		3 p.	51·2	45	·06						
		8 p.	45	41·5	·10						
	Feb. 17th	8 a.	45	42	·08	...	34	*m*	0	...	Drizzling v. fine rain.
		9.30 a.	45·5	42·5	24	...	..	*m*	1	N.W.	
		11.30 a.	45	43	24	...	...	*o*	1	N.E.	Raining since 11 moderately.—Faster.
		Noon	44·8	43	23·98	...	...	*o*	0	...	
		1 p.	43·8	41·2	·975	...	...	*o*	3	N.W.	Rain.
		2 p.	44	42·3	·98	...	...	*o*	0	...	Steady rain.
		3 p.	43·5	42	·98	...	...	*o*	½	N.W.	Steady rain.
		4 p.	42·5	41·3	·99	..	...	o	0	...	Rain very light.
		5 p.	42·8	41·5	·98	...	...	o	0		
		6 p.	43	41·5	·98	...	...	*o*	...	...	Rain light.
	Feb. 18th	7 a.	40	37	24·03	...	31	m c	0		
		8 a.	41	37	·03	...	...	b v c			
		9 a.	40·8	38·2	·03	...	...	b v c	0		

1877, FEBRUARY.—AIN SHIRWAN TO BAGHDAD (*continued*).

Place.	Date.	Time.	Dry bulb.	Wet bulb.	Aneroid Bar.	Max.	Min.	Sky.	Wind.		Remarks.
									Str.	Dir.	
Dowlet-abad	Feb. 18th	10 a.	...	...	24·035					...	
		11 a.	42	39·2	·035	...	...	*o.*	½	N.	
		Noon	42·5	40·2	·04	...	...	*o.*	½	N.	
		12.40 p.	42	39	·02	...	...	s.*o*.q.	5	N.W.	
		1 p.	41	38·2	·02	...	...	s.*o*.*q*.	4	N.W.	
		2 p.	41·2	39·2	·02	...	...	*m.*	1	N.W.	
		3 p.	41·2	38·2	·03	...	...	q.*m*.	3	N.W.	
		4 p.	41·2	38·5	·025	...	...	b.v.C	3	N.W.	
		5 p.	40	38	·06	...	...	b.C.	3	N.W.	
		6 p.	39	37	·06	...	...	b.v.*c*.	1	N.W.	
		8 p.	38·5	36·5	·07						
	Feb. 19th	9 a.	37	dry	·11	...	25	b.*v*.*c*.	1	E.	
		11 a.	37	34	·12	...	...	b.v.*c*.	3	N.W.	Icy cold wind.
		12	37·5	34·2	·125	...	...	q.b.v*c*	4	N.W.	Icy cold wind.
		1 p.	37·5	35·5	·125	...	...	q.b.v*c*	4	N.W.	Icy cold wind.
		3 p.	39·5	35·5	·1	57*	...	q.b.v*c*	4	N.W.	Icy cold wind.
		5 p.	39	35	·12	...	...	b.v.c.	2	N.W.	* In sun.
		7 p.	37·8	35·2	·14	...	...	b.*c*.	1½	W.	
	Feb. 20th	7.30 a.	34·5	frozen	·195	...	24	m.	0		
		9 a.	...	...	...	...	..	b.v.c.	1	N.W.	On road.
		Noon	40	...	...	...	...	b.v.c.	2½	W.	On road.
Kangiwar	Feb. 21st	6 p.	46	42	24·95	...	...	m.*c*.	0	...	Max. and min. stolen.
		7.30 p.	42	40	·98						
		9 p.	42	38	·95	...	...	*m.*	0		

1877, February.—Ain Shirwan to Baghdad (*continued*).

Place.	Date.	Time.	Dry bulb.	Wet bulb.	Aneroid Bar.	Max.	Min.	Sky.	Wind.		Remarks.
									Str.	Dir.	
Kangiwar	Feb. 21st	10.40 p.	37·5	36	24·98	...	...	*m*	0		
	Feb. 22nd	7 a.	39	38	·95	...	...	C	0	...	Rained hard 8.30 a. to 4 p.
		9 a.	42	40	·96	...	...	O			
Sahna		6 p.	48	45·5	25·15	..	...	O	0		
		7 p.	50	45	·15	...	...	O	1	S.W.	
		8 p.	50	44	·17	...	...	C	1	S.W.	
	Feb. 23rd	8 a.	48	42	·28	..	...	b m v c	0		
		9.30 a.	49·5	44·5	·28	...	...	b m v c	2	W.	
Bisitun		9 p.	47	43·5	·53	...	...	b c	0		
		10 p.	45	42	·54	...	...	b c	0		
	Feb. 24th	2 p.	59	48	·5						
		6 p.	55	45	·49	...	...	b *c*	0		
	Feb. 25th	6 a.	40	38	·53						
		6 a.	40	38	·53						
		8 a.	41	43	·56	...	...	*m*	0		
Kirman-shahan	Feb. 26th	11 a.	51	50	·39	...	...	m	0	...	Max. and min. recovered, quicksilver split, shook it together, and the max. and min. observations, commencing 27th, 1.15 p.m., are taken with it in that state, to see if any regular error could be established.
		1 p.	57	50	·39	...	...	m	0		
		3.30 p.	57	51	·33	...	...	m	1	N.W.	
		5 p.	56·5	50	·34	...	...	b c	0	N.W.	
		10.15 p.	54	49	·40	...	...	*m*	0		
	Feb. 27th	7.15 a.	52·5	48	·36	...	...	*m*	0		
		9 a.	54	49·5	·365	...	...	*m*	0		
		1.15 p.	60	52·5	·3	58·5	50	*m*	0		
		3.52 p.	58·5	50	·24	57	51·2	*m*	0		
		5 p.	57·5	55·5	·245	57	51				

1877, FEBRUARY, MARCH.—AIN SHIRWAN TO BAGHDAD (*continued*).

Place.	Date.	Time.	Dry bulb.	Wet bulb.	Aneroid.	Max.	Min.	Sky.	Wind.		Remarks.
									Str.	Dir.	
Kirman-shahan	Feb. 27th	5.30 p.	59	54	25·23	57·8	51	*c*	o		
		11.30 p.	59	51	·25	58·51	50	C	o		
	Feb. 28th	11 a.	56·2	52	·235	58	50	*r o*	o	...	Raining steadily since daylight.
		1.30 p.	56·5	53	...	57	50	*r o*	o		
		3 p.	58·2	54	·2	58	49·5	*c* b v	o	...	Sun came out, rain stopped.
		5.15 p.	58·8	53·8	·185	59	49	*c* b	o		
		7 p.	57·5	53·2	·2	58·2	49·8	*c*			
	March, 1877 Mar. 1st	10.30 a.	55	51	·175	56	...	*r o*	o		
		1 p.	56	52	·18	...	...	*r o*			
		3.15 p.	55	51·2	·18	...	...	r *o*			
		5.45 p.	55	50	·19	...	...	*c*	o	...	Stopped raining.
		9.45 p.	55	51	·23	...	...	b c	o		
	Mar. 2nd	7.30 a.	53	49	·29	...	...	m			
		9.30 a.	54	50	·32	...	...	b *c*	o		
		Noon	55	51	·29	...	...	b m	o		
		2 p.	56·8	52·2	·26	...	...	*m*			
		3.30 p.	57	52·8	·255	...	...	*m*			
		5.30 p.	60	55	·26	...	...	*m*			
		11 p.	57	52·5	·31	57	...	*m*			
	Mar. 3rd	8.30 a.	56·5	53	·35	...	...	r *m*			
		11.10 a.	59	55	·325	...	...	*m* r			
		1.15 p.	58·8	54·5	·315	...	...	*m* r			
		3 p.	58	54	·305	...	...	r m o	o		

1877, MARCH.—AIN SHIRWAN TO BAGHDAD (*continued*).

Place.	Date.	Time.	Dry bulb.	Wet bulb.	Aneroid.	Max.	Min.	Sky.	Wind.		Remarks.
									Str.	Dir.	
Kirman-shahan	Mar. 3rd	10.40 p.	58	54	25·27	...	...	m	0		
	Mar. 4th	9 a.	59	55	·2	...	...	*m*			
		12.30 p.	61	56·2	·195	...	...	*c q*	3	S.W.	Sun visible at intervals.
		11 p.	58	53·5	·2	...	...	b c	0		
Mahi Dasht	Mar. 5th	6.30 p.	51	43	·16	...	...	b *c*	2	S.W.	
	Mar. 6th	8.30 a.	46	44	·29	...	...	m	0		
Harunabad	Mar. 7th	8 a.	38	37	·42	...	...	b	0		
Kurind	Mar. 8th	10 a.	46	39·5	23·8	...	...	b	0		
		11 a.	49·5	45·5	·8	...	...	b	0	...	Marestails
		Noon	51	45·5	·8	...	...	b	0		
Baghdad	Mar. 18th	6.20 p.	59·3	51·3	29·93	...	...	m	0		
		10.10 p.	56·2	50	·97	...	...	b v	0		
	Mar. 19th	6.30 a.	50·5	41·5	·93	...	...	m	0		
		4 p.	68·8	54·5	·85	...	...	b v	0		
	Mar. 20th	7.30 a.	59	53	·84	...	...	b v	0		
		Noon	66	58	·81	...	...	...	0		
		9 p.	67	...	·77	...	...	b m	0		
	Mar. 21st	10 a.	66	58	·84	...	...	m	0		
		4 p.	69	61	·77	...	...	m	0		
		8.40 p.	69	62	·8	...	...	m			
		10.15 p.	69	62	·8	...	...	m	0		

APPENDIX E.

Firman from the HISSAM À SULTANAH, the Commander-in-chief of the Persian Army, and uncle of the Shah of Persia.

(TRANSLATION.)

H. H. THE PRINCE OF PERSIA.

To all those in high official positions, officers, scheikhs, and officials of the town of Kirmanshahan, officers of the public highways in Persia, etc., etc.

Mr. Floyer, a British subject, is leaving for Baghdad, and about to make a voyage in Persia. We request you all to prepare for him comfortable lodging in the different places he may pass through, and to render him every service, so that he may be comfortable and contented; therefore, on receipt of this, you will prepare to assist him and to render him every assistance, and to accompany him from one place to another, for his proper protection and safety.

(TRANSLATION.)

MEMORANDUM OF AN AGREEMENT

made this 15th day of Moharam el Haram 94, between Mr. Floyer on the one part, and Ali Akber, muleteer, of Isfahan, on the other.

It is agreed that the said Ali Akber engages to hire a saddle horse and three mules to Mr. Floyer, for himself and baggage, from Isfahan to Kirmanshahan, for fifteen days, for the sum of eight tomans (£3 16*s*.), being at the rate of two tomans each, half of this sum to be paid in advance before starting, and the remaining half at the termination of the journey.

It is also agreed :—

1st. In the event of any delay taking place, no allowance will be made for such delay.

2nd. Should Mr. Floyer make any stoppages on the journey, he agrees to pay 3 krans per day for fodder.

3rd. At the termination of the journey, providing this contract has been fulfilled, and Mr. Floyer is satisfied, he will pay Ali Akber two tomans (19*s.*) as a present.

(L. S.) ALI AKBER.

DARPAHAN AIR.

JASK SENTINELS' NIGHT SONG.

TELLING MINSTRELS' AIR.

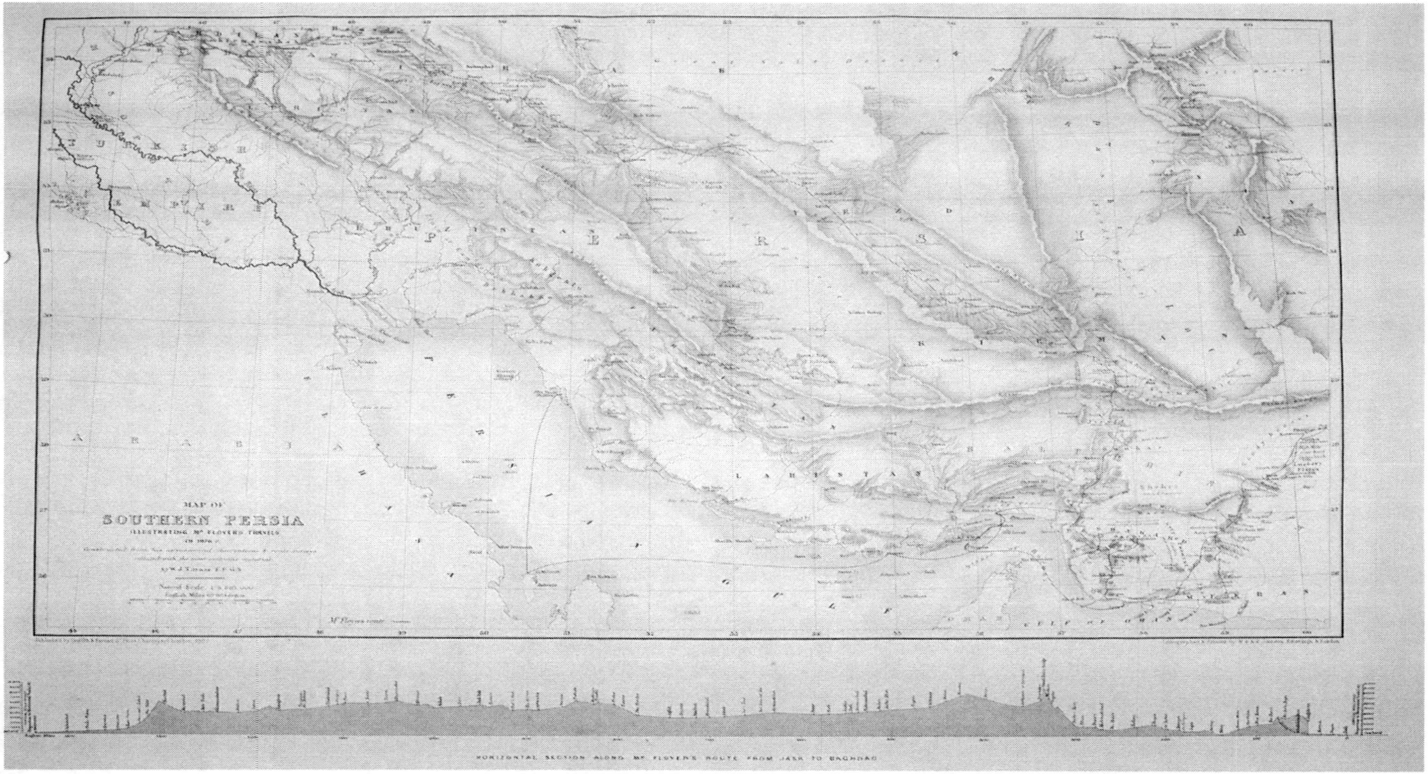
MAP OF
SOUTHERN PERSIA
ARABIA
PERSIA
LARISTAN
TURKISH EMPIRE
GULF OF OMAN
HORIZONTAL SECTION ALONG Mr FLOYER'S ROUTE FROM JASK TO BAGHDAD